QUEMOY

ng

FORMOSA

3_

D0397489

N

E

S

Southeast Asia

author's route o o o

0   100   200   300
scale of miles

LUZON

Clark Field ·
CORREGIDOR I.
Manila

THE
PHILIPPINES

SULU SEA

MINDANAO

KINABALU

BASILAN

PACIFIC
OCEAN

CELEBES

WEST
IRIAN

Makassar

E   S   I   A

An Eye for the Dragon

By Dennis Bloodworth

THE CHINESE LOOKING GLASS
AN EYE FOR THE DRAGON

An Eye for the Dragon

Southeast Asia Observed

1954–1970

Dennis Bloodworth

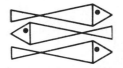

FARRAR, STRAUS AND GIROUX
New York

For Ping

Acknowledgments

I would like to acknowledge my debt to the writers, translators, and publishers of works from which I have quoted or taken extracts. These include *Sinister Twilight* by Noel Barber, published by Houghton, from which I have condensed material and quotations about the fall of Singapore (pp. 21-23); *The Golden Chersonese* by Isabella Bird, published by the Oxford University Press (pp. 13, 18, and 331); *A History of South-east Asia* by D. G. E. Hall, published by St. Martin's Press, (p. 19); *The Travels of Marco Polo*, translated by Ronald Latham and published by Penguin Books Ltd. (pp. 8, 12 and 296); and the *Encyclopaedia Britannica* (p. xvi). I am also indebted to David Condé and the *Far Eastern Economic Review* for some of the material on "Japlish" (p. 381); to Estelle Holt for permission to use two anecdotes about Laos (p. 114); to Bernard Kalb, now of CBS, for permission to use his Bali anecdote (p. 72); and to Mark Frankland and John Stirling of *The Observer* and Stanley Karnow, now of the *Washington Post*, for their permission to use quotations from their files.

I would further like to thank Stanley Karnow, Hugh Mabbett of the *Straits Times*, Harvey Stockwin of the *Financial Times*, and the two freelance journalists, Alex Josey and Ramsay Williams, for reading parts of the book and for making many valuable suggestions and corrections. My debt to *The Observer* and the *Observer Foreign News Service*, acknowledged with gratitude in the introduction, should again be registered here. Finally I must express my sincere thanks to my assistant Edward de Souza, who typed and checked the manuscript so efficiently and conscientiously.

Contents

Glossary   *xi*
The Taste of Durian   *xiii*

1   As the Curtain Rises   3
2   The Contract Breakers   14
3   The Carbon Copies   26
4   God's Other Country   35
5   The Mask of Democracy   45
6   Danger: Mao at Work   53
7   The Odd Couple   65
8   The Millionaire Friends of Mao Tsetung   76
9   The Fallen Domino   85
10   Poverty's Child   94
11   "Bonjour, Altesse"   105
12   The God-Kings   119
13   A Question of Identity   133
14   The Sweet Smell of Corruption   146
15   The Traffickers   159
16   Mumbo-Jumbo Makes History   164
17   Three Thousand Million Born Losers   172
18   Wars of Religion   181
19   Ladies Only   192
20   The Broken Lands   203
21   Our Men in Saigon   208
22   Their Men in the Sticks   223
23   Two Buckets of Blood   232
24   The Good Guys   247

25 Civilizing the Natives 256
26 My Country Right or Left 267
27 Cock and Bull 279
28 The Tortoise and the Terrapin 291
29 The Numbers Game 304
30 Small Brother Is Watching You 316
31 The Wandering Chinese 327
32 The Mythical Malaysians 336
33 The Seventies: Adults Only 351
34 The Adhocracy 362 /
35 Dangerous Liaison 372

Synopsis of the Plot 385
Bibliography 401
Index 409

Glossary

NOTE: Definitions of peoples and places—Lao, Laotian, Malaya, Malaysia, Vietcong, Vietminh, etc.—are given under the respective countries in "Synopsis of the Plot" at the end of the book.

AO-DAI   Vietnamese women's dress of a long, high-collared silk coatee and trousers.

BARONG TAGALOG   Filipino man's national dress: usually a cream-colored embroidered shirt, worn loose.

BARRIO   A Filipino village.

BATAK   A minority people of Sumatra.

BOMOH   A Malay medicine man.

BONZE   A Buddhist monk.

BUNG   An Indonesian word for brother.

CONFRONTATION   Indonesia's undeclared war against Malaysia: 1963–1966.

CYCLOPOUSSE   In Francophone territories, a trishaw or tricycle rickshaw.

DAIMYO   Japanese feudal lord.

DONG   Vietnamese piaster: the rate of exchange of the North Vietnamese dong in Hanoi in 1955 was 10,000 to the pound.

DUKUN   Malay medicine man (*cf.*, bomoh).

GAMELAN   An Indonesian orchestra, in which the most important instruments are drums and xylophones.

KAMPONG   Malay village or homestead.

KARMA   According to Hindu belief, our destiny as it evolves from the sum of all our actions, good and bad, in all previous lives, and the impact of the karma of others upon it.

KEMPETAI   Japanese secret police.

KRIS The Malay dagger, often with a twisted, winding blade like a snake.

LONGGYI Burmese equivalent of a sarong. *See* sarong.

MAHAYANA BUDDHISM "Great Vehicle" Buddhism from North India, whose canon is in Sanskrit and whose sects postulate saints, heaven, and the power of faith. *See* Theravada Buddhism.

PARANG A Malay chopping knife, or machete.

PITJI A short Indonesian velvet cap, usually black. *See* songkok.

PRAHU A Malay boat.

SAMPOT Cambodian equivalent of the sarong.

SARONG A long, voluminous Malay step-in skirt, whose slack is folded across the body and tucked in to give a tight, sheath-like effect.

SONGKOK The Malay black velvet cap. *See* pitji.

STENGAH (satengah) A Malay word literally meaning half. In colonial drinking terms, a small whisky.

THERAVADA BUDDHISM Sometimes known as Hinayana ("Little Vehicle") Buddhism. It originated in South India, its canon is in Pali, and it promises only the bliss of extinction if after many incarnations a man achieves enlightenment.

TRISHAW Tricycle rickshaw.

The Taste of Durian

It proved difficult to find a title that would label this book concisely yet accurately, for its subject is not just the anguish of Vietnam or the delights of Bali. It is the whole, seemingly unrelated miscellany of states that lie between the familiar shapes of India to the west and China to the north, and look like nothing so much as a man leaning out of the ballooning continent of Asia to fling a large armful of litter into the sea. But perhaps a few basic details will help to knock them into perspective.

As Florida noses down from the southeastern tip of the North American mass toward the Antilles and the Bahamas, so another peninsula probes outward from the southeastern tip of the Asian mass toward the three thousand islands of Indonesia to the south and the seven thousand islands of the Philippines to the east. And the modern code name for this pattern of land and water is Southeast Asia.

Southeast Asia is as wide as the United States and stretches across the equator from the latitude of New Orleans in the north to that of Bahia in the south. The mean temperature is usually in the eighties all year around.

Extending southeastward from India, the states on the mainland peninsula are the Union of Burma, the kingdoms of Thailand, Laos, and Cambodia, and the two Vietnams, while down its long thin western arm lie Malaya (the western half of the Federation of Malaysia) and the small island republic of Singapore, which is joined to it by a causeway.

Across the Straits of Malacca and the South China Sea, the Indonesian archipelago alone is scattered over three thousand miles of lukewarm water until it meets the Philippines and Australasia. Its islands include the great bulk of Borneo, along whose northern edge are the East Malaysian states of Sarawak and Sabah as well as the tiny oil-sultanate of Brunei.

The area is even vaster than that of the United States, and to fly from Burma to Manila via the Indonesian capital of Djakarta is like flying from Los Angeles to New York via New Orleans. As most of it is water, however, its greater population of some 260 million (112 million in Indonesia alone) live on only half as much land. Nevertheless, many parts are sparsely peopled. Laos, one of the five riverine states of the great river Mekong that bisects the peninsula and is nearly 250 miles longer than the 2,348 miles of the Mississippi proper, is as big as the United Kingdom but has only about three million inhabitants.

A pack of independent countries today, Southeast Asia can be cut several ways. The fundamental Western colonial influence in Burma, Malaysia, Singapore, and Brunei has been British. In Indonesia it has been Dutch. In the Indochina states of Cambodia, Laos, and Vietnam it has been French. In the Philippines it has been Spanish and American. Ethnically, however, Malaysia, Indonesia, and the Philippines are linked and largely inhabited by brown people of "Malay" stock. Similarly, Thailand (formerly Siam, the one state that was not colonized), Laos, and the Shan States of north Burma are all peopled by yellow men of "Thai" origin. But there are many other strains. The dominant race in

Burma is related to the Tibetans; in Cambodia it is the darker "Khmers"; and Vietnam is inhabited by "Viets' from South China. Culturally, it is in Vietnam that the "Indo" cf "Indochina" ends: people no longer build houses on stilts, and the sarong, which is the costume of Southeast Asia, gives way to Chinese pajamas and the fetching *ao-dai*, itself a variant of the Chinese *cheongsam*. For the Indian culture which in early centuries gave most of Southeast Asia coherence did not impose itself on northern Vietnam, for so long a vassal of China.

Religion helps to bring out the two main themes of the subcontinent. The brown Malay world of Malaysia-Indonesia-Philippines is almost entirely Muslim (with the important exception of Christian Luzon). On the other hand, the countries that make up the main blob of the peninsula itself—Burma, Laos, Thailand, Cambodia, Vietnam—are Buddhist.

The majority of Singaporeans are immigrant Chinese, who also account (with immigrant Indians) for about half the population of Malaysia and constitute a small but powerful economic minority in other countries of this area, which is backward but not poor in resources. Southeast Asia produces most of the world's rubber and tin, and much of its teak, tea, coffee, pepper, palm oil, kapok, pineapple, sugar, and spices. It is also rich in oil.

North Vietnam is the only Communist state in the subcontinent, and while all others (except South Vietnam) would welcome better relations with the Communist powers, all fight Communist subversion at home. As I write, elected politicians govern in Laos, the Philippines, Malaysia, and Singapore, but army generals dominate the administration in Burma, Indonesia, Thailand, and South Vietnam. Cambodia was ruled by its royal head of state, Prince Norodom Sihanouk, until 1970, when it was declared a republic.

But I must stop there, for this is no textbook. There are many excellent works on the history, the geography, the cultures, and the current political problems of the countries of Southeast Asia for those who want more data. Moreover, a good encyclopedia will cover every aspect of the area from philosophy to fruit.

Take, for example, the durian. *Durio zibethinus,* you may read, "is of the family Bombacaceae, and can grow to a height of eighty feet. It is found in Sumatra, Celebes, and Java, and is cultivated in Malaya and Thailand as far north as the 14th parallel. The fruit is spherical, measures up to eight inches in diameter, and may weigh eight pounds. It has a hard green external husk armed with pyramidal tubercles terminating in sharp points. Inside, it is divided into five oval compartments, each filled with glutinous pulp and containing up to five large, edible seeds. Of exceptionally high protein value, it is noted for its delicious flavour and for its offensive odøur."

Now you have been told all about the durian, and you know nothing. For you have neither smelled nor tasted it. In the words of someone who did so one hundred years ago, a "rich, butter-like custard, highly-flavoured with almonds gives the best idea of it, but intermingled with it come wafts of flavour that call to mind cream cheese, onion sauce, brown sherry." Let me add that the smell is sweetly fetid, a loathsome compound of rotten onions and rotten meat. But men cheat and steal and fight over durians, as I know, for a big durian tree overhangs my garden in Singapore, and every year thieves smash down the fence to get at the stinking fruit.

Southeast Asia is like the durian—prickly, strange, smelly and beautiful, revolting, enchanting, an offense and an addiction. I am not an academic with all the facts and figures at my fingertips and my fingertips eight thousand miles away from the reality. But I have made the Far East my diet for sixteen years. My object, therefore, is not to measure it and weigh it and put it into Latin but to break it open for the ordinary reader who has never seen it, and to offer him a taste.

Certain Chinese artists, it is said, put the eyes in last when they painted a dragon, for this brought the formidable creature to life. Others have drawn the region for the western world; I would like to try to give it an eye in which the reader may glimpse something of its awakened spirit (leaving him to put in the other himself).

So this is not a country-by-country analysis of the region, with

a chronological account of postwar political developments. I have
in fact provided a separate Synopsis of the Plot at the end of
the book, to which the reader can always refer to find his bear-
ings, in order to free the book itself from the burden of narrative
form (to paraphrase from Lawrence Durrell's *Justine*).

I have tried, rather, to explain the nature of the East through
the eyes and experience of a minor character (myself), and to
let the contemporary drama of Southeast Asia emerge naturally
from the beliefs, customs, prejudices, and traditional patterns
of thought of the principal players—the peoples themselves.

The book is mainly about Southeast Asia, although there are
asides on Korea, Japan, and, of course, the great cultural god-
fathers of the subcontinent, India and China. It attempts to
bridge the generation gap between the old, established Asia and
the new, emerging Asia, and also to describe the sometimes
clumsy love-hate-play between East and West. Much of the
material has been drawn from articles I have written in the past,
and I am particularly grateful to the editors of *The Observer* and
the *Observer Foreign News Service* (OFNS) for allowing me to
take extracts from them.

My references are those of a Far Eastern correspondent, not
a research scholar, and my target is not the Asian specialist but
a far more important person in the West—the man who does
not know Asia at all. And since the book must have more to it
than the dry bones of academic study if it is to be fit for human
consumption, I make no excuse for the color and comic relief.
There are no footnotes or acknowledgments in the text to worry
the reader, quotations have been condensed, and the number of
names—whether of Eastern politicians or of Western journalists
—has been kept to a minimum. As in the case of *The Chinese
Looking Glass*, this book has been designed for reading.

D. B.

Singapore
February 1970

An Eye for the Dragon

When you have heard, you must listen;
When you have seen, you must judge in your heart

Lao proverb

1 : *As the Curtain Rises*

Like all the best cables, this one arrived in Singapore at two o'clock in the morning. Couched in the usual sibylline idiom of the editorial staff, it read: COULDST INFIT QUICK TRIP MACAO VIEW FILE COLOURFUL BACKGROUNDER GOLD SMUGGLING RACKET FOR SWEEKENDS PAPER QUERY CHEERS NEWSEDITOR.

Two can play at this game, which depends on the six-and-a-half hour time lag between Singapore and England and is contested with the politely concealed malice of club croquet. It was not until eight o'clock, therefore, that I propped my dog-eared school atlas against the marmalade and prepared to send my opponent on the desk in London an urgent telegram which, I calculated, would get him out of bed at about 0230 hours the previous night.

Not only time but space was on my side, moreover. Macao,

the tiny Portuguese colonial "province" that protrudes from the gross abdomen of Communist China like an insignificant wart, was fully five and a half inches from Singapore according to my map, or 1,750 miles as the crow flies. But it was only forty miles from Hong Kong, where my colleague Rawle Knox was then based. Accordingly, I wired briefly: WHY SEND ME AND NOT RAWLE QUERY BESTEST BLOODWORTH. To which I received the unnerving, even briefer reply: BECAUSE YOU ARE NEARER LUV FRED.

A further exchange of sardonic endearments revealed that someone in London had confused Macao with Malacca, on the west coast of Malaya, which was a little like mistaking Budapest for Bristol. There was nothing really startling about this, however. People in the West still send letters to "Hong Kong, China," even to "Singapore, China." Men may know something of the Further East, a relatively simple affair dominated by easily recognizable geographical clichés like China and Japan. But the states of Southeast Asia appear to the stranger as an ambiguous, almost obscene muddle of shapes dangling from the world's bulkiest continent and then trailing off vaguely into an untidy mess of ten thousand tropical islands. Africa may have renamed its component parts and disconcertingly changed all its postage stamps, but Africa at least has always been Africa. In the mind of any man west of the Indian Ocean, however, Southeast Asia did not even exist thirty years ago. It had to be invented.

Early mapmaking of the region was understandably hit-and-miss, but the cartographical squint that in 1562 put the Stretto di Anian—and so today's Vietnam—to the north of China instead of to the south would not have raised the well-tended eyebrows of the special envoy from Washington who arrived in Saigon nearly four hundred years later during a tour of Southeast Asia. While she was being escorted by an American embassy official from the airport to a room reserved for her in the Hotel Majestic, this lady (for such she undoubtedly was) commented affably: "My, it certainly feels good to be in Indonesia." "Excuse me, ma'am," corrected the other, "but this is not Indonesia. This is Indochina." "Jesus," breathed Her Excellency, visibly moved by something, "where the hell have I just come from, then?"

Later, rioting Vietnamese, although ignorant of this conversation, broke into her hotel bedroom. "But I am your friend," protested the anguished ambassadress to the mob. "I am an American." Thus goaded, they threw the furniture out of the window.

How does that contradiction in terms, the Western Far East correspondent, explain the one unknown world to the other? Between chains of theatrical mountains, a simple, often indolent civilization graces rich rice-growing flatlands veined with waterways and bisected by the great yellow Mekong River. The golden-tiled temples, with their fantastical, upcurling roofs, tower over settlements of little wooden houses on stilts. The mop-headed palms and shady tamarinds stand motionless under a steamy sky. Sarong-clad women bicker in the marketplace. This may seem to be no more than the setting for the Coke signs and the Cadillacs and the TV commercials, the flashing jets and mechanized armies and student strife, for mushrooming hotels and mushrooming high explosive. But the comforting familiarity of all that shiny Western veneer does not help.

For the dubious purpose of writing these reflections I have lined up seventy old notebooks, and now, picking one at random, labeled "Laos, July 1957," I find myself staring, appalled, at a page of almost incomprehensible scribble reading: "*Democrats angry Leuam not retained by Katay as Min. Fin. Also brother murdered in mistake for Phoui (plot with Pau and Bong) and tend blame Sananikones. Prog. party vote 8 K, 5 SP, 4 abstained. SP and Pet not deputies. Vorovong says Katay must fail. Nou Ing also left out last cab.*" Pages of it. What does it, or did it ever, mean? Yet on some sad and sweltering evening in the rapidly receding past, I must have unpicked the tangle and knitted it into six hundred words gently explaining the vital importance of this whole grisly Oriental vendetta to unconvinced *Observer* readers eight thousand miles away in Windsor Castle and Wormwood Scrubs. How else would I have received in Vientiane an acknowledging cable from London saying: THANKEST YOUR LUCIDEST LAOS REGRETFULLY OUTSQUEEZED LATER EDITIONS OWING NEWS PRESSURE CHEERS NEWSEDITOR.

I could hardly blame him. It became an exacting task to try

to explain clearly in half a column a series of obscure crises in which, for a start, the name of the neutralist leader Prince Souvanna Phouma appeared to be a deliberately contrived anagram of the name of his "pro-American" rival, General Phoumi Nosavan. Anyway, as some mythical ambassador is said to have declared of every capital from Saigon to Djakarta: "Anyone who thinks he understands the situation here simply does not know the facts."

The ignorance cuts both ways. In Phnom Penh once a young Cambodian Buddhist bonze with shaven head and begging bowl stopped me under the shadow of the sun-baked wall of the royal palace and in stilted English asked for a light for a cigarette, which he fished from somewhere under his saffron toga. "And you are what nationality?" he demanded, with cool monastic insolence. "British," I replied defiantly, and almost without a moment's hesitation. The naked face sharpened with faint puzzlement, so I repeated: "British—you speak English, you must have heard of it?" The monk shook his head disdainfully. "No," he answered, and left the monosyllable hanging limply in the air as he shuffled on, puffing. I watched him go, consoled by the memory of the chagrined Washington diplomat who discovered that a Malay he was talking to on the island of Langkawi had never heard of the United States. It might be difficult to put Laos across in Lambeth, but at least I was spared the frustrations of putting Lambeth across in Laos.

Too much language and too little learning make an unstable compound for a human relationship, for they produce a synthetic sense of understanding which can be as dangerous as dynamite. Thomas Stamford Raffles, the liberal and humanitarian founder of Singapore, discovered this to his cost when in 1811 he wrote to the sultan of Palembang urging him to force the local Dutch garrison to leave. His scribe translated this into Malay as "beat them out conclusively" and the Sumatran potentate, adapting it to his own vocabulary of violence, thereupon had the Dutch massacred to the last man. Very wisely my Chinese wife, Ping, refused to teach me any Mandarin before she had first put me through a crash course in Chinese history and philosophy (as well as the Singapore Registry Office). But knowledge limited to acts and facts can be as hazardous as knowledge limited to mere words.

There is an elusive, now-you-see-it-now-you-don't character to man's similarity to man that can be almost shockingly deceptive. Southeast Asia can only be interpreted in terms of the mental idiom peculiar to its peoples, the idiom that has evolved over the slow centuries and the fleeting years.

An old philosophical limerick best poses the initial puzzle:

> There once was a man who said "God
> Must find it exceedingly odd
> That that sycamore tree
> Continues to be
> When there's no one about in the quad."

Before *The King and I* and *The Ugly American,* before Joseph Conrad and Somerset Maugham, and before the first Western tradesman set his big round eyes upon it and staked the first colonial claim, this obscure subcontinent must have existed. But what was southeast Asia before it was ever Southeast Asia?

Like spectral figures that materialize in a gloomy corner of the canvas when a masterpiece is cleaned, the outlines of old, lost kingdoms emerge slowly from the dark, featureless map as a century of scholarship begins to dissolve our ignorance.

"The people of Funan are cunning and astute" mumbles a Chinese chronicler, bent over his brush fourteen hundred years ago. "They trade in gold, silver, and silks. When the king travels, he rides on an elephant, and women may do the same. For distraction, the people arrange cockfights and pigfights. They have no prison. They judge by heating a chain red-hot which must then be carried seven paces. The hands of the guilty are scorched, but the innocent man is not hurt. Or else they duck one in deep water. He who has right on his side does not sink; he who is wrong, does." The people lived in thatched wooden houses with tall palisades, but the king reigned from a storied pavilion, possessed many gold vases, incense burners, and foreign slaves.

Only dimly perceived from this distance, Funan dominated the subcontinent for five hundred years after the death of Christ, and at the zenith of their power its kings were overlords from the Mekong Delta in the east to the Malay peninsula in the west. But all that has been found of it has been a few gold and bronze objects, some of them inexplicably inscribed with the name of the Roman Emperor Antoninus Pius—as was the wall he built between the Forth and the Clyde in Scotland.

To the north lay Champa, its monarchs masters of the littoral that now includes Central Vietnam. First glimpsed in the days of Marcus Aurelius, Champa survived seventeen centuries of uneasy and fluctuating fortune. "You must know that in this kingdom," relates Marco Polo, "no pretty girl can marry without first being presented to the king for his inspection. If he is pleased with her, he takes her to wife. If not, he gives her a sum of money appropriate to her station so that she may take another husband. I assure you that when I was in this country the king had 326 children . . ."

The Chams built grand and durable temples as smooth as sandstone, for they used no mortar but baked the bricks after they had been laid, as part of a process now lost, so that a knife cannot be inserted between them even today. The men themselves proved less durable, however. The great realm, its center earlier in the region of Hue, gradually shrank southward like a fizzling balloon, and finally disappeared into the swamps west of Saigon.

By the time Champa sank into history, Funan was long gone, overthrown in the sixth century by a Khmer power which China knew as Chen-la and which extended in its heyday to the Chinese border in the north, to modern Tonking in the east and modern Cambodia in the south. Its royal palace may well have been at Vientiane, the bucolic temple-strewn little capital of Laos, but if so, its former magnificence is lost in the drains and dust.

"Every three days," wrote a Chinese during the seventh century, "the king goes in solemn procession to the Hall of Audience and seats himself upon a bed made of five sorts of perfumed

wood and decorated with seven precious things. Above the bed
rises a pavilion of magnificent materials, of which the columns
are of veined wood and the screens of ivory sewn with flowers
of gold. A golden incense burner, tended by two men, is placed
in front. More than a thousand guards clad in mail and armed
with lances are ranged at the foot of the steps to his throne, in
the halls of the palace, at its gates and peristyles." Men always
go about armed, and a simple tiff may lead to a bloody fight, he
goes on, but: "They wash every morning, brush their teeth with
small pieces of wood, and do not fail to read their prayers." They
write from left to right, not from top to bottom as in the Celestial Empire itself, it is noted later, disapprovingly. But they also
hold fireworks displays on New Year's Eve, honor twelve signs
of the zodiac, and observe leap years, "for their men are learned
in astronomy and able to calculate eclipses of moon and sun."

In the ninth century a new master of Chen-la moved the
Khmer capital to a new site at which, for nearly four hundred
years, a line of prestigious kings was to direct the work of thousands of elephants and hundreds of thousands of men in the
construction of one of the most awesome manmade wonders of
the world, the gigantic complex of stone and tombs, temple
mountains and intricately sculptured memorials of Angkor. For
half a millennium after the final decay of the kingdom these
fantastic monuments of "Kambuja" slowly crumbled and sank
into a greedy sea of encroaching jungle whose banyan trees
crushed whole shrines to rubble between their monstrous roots.
In 1863 a French naturalist uncovered a corner of the colossus,
and since then his compatriots have painstakingly rebuilt much
of it in all its magnificence.

Angkor Wat, tomb and temple for a god-king who personified
Vishnu on earth, was surrounded by about four miles of moat,
and is still approached by an immense paved causeway. The
structure itself, its successive tiers of terraces and cool, colonnaded
galleries, pavilions, and steep stairways surmounted by five tall
towers, was made without mortar, every stone being set precisely on the next. The whole marvelous artifact is a running
riot of bas-relief, of gods and heavenly dancing girls, battle scenes

and naval pageants. The first gallery alone has an inner wall of polished sandstone carved into a brilliantly executed frieze seven feet tall and more than six hundred yards long.

The kingdom, which straddled the subcontinent of Southeast Asia by the eleventh century, declined as inexorably as the waning moon. Harassed by vigorous Siamese newcomers from the north, it collapsed beneath the weight of its own monuments and the exhausting effort required to build them. By 1431 the time had come for the Khmers to move south and soon they abandoned the whole gorgeous growth to the weeds.

There were nevertheless men across the uneasy seas that separated the mainland from the fragmented jigsaw of islands to the south who had looked upon Chen-la as little more than a vassal. The Indonesian archipelago had thrust up its own great realms, and in the manner of arrogant islanders from Cornwall to Kyoto, they regarded the adjoining continent as their footstool. In the sixth century Srividjaja emerged as an ambitious maritime trading empire whose hegemony extended to the coastal corners of Malaya, Cambodia, and the Philippines, and six hundred years after that a visitor to the capital at Palembang in South Sumatra remarked that it was still a thriving center of sea power in which, rather typically, "eight hundred moneychangers are busily engaged."

Two centuries later, however, the might of Srividjaja was only a memory, eclipsed by the new, formidable Javanese empire of Madjapahit, which claimed suzerainty over Siam, Cambodia, Annam, and Malaya, and also—if with questionable bravado— the entire Indonesian archipelago. It was to hold sway until after Columbus had discovered America and Bartholomeu Dias had sailed around the Cape of Good Hope to put the white man and his white ships into the Indian Ocean for the first time.

Nevertheless, just as the pressure waves in Europe flowed in from the east and finally petered out on the beaches of the British Isles to the far west, in a supine Southeast Asia overhung by the mass and might of China, the main pressure flowed from north to south.

The light-yellow men who compelled the Khmers to abandon

Angkor had been unceremoniously pushed out of their own private
kingdom in South China by the Mongol hordes of Kublai Khan
in the thirteenth century and had therefore pioneered all the
more boldly into the ill-lit subcontinent to their south. They
were the Thais, who became known as the Shans when they overran north Burma, the Laos when they dominated what is now
Laos, the Siamese when they obliterated the memory of Angkor
and later established the kingdom of Siam. (But they remained
the Black Thais and White Thais in the mountains of North
Vietnam, where they preserved their simple hill-tribe habits and
their respect for formal, traditional dress.)

Other small, pale Northerners edged down the Indochina
littoral, the name of their state changing as they crept southward:
Nam Viet, Dai Viet, Annam. In some ways reminiscent of the
conquest of the West in a newer continent, their armed migration was to obliterate the Chams as a nation, but they themselves
were to lose an old identity in order to gain a new one, finally
emerging as the people of "Vietnam."

Meanwhile, as the deep dyes of Greco-Roman and Christian
culture seeped across the fabric of primitive Europe, coloring
earlier patterns of repulsive custom and improbable belief, the
East was absorbing spiritual light and shadow from two great
presences on the frail fringes of the subcontinent: China and
India.

Confucian China offered no gods but the down-to-earth ethics
of a benevolent society. Harmony with the universe depended on
harmony among men, and so salvation lay in the careful study
and emulation of ancient sages, in whose goodness and wisdom
lay the secret of human and cosmic concord. The Chinese therefore bequeathed to their Korean and Vietnamese vassals the
concept of an empire administered not by blue-blooded dunces
but by a civil service of scholar-mandarins steeped in improving
reading.

China's suzerainty was inspired by a philosophy which taught
that there was no other civilization but the Confucian state and
that its emperor was not only vicar of heaven but viceroy of all
the earth. Other rulers were not fellow princes but mere feuda-

tories. They must at least go through the motions of swearing loyalty and sending tribute to the Son of Heaven, and so spare a sometimes embarrassingly weak Celestial Empire the undignified necessity of proving who was the master.

China conquered Tonking a century before Christ was born, and kept it for a thousand years, and during His lifetime a usurper on the Dragon Throne sent an expedition as far as North Sumatra to acquire a rhinoceros for his zoo. The impression it made is not known, but twelve centuries later Marco Polo had occasion to describe its Javanese cousin, for the armies of Kublai Khan not only invaded recalcitrant Burma and Annam but crossed the seas to Java to teach a temerarious king that he could not expel the Son of Heaven's ambassador with impunity. ("These unicorns," he relates disgustedly, "have the hair of a buffalo and feet like an elephant's. They have a single large black horn in the middle of the forehead. They are very ugly brutes to look at. They are not at all such as we describe them when we relate that they let themselves be captured by virgins, but clean contrary to our notions.") Later the eunuch-admiral Cheng Ho, castrated commander of China's greatest fleets, seized "rebel" kings in South Sumatra and Ceylon and removed them to Peking to encourage a proper respect for the emperor in others.

The Confucian view of heaven as an enigma about whose nature it was obviously absurd to ask at all complemented, if a little uneasily, the smoky imagery of Hindu and Buddhist mysticism that curled upward from a philosophical conviction that, on the contrary, a sensible man should devote his attention to a metaphysical cosmos whose story was to be measured in "kotis of kalpas" (tens of millions of cycles of 4,320 million years each). It was the world that was a waste of time.

Appropriately, Indian suzerainty over Southeast Asia was spiritual, for the cults of Buddhism and Brahma-Vishnu-Siva, the trinity of Creator, Preserver, and Destroyer, had been brought by the Brahmins from India and the Indies. They held in their many-armed embrace almost all of the gorgeously named kingdoms of the region—Funan, Champa, Chen-la, Angkor, Srividjaja, Sailendra, Madjapahit—and Sanskrit was to the learned of

Southeast Asia what Latin was to the prelates of Medieval Europe.

In Funan, inscriptions recorded the legends of North India, and today Hindu epics still provide the themes for Indonesian shadow plays, for the dances of Bali and Bangkok and the Royal Cambodian Ballet. Their mythical half worlds are endlessly re-created wherever Javanese puppeteers perform to village audiences and Thai dancers, sewn into their scintillating confections of gold and silver brocade, arch their long-nailed fingers in the curlicued gestures of a wordless dialogue.

As one coat of lacquer is laid on another, the new faiths of Buddhism and then Islam were added to the map of Southeast Asia, half obscuring the old, and leaving only Bali as the last stronghold of the earlier Hinduism. The teachings of the Prophet Mohammed spread to Southeast Asia as converted Indian merchants from Gujerat sailed to Sumatra and Malaya and the further islands, until the powerful Hindu Madapahit Empire was overthrown in Java and two new Muslim kingdoms arose in its place. They were just in time to face the Protestant Dutch in Java, as the Moros faced the Catholic Spaniards in the neighboring Philippines to the east. The Christians had arrived to save the Orient from itself.

2 : The Contract Breakers

West and East do not speak the same language, even when it is English. To the half-educated, half-heathen product of the British school system, medieval "Islam" evokes a vision of Holy Wars, of flames, scimitars, and angry young men in turbans slaying infidels from one end of the Mediterranean to the other in their earnest and impartial attempts to propagate the Word of the Prophet. Early "Christianity," on the other hand, is St. Augustine and the humble heritage of Iona, the soft progress of peaceable barefoot friars opening the eyes of the ignorant to the glory of heaven and their nostrils to the rather objectionable odor of sanctity.

In much of the Malay world of Southeast Asia, however, Islam meant the sufi, the emotional yet gentle missionary who sailed through the islands, adapting the sharp edges of his faith to the curves of the cults he found, and reconciling them through their common denominator of medieval mysticism. Christianity, on the other hand, was carried to the East with cutlass and cannon, and if the white men that so unfortunately seemed to go with it were not gratuitously bullying the benighted, they were using any local display of enmity toward their priests as a pretext for laying violent hands upon kings and their countries. In this way the persecution of Christian missionaries by two emperors of Annam lit a powder train of events that ended with Paris writing "French Indochina" across the entire eastern half of the Southeast Asian mainland. This was an age in which even de Gaulle would not have been an anachronism, for French nineteenth-century colonialism was characterized by a chauvinistic hysteria and greedy obsession with Gallic *gloire* which was further stimulated by a perfidious British presence in the western half of the subcontinent.

First in the field, however, were the Portuguese, who seized Malacca in 1511 in order to stop the spread of Islam and Arab trade. Their methods were inspired not so much by the teachings of St. Francis Xavier, who rode through the streets of the port ringing a bell and calling on all to pray for "Jews, Turks, infidels, and heretics," as by the exacting example in savagery set by Vasco da Gama when he encountered an unarmed Arab ship in the Indian Ocean a little earlier. The ship was found to contain many pilgrims from Mecca among the three-hundred-odd men, women, and children aboard. So, after carefully removing the cargo, the Portuguese locked all the passengers in the vacated hold and set fire to the ship. And when the hapless inmates obstinately broke out on deck again and tried to beat back the flames, the great navigator sailed his squadron around and around the floating bonfire, bombarding it with cannon while women held their babies up in their arms in an absurd attempt to wring a little Christian mercy out of him. With sour if saintly humor, St. Francis himself wrote that the knowledge of the Portuguese in Amboina seemed to be confined to the verb *rapio*, in which his countrymen demonstrated "an amazing capacity for inventing new tenses and participles." The Spanish, who landed in the

Philippines later in the century, showed the same deadly diligence in pursuing their colonial crusade against the Muslim Moros in the southern islands of the archipelago.

"If the Portuguese were little better than buccaneers, the Dutch who drove them out were little better than hucksters," was the uncharitable verdict of one of those intrepid middle-aged English ladies who always seemed to be penetrating jungles in the nineteenth century when they were not presiding over tea and thin-cut sandwiches on the lawn.

The verdict of Miss Isabella Bird (for such, almost inevitably, was her name) was presumably based on accounts of the way in which, with the commendable thoroughness of the Dutch burgher, the Netherlands exploited the Indies. The Dutch founded Batavia in Java and seized Malacca from the Portuguese in the early seventeenth century, and thereafter systematically fleeced the sprawling dependency which is today the Republic of Indonesia. The principle was quite simple. The native farmer was told what to grow on much of his land and was obliged to deliver the crop for a fixed price to Dutch merchants who held a monopoly on its fantastically profitable export to the Netherlands. Since local chiefs also took their cut, it has been estimated that during the eighteenth century a Javanese planter had to supply double the quantity of coffee that was actually shipped, for which he would receive little more than one-twentieth of the sale price in Holland. This "coffee culture" racket was still operating during World War I, and ten years after it Dutch government monopolies in pawnshops, opium, and salt in the Netherlands East Indies were still bringing The Hague a respectable revenue of more than £8 million a year.

Like the French, the Dutch were reluctant to groom their golden-brown wards for authority, and when the Japanese invasion of Java in 1942 brought them their first false scent of independence, there were fewer than 250 Indonesians holding senior posts in the civil service throughout the entire archipelago, compared with nearly three thousand Dutch.

To the British, one of the most irritating characteristics of the British is the irresponsible fashion in which they will invent something and then leave others to exploit it on a mass-produced basis (tanks, jet aircraft, and counter-insurgency immediately come to mind). Colonialism is the exception. The British left the Portuguese, the Spanish, and the Dutch to do the pioneering, and only then went into the business seriously themselves, emerging with a controlling interest in the biggest cartel of all. By 1824 they were still limited to modest beginnings in Southeast Asia: Penang, Malacca, and a spit in the ocean off the point of the Malayan peninsula, called Singapore. The robust and enterprising spirit of the men on the spot, however, was exemplified by the official of the East India Company who acquired this 225 square miles of unprepossessing jungle and mangrove swamp with little more than a handful of primitive Malay fishermen clinging precariously to its malarial fringe. Thomas Stamford Raffles, finding the sultanate which controlled Singapore in dispute, installed a dispossessed claimant on the island and at once concluded an agreement with its new, grateful, but impecunious master whereby the company would pay him $5,000 a year for the right to establish a settlement. For he foresaw that this mud bank in the gullet of the Straits of Malacca, commanding the strategic water gate between East and West, would one day outstrip all neighboring territories in importance. And he was right.

The coy attitudes of British officialdom toward the acquisition of empire were also reflected in the company's reaction to the Singapore takeover. Raffles was castigated for exceeding instructions and for annoying the Dutch, and when he died the company dunned his impoverished widow for £10,000 to cover various expenses he had incurred, including those of his original mission to the island. The same spirit diluted the policy of the government of British India toward Burma, which was only acquired piecemeal after the initial moves had been provoked by the repeated threats of an ill-tempered Burmese monarch to take over bits of India. (This characteristic of grasping more power under protest has been complemented by the deceptive aggressiveness of Peking, which many believe to be no more than a well-developed defensive reflex thoroughly justified in a world in which three out of four people are not Chinese. The Reluctant Lion, it could be said, has been matched by the Reluctant Dragon.)

Piracy along their trade routes, and the routine state of "robbery, battle, and murder" in the interior behind their finger-holds down the steep Malayan coast, drew the British into pacifying and accumulating more and more territory unwillingly in accordance with some sort of imperial variation on Parkinson's Law, it is claimed. There is certainly evidence to support the contention. When a British Resident experimentally appointed to the Malay state of Perak in 1875 was promptly murdered, and the governor in Singapore launched a sharp "little war" of reprisal, there was uproar in England, and irresponsible colonial officers who added to the burden of empire by conquering territory without parliamentary approval were roundly condemned.

Despite all the ostensible timidity in London, however, it is to be remarked that with the passage of healing time Britain found herself virtually in possession of the whole of North Borneo and the peninsula of Malaya. The British Resident to a Malay state, originally sent as an "adviser" to the ruling native prince, became the government itself. "Captain Murray," Isabella Bird tells us briskly of one Resident, "is Judge, Superintendent of Police, Chancellor of the Exchequer, Surveyor of Taxes, besides being Board of Trade, Board of Works, and I know not what besides." Local rajahs attended by such Residents she describes as being virtually "pensioned off." But in a fetid and lawless land in which personal feuds and rival claims to power were summarily settled with the snake-bladed kris, white protection could be a serviceable counterbalance for the blackest reputation. In Perak the British upheld as ruling prince an unamiable fellow who is said to have poured boiling water over the back of a runaway woman slave and then put a red-ants nest on it. Generally detested by his fellow Malays, he not unnaturally turned out to be "a proved man as to his loyalty," records a tongue-in-cheek British official.

Striving to run their states on a sound financial basis, Residents relied upon well-tried and conventional sources of wealth like farming, taxes, and licenses. They needed no knowledge of agriculture, however, for the "farmers" were enterprising business-men who were sold monopolies in such estimable services and commodities as gambling, drink, and opium (happily for the exchequer, "every coolie smokes his three whiffs every night"). It would nevertheless be grossly unjust to suggest that there was no other farming. Plantations were not, on the face of it, unat-tractive investments, for coolies were paid a shilling a day and it cost only five pounds to build a barrack into which you could cram fifty of them.

This was no continent of primitive jungle dwellers, however, and what the white man was rearranging to suit his own con-venience, much as one may convert an elephant's forefoot into a wastepaper basket or a Chinese bronze drum into a barbecue, were the shards of great civilizations with intricate administrative systems as well as profound religious beliefs. At Angkor the enormous hydraulic network that irrigated the country had in its own way been as wonderful as the monuments to its god-kings. The whole region of more than twelve million acres, served by ingenious devices for controlling the movement of water from and to reservoirs of immense capacity, was squared off into rice fields capable of yielding three and even four crops a year.

The European was constantly to be astonished, and on first seeing the Shwe Dagon Pagoda in Rangoon four hundred years ago, a British merchant-adventurer wrote: "It is called Dogonne, and is of a wonderful bignesse, and all gilded from the foot to the toppe. It is the fairest place, as I suppose, that is in the world: it standeth very high, and there are four ways to it, which all along are set with trees of fruits, in such wise that a man may go in the shade about two miles in length." The arrogant Spanish were chastened to observe not only the excellent craftsmanship of the Filipinos, who built galleons for them of up to two thousand tons out of splendid hardwood, sailcloth, and manila hemp rigging, but also what masterly seamen they were when they handled them.

To these peoples Western conquest brought not only war but peace. The mayhem subsided and across the face of Southeast Asia there slowly crept an unaccustomed expression of catatonic calm, broken by an occasional nervous twitch here and there but utterly unlike the jerky fits expressive of greed, treachery, violence, and hatred that had convulsed it before. This was the hypnotic imperial pax imposed by the new white masters of the subcontinent. But the first catch in any colonial contract is the *noblesse oblige* clause in small print which stipulates that the superior must be seen to be superior, and the right to plunder must be matched by a readiness to protect. This clause was invoked in 1941 when the Japanese attacked, and the West was exposed as a common cheat.

The admiral, who had studied aboard the training ship *H.M.S. Worcester*, showed the usual national genius for copying others and on the eve of battle dispatched the signal: "The destiny of the Empire depends upon this action; you are all expected to do your utmost." This Japanese Nelson then engaged the Russian Baltic Fleet, which had come halfway around the world to challenge him in the narrows of Tsushima, and sank, captured, or disabled every one of its thirty-eight ships.

Admiral Togo's decisive victory at sea in 1905 and the defeat of the tsar's armies in the Russo-Japanese War sent a faint quiver of expectancy through the Far East, for an Asian power had for the first time whipped the whites at their own war game. But although, in the thirty-six years that followed, twinges of nationalism animated the subcontinent's soporific countenance—there were riots in Burma and there was bloodshed in Tonking and Indonesia, where uprisings were suppressed with nervous brutality —the domesticated dragons of tropical Southeast Asia for the most part remained reassuringly tame.

When for the second time the Japanese displayed the same military vices and virtues by attacking without declaring war and then crippling an enemy fleet with praiseworthy economy, confidence in Western supremacy at first remained unshaken. Nowhere was this more true than in Singapore. The Japanese, having struck the first blow at Pearl Harbor in December 1941, lashed out in all directions at bewildering speed and within three weeks had taken Wake, Guam, and Hong Kong, had landed in Thailand and Indochina, invaded the Philippines, Burma, Bali, and Sumatra, sunk the *Prince of Wales* and the *Repulse*, and established a beachhead in north Malaya.

Lolling in the rattan chairs of Singapore clubs while forty-year-old Chinese "boys" sidled up with the day's first iced *stengah*, a man of the right creed and color could nevertheless scribble his name on a chit and see things in their proper pink perspective. Singapore was an impregnable fortress. Hills had been flattened and rivers deflected to build the mighty £63 million naval base, with its twenty-two square miles of anchorage, its giant floating dock, and seventeen football fields. The island was defended by 88,000 troops, and the R.A.F. were operating from four airfields in machines which, it had been solemnly promised, were "more than a match" for Japanese Zeros. To reach Singapore, moreover, the enemy had to fight his way through four hundred miles of impenetrable jungle against British defending forces, and it simply could not be done, old boy.

In fact, the indefatigable little men from Asia's offshore islands covered the distance in just over two months, and were decapitating their first Chinese victims on the Singapore waterfront under the eyes of the helpless British by mid-February 1942. The naval base had proved a fabulously costly white elephant, for, as it was belatedly remarked, its 15-inch guns pointed "in the wrong bloody direction" and could not traverse enough to bear fully upon an army invading overland from the north. In any case, they had no high-explosive ammunition suitable for the task of mincing up men, but only armor-piercing shells for knocking holes in absent enemy warships. The R.A.F.'s aging collection of aircraft was soon shot out of the air, leaving one squadron of Hurricanes to face more than two hundred Japanese planes. When it was all over bar some defiant shouting that "There'll always be an England," the Japanese had lost 10,000 men (and the British 139,000 one way and another).

Some of the besieged fought brilliantly, above and below, and many British men and women acted with a gallantry that matched the stoical courage shown by the Asian poor amid the wreckage and mangled horrors of devastated Chinatown. But as morale crumbled and the dispirited and defeated army filtered down from Malaya to join the final dregs of the defense in Singapore, the island stood exposed, both naked and ashamed. And when orderlies piling corpses into a forty-foot trench outside the General Hospital put Asians at one end and white men at the other, it was somehow symbolical. Not all were brothers even now, and the men were still to be separated from the "boys," it seemed.

First the white wives began to leave—two of them successfully insisting that their cars must be loaded on the same ship with them, although every inch of space was precious. Next, Harbour Board officials and naval technicians were furtively evacuated, and finally a "secret" operation to slip out three thousand "key young men" who must run away to fight another day was mounted on Friday the thirteenth of February. The definition was liberally interpreted, and an incongruous flotilla of forty-four boats sailed for Java, carrying among others eighty-seven members of the Public Works Department headed by a man who had been expressly ordered to stay behind—and his wife. They were to be followed within forty-eight hours by Lieutenant-General Gordon Bennett, Commander of the Eighth Australian Division, who crept away without permission, having issued a last order to his troops to stay stanchly at their posts before he made for the docks.

In the heavily bombed and shelled General Hospital, Asian civilian nurses, who could have faded back into their kampongs without trace, were firmly told that neither their civilian director nor the British Army sisters were going to leave, and chanted "Then we stay too." And they did—working with a marvelous devotion to duty. A few days later the British Army sisters nevertheless silently disappeared. Abandoned by the absconding white man to a yellow conqueror with the leniency of a locust, the island's immigrant Chinese, Malays, Indians, and Eurasians stayed put, for they had nowhere to go.

"Don't worry about me—I'll become part of the scenery," smiled a Eurasian journalist as his white colleagues took off. He did—but he also operated a short-wave radio and smuggled thousands of messages to British internees in Changi jail, using a Chinese plumber as his courier. Finally betrayed from inside the camp, he was seized, beaten, starved, and sadistically tortured over a long stretch of months but never gave away a single accomplice. Eddie de Souza, my Eurasian assistant, who could also have melted into the shadows easily enough, refused to discard his uniform as a volunteer and was duly taken prisoner and sent to work on the infamous "death railway" the Japanese were building from Siam to Burma.

First known as Timasek, then as Singapore the Lion City, the island was called Syonan by its new Japanese proprietors. There never had been any lions, people realized, and the settlement was now insecure, unsure of its identity, in shock after its traumatic experience. If the British could return to Malaya and Singapore without blushes or bloodshed in 1945, it was because the Japanese had not only behaved so atrociously, but had opened the bidding in brutality on arrival by butchering with bayonets nearly everyone they found in the British military hospital on the island, and the Asian observed in time that the white man was to suffer with the yellow and the brown after all. In work camps, on the death railway, men of all shades perished of starvation and the systematic savagery practiced upon them by the dreaded Kempetai. The Japanese beat prisoners until they were "as raw as liver," made them kneel and then jumped on their exposed soles with army boots until the fractured bones appeared, or with fiendish simplicity denied them all food and all sleep for days on end. "We suddenly feel the British are not bosses but human beings like us," a Chinese woman told me. A common suffering and a common hatred blurred the colors and brought the races closer.

But the white man had forfeited his right to rule. To Asian nationalists, who by now had had quite enough of brick-faced barbarians from the West, the ugly Japanese had held out one beautiful promise—the magic which Malays call "Merdeka" and Vietnamese "Doc Lap" and which smells as sweet by a hundred other names: independence. Since this promise must be made to come true whoever won, nationalists supported first one side and then the other as the fortunes of war fluctuated, and sometimes divided the labor between them and backed both at the same time. In Burma the sarcastically self-styled "Thakins" ("Sahibs") first helped the Japanese and harassed the British, and then backed the British once it looked as if the Japanese would lose the war. In Indonesia, Sukarno and Mohammed Hatta collaborated with the Japanese and were made responsible for recruiting 120,000 men into auxiliary forces, which ostensibly served the ends of Tokyo but in fact became the core of the Indonesian People's Army. Other nationalist leaders were simultaneously organizing resistance against the invaders in accordance with the sound principle of heads-I-win, tails-you-lose.

Peace came like the last, revealing chapter of a farcical whodunit, with the glaring suspects unmasked as sound security risks after all and the crime pinned firmly on the hero's best friend. The chapter begins with a comic semantical misunderstanding, the Americans and British calling anyone who backed the Japanese "collaborators" and "quislings" while Asians are calling them "patriots." General MacArthur swears he will run "every disloyal Filipino" to earth, and in Burma General Slim reminds the Thakins, who are asking London to recognize their provisional government, that under British law they are nothing but traitors.

This makes for a strong dramatic opening, but the reader must not be misled. MacArthur proceeds to give a certificate of good conduct to Manuel Roxas, who served Tokyo's puppet government in Manila by procuring rice for the Japanese, and in the year after their surrender he is elected president of the Philippine Republic and hailed as a loyal friend of the United States. In 1948 he proclaims an amnesty for all "traitors" who have not committed serious crimes. Marshal Pibul Songgram, who declared war on the Allies and allowed the Japanese to use Thailand as a springboard for their assault on Malaya, is back in power by early 1948 and assiduously courted by the Anglo-Saxons. The British recognize an interim government of Burma dominated by the Thakins, just eight years after these gentlemen are taken to Japan for military training and return to Burma with the invading Japanese army.

Magnanimity cannot safely be extended to all those who showed themselves "pro-Ally," however, for they are now politically suspect. MacArthur's disapproval is deflected to the Hukbalahap movement—the People's Anti-Japanese Army whose thirty thousand guerrillas, supplied with American arms by submarine and parachute, successfully sabotaged Japanese administration in many provinces of the Philippines, but also sovietized them as a sideline. In Bangkok, Pridi Panomyong, Pibul's rival who led the anti-Japanese "Free Thai" underground, is out in the cold and will end up as a permanent guest in Communist China. At this moment the lesson of the whole absurd paradox is: we can deal with our former enemies, and their possible role in the future deserves sympathetic perusal. But heaven preserve us from our friends. Most of them may have to be taken as Red.

3 : The Carbon Copies

As they marched past the general, the two tall Indian officers, their mustaches as stiffly horizontal as the swagger sticks tucked neatly under their rigid left arms, threw up a clockwork salute in perfect unison as if they were Grenadier Guardsmen crossing a barrack square. They were, in fact, crossing Rue Catinat on their way to the terrace of the Hotel Continental in Saigon and a lanky glass of *citron pressé soda*. "Crumbs," said a British correspondent rather nastily (he had served in the Royal Navy). "Look what a marvelous bunch of carbon copies we've made of ourselves."

It was 1955 and high summer, and he should have saved his breath to cool his beer, for he was talking about the new lords of Asia, the Western-educated native elite who had so naturally assumed the mantle of the outgoing white master in their respective countries. They were often few, but by 1963 they were running every ex-colony east of Persia, and the most important Oriental languages for any Far East correspondent to know were English, French, and Dutch.

The chanceries of Indochina ring with their voluble if slightly glottal Parisian. The flamboyantly patriotic Sukarno will sign his name in Dutch fashion "Soekarno" to the end of his days. When he met Tengku Abdul Rahman of Malaysia, the two champions of Malay culture dropped quite naturally into English (which they both used again when they criticized each other fiercely in separate private conversations with President Macapagal of the Philippines, the third Malay power in the region). Mutually hostile ministers from opposite ends of the continent belong to the same exclusive club as those who took their law or leisure at Oxford and the Inns of Court, their economics at London.

The products of cultural cross-pollination are sometimes singular mutants whose voices and faces do not match. Introduced one day in Formosa to an elderly Chinese with ivory skin and eyes like ebony splinters, I felt my hair rise on my scalp as the idiom of a dead tongue rolled from his mouth in the accents of Bertie Wooster. "Howd'yedo, my dear fellah," he said pleasantly enough. "Nice runnin' into you. By Jove, isn't it simply rippin' weathah we're havin'?" Medium? Ventriloquist? Fiendishly possessed puppet? He actually said "Well, pip-pip, cheerio" when he left, and I learned that he had come down from Oxford nearly half a century before and had not been back to England since.

He was a well-adjusted old gentleman, however, versed in the history and art of his own country, and therefore equally at home in East or West—the East of 1968 and the West of 1923. But when a group of Russians visited the University of Singapore shortly afterward, they created a crisis in communication by innocently addressing a Chinese member of the staff in fluent Chinese. She belonged to the sad band of English-educated who cannot speak their own language and who, in terminal cases, not only know nothing of their own history but would rather eat sausages and mash and raspberry jelly than a curry or Cantonese rice.

The French and Dutch failed miserably to train their subject peoples for administration against the day when they must rule themselves, for they had no intention that such a day should come. The British have a brighter record, but they stand accused of educating nations of dusky clerks into whose minds has been crammed an indigestible porridge of alien fact and fiction such as the dates of Wellington's victories and "Oh, to be in England now that April's there."

In stove-like cities they talk of "being snowed under" and "walking on thin ice," and when the anti-colonialist People's Action Party came to power in Singapore in 1959, its official organ, the authentic voice of equatorial nationalists sweating happily for the first time over the problems of self-government, could only say "The dark stormy nights of winter are passing away. The clean, keen scent of spring begins to fill the air" in a land that knows neither winter nor spring and in which night falls like a cloak at about seven o'clock all the year round. I pick up a little book entitled *Malayan Songs for Malayan Children* and find that the first page carries the words and music for "D'ye ken John Peel," not one line of which could possibly mean anything to any child in the country.

Not all transplants are incongruous, however. The Oriental judge in robes and wig may look ridiculously hot, but the equitable law which the British originally imposed on Singapore and Malacca soon had immigrants streaming into these settlements from Malay states where justice was often as uncertain as it was sudden. It was the British Residents who later introduced prisons in the interior, where formerly culprits were just shot, krissed, or flogged, to save house room.

From common law to cricket, and from equitable government to driving on the left, the British—as did the other colonial powers in their territories—cut a new and exotic pattern into the original design of Southeast Asian society. And their Western-educated heirs, hesitant to indulge in too much freehand drawing at the outset, usually begin by following the grooves. In consequence, he who runs eight thousand miles from the freezing rigors of British taxation may read, on his first Singapore assessment form, familiar-looking crossword clues like "An individual who is resident for the basis year for a year of assessment is ordinarily resident for that basis year unless he is not ordinarily resident for that basis year."

Faced with a similar brain-teaser in Vietnamese financial regulations in 1955, I took the trouble to see the minister in Saigon and ask him what it meant. "To tell you the truth," he replied at length, avoiding my eye and grinning frantically at a hideous lacquer mural on the far wall, "I don't really know myself. But it was in the original French document, it was well phrased, and so when we drew up our own laws we thought we had better include it in case it was important." I slunk out, feeling like a man who had addressed the wrong Chinese in Chinese.

Paradoxically, it was the colonial powers themselves that schooled their Asian wards in the elements of nationalism and so signed their own expulsion orders. At Oxford and Cambridge, Indians and Malays and Burmese were conscientiously instructed in those ideals of freedom inherent in a scepter'd isle that "never did, nor never shall, lie at the proud foot of a conqueror." At the Sorbonne young Vietnamese and Cambodians (along with Chinese like Chou En-lai) were inspired by the French Revolution but noted that "Liberté, Egalité, Fraternité" stopped at the Suez Canal. At Leyden, thoughtful Indonesians began to realize that there were lessons to be learned from the fine tale of the rise of the small but sturdy Dutch Republic among the bullying monarchies of sixteenth-century Europe. From a continent in which men hardly understood the concept of nation, the young flocked to the capitals of the West to hear for the first time of nationalism, revolution, and a man buried at Highgate called Karl Marx.

While white men in Europe were teaching the Western-educated Asians to throw them out of the East, more white men in the East were literally digging the grave of colonial domination. Archaeologists and scholars from the West drew from the forgotten recesses of Asian history the splendors of Angkor and the might of Srividjaja which were to fire the Khmer and the Malay with their intimations of glorious national heritage. Before they came with their spectacles and spades, Angkor was no more than a fleet of stone wrecks in a Sargasso Sea of jungle, and nothing was known of Srividjaja but its name—in 1908 one Dutch scholar still believed it was a historical person, not a power, and no Indonesian contradicted him.

In Dutch Indonesia and French Indochina men newly armed with ancient pride and modern liberal ideas fought their colonial tutors to a standstill after World War II, and then negotiated their independence. Yet by virtue of their Western education, they were often isolated from the millions.

In 1956 I moved house (two maltreated suitcases and a middle-aged typewriter) from Saigon to Singapore because, incredible as it now may seem, the story in South Vietnam had gone as flat and damp as one of its own paddy fields, while in swinging Singapore the current chant ran: "See you later, Agitator," to which the with-it response was: "When it's quieter, Rioter." First deflected to cover right-wing secret-society disturbances in Hong Kong before covering left-wing anti-colonial disorders in Singapore, I found myself flying from one British colony compounded of barbed wire, broken glass, and burning cars, to land punctually in another British colony of barbed wire, broken glass, and burning cars. By the time I could pick up the contacts warmly recommended to me by my predecessor, the Singapore Special Branch had flung nearly all of them into the same historic Changi jail where the Kempetai had practiced its plastic arts on an earlier generation of prisoners.

I nevertheless managed to meet one disconsolate anti-colonial mobster whom the police had ruthlessly left at liberty. "They know that what I should like now would be a year or so in the clink, and so they won't arrest me, confound them," he ground out venomously, as if that, too, must be added to the long list of their towering crimes. I murmured a few words of polite condolence, for this was like failing an entrance examination or being dropped from the team. Few who did not qualify for a colonial jail today could hope to qualify for a cabinet seat in the independent Asia of tomorrow. A man who was denied the accolade of arrest and was allowed to slink about the city in dishonorable freedom might even be suspected of being a police informer.

"You see, if I don't have a year's peace and quiet I shall never find time to learn Malay," he went on. He had another point there. Chinese and Malay were taught in Changi five times a week, and his great handicap as an Asian rationalist was that he was English-educated, a suspect carbon copy of the colonial master, and he could not hope to enjoy real communion with the uneducated masses of this stirring subcontinent until he could speak to them as a fellow Asian in the language of a fellow Asian.

He was far from being an exception. Lee Kuan Yew, Singapore's youthful and astute Cambridge-educated premier, who is only rarely anyone's fool, long ago threw himself into the task of learning fluent Mandarin and Malay in order to persuade the Asian populace he was one of them. His problem was brutally simple. The Chinese-educated Chinese, soaked in tea and Mao and a three-thousand-year-old tradition of contempt for foreigners, saw him as a beer-drinking, golf-playing barbarian despite his Chinese face.

Nationalism is not rationalism, and its devotees will practice its rites without counting the cost. The compulsive urge to have a national language where the country's nerve systems have hitherto functioned in English, or French, or Dutch has prompted the new masters of the East to embark eagerly upon the endless hazards and complications and disadvantages of enshrining Malay in Malaysia (where the Malays are in a minority), Hindi in India, and "Pilipino" in the Philippines as the shibboleth of the patriot. This nevertheless involves adapting foreign words in order to update their somewhat basic vocabularies, and the results are not always felicitous. "Taliveshen," "talipon," "ois," "chek," and "teksi" get by in Malay, but "semen" is a little unfortunate for "cement." There has been much minting of words, of indiscriminately mixing Malay, English, and Arabic into philological alloys until some so-called Malay has become incomprehensible to Malays themselves. In Pilipino, we have "telebisyon" and "besbol," but apparently it was unpatriotic to borrow "cher" for "chair," and so the word "salumpuwit" has been coined—a good, earthy phrase derived from the native Tagalog which Filipinos more addicted to English say means "something to stick your ass on."

In the fifties the signboards began to change all over Asia. In Saigon and Phnom Penh the streets called after the tongue-twisting but musical names of the heroes of the French empire— Chasseloup-Laubat, Lagrande de la Liraye, Doudart de Lagrée— gave way to Vietnamese monosyllables set to three-four time like Phan Thanh Gian and the rolling, gong-like Khmer notes of Norodom and Monivong. But for years this bedeviled circulation, for even the skinny, knot-calfed drivers of the ubiquitous *cyclopousses*, or pedal rickshaws, stuck treasonably to the old names and did not recognize the new.

The first elected mayor of Singapore, Ong Eng Guan, attempted to insure that freedom would mean confusion by exuberantly planning to rename all streets that "perpetuate the memory of ex-governors and colonial officials." Since the most sacred word at that moment was "Merdeka" (Independence), which had already given the island Merdeka Bridge, there would also have to be Merdeka Circus, Merdeka Highway, Merdeka Way, Merdeka Quay, and others. Those with a smattering of vulgar French voiced their own terse comment on these proposals, which in any case quite unsuitably aped the infuriating inability of the British to think of a name, so that in the same area of London there will be Belsize Park, Belsize Gardens, Belsize Lane, Belsize Crescent, and so on, *ad nauseam*. (He was fortunately restrained.)

Nationalism, like yawning, is highly infectious. The mood was established in Singapore in 1959 that would later prompt a mild, somewhat inexperienced party official to pronounce the howler of the academic year. Told that a patient he saw during a tour of the General Hospital was to be given a local anesthetic, he remarked approvingly: "Excellent, let us rely on our own rather than on foreign resources wherever possible."

But for many the phase passed. As knife sharpens knife, nothing quickens mutual understanding better than a long, thoroughly abrasive relationship, and once the new nations of Southeast Asia had joined the none-too-amiable club of sovereign states on an equal footing with all others, it was often a relief to their Western-educated leaders to see the familiar faces of their former colonial *bêtes-blanches*. Their souls, however different, were at least clothed in the same ill-fitting cultural uniform that they had been unceremoniously thrust into at school, and they enjoyed a certain rough-and-ready understanding, even mutual regard. The horrors of their prefect-and-fag days were over, and they were both old boys of the same alma mater in an alien world.

Sutan Sjahrir, the Indonesian revolutionary leader, expressed the sweet-sour taste of the West on the tongues of Dutch-educated Indonesians when he recommended the "forceful, dynamic, and active life" of European civilization, despite its "brutality and coarseness." After two bloody "police actions," the Round Table Conference at which The Hague grudgingly relinquished Indonesia to the Indonesians in 1949, and the ignominious expulsion of all Dutch from the republic in 1957, the Hollander whom the Javanese had earlier found such heavy going was given the warmest welcome when Western influence filtered back into Indonesia in the mid-sixties. Here was a foreign devil they knew, and he was trusted more than those they did not for everything familiar about him from his aspirates to his aspirins.

In Indochina, where the blue-blooded nationalist movements of royal princes had been inspired by dreams of independence and not the damnation of the French, leaders like Souvanna Phouma in Laos and Norodom Sihanouk in Cambodia sent their children to French schools once they were kings of their own castles, the French planters remained, and the French professors poured back into the *lycées* of Vientiane and Phnom Penh. When in November 1963 Sihanouk announced that he was kicking the Americans out of Cambodia, he told me that French experts in the fields of education, administration, justice, and even national defense could all stay. "We are rejecting all American aid in future," he said a little shrilly, but added in a confidential tone:

"However, if Washington wants to send us money through the French, as representatives of the West here . . ." The Americans did not avail themselves of this unique opportunity to give something for nothing.

No one has personified the post-colonial kiss-and-make-up more than Lee Kuan Yew of Singapore. This English-educated revolutionary was in close contact with members of the Communist-led Anti-British League in 1951 and went puce as if the venom were in his very veins when I first heard him inveigh against the iniquitous white man before a multi-colored mob of trade unionists in 1956. But thirteen years later he was telling the entire Commonwealth that Britain was not unnaturally frustrated by "the attitudes of European countries she helped save in the last war and the querulous colonies she nurtured to independence . . . and in return received churlishness and sometimes abuse."

My irrepressible Indian friend James Puthucheary, three long spells of political detention for left-wing activities behind him, watched his anti-colonialism fall out of fashion from behind the wire. He has since taken his own revenge on the treacheries of passing time by qualifying as an advocate and joining a prosperous partnership in Malaysia. "For law," he explained to me happily, "is the last resort of the scoundrel." Harry Lee Kuan Yew reversed the process by moving from law to politics, but he also has come to terms with his former white tutors and tormentors. Except that you do not call him Harry these days. You must call him Kuan Yew.

His equilibrium is, however, denied to men in whom the clash of cultures provokes that most harrowing of all questions: "Just who am I, anyway?" And these are to be found in quantity in the Philippines.

4 : God's Other Country

His name is González. He wears a gold medallion of the Virgin
Mary, a gift from cousins in Madrid whom he visited two years
ago. But it is partly concealed by his *barong tagalog*, the embroidered cream shirt of pineapple fiber which is the Filipino
national dress. From his beringed hand dangles a leading Manila
newspaper. A headline is visible: "Cops Air Meal Pay Gripe."
He ignores this mystery, however. "Don't kid yourself," he says in
his Spanish-American English. "All this trouble will blow over.
The Philippines and Indonesia and Malaysia are gonna be
friends. We Malays have to stick together."

The Philippine Republic consists of thirty-seven million Asians
sitting on seven thousand Asian islands whose pressing postwar
problem has been to prove that they are Asians at all. It has not
been easy. Four hundred years ago the Spaniards began coloniz-

ing the archipelago, and although they were obliged to chasten the Muslim south with the sword, they found that they could carry most of the rest with the Cross. In 1898 the Americans took over, and a new army of missionaries preaching private enterprise, democracy, and the virtues of rye whiskey swarmed over the land. From this confusion of Madrid and Manhattan, the Philippines emerged in 1946 as an independent republic, an ostensibly Asian nation of Malay stock which took its very name from a dead European monarch.

Nor is that all the Spaniards left behind them. During Holy Week the Catholic churches of Manila are crowded and penitents parade the streets, flagellating themselves with whips laced with ground glass, and carelessly splattering the bystanders with blood. The language and the literature of the older generation are Spanish. So are most of the traditional dances, like the formal *rigodón de honor*, performed by ladies whose national dress belongs to eighteenth-century Castile.

It is upon a gracious if politely corrupt Iberian foundation that this most distant outpost of twentieth-century America has been erected. After four hundred years in a convent and fifty in Hollywood, as some wag once observed, the Filipino raised on Spanish, English, and his native Tagalog and surrounded by bananas is ever fearful that his country will be dismissed as a displaced South-American republic out of an O. Henry short story. He is eager above all to be taken for a regular member of the all-Asian anti-colonial team, and although full of much misleading American sass, he is in fact seismographically sensitive about his equivocal identity and his national dignity.

In 1968 President Marcos was urged to cut short his visit to the United States when the Americans treated him "like a vassal" by sending only a "second-rate dignitary" to meet his plane. Marcos himself was drubbed by his opponents in Manila for describing President Johnson as the "Liberator of Asia," for this added dimension to the grinning little image of the Philippines as a sycophantic satellite of the West, populated by cut-price Americans.

Fury is aroused by the "special relationship" between the two

countries which enables American soldiers to shoot a Filipino or
two from time to time and get away with it, thanks to their
extraterritorial rights in the republic. In 1965 thousands of
torch-bearing demonstrators burned Uncle Sam in effigy outside
the United States embassy in Manila, after marching through the
streets bearing thirty-two cardboard coffins symbolizing the alleged victims of an American's inalienable right to the pursuit
of trigger-happiness. This hateful manifestation was provoked
by the killing of a fourteen-year-old Filipino boy caught scaveng-
ing for scrap metal at Clark Air Base, nerve center of the United
States Thirteenth Air Force north of Manila, and the street was
filled with placards reading "Go Home Yankee Dogs," "Go
Home White Monkeys." In early 1969 the scene was repeated,
with the placards saying "Johnson is a murderer," after an American court-martial had acquitted a lance-corporal of killing a Filipino inside another U.S. military establishment. The United
States authorities have been known to pay compensation to a
victim's family, but this has inspired the steely Manila headline:
"Shoot a Filipino for $787."

From the very beginning of their relationship, the Americans
showed their new Asian friends that they were up against com-
mendably sharp minds, for their first act was to relieve the Filipinos of the Philippines. During the Spanish-American War of
1898, anti-colonial revolutionaries under General Emilio Aguinaldo rose against their Spanish masters in the Philippines in
secret agreement with the United States, on the understanding
that they were fighting for Philippine independence Once the
war was won, however, it transpired that the Filipinos had been
laboring under a slight misapprehension. The white man's burden
was shifted straight from Spanish to American shoulders, and
the United States proceeded to suppress a revolt by Aguinaldo,
who had been sworn in rather forlornly as first president of a
sovereign Philippine republic at his headquarters northwest of
Manila.

Forty-eight years later the Americans did indeed grant the
Filipinos their freedom, but, true to their own exotic tradition of
equality, bound their two countries together with constitutional

provisions and reciprocal agreements which gave Americans the same rights as Filipinos in the republic until 1974, allowed the United States to maintain military bases in the islands in exchange for defending them, and provided each country with a duty-free market in the other. The golden handshake had become an iron grip.

However, if imitation is the sincerest form of flattery and not just the lowest form of humor, no one can doubt that beneath the stinging spindrift of anti-American agitation that blows fitfully over the surface of Philippine life lies an ocean of harmonious fellow feeling. Manila is a city of cheeseburgers and back-yard barbecues and hotdog stands, of motels and curtained day clubs with soft lights and soothing singers for businessmen prone to fatigue at two in the afternoon, of memorial parks in California style where mortal man may buy his plot, erect his own engraved mausoleum, and have nothing left to do but die. Its money looks like the American dollar, and its newspapers use type faces once dear to Times Square.

A reverence for the past is always touching. A sensitive Chinese delights to find in Japan ancient customs borrowed from his own country more than a thousand years ago but long since abandoned in China itself. An Englishman in New York is refreshed to be addressed in the archaic argot of World War I by some native joker who fondly believes he is mimicking contemporary British slang and would get along splendidly with my venerable Chinese friend in Formosa—I mean to say, old chap, what? In Manila the happy American finds himself nostalgically reminded of his own great heritage of the twenties.

"Two Cops Slay Four at Fiesta" scream the streamers. "Co-ed Taps Frat Sweetheart." History in headlines nevertheless tells us that in 1957 there was a municipal resistance to the soft-drink civilization, for we had "City Dads Cool on Pop Plant Plan." "Check your firearms here" reads a notice at the entrance to congress, and I duly check with a gentle, corpulent official wearing yellow shoes, an olive shirt, and a small straw hat with a tartan ribbon. "Deposit your lethal weapons" says another at the municipal waterworks, with its charming children's playground.

For the republic is a colorful garden of variegated violence with an average annual yield of from ten to fifteen thousand murders.

The administration is only faintly sketched in over much of the archipelago and is hampered by a carefully cultivated contempt for the law common to the city gunman and the flick-knife boy in the shantytowns of Manila, the Christian and Muslim in the deep south who settle ideological differences in blood, and scantily clad Igorot tribesmen who develop an urge to collect human heads each year when the flame-of-the-forest blooms again. That does not take into account rival police in neighboring suburbs, who have been known to shoot it out between them while the hoodlums looked on at this somewhat unusual form of gang war. There are about 320,000 licensed firearms in the country, and perhaps half a million more whose owners are not authorized to kill at all. In 1968 a report before congress disclosed that syndicates would commit a modestly priced murder to order for approximately $250, and I have even heard $25 mentioned as a deposit.

A bulge in the waistband feels natural to many Filipinos who believe that it is up to the citizen to heel himself. At a small but well-thought-out diplomatic dinner a gentle, bespectacled Filipino academic leaned over a centerpiece of cut-glass palm trees and inquired diffidently whether I had heard of the Balisong, or Batangas butterfly knife. This, it turned out, was not some sort of lepidopterist's scalpel but a beautiful and ingenious weapon which he pulled from his pocket and forthwith demonstrated to the entire table. No blade was visible, but the silver-studded blackwood handle was split down the middle into two legs joined by a hinge. Holding one leg, the professor deftly jerked his wrist so that the other swung around fan-wise and back into his hand, leaving exposed five inches of serviceable-looking steel which had emerged in a symbolically phallic fashion from between them.

"Have you a knife with you?" he asked and, when I said no, generously pressed it upon me. "You may need it," he urged. "And I have plenty of others anyway." He was a professor of English, and a man of unquestioned propriety, soberly dressed but for this one ornament. He was also a small man, probably weighing no more than the 110-pound farmer named Benito Fidel who killed four bandits and wounded two more with a .22 rifle when they tried to steal his six head of cattle in 1969. Fidel had the same instinct for do-it-yourself protection as the Manila politicians, among whom armed bodyguards—preferably ex-thugs themselves—have become status symbols.

The underpaid and undereducated police have been accused publicly of incompetence, brutality, and widespread corruption, and as I write, more than one thousand officers and men of the Manila Police Department are at their posts but under investigation for conduct unbecoming to the fuzz, ranging from graft to murder. It is characteristic of Oriental thought that opposites are seen to complement each other: there can be no light without dark, no good without evil. Perhaps in accordance with this principle, many of the Manila police look upon protection racketeers and smuggling syndicates as natural partners whose elimination would automatically mean their own elimination too, and who must therefore be cherished.

Around the scimitar-like curve of the Manila Bay strip on Roxas Boulevard the supper clubs rival each other in legitimate luxury but are flanked by plush little gambling casinos with entrances like double airlocks in an H-bomb shelter. I tap on an outside door and a small panel opens to reveal a pair of half-closed eyes, to which I say softly and forgivingly, "Jesus sent me." The door opens to let me in, but behind it is a black curtain, and when I have fought my way through that, I am in a cubicle about the size of an upended cabin trunk, facing a very fat man indeed in barong tagalog with much fancy weaving on it, while a small, candle-faced accomplice leans against what is left of the space. The fat man frisks me, and I am passed through a sliding door—only to find myself in a second cabin trunk with another fat man who also frisks me. I am then allowed into the club to lose a little money.

A shocked congress, hearing that one of their number had actually been detained by the National Bureau of Investigation when caught frequenting an illegal gaming house like this, reacted vigorously in 1963 by cutting off the N.B.I.'s entire budget allocation. But not far from here the son of the Speaker, José "Banjo" Laurel, was arraigned in 1969 for allegedly slapping and then shooting a policeman in the chic Bayside nightclub, while his bodyguards followed up with a fusillade that wounded two others. The Speaker himself had been winged by a bullet in a nearby steakhouse two years before.

Sometimes one is tempted to ask what this vast archipelago of thin men and private eyes would have done without the culture and the drama delineated for its inhabitants by Dashiell Hammett and Raymond Chandler. But there is, of course, far more to the Filipino-American love-loathe than that. Manila man in the eyes of an Indian is similar to a Madison Avenue account executive in the eyes of an Englishman: they both believe in Dale Carnegie and democracy à la mode, they push the same ballyhoo with the same disarming spirit of dedication, and they live in the same half world of man-to-man, dog-eat-dog relationships that the deferential Asian or European, imprisoned by his own caste system, would give much to copy. The Spanish-American mastermix may have given the Philippines flagellating exhibitionists and air-conditioned cells for Dominican monks, but it has also created the charming illusion that human equals human.

I remember my first humiliating attempts to see Vice-President Emmanuel Pelaez in Manila by applying ingratiatingly through the correct official channels, to be rightly regarded with contempt by all the bureaucratic flunkies in my path. One day I told a Filipino colleague of my problem: Pelaez was giving me the anti-British brush-off. He at once made a telephone call which established that at that very moment the vice-president was on his way to a private room in a smart downtown restaurant, where he was throwing lunch for most of the senior members of the diplomatic corps. "Okay," said Benedicto David. "We go too."

Frilly with my old-world servility, I protested that we could not barge in on a formal vice-presidential lunch, but David simply jeered, and before I knew where we were, we were thrusting our way through a phalanx of lackeys and two swinging doors into an air-conditioned anteroom full of dignified middle-aged gentlemen conversing politely in subdued tones and conservatively cut suits. Without hesitation, David dragged me toward a tall, graying figure who was gazing at him rather blankly from the very middle of this concourse, like Nelson in Trafalgar Square. When we arrived before him, however, David said: "Hi, Mani, I want you to meet Dennis Bloodworth of the London *Observer*." The vice-president said, "Hi there, let's go sit over in the corner away from the mob," and we were in.

This is free-and-easy catch-as-catch-can democracy. No punch lines are pulled in or out of congress, and Asia's shrillest, most uninhibited press will call the head of state a "liar" or "a coward and a poltroon." On weekly "Common Man's Day" I have watched shabby old peasant women, youngsters in aggressive Hawaii shirts, and personable girls in well-starched cotton frocks as they shuffled forward patiently across the gaudy gardens and the cool, tiled floor of the Malacanang Palace to speak, one by one, with the president. The president sat behind a plain wooden desk, and while some just shook his hand, others would launch into a long, winding tale of bureaucratic injustice in their *barrio*. Often the president scribbled a note and handed it to an aide, and a Filipino who had thought himself pitted hopelessly against the inert mass of an uncaring administration would suddenly find that all the corners had been cut and his problem was solved. "He is an honest man," said one of his admirers. "He is atoning for the sins of corrupt governments of the past." "Yeah," cut in a detractor neatly. "He always did think he was Jesus Christ."

President Macapagal had just aroused a little ire in some quarters by accusing an opposition candidate of accepting a million dollars from Communist countries, notably China, to finance his election campaign. No one seemed to think it odd of him to make such a preposterous charge, for in the Philippines money makyth man and anything is just possible. At one end of the scale, a congressional bill to nationalize the rice industry is held up for twenty-four hours so that desperate private dealers who stand to lose fortunes can be squeezed stone-dry when they make their last-minute cash bids to have it thrown out; at the other, Filipino firemen let shops and houses burn while, hoses idle, they haggle with distraught Chinese owners over the prevailing price of water. Why should not Macapagal suggest that a rival had been paid by the Communists? An admirer and well-wisher of his own had ruthlessly eliminated another candidate by hitting him in the hip pocket with half a million dollars.

A Philippine election campaign has been known to cost four times as much as its American prototype for each ballot deposited. Fat bank rolls are reserved for the hearts and minds of those party delegates who astutely hesitate in their choice of presidential candidate, and rivals who conveniently withdraw their nominations are generously compensated. Voters are won over by putting them on the payroll or by feeding them at campaign parties with "peso sandwiches" consisting of two thin slices with a bank note in the middle (for, as is well known, man cannot live by bread alone).

These one-dollar-one-vote elections are a free-for-all fought with bullets as well as ballots, however. During polling in 1965, troops and constabulary moved into the most inflamed parts of the country to stop the slaughter on the ground. In the worst single incident, seven died in a gun battle when in the center of one town heavily armed "fortresses" were set up only two hundred yards apart by hangers-on of two political rivals. The rivals were both congressmen of the Liberal Party. The opposition Nacionalistas were merely interested, discreetly approving onlookers. During partial elections two years later, nearly one hundred unfortunates were shot, stabbed, or killed with coshes, and in the presidential elections of 1969 more than eighty died violently.

The temptation to look upon democracy in the Philippines as a tragi-comic circus inspired by Li'l Abner is not blunted by the behavior of congressmen like the one who submitted to the Speaker's office a bill for outlawing typhoons. But it is to be noted that the military *coups d'état* that shake most of the capitals of the Far East like recurrent earthquakes are unknown in this republic, that the peasant in the *barrio* is the most politically aware villager in Southeast Asia, that the parliamentary structure is firmly based on two main parties, and that—an almost unique phenomenon in the region—power actually does change hands constitutionally whenever the ballot dictates. Filipinos enjoy the most exhilarating, irreverent experiment in freedom in Southeast Asia. Manila may seem to combine Tammany Hall with prohibition Chicago, but then so did the United States only a few years ago.

Democracy is an American graft on an Asian trunk, however, and it does not mean in Mindanao what it means in Massachusetts. The Oriental Filipino often sees political power simply as a means to advance family interests, and to stop short of cheating may be selfishly to deprive one's dependents for the sake of one's own lily-white soul. The men already on top are expected to be grasping, but there may still be a good reason for not voting for the others, since "the mosquitoes inside your net have sucked your blood, but think how much hungrier those outside would be."

Graft, corruption, conflicting business interests and pressure groups, political jealousies, and a dilatory congress provide enough cotton wool to turn any reforming presidential punch into pat-a-cake. Student rioting which broke out in Manila early in 1970 was prompted by fury with the sick Filipino system more than resentment of American privilege. The conditions for revolution are present and, given enough license, democracy may still dig its own grave. Much depends on whether the Filipino truly believes in the almost limitless authority of elective bodies—so succinctly evoked by a Manila headline which appeared the day after an important announcement from the Vatican and read: "Sainthood okayed for five."

If the Filipino cannot keep faith with democracy, what of his neighbors?

5 : *The Mask of Democracy*

The dignified gentleman in the blue mohair suit, the restrained club tie, and the well-polished black shoes threaded his way toward me through the mob in the air-conditioned Sarawak bar and we shook hands. He ordered lager, and as he raised his glass to drink, the tattoo marks on his finger joints told me he was that uncommon type of collector, the successful head-hunter, for each blue knuckle in North Borneo is equivalent to a notch on a gun in the old West.

A paramount chief of Sea-Dyaks, or Ibans, a native people of Sarawak whose otherwise unexceptionable manners have been marred by the pursuit of this regrettable hobby, he had been presented to Prince Philip in Kuching earlier that evening. On the morrow I was to watch one of his colleagues, lightly clad in a straw hat, a khaki jacket, and an intricately tattooed bare backside, deliver a loyal address before the colony's distinguished visitor in the legislative council. It was 1959, and the spread-eagled territories of North Borneo, acquired by Britain in grosser days with the irritating ease of a millionaire making yet more money, were still colonial dependencies. Despite the march of time, it hardly seemed likely that these amiable but illiterate gentlemen with their Beatle cuts and illuminated bottoms would one day sit in the federal parliament of an independent Malaysia. But within five years one of them would in fact be a minister.

This future lay dark before us, however, and the duke and I (among others) were able to see tomorrow's electorate without any qualms about the one-man-one-vote system. For from the moment when the first chanting Dyak maiden, dressed in nothing but an elaborate silver tiara and a long flashing fish-scale skirt of overlapping silver medallions, ceremoniously offered Prince Philip a rice beer in a thick-rimmed kitchen tumbler, the people stole the show.

Behind the frill of steaming swamp tacked along the North Borneo coast lies a lunatic interior, an almost impenetrable confusion of rain forest and mountains striated by twisting, rock-strewn rivers on which the hard-drinking Dyaks, Dusuns, and Muruts build their longhouses on stilts, and hunt, fish, and culti-vate small patches of rice and manioc. And as the duke pilots his Heron aircraft from strip to dusty strip across this archaic wilderness, followed by twenty cursing correspondents rammed into two flying biscuit tins, the kaleidoscope spins with gathering momentum.

At Sibu the Iban chieftains line up for his touchdown—gaudy ornithological freaks clad in monkey skins and beads and bangles and stuck all over with feathers, whose bare-breasted womenfolk jingle like caparisoned ponies every time they shift their feet. At Miri the Dyak dancers squirm and yelp endlessly into the night, monstrous black-and-white hornbill plumes streaming from their hair. In Jesselton the duke watches Bajau pirates assault the coast, leaping from their prahus with drawn cutlasses, and Dusuns shooting stuffed monkeys out of trees with long blow-pipes and poisoned darts. He is asked to celebrate by drinking homemade palm toddy out of a grimy earthenware jar with all his new cronies, and for the first time he appears to lose a little of his aplomb (he does not know that etiquette allows a guest to appoint some only-too-willing "mouth" to do the drinking for him).

The Queen's husband is of widespread interest, especially among the Muruts. The chiefs of this diminishing uxrive people, alarmed by their falling birth rate, discuss a romantic proposal based on their traditions of open and polygamous hospitality, whose adoption would serve the double purpose of doing honor to the royal visitor and of multiplying their number considerably. The suggestion is put to the women of this tribe and meets with a more than favorable response. But, alas, their paramount chief is dissuaded by some officious British bureaucrat from broaching the subject to the duke himself. The Muruts continue to decline.

Many of the natives, brought to the coast to be shown to the duke, are seeing a water tap, a bicycle, an electric light bulb, sarsaparilla and the sea for the first time. But the moment is to come disconcertingly quickly when these territories will be faced with the strange business of electing forty representatives to the Malaysian Lower House in Kuala Lumpur. Like most of Southeast Asia, they are hardly ready for the experience.

The knowledge of tribesmen in Borneo and Central Vietnam alike is often limited by the distance they can paddle or walk in one day. There are Laotian villages in which even the headman cannot quite remember the name of the prime minister, and where the ordinary voter may not know the name of his own country, or where it is, or that other countries exist at all. In Thailand the peasants recognize their king, but may look blank if you mention any "strong man" who has been bedeviling Thai politics for the last quarter of a century. In Vietnam in 1967 there were isolated villagers who were still unaware that President Ngo Dinh Dien had been butchered four years before, and who knew nothing of their latest rulers. In small, smart-aleck Singapore, Ping once asked two women construction workers, in their red headdresses and faded blue denims, what they thought of Premier Lee Kuan Yew. They gazed at us thoughtfully for a moment, faces of cigar-box wood tilted slightly upward. Then one lifted a hand like a old meat board and asked carefully: "Do you mean the short fat one or the tall thin one?"

In earlier Singapore elections, wily canvassers were known to have told the illiterate that all they had to do was put a cross against the second name on the list when they entered the polling booth. This would be their own candidate, and the ruse worked— except when the voter unintentionally double-crossed them by holding the ballot paper upside down. When voting is not compulsory, up to seventy percent of the electorate may not bother to go to the polls, and democracy becomes the business of sharp professional power seekers and pressure groups—if it is allowed to survive at all. "We can't afford it," a Vietnamese whiz-kid once told me, glaring gloomily at the gun flashes across the Saigon River over his dry martini. "It is not just the Vietcong. The peasants are too ignorant, too easily misled." What he meant was that they were amateurs who should be kept out of the club. The 1967 elections in South Vietnam, hailed as a triumph of the people's will, were in reality a modest mechanical success. Many voted only because they were told to, and then for the man their village heads or religious mentors indicated.

There have been other causes for the demise of democracy in Southeast Asia during the postwar years. High on the list must stand man's genius for disagreeing with man, and the popular conviction among politicians that two parties are better than one because then there will be twice as many jobs for the boys. The modest Vietnamese have never had more than fifty parties at a time, and the Thais twenty-five, but in the 1955 general elections in Indonesia 169 political groups formed up to fight for 257 seats, which were eventually shared among twenty-seven of them. Nor have Asia's parliamentary representatives always preserved the dignified mien popularly associated with both Westminster and the Wisdom of the East. In 1966 an elected legislator in South Korea lowered the tone of debate by indecorously flinging a badly secured parcel of human ordure at the government benches, while in Malaysia a state assemblyman brandished a naked kris and challenged a colleague to a duel on the floor of the House. At the turn of 1970 a woman deputy in Saigon tried to shoot a tiresome colleague in mid-session.

In 1958 Marshal Sarit Thanarat of Thailand, saddened by the rising price of parliamentarians and the high cost of legislating, suspended the experiment in democracy for ten years by dismissing the national assembly in Bangkok and ruling through a "Revolutionary Party" of military officers. Few voters were really outraged. Most of the candidates who had won seats in the previous general election were not so much the people's choice as creditors to whom peasants and shopkeepers owed money. When it looked as if their days were numbered, they hastened their own end by becoming more and more expensive to buy, urged on by the need to make quick profits before they lost their jobs.

If the Americans are sometimes blamed for molding their client states into monstrous mutants of modern democracy, it must be admitted that they have often had poor clay on which to work. The old Vietnamese political parties consisted mainly of sharp little revolutionary splinters engaged in conspiratorial intrigues and an occasional act of slaughter. The intellectual opposition that courageously challenged the oligarchy of President Ngo Dinh Diem and his family in 1960 with the "Liberty and Progress Bloc" proved to be a different sort of anachronism, however.

Having missed its press conferences in the air-conditioned opulence of the Caravelle Hotel in Saigon, I visited the home of one of its leaders to find myself amid a curio-shop clutter of gorgeous, horribly valuable antiques, listening to a smooth denunciation in well-polished French of the iniquities of the president's land-reform program. These iniquities, it rapidly emerged through the slightly perfumed cigarette smoke and the tinkle of liqueur glasses, had been committed not against the peasant but against South Vietnam's powerful and wealthy landlords, of whom he was one. Restore them their land, and the peasant would once again be happy under their benevolent patronage, I was told. As a program, it seemed a trifle to the right of Magna Carta.

One successful Asian politician with emotions as ungovernable as his thirst attacks his critics with his fists or furniture, has been known to beat up his wife (with the help of his mother), shows all the symptoms of a megalomaniac ("practically certifiable," as one of his friendlier colleagues told me), and only ended up in politics because he was sacked from a minor post in the judiciary for brutally abusing his powers. ("And lucky I did," he told us smugly when he became a minister.)

I have seen the Montecittorio in Rome and the Assemblée Nationale in Paris turned into close-packed battlefields as aging deputies launched themselves at each other, kicking, punching, tearing viciously at each other's throats, and ripping up woodwork for weapons when a whole company of police charged in to quell the riot. Nor are corruption, graft, sex scandals, drug dramas, and ballot fixing entirely unknown among the voting systems of the West. But whereas Europe acquired democracy, Asia had democracy thrust upon it, and many of Asia's masters look upon a parliament much as their forebears looked upon a well-turned-out elephant: it should be thoroughly domesticated and docile, and there must be no doubt as to who rides whom. It may then be an ornament to the state and a symbol of national integrity and prestige, conveying unquestioned authority. But if it goes wild, it should at once be curbed, and if necessary liquidated.

Having taken brutal, furtive punishment in the back alleys of the subcontinent, democracy is still somewhat unfairly in the dock as a delinquent suspected of breaking the peace in the first place, its egalitarian ethics under gloomy scrutiny. Its most implacable enemy has not been the substance of Communism, but its shadow. By 1959 military leaders had seized power from ineffectual or corrupt politicians in Pakistan, Thailand, and Burma. Indonesia was well on the way to becoming a dictatorship, and in Laos a conservative prime minister had armed himself with special prerogatives which reduced parliament to a cipher. General elections due to be held in three different countries of Southeast Asia in that year were postponed. And all those responsible had the same ready-made excuse: the threat of revolution.

Communism wages a far more subtle and effective ideological struggle in the counsels and consciences of its most bitter adversaries than it does in any tangle of jungle or secret city cell. The Communists are dedicated to the overthrow of government by fair means or foul. A young Asian state that tries to fight them with constitutional liberty, therefore, is like an inexpert adolescent who tackles an armed thug according to Queensberry rules, many Asian politicians say, and he should be rescued from his own scruples. Which is worse, they ask, to betray democracy by allowing freedom to those who will destroy freedom, or to betray it by restricting their rights as citizens? The argument provides would-be dictators with respectable reasons for having all their political adversaries eliminated as dangerous subversives, and persuades even honest but prudent Asian leaders to whittle down democracy in its own defense. The Communists do not have to discredit their enemy: the anti-Communists do it for them.

In South Korea a National Security Act sweepingly outlaws any action or speech which "might lead to results advantageous to Communists," and in 1968 the comfortless jails of Thailand still accommodated those who had been thrown into prison without trial ten years before on the simple charge of "hooliganism," as martial law allowed. Moreover, the new Thai constitution which restored democracy to the kingdom in 1969 is also well perforated with funk holes. It guarantees the rights of the citizen (except where they affect national security), and it guarantees freedom of speech (except where the government rules that it may be harmful to the national interest).

In an Indonesia still queasy with Communist unrest, President Suharto, having armed himself with special prerogatives, repeatedly postponed long-promised elections. The People's Action Party in Singapore and the Malaysian Alliance in Kuala Lumpur have preserved the special security ordinances introduced by their former British colonial masters: in Malaysia hundreds of political suspects are held under lock and key without trial, in Singapore more than fifty leftists still languish in detention. It is not always easy to say whether all these maneuvers are designed to save democracy, the state, or just the ruling party in each case, but the psychological effect is much the same.

To the Western democrat, however, the reaction of many Asians of the older generation might seem as startling as his own inverted image in a concave mirror. For these do not cry out at the bruised visage of democracy; they see it, rather, as a specious papier-mâché mask of deceit which in recent years has often been clamped over the homely, familiar visage of Oriental autocracy. "It is not so much the dictatorship that infuriates me," one Vietnamese told me of Diem before his death, "but the hypocritical imitation of democracy we have to conceal it with in order to please the United States."

When the free West first peddled a vote for every man as the panacea for past ills, the colonized East had been suffering not from despotism at home so much as from domination from abroad. It was not dying for democracy but living for the day when it would be its own boss. The Americans may have attracted numerous rice-democrats who came to pray so that they could stay to scoff, but the mainspring of Asian ambition was something the East had already learned from the West—nationalism. And this could be "pro-Communist" or "anti-Communist," according to taste.

6 : Danger: Mao at Work

"We settled into our ambush positions in the jungle," the major told me, wiping the beer from his bristle, "automatic weapons trained on the path, and waited for the Communists to come. Suddenly we heard quick, light steps up the track and—" he paused, banging his pewter tankard down on his knee with restrained violence—"hang it if fifteen chaps in vests and running shorts from the local harriers club didn't come trotting past as if they were on Hampstead Heath."

I nodded sympathetically, for I too had suffered from the frustrations of this dying war, in which the eager and the bloodthirsty were frequently made to look foolish when dramatic danger zones became disconcertingly peaceable stretches of real estate almost overnight. The Malayan Emergency, declared in 1948 after Communist killers had tied up three white planters in Perak and then shot them down in cold blood, was now nine years old and fading before our eyes. Communist guerrilla forces had been systematically pared down to fewer than one thousand men. Chin Peng, secretary-general of the Malayan Communist Party, had long since crept out of Malaya and across the border into the sanctuary of the jungles of Thailand. By 1960 it would officially all be over.

This was the end of another act in the tragi-comedy whose ironies had so far been well sustained. For just as Western ideas and Western historians had inspired the Asian nationalist to demand independence, so Western military organization and Western weapons generously helped the Asian Communist to try seizing it through armed revolution.

Like a man plunging further into debt, the defeated white man armed the Asian and organized him to continue the guerrilla struggle against the Japanese all over the subcontinent after his own conventional defenses had crumbled in 1942. In Malaya the Japanese had to cope with disrupting sabotage carried out by a *maquis* of seven thousand men armed and supplied by the Southeast Asia Command in Ceylon. Most of them were Chinese immigrants of whom one British guerrilla officer wrote: "The rank and file were absolutely magnificent. I can hardly find words to express my admiration for their courage, fortitude and consistent cheerfulness in adversity." They were members of the Malayan Peoples' Anti-Japanese Army, and when a British party from India, secretly landed by submarine, contacted them in 1943 in order to reach a working agreement against the common enemy, the most cooperative leader they dealt with was this same Chin Peng. For the M.P.A.J.A. was the military arm of the Malayan Communist Party.

The British air-dropped weapons and supplies to these willing fighters; a high percentage of which, however, they were later blandly told had been "lost." The M.P.A.J.A. regiments, preparing for the war that was to follow the war, had carefully buried them for future use against their friends the donors. In Burma the British also armed the Thakins; in Thailand the Americans armed the "Free Thais" of Pridi Panomyong; in the

Philippines they armed the Hukbalahaps; and from Kunming in southwest China, which was still in Chiang Kai-shek's friendly hands, the American Office of Strategic Services supported a growing guerrilla movement in Tonking organized by the League for the Independence of Vietnam, the "Vietminh." The leader of this group was a Comintern agent who hid himself behind the name of Ho Chi Minh.

For three years after the war the Communists adopted a smiling and seductive mien in order to form "united fronts" with non-Communist political organizations which they could "capture" from within, and so worm their way into power constitutionally. But in 1948 the Cominform once more identified the West as the enemy in plain terms and damned the new nationalist governments of Asia as imperialist puppets. Dropping their best Party manners, the Communists turned to violence—and the Allied weapons they had kept for this very day. Within months Sukarno faced an uprising at Madiun in Java, the terrorists had struck down their first victims in Malaya, and the Burmese Communists were in armed revolt against the new and shaky nationalist administration in Rangoon.

In Malaya the agony was sharpest, and it lasted twelve long years, for Malaya was a British dependency during most of them, and the struggle was therefore "anti-colonial." Two-thirds of this country as big as England lay under a rough coat of jungle in which a man might not see more than a few yards ahead of him and in which it could take him a whole day to hack his way through a mile or two of undergrowth with a parang. That jungle was the haven of ten "regiments" of Communist guerrillas, nearly all of them Chinese, who had moved into hidden forest encampments, some capable of sheltering five hundred men. Often living on cassava or wild tapioca, which can be the source of sudden death rather than the staff of life if it is not carefully washed and heated to cleanse it of prussic acid, Communists with campfire in their bellies blew up trains and ambushed vehicles, launched large-scale assaults against rubber estates, or murdered miners, planters, government officials, and "uncooperative" civilians at will. Armed with machine guns, grenades, and carbines, they could shoot it out with army patrols and military convoys, and burn down police posts.

Paramilitary police and twenty-three battalions of regular troops were deployed on the "inside," pushed into the heart of Malaya's green hell in small "jungle-bashing" hunting parties that hit the guerrillas on their own ground. It was coldly calculated that the average British tommy, Malay private, Gurkha, or Fiji Islander would spend twelve hundred hours soaked through, bitten mercilessly by leeches, and forbidden to smoke or talk above a whisper, before he would get his first shot at a terrorist.

As the maddening hide-and-seek war went on year after year, however, the noose made up of some 360,000 men slowly tightened. The guerrillas were isolated from their supply lines, sector by sector, permitted to starve and then trapped as they emerged for food. Police services weaved an intricate web of intelligence until they held a dossier on every man and woman on the other side. R.A.F., Royal Navy, special constabulary, and home guards all played their conventional roles. And then to the long bow and the broadside, which had in other centuries given the British mastery on land and sea in the course of their regrettably lurid island story, was now added another unconventional weapon: independence.

It is the white-hot August of 1957. Architecturally, Kuala Lumpur is a fine example of late Victorian Haroun-al-Raschid, a city rich in bogus domes, in minarets and Caliphate colonnades. Even the railway station looks like a palace in old Baghdad (from the outside), and all would be well if some joker had not put down in the very center of the town a great rambling country club in glorious technitudor. However, on this auspicious day the focus of attention is the new stadium, which stands aside and aloof from that confused riot of arabesques and old oak beams as it gathers into its great dish the colorful crowds and the actinic rays of Malaya's relentless sun.

The ceremony follows its inevitable course. The brass bands play, the usual soldier faints. Then, one by one, each under a great yellow silk umbrella carried by a gaudy flunky, the sultans

of Malaya are escorted across a red carpet to their special dais
in the arena, corpulent gentlemen bobbing along in their gorgeous regalia, chatting in a dignified way on this solemn occasion,
doubtless about horse racing and H.R.H. And when all are in
their place the Duke of Gloucester (for it is he) makes a graceful
little speech in that high, agonized voice common to so many
of the House of Windsor, and surrenders the documentary "instruments" which confer full sovereignty onto the Federation of
Malaya as of midnight. The huge concrete bowl vibrates with
the cry "Merdeka!" as if it would crack. I withdraw to the lobby
for lime juice, and run into Hamid.

Hamid is a professional Malay "student" in his mid-thirties
whose normal uniform is a frayed white shirt, an elderly sarong,
and two bare feet, and whose normal cronies are two baby-faced
Chinese Communist militants and a fierce little Indian Marxist
tiresomely long in the tongue. I see him only intermittently, for
he has a fondness for traveling, his journeys sometimes taking
him as far afield as Peking and Moscow. Today, however, his
face is split by a melon slice of a grin, and he is resplendent in a
glossy black *songkok* (the short, soft Malay fez), a faultless pearl-
buttoned silk blouse, and a magnificent brocade sarong in blue
and silver. We exchange only a few words, but I somehow sense
that for him the fight is over. More than violence or votes, most
Malayans had simply wanted their independence. And now they
had it.

Terrorism smoldered on like a dwindling fire for three more
years, but there were too few to stoke it any more. The Malayans
quietly assumed the administration of their country as their
own native Paramount Ruler moved into his new palace, a for-
tress-like mansion which had originally been built for a Chinese
millionaire and his thirteen wives. The British expatriates were
thinned out of the ranks of the civil service like white hairs, but
no conspicuous bald patches appeared.

Communist leaders had meanwhile realized that the struggle
for world supremacy had become an exercise in isometrics:
neither side could win with brute force in any form, from
banditry to the Bomb. However, the Western powers could be

discredited. Already tarnished by their acquisitive colonialist record, they were now the authors of a series of bellicose acronyms—NATO, CENTO, SEATO—which betrayed their chronic aggressions. It was therefore decided that in contrast to these compulsive gangsters the Communists must emerge as respectable, peace-loving champions of national sovereignty and neutralism. An already suspicious Asia could then be enticed away from the West with a little soothing sympathy (and mugged later). While the Communist states befriended the new nations of Southeast Asia, the local Communist movements must once more enter into broad alliances with the local nationalists.

But the Chinese soon abandoned this ploy, and by 1960 quarreling ideologues in Moscow and Peking were no longer troubling to keep their voices down. Peking condemned all peaceful coexistence advocated by the Russians and upheld the hallowed principle of permanent world revolution. For the young new nations of Southeast Asia had formerly been tributaries of the Celestial Empire, and just as Imperial China had brought the word of Confucius to those in outer darkness in this region, so Communist China must now imbue them with the Thought of Mao. However, as the Chairman's guerrilla precepts were founded on the conviction that native peoples win "wars of liberation" when the foreigners and mercenaries are all on the other side, China would not risk an international conflict by pouring her own troops into Southeast Asia to fight their battles for them. Communist terrorism had nonetheless won a new lease of death, and what followed was predictable.

On August 5, 1966, Inspector Solomon Samy wrote with brutal irony to his bride-to-be: "This is probably my last letter to you addressed as Miss Mary Ann Peh." He was right—not because his marriage took place as planned on the twenty-seventh, but because Miss Peh was to read the letter while sitting by his coffin. Forty-eight hours after he posted it, the Malaysian Special Branch officer was shot dead when thirty Communist guerrillas ambushed a joint security patrol on the Thai-Malaysian border, killing or wounding everyone. At the end of the year it was estimated that there were nearly one thousand hard-core armed

terrorists of the "Malayan National Liberation Army" lurking in
the wild sea of jungle on the Thai side of the frontier. They
were being given close support by about two thousand militants
drawn from the younger generation of local Overseas Chinese,
who in turn collected dues, food, and information for the guerrillas from twice that number of active sympathizers.

For the Malaysians, the new "armed struggle" of the Communists was like the familiar gray opening of a recurrent nightmare. Lacking wide popular support, it was on a reduced scale,
and some critics protested that the menace was exaggerated.
Others agreed that Mao's theories on peasant revolution could
never apply in the game-and-rubber economy of Malaysia's
jungles and industrial plantations. But it was obviously time to
wake up.

Police were soon to raid the first Malaysian "People's Commune," organized by local Communists in emulation of those
formed in China ten years before, when Mao tried to brigade the
peasantry into disciplined, self-sufficient collectives in which all
property was pooled. The commune threatened to become the
wagon circle of the Maoists in imperialist badlands where Communist writ did not yet run, it appeared, and on the Malayan
peninsula militant leftists set out to develop a rash of these small
red enclaves across the countryside until the revolutionary moment arrived for "using the villages to besiege the towns." They
had meanwhile deeply penetrated Chinese schools, at least four
big trade unions, and two opposition parties. The activists took
their general directives from Radio Peking, carefully tape-recording the broadcasts and distributing them to party cells. The
Quotations from Mao were being smuggled into Singapore at the
rate of eight thousand copies a month, and they were trickling
into the North Borneo states of Sabah and Sarawak, where stubborn Communists among the immigrant Chinese waged their
own will-of-the-wisp war.

Peking announced the creation of a "Patriotic Front" in Thailand in 1964, and by the beginning of 1969 subverted Meo
guerrillas in the north of the country were using rocket launchers
against the security forces. Taking their cue from Radio Peking,

the gunmen of the Patriotic Front numbered between twenty-five hundred and three thousand men, supported by about twenty-five thousand sympathizers. Over the border in Cambodia, Prince Norodom Sihanouk now described the struggle against "Red Khmer" terrorists as an "all-out war" against a "foreign-inspired" enemy within, while his hill tribesmen to the east were a prey to the bullying and blandishments of the Vietcong next door. As more red patches of Communist inflammation discolored the map of Southeast Asia, pessimists began to prophesy the sepsis of a subcontinent from the wound of Vietnam.

Nowhere did this seem more obvious than in Laos. "Any settlement over Vietnam reached at the Paris talks must include a settlement here too," William Sullivan, Washington's supercharged ambassador to Vientiane, told me in 1968. But appearances are deceptive. Sullivan lived twenty-four hours of the day with the nagging knowledge that North Vietnamese battalions already operating inside the country could cut right through to the frontier of Thailand and take the Laotian capital itself within a week. Yet he remained unruffled.

For although Laos was a pushover, Hanoi did not push. Some forty thousand North Vietnamese regular troops and up to twenty-nine thousand pro-Communist Pathet Lao guerrillas dominated much of the territory, but they were not deployed to conquer it. Their task was to hold a protective lining of geopolitical fat in the northern and eastern provinces of the kingdom, covering the frontier of North Vietnam and the vital Ho Chi Minh trails that served as a pipeline for men and guns fed into South Vietnam. Their forays into the Laotian plains from the foothills of the high Annamite Chain, through whose vulnerable passes the Communist reinforcements must file, were mainly intended to keep the Royal Laotian Army at a safe distance. Moreover, in the northern provinces of Laos it was the anti-Communist Meo hill tribesmen who were the hit-and-run native guerrillas, moving easily among their own folk "like fish in water" as Mao had taught, and the North Vietnamese conventional troops who were the hated alien intruders. They could fight no "patriotic" war on this soil.

In Hanoi Communist spokesmen have revived the old term "Indochina," and there can be little doubt that the North Vietnamese dream of a day when they can act the big brother to a Communist Cambodia and a Communist Laos. But their first concern will be South Vietnam, not the lands across their border, and although the seepage into the fringes of Thailand looks dangerous, there is in fact a damp course of devotion to king and Buddha in the interior which may stop the rot. As the Vietminh marched into Hanoi in 1954, gloomy analysts predicted that all Southeast Asia would go Communist within ten years. But fifteen years later not a single country had done so. China, the biggest domino of all, had fallen two full decades before, yet only North Vietnam had been knocked over since.

Maoism was losing its looks. When the "Great Cultural Revolution" broke out in China in 1966 and Mao Tse-tung loosed the Red Guards on everyone from his Foreign Minister to foreign nuns, the whole mystifying domestic upheaval appeared to most Asians to present the unedifying spectacle of a mad god biting its own tail. They became further disillusioned as the Chinese began to export their ideological convulsions, and Peking's novel diplomatic dictum that any mob wearing Mao in the buttonhole was right wherever it rioted began to reap brusque responses.

Accordingly, Burma, Ceylon, Nepal, and Mongolia were all accused of insulting portraits of Chairman Mao, or unwarrantably holding up imports of inflammatory Communist propaganda, or unpardonably stopping "patriotic" Chinese from rampaging through their respective capitals. In Peking nine foreign embassies were successively besieged by Red Guards, and Indian and Indonesian diplomats were forced to leave China under humiliating conditions. In all, China quarreled with seven of her immediate neighbors and nearly thirty countries around the world before revolutionary rage gave way to some semblance of reason, and the Maoists began to mend their diplomatic fences. But throughout the area the damage had already been done. It is enough to see a man foam at the mouth just once.

It is very doubtful whether anti-Communists could have slept as easily in their beds if China and the Communist parties of

Southeast Asia had everywhere practiced the peaceful coexistence which produced such solid dividends in Indonesia. In Djakarta the Communists paid unswerving lip-serivce to President Sukarno, who needed them in turn to counterbalance the Indonesian army and the Indonesian Muslims. This symbiotic relationship between the "Bung" and the Partai Kommunis Indonesia enabled the P.K.I. to rally some sixteen million people to its front organizations, to penetrate the army and to subvert the air force, to win widespread sympathy in the left wing of the Indonesian Nationalist Party, to acquire three seats in the government, slots in the Supreme Advisory Council, and the ear of the aging master. Sukarno himself denounced "Communist phobia" and coined the term NASAKOM for an administration in which Nationalism, Agama (religion), and Communism would all be represented.

In 1963, while plans were being laid that would raze the new British embassy in Djakarta to the ground in a few weeks' time, I asked M. H. Lukman, deputy secretary-general of the P.K.I., what would happen to the Father of Indonesian Independence "after the revolution." He looked around the shabby little anteroom at party headquarters, sipped his coffee to cover the pause, and said softly, "The way President Sukarno is thinking now, we don't see why he should not remain in office when we are in power."

Sukarno was flouting the United Nations and threatening to set up a rival organization for states that resented the prerogatives of the Big Five in New York. He had declared anti-colonialist cold war on the white and wealthy West and might well line up the leaner Afro-Asian nations against Washington and London far more effectively than could a Communist behemoth like China, which inspired distrust and fear in so many. His militant policy of rallying the have-not countries as New Emerging Forces against the Old Established Forces of capitalist and colonial powers promised a new polarization that would isolate the imperialists. The Bung was most conveniently chalking out the pitch for a Communist victory later.

Then, having won all this with their smiles, the P.K.I. threw it away in an abortive *coup d'état* on September 30, 1965, in which six Indonesian generals were murdered and mutilated and pitched into a well. A palace colonel ostensibly made his foolhardy, grand-slam bid for power, but it was obvious that he was playing with Party cards, and he later revealed that the Communists, who had been sent arms from China, would have kept Sukarno only as a paper president once they had taken over. It is believed that Chinese doctors attending the Bung's troubled kidneys in Djakarta had whispered (on orders from masters in Peking over-impatient for revolution) that he would soon die. This supposedly prompted the hesitant Indonesian Communists to rise before he no longer stood between the P.K.I. and the army, for the generals were reputed to be planning their liquidation. If they were not very quick, ran the argument, they would be very dead.

There had been a gross miscalculation, however. Njoto, second deputy secretary-general of the P.K.I., once assured me in the same shabby room in which I saw Lukman that eight out of ten soldiers were sympathetic to the Party because they were loyal to Sukarno. This *non sequitur* was now to cost the Communists dear.

The soldiers did not wait for Sukarno to die All over the republic the military and the Muslims set about exterminating the P.K.I. (and their own private enemies) with such a show of stamina that everyone soon lost count of the corpses, and vague estimates of the dead still range from a hundred thousand to half a million. As for the much-subverted Indonesian air force, General Abdul Haris Nasution, then Defense Minister, told me in the front lounge of his home in Djakarta (where on that black day in 1965 assassins were to miss him but shoot down his five-year-old daughter): "I am not afraid of Communist penetration in that quarter. The man who controls the ground troops controls the situation. It is a small matter to isolate a few military air-fields, cut off the fuel supplies, and ground the MIGs for good." And he was proved right.

By 1968 Sukarno was out and the anti-Communist President Suharto was in. The army was patiently winkling Communist guerrillas out of limestone fissures and caverns in East Java. Most of the P.K.I. leaders were dead, had fled, or were behind bars. For at least the third time in its checkered history, the impulsive Indonesian Party had tried to jump the gun and taken a bullet in the back for its pains. Peking was back to square one. Coexistence might pay. Crime had not.

7 : The Odd Couple

Mirnoye Sosushchestovaniye. I had learned the Russian phrase that morning, and perhaps learned also a little of its real meaning —a cat-and-dog life without conflict—as I trailed Mr. Peaceful Coexistence himself across the volcanic piecrust of Java. It was February 1960, and the second day of Premier Nikita Khrushchev's visit to President Sukarno of Indonesia. At Tjipanas, the mountain resort in the hills south of Djakarta, the principle was expressed in a simple tableau. The two men sat side by side, plump thigh to plump thigh, like an ill-assorted bride and groom at an Oriental wedding. Khrushchev was pink, sweating, and glum in his hand-worked Georgian shirt, his cream-puff suit with its cornucopia trousers, possibly wondering what on earth he was doing in this, the third presidential palace he had visited in twenty-four hours. Sukarno was immaculate in his black cap and beribboned uniform, his fastidious drooping lips and large dark glasses otherwise giving him the air of a slightly passé Hollywood co-respondent on the beach at Cap d'Antibes. One had emerged from the gray, winter backcloth of Moscow and mechanistic revolution; the other from the torrid, fleshy riot of a Balinese landscape. They seemed to have little to say to each other.

A radio reporter tape-recording the tinkling Javanese music in the background was suddenly accused of trying to pick up their heavily starched conversation, and a few minutes later my arm was also seized as I stood with other correspondents on the steps of the open-sided pavilion to which they had so pointlessly been flown by helicopter just to sip coffee. I turned, to meet the accusatory glare of a tall young thug with eyes of slate who rapped out something in Russian and jerked his thumb over his shoulder. His meaning was obvious, and it was not Peaceful Co-existence. Harsh words were then exchanged in the language of Lenin and Lady Chatterley with neither of us understanding the other, while Khrushchev watched impassively, his small blue eyes unblinking.

Only afterward did it occur to me that I had been wearing a rather nasty dacron suit that might have been run up in Bratislava, and the bodyguard had therefore probably taken me for a Soviet or satellite journalist unwarrantably hobnobbing with undesirable Western colleagues. But his behavior was typical of Khrushchev's secret service men, who treated Indonesia as if it were an insecure dependency of the Soviet Union and ignored the susceptibilities of their hosts. They persuaded the Soviet premier that he should not risk traveling around the country in the aircraft Sukarno hospitably put at his disposal but should fly in one of the Ilyushins that had brought the Russian party from Moscow. They also urged him to reject as unsafe the Indonesian program for him to travel by road to Bandung (but he overruled them).

Khrushchev had already shown his temper on his arrival in Indonesia, and the sunny atmosphere at Djakarta airport, where a grinning Sukarno planted himself on the rolled-up red carpet ready for the occasion and tilted his black *pitji* to one side of his head like some equatorial Maurice Chevalier, had soon been dispersed. The Russian premier, it seemed, liked neither the arrangements nor the rumors provoked by his acceptance of Sukarno's invitation, and the first thing he did was to fire the Soviet ambassador to Indonesia straight back to Moscow. It was a poor beginning for a goodwill visit. Khrushchev did not go to the Indonesians in order to entice them into the Soviet bloc, but his purpose was certainly to dissipate distrust of the Communists aroused by Peking's aggressive foreign policy at this time, and to depict them as men of probity who had found the formula for making modern powers out of backward Asian nations.

In fact, the meeting of minds was no greater than it would have been if President Eisenhower—whose failure to go to Djakarta Khrushchev was neatly exploiting—had been there in his place. Listless, taciturn, wilting in the heat, the Soviet premier dutifully played his role of "Prince of Peace" when he faced Indonesians in the mass, perching himself on the back of an American convertible beside "Bung" Karno to wave at a populace that waved back a million identical replicas of the Indonesian and Russian flags printed on poor-quality paper. But his welcome was well organized rather than warm, and the crowds were thickened by long lines of shrill schoolchildren turned out in force to greet the latest of a long line of foreign faces. He was no more than that to most. Sukarno's quick succession of state guests somewhat bewildered simpler people, and a correspondent who pointed to a poster of Khrushchev's head in Djakarta and asked provocatively "Who is that fat Dutchman?" was solemnly told by a confused trishaw driver, "That's no Dutchman, that's the King of Thailand."

It was small wonder that Khrushchev was displeased with the program, for he and the Bung seemed to be completely at cross-purposes, and he found himself unfairly trapped on a de luxe cultural rubber-necking tour during which he would see no plantations or power stations or other Marxist musts. Instead, Sukarno gave him the standard treatment.

First they set off from the capital for the president's sugar-white colonnaded palace at Bogor, where Sukarno showed the

Khrushchev family around the deer park and the botanical gardens, while I contemplated the Bung's private rhinoceros. (The rhinoceros is much prized among the more lubricious Asians for the propensities of the horn, which, when ground up and swallowed, is erroneously believed to stiffen the determination of aging men to show how young they are. I do not know Sukarno's views on these matters, but they would surely be well informed. It appeared to be a Sumatran rhino and therefore originally endowed with two horns. Both were missing.)

Their next stop was Bandung, the city of peaceful coexistence itself, where the Soviet visitors and their camp followers were dragooned into playing the *angklung*. It was Sukarno's custom to make foreigners perform for him, and at numerous interminable presidential parties ambassadors have warbled shakily and counselors have capered at his bidding. He could hardly order the Soviet premier to sing a solo somewhere along the line, but Khrushchev was not to be let off altogether. The Indonesian *angklung* is like a big bamboo rattle. Shake it, and it gives off a sweet tremolo of two harmonious notes with a hollow, wooden xylophone quality to them. Herded into rows of chairs in a hotel ballroom, we were handed *angklungs* graded to cover the entire scale from A to G and so converted into a living keyboard. A music-master on a dais displayed placards on which the chords of some simple tune were shown alphabetically, and by moving his pointer progressively from one to the next in correct time, he set us all jingling in turn as our notes were indicated. Khrushchev sat well forward in this adult bell-ringing class, attentive to the conductor's gestures but patently ill-at-ease in so unaccustomed a form of collective.

He then flew to Jogjakarta to address the students of its old university, and that was the only occasion on which he woke up with words. "By 1965," he shouted, a trifle erroneously, "the Soviet Union will be producing more than half of the world's goods. You students should come to Russia to see for yourself. I will give you a guarantee that no one will be forced to accept Communist ideals against his will." Much laughter and applause. I did not see this, however. A time comes on all these tours when the wise correspondent opts out, leaves it to the TV cameramen to record the inch-by-inch progress of prince or premier, and goes overland instead of flitting across foreign countries by air. For it is written: "A rider must dismount to look at the flowers." With two American colleagues, I had hired a battered old Chevrolet with a sulky carburetor and a leaking radiator, and we set off across Java by road.

From the terraced rice fields that provide the West Java volcanoes with their brilliant settings of jade, we headed for Semarang along the north coast of the island, bouncing over ribbed and potholed roads through stricken flatlands of scrubby gray-green fields listlessly manured by skinny cattle. The villages were miserably poor, their streets sullen. This was Sukarno's other island, which Khrushchev was not going to see, the ugly consequence of economic irresponsibility, inefficiency, corruption, and presidential megalomania.

On these roads cautious men traveled with a full car, so that armed hitchhikers might legitimately be refused a lift with a shout of "no room" and a shoe on the accelerator. The Chevrolet struggled over the 250 miles to Semarang, where this skeletal scenery vanished and we took the road south for Jogjakarta. The world tilted over as we climbed, the sun fell from sight, and the dry sky took fire until the whole vault was in flames. Against this lurid light there swung into line the great dark cones of five majestic volcanoes. It was as if this were the hot heart of the world. No one could fail to sense the lush, sweating life in the lowlands below that was Sukarno's vision of Indonesia, and turned even his love of country into a voluptuous passion incomprehensible to men conditioned to the Kremlin and the Caucasus.

The next morning we followed Sukarno and Khrushchev out of Jogjakarta. To the north across luscious rice lands fringed with coconut palms, the perfect cone of Merapi rose distantly from the plain like an aloof Vesuvius, a flat sliver of cloud half-severing the summit from the base. Ahead, the Soviet leader stood at the foot of its manmade reflection, the magnificent temple-mountain of Borobodur, and Marxist and monument confronted each other stonily, as if each perceived the challenge of the other.

Borobodur was built during the Sailendra dynasty in the eighth century—one hundred years before the Viking chieftain Rurik made his base on the Volkhov, and a primitive Russian state was first founded on a policy of plunder and piracy. Rising to a bell-like summit, this colossal sermon in stone ascends heavenward in nine narrowing tiers of galleries three miles long and intricately sculpted with bas-reliefs. The whole vast crown of rock symbolizes the Buddhist belief that man climbs through his many incarnations to the perfection whose reward is the bliss of Nirvana. It expresses the hierarchical Hindu-Buddhist society whose principle was the higher, the better, until the king at the apex of the system was the perfect earthly incarnation of Vishnu or Siva.

Excavated on the orders of Raffles when Britain occupied the Netherlands East Indies during the Napoleonic Wars, Borobodur was another example of the Asian nationalist's debt to the white archaeologist. But in this case the colonialists had, with unconscious malice, restored to the Indonesians a huge hill of a talisman whose magic impassively repudiated the egalitarian and atheistic tenets of the perspiring Russian visitor. Khrushchev and family gave it their suspicious attention, and then took off for Surabaya.

In Surabaya the Soviet prime minister's dull speech received a dull reception from the crowd carefully assembled in the local stadium. But when Sukarno rose to address the microphone and the concourse of forty thousand young people beyond it, describing his guest as "not exactly tall and a little fat, but the leader of a billion people," and then launching into one of his silver-tongued harangues—violent, simple, and repetitive like all war dances—he was given an ovation. Khrushchev sighed, and they went on to Bali.

At Bali airport the Russian was greeted by a great bouquet of bare-shouldered beauties in patterned sarongs of silver and blue and red and purple, their sleek heads crowned with flowers of golden filigree, their delicate hands holding bowls of petals to strew in the path of "Bung" Karno and the white alien. Running through my slides, I see Khrushchev being blessed by some local guru. He is bearing up well, grinning gamely, straw hat in hand

and a *lei* of red hibiscus about his neck. But in Bali above all
the mass of great square men from Moscow boxed up in great
square suits, the paper flags and pomp and the metallic blaring
of banal national anthems over scratchy loudspeakers were an
incongruous affront, and the age of cancer and the coronary
suddenly appeared at its very silliest.

Beyond the protocolaire frills and the security fuss, the blue
breakers rolled timelessly in to a silver shore, and behind the
lackadaisical palms and the iridescent rice fields stood the silent
volcanoes of the hinterland, wreathed in cloud. In villages where
palm-thatched pavilions alternated with gracefully worked gate-
ways and temples of rose-red stone, copper-breasted women in
peacock-bright sarongs undulated bonelessly as they bore head-
loads of fruit and rice down the dusty streets, naked children
played idly on the verges, and craftsmen squatted to carve somewhat repetitiously from sandalwood, teak, and ironwood the
elongated deer and elongated women, the demons and angels of
this haunted animist paradise.

One night I stood among the crowd in a village square while
three gorgeously dressed Balinese girls, their heads capped with
tiaras of flowers and golden ornaments, their long-nailed, taper-
ing fingers curled back almost to the wrist, twisted and swayed
to the measured, limpid beat of a gamelan orchestra. But into
this idyll there inevitably burst a black American limousine from
the palace above decorated with Indonesian and Russian national
flags, raising the dust and ripping the velvet night with its in-
sistent horn and headlights. We were back in the twentieth century, and "back" undoubtedly seemed the right word.

The next evening we went up to this palace of Tampaksiring
to watch Khrushchev watching the Ketjak. The Ketjak is the
famous monkey dance from the great Hindu epic, the *Ramayana*,
which tells how Hanuman, king of the monkeys, helped the good
King Rama to rescue his wife from the clutches of the evil ruler
of Ceylon. Some seventy half-naked men, their glistening backs
almost black in the uncertain, smoky light of flaring torches, sat
cross-legged in concentric circles, their hands making a dark
forest of fingers as they waved them toward the hub of their

human wheel and chanted the chattering monkey chorus in explosive unison. Fantastic figures of fable capered among them, as the voices of the soloists—grating and nagging as if from the grave itself—rose and fell in their narration of the ancient and sinister legend. The Ketjak, performed under these optimum conditions, is a weird and wonderful thing, but the elderly Russian gazed fixedly at nothing, hot, tired, and bored.

Outside, it was a night of stars, and after the dance Bernard Kalb, then of *The New York Times*, took a stroll in the luxuriant moonlit palace grounds with an impeccably dressed Indonesian acquaintance. Suddenly a Russian security officer stepped out of the shadows and ordered Kalb out of the garden. "But this is the chief minister of Indonesia," he protested, gesturing toward Doctor Djuanda, who stood at his side. The Russian security officer ignored Djuanda and gazed for a moment at the big American's fine semitic head, so reminiscent of some discredited Babylonian monarch. "I don't care who he is," he barked tautly. "Get out." In deference to Djuanda, Kalb complied. We were back at the beginning again.

"Who's that fat Dutchman?" As the Khrushchev family, including his daughter and son-in-law, Aleksei Adzhubei, disported heavily in the tepid surf at our beachside hotel, they must have looked compromisingly like the former colonial *Herrenvolk* to undiscriminating Balinese. Although Sukarno screamed at Surabaya that Khrushchev could speak for Asia at the next summit meeting, and although the Bung was to borrow a billion dollars from Moscow within the following five years, Russians were forever white men in the eyes of Indonesians and of all the other prejudiced and pigmented peoples of the subcontinent.

Aid and trade did not generate greater affection for the Communist half-world. Soviet earth-moving machinery worked badly in Indonesian soil. Soviet building specifications did not meet local requirements, subsidences occurred, cracks appeared, and tempers frayed. A Czech agricultural machinery plant proved entirely unsuitable for the tropics, and Prague could supply no spare parts. A Czech tire factory turned out to be ten years out of date, and Polish equipment for new shipyards rusted on the site because no local currency was available to pay for construction work.

The Iron Curtain experts were exasperated by inefficient Javanese labor and the impractical ministerial plans of Djakarta, but for the sake of political goodwill agreed to projects which the Western powers had turned down as misconceived. In Makassar, the Czechs found themselves trying to build a cement plant at a point where the wharves, the roads, the bridges, and the vehicles that were supposed to run on them were all too small and too weak to carry the machines, which in consequence remained in their crates for months on end. Moreover, the cement was not required in Celebes but in Java, four hundred miles away across the sea. In order not to offend their protégés, the Russians also insisted on Indonesian participation in their engineering and construction projects, and this simply made for more bad blood, for Javanese civil engineers interpreted Russian plans and work schedules in their own way—and at their own maddening pace.

The sad story was repeated elsewhere, as sad stories always are. In 1964, I found that Communist benefactors had initially given Cambodia a paper factory with the wrong sort of machinery for making paper out of the ubiquitous Cambodian bamboo, a sugar refinery with the wrong sort of machinery for making sugar from the ubiquitous Cambodian sugar palm, a cement works which was erected on a site twenty miles away from the nearest water, and a plywood factory whose original glue came unstuck in the heat.

The white elephant is a royal beast well known to Cambodians, for small ones may be seen today, chewing away meditatively at lengths of succulent sugar cane in the precincts of the palace at Phnom Penh. They look harmless enough, but it was the custom for an Oriental potentate to show displeasure by presenting one of these slightly pink pachyderms to hapless servitors who had incurred his wrath, and this backhanded compliment spelled ruin. The beneficiary could not neglect the animal without committing *lèse majesté*, but must keep and clothe it in the style to which it was accustomed, and in time it simply ate him out of house and home.

"And that precisely defines the generous gifts showered upon us by our Russian patrons," one Cambodian minister told me sarcastically. "Are they, too, angry with us, then?" It was a malicious Asian reaction to the munificence of the Soviet Union, which had presented Cambodia with a five-hundred-bed hospital and a technical institute, and then left it to the Cambodians to find most of the skilled staff and the money to run them. There was at the time a tendency among Khmers in the know to find that whatever the Russians gave them free was embarrassingly expensive, and some were secretly a little envious of the Indonesians, to whom Moscow had made only one outright gift of a much smaller hospital.

The Indonesians had their own headaches, however. Capitalist aid was designed to enslave underdeveloped countries, Khrushchev had warned them. Soviet assistance, on the other hand, was designed to enable young nations to consolidate their independence. "Through Communism and Communist friends, you too can grow muscles like ours," he seemed to say. It was in theory heady stuff for peoples sick of having sand kicked in their faces, and Khrushchev's visit to Indonesia was deceptively productive. By 1965 Sukarno was spending the last of his billion-dollar Russian credits, Djakarta was the proud possessor of the biggest collection of obsolescent Soviet warships and jets in Asia, and the Indonesian government was having to sacrifice more than $150 million a year—nearly one-third of all national foreign-exchange earnings—simply to pay off the interest on the Russian loans.

By 1969, 115 of the 200 fighters and bombers so handsomely provided by Moscow were grounded for lack of spares, and the 19,200-ton Sverdlov-class cruiser renamed *Irian* could not put to sea because the refrigeration system, on which it was completely dependent, had collapsed. Inert Soviet-designed destroyers, immobilized for want of maintenance and replacements, cluttered up the quays at Javanese ports like so much scrap metal, and there was talk of towing off some of this outdated ironmongery and sinking it, to make more space for calling freighters. Indonesia's military debt to Moscow still stood at $800 million.

The generosity of Mr. Peaceful Coexistence had brought Indonesia to the brink of ruin. But ruin, of course, means poverty, and Asian poverty is the friend of Asian Communism—when Communism is the devil the poor don't yet know.

8 : The Millionaire Friends
of Mao Tsetung

It was somehow inevitable that while most of the West chose wheat, most of the East chose rice, since the principle that to him that hath shall be given applies to toil as well as treasure. Good rice is first planted in nursery beds, where it must be constantly manured and watered. When the monsoon breaks and the main paddy fields flood, the peasant plows and replows them thoroughly behind his water buffalo and then tenderly and meticulously pulls up his thousands of young shoots from the nursery and replants each by hand in small clumps in these inundated fields. And for this he and his family will bend day after day in the steam heat of the tropical plains, standing in a foot or more of water, and patiently thrusting each bunch into the sodden soil beneath.

Like rice, like men. If there is no tender transplant from

colonialism to independence under a native administration that has been properly prepared to receive and nurture the millions, stunted nationalism may succumb to Communism, the victim of neglect and poverty.

In prewar Tonking, only four Vietnamese farmers out of ten owned more than an acre of paddy field. But most were better off than their brothers in the Mekong Delta, where the rice-growing peasant paid forty percent of his hard-won crop to his landlord (in addition to other "gifts" and services exacted from him), and up to 120 percent interest a year on the money he had to borrow between harvests. These are the sort of statistics that push the poor into the red in more senses than one. In northeast Thailand, where the left-wing "Free Thai" guerrillas first trained during World War II and Communist insurgency discolors the map today like a bruise on a green apple, a man may make as little as thirty-six dollars a year. During the wet season half of the villages are marooned by floods and are inaccessible, while in the dry season the mean soil crumbles to dust and the land is afflicted with drought.

Rising Thai doctors, technicians, or agronomists decline to waste their time and talents on this unrewarding outback, and it has inspired little interest in its administrators. When the Communist insurgency began, one loyal village chief went three times to the district authority to report the presence of armed terrorists, and was finally assassinated for his pains before any move was made against them. Isolated and seemingly abandoned, most villagers from this remote rural slum connived at the Communist insurrection not for love of subversion but of survival. The first task of the Thai government, when it was at last persuaded to stir itself by a grant of special American aid worth about $100 million a year, was to show that it existed at all, and to "do something" when the people retailed their needs and fears. Only a program of faith and works, of protecting the peasant to give him confidence and providing him with roads and wells and drugs and schools, could win him back.

In a frustrated world darkened by the proposition that unbridled sex breeds overcrowding and undernourishment, however, the prolific poor become poorer, the rarer rich richer. By the year 2000, it has been estimated, Asia will have to feed more people than there were in the whole world in 1968. In Malaysia three babies are born for every two covered by an increase in the national income, and despite an imaginative campaign in India to sell 600 million attractively packaged, government-subsidized condoms for about a halfpenny each by 1973, the population of 500 million may well double by the turn of the century. Furthermore, the most efficient plans for making a "developing" country richer often widen the gap between the haves and the have-nots, for in the semi-automatic world of the supermarket and the super-container, biggest is thought best, and small shops and ships may be lost without trace. The same is metaphorically true of small farmers and small cottage industry.

The well-to-do West can afford inequality, because most of the poor can afford to be poor. "Don't show me more museums," Ping said to me on her first visit to London. "Show me poor people. I want to see how poor people in West live." I showed her— the blackened brick and scrawled graffiti, the dirty concrete stairways, the sniveling brats in mean back alleys, the blowsy drabs and the rusty railings. "No," she said with a sort of exasperated finality. "It's no good. You don't understand. I mean poor people, *reary* poor people." I looked down at my shoes in shame and mumbled, "I'm sorry. These are the best I could find." I knew what she meant.

Asia cannot afford inequality, for the poor cannot forever bear to be so poor. The development of miracle strains of seeds like IR-8 in the Philippines may mark the beginning of an escapist from-rice-to-riches fairy tale, but experts have calculated that it would cost two and a half billion dollars a year for a whole decade to make it come true. Otherwise, there may still be widespread ·famine.

Meanwhile, at one end of the region the leaking, crate-sized hovels cling to the steep hills of Hong Kong, their flat roofs of tin and tarred paper like tired eyelids on the face of the rock. At the other, the destitute of Djakarta swarm in shantyvilles that look like oversized rubbish dumps, or bed down temporarily in highly desirable four-foot-in-diameter water pipes waiting to be laid. Their plumbing is the stinking city canal, in which they bathe, clean their teeth, and wash their sarongs, while others squat meditatively upstream, waiting for nature to take its course.

Until recently there were only eight fully qualified Laotian doctors in the whole of Laos. But that was already a great improvement, for when the famous and lamented Dr. Thomas Dooley first took a medical team into the remote villages in 1958, there was only one, and he was the Minister of Health. Dooley gave crash courses in first aid and hygiene to "glorified dressers," and Laos made full use of every failed medical student with three years of skipped lectures to his credit who would stay in the country and "practice." I have seen wards in Laotian hospitals that would have looked unreassuringly familiar to the *younger* Florence Nightingale, the patients lying on bare boards, sometimes without a stitch of clothing on them, or trussed up in dirty dressings in the usual miasma of urine and stale sweat.

"Fifty percent of pregnancies do not go to completion," wrote Dooley. "Of one hundred babies conceived, only fifty will be born alive. Of these fifty, twenty will die during infancy. Of the thirty left, ten will die during childhood."

In 1968 bubonic plague was reported in Vietnam, Burma, Thailand, and Indonesia, and was threatening the Philippines, where huge armies of rats had invaded the countryside, consuming millions of dollars' worth of grain. The Filipinos were encouraged to look on rats as a treat, to start eating them in order to supplement their diet and rid themselves of the vermin at the same time. "If locusts can be made a delicacy, why not rats?" one provincial councilor asked illuminatingly, and a home-management expert produced a variety of recipes for dressing them up with sauces and chili and curry for the queasy.

All this promotion may have been quite unnecessary. Most Filipino housewives have to cater for seven mouths on a family income of about ten dollars a week, and some sharecroppers earn as little as ten dollars a month (if they are not cheated by their landlords). While the big American sugar-daddy buys up the cane crop and keeps the wives of the Philippine plantation barons dripping in diamonds, the small peasant is slightly worse off than was his Vietnamese fellow farmer: he is left with only half his yield and must often pay more than one hundred percent interest on any loan to buy seeds, tools, or fertilizer. Land reform may be a grim reality today in Communist North Vietnam, but it is still only a delectable dream in the free Philippine Republic.

This is not surprising, for the paper-thin upper crust in the Philippines remains true to those comforting capitalist philosophies which teach that, like *yin* and *yang* and cops and robbers, there cannot be haves without have-nots. In his affable, princely way, Tengku Abdul Rahman of Malaysia once comforted President Macapagal by telling him that Filipinos did not have to be left-wing to become Asians. But it cannot be said that their men of moment have shown much inclination to choose socialism as a cure for their schizophrenia anyway. The worship of private enterprise and unhealthy competition is as devout in Manila as it is among the million-eyed stone gods of Manhattan. And the distance between the poor and the rich strains the eyes.

In 1945 the Filipino capital was the scene of some of the most savage butchery and ruthless destruction of World War II, and by the time peace came, it was a wreck. Today troglodyte communities still live in the black holes that pockmark the crumbling walls of the old Spanish town, cave dwellers in the heart of the city, while newcomers drifting in from the poverty-stricken *barrios* raise their own hideous shacktowns of packing cases and hammered-out petrol cans and fragments of tarpaulin and tent. A whole family of these may earn only a few dollars a week. Yet in 1968 the vice-president gave a party for a few friends in Manila which reputedly cost him half a million American dollars. It lasted only one night, but the friends had been flown in by jet from Texas and Madrid to drink his champagne—not by the glass, but by the fountain.

"And here," one ambassador said, pulling a bottle of whisky out of his desk drawer like any West Coast private eye, "I have for the first time in my life seen gold bath taps." He went on to tell me of a Filipino family of five with sixty servants and thirty-two cars, of a woman whose huge wardrobe, housed in an extensive gallery in her Manila house, could be used only in conjunction with a card-index system which listed hundreds of toilettes and was carefully cross-referenced so that dresses might be matched with the right accessories. That was a few years ago. By now she may have a computer.

The talk that season was of an elegant party thrown to honor an outgoing Portuguese ambassador, for which the hostess had erected seven pavilions to house seven tables, each one re-creating a different age in a different country in its furnishings, its table-ware, and its food and drink. The guests were provided with costumes appropriate to their time and place, and an authentic and lavish banquet of the period was served in each case. There was a pavilion for the Ming dynasty in China, for which the delicacies of five hundred years ago were brought in from Hong Kong. There was a table of King Arthur's doubtful days, at which guests ate and drank from heavy silver platters and goblets. There was a dinner of the Directoire in Paris, a Russian banquet of the reign of Catherine the Great. Ming trimmings for the Chinese tent had been shipped especially from Japan, caviar was flown from Persia, and the hostess supervised seven teams of seven cooks preparing seven different feasts in seven kitchens, as if some crazy hypothesis of the Walrus and the Carpenter had somehow been given reality. And heaven knows what else was produced in the King Solomon pavilion.

One fancy dress party may provoke another, however.

The group of rather unprepossessing Filipino ladies, a trifle too thick at the ankle and flat at the thorax, bowled down the road in central Luzon in two "Jeepney" minibuses. But although their clothes may have been ill-fitting, and their figures somewhat angular, they were most certainly dressed to kill. As they rounded a blind bend and spotted a checkpoint ahead, the drivers accelerated and guns came up from under the drag. The buses crashed through the barrier with deafening bursts of fire which killed one constable and subsequently riddled a pursuing police car with bullets. Tragedy had hit one man and his family, but the incident had the flavor of farce about it, with the "Huk" terrorists in their borrowed feminine finery bouncing along like characters in a comic film.

It was the sort of episode that conspires with the cry-wolf school of excitable journalism in the Philippines to persuade the skeptical public that nothing serious ever happens there except on paper. If Communist bandits are reported to be active again, it is simply to justify more military expenditure. "Every time congress discusses the armed-forces budget, the number of top Huk commanders increases geometrically," a cynical commentator once remarked. But the Huks are more than a hoax.

"Huk" was the first syllable of the Tagalog for People's Anti-Japanese Army, the Communist-led Filipino guerrilla movement which the Americans supplied so plentifully with arms during World War II. Today it is the first syllable of the Tagalog for People's Liberation Army. Looked upon askance and then cheated of seats in Congress once peace was restored, its leaders took to their weapons again.

There has been no shortage of these. The United States has continued to supply the movement, so that today it is well furnished with submachine guns and armalite rifles. The difference is that in wartime the Americans delivered the arms, but in peacetime the Huks collect them from store. It is not easy to stop a Filipino once he sets his heart on something belonging to someone else, and on one occasion American officers investigating a theft of arms from the conveniently located Clark Air Base north of Manila were baffled to find the perimeter wire intact—until one of them counted the gates. There was an extra one, complete in every detail, which had no business to be there at all.

Clark Field also supplies the Huks with much of their money. In nearby Angeles City they are the real rulers of an empire of gambling clubs and girlie bars, bus services, barbershops, and straightforward old-fashioned bordellos that any United States military complex grows like fungus, and from all of which they exact taxes. The Huks run bingo games and boxing matches, cockfights and clip joints and car services for American tourists, and no one knows how much of the $75,000 a day that pours out of the air base and into Angeles City is siphoned off into their "socialist" movement by shopkeepers and prostitutes and cab drivers ready to pay for a little peace. In addition to their own potential for punishment, the Huks subcontract assassination to juvenile murder squads on a strictly cash basis.

Operating with a jarring combination of principles drawn from Marx and the Mafia, the Huks blackmail and intimidate politicians and big business, and buy up provincial officials or police, slaughtering the uncooperative where it is sound policy to make an example. They have been known to chasten the neighborhood by presenting the legs of an enemy to his wife and the head (wearing sunglasses) to his mother. A killer squad known as The Beatles specializes in lethal attacks on police and the liquidation of informers in various distasteful ways.

On the other hand, the Huks have been praised as the champions of justice in the past. Not only has their "invisible government" administered hundreds of villages in central Luzon, but in Huk territory no man steals a water buffalo or rapes a girl without risking swift retribution from these friends of the farmers. Their four-hundred-strong guerrilla force in this region has been supported by at least thirty thousand peasants ignored by the government, beaten by corrupt police, and robbed by landowners. The Huks charge a modest fee, payable in unhusked rice, for their services as protectors, and these services include helping with the harvest and reasoning with the more rapacious landlords at gunpoint on behalf of the victimized sharecropper. Huk Law was for long the only equity the Philippines knew.

Luis Taruc, former Supremo of the insurgents who surrendered in 1954, explains the two faces of the movement by saying that there are anti-feudal "ideological Huks," who should be granted an amnesty, and "fake Huks," who are common bandits and should be exterminated. A pretty, fifteen-year-old Huk Amazon, captured at the beginning of 1969 when her teenage husband, two uncles, and a grandfather were killed in a clash, described how her group of guerrillas had listened every night to an instructive course in Communism broadcast by Radio Peking in Tagalog, and added that the leader of the local liquidation squad was a graduate from a secret "Stalin University." She was proud of the Huks, she told President Marcos personally in Luzon. "They are the army of the poor, and taught to help the people," she said simply.

But the Huks cannot be divided so easily into red and rogue. Bandits are as much part of the raw scenery of Southeast Asia as browbeaten peasants. In the Philippines as elsewhere, poverty may fuse an incongruous mixture of discontented elements into an explosive compound. In at least one case in modern political history, a Communist leader has found his early allies among farmers and footpads. His name was Mao Tse-tung, and subsequent events proved that he knew what he was about.

9 : *The Fallen Domino*

At Saigon Airport in November 1954 I boarded an elderly Dakota
with that unmistakable beaten look about it of those whom life
has treated unfairly, and flew northward to Haiphong in a desperate attempt to reach Hanoi that same midnight. At midnight all
movement into the city would stop, and thereafter I might never
be allowed to go there again. On the morrow the French were
moving out, the Vietminh were moving in, and Hanoi was to
become the capital of a Communist and possibly unapproachable
Democratic Republic of Vietnam. Stunted nationalism and poverty had claimed their first victim in Southeast Asia.

The eight-year-long Indochina War between the Vietminh and
the French was over. The folly of Dien Bien Phu and the frustrations of the Geneva Conference were behind us. Vietnam was
irrevocably sawn in half at the 17th parallel until the day came

when some magician could show that it had been only an illusion after all. Tomorrow the North would have to be abandoned to the Communists, except for the port of Haiphong, which the French would keep until April 1955. In two years' time, elections were to be held in both the northern and southern "zones" of Vietnam, which would then be reunited into one country under the government of the party that won them. This was not among the best-laid schemes of mice and men, and the consequences were predictable.

The Dakota was not. Fitted along the sides with green metal bucket seats like a set of mildewed dentures, it was filled with displaced peasants who had been packed off to their home villages in the north before they needed visas to get there. The center of the cabin was a mound of those obese cloth bundles and baskets and bulging paper bags that are Asian for luggage, the whole straining and groaning and shifting uneasily like some captive beast. Outside, darkness had fallen, and like some half-blind old dog, the Dakota had blundered into a wall of rain intricately cracked and seamed by glimmering explosions of forked lightning. The plane jinked and bucked in a merciless headwind, and I wondered if God would speak Vietnamese. It was all very ominous.

We crawled out at Haiphong into heavy flapping sheets of rain. The airfield was in almost total darkness and seemed deserted. Hanoi was about seventy miles inland to the west. These are the moments when the lonely correspondent, typewriter in one hand, hold-all in the other, rain streaming down his neck, enjoys that most reassuring of all human sensations—hitting rock bottom. He will not starve, he will not freeze to death. Somewhere beyond this fifty-acre field of twisted and uneven metal runway on which he has just tripped painfully there is another deadline.

We all trudged off to the carpark and there, miraculously, was a glorified station wagon converted into a minibus, and a bearded young Frenchman in minishorts asking if anyone with 1,500 piasters (about seven pounds ten) wanted to go to Hanoi. By eleven we were rattling over the one-mile-long Paul Doumer road-and-rail bridge that crossed the Red River and led into the dead city. I found a bed in an empty brothel (all the girls had fled south).

On the next morning I saw *them* for the first time. They moved through the gray streets firmly but softly in their rubber sneakers, their small solar topees covered with camouflage nets, their buttoned-up denim uniforms, and with their packs and blanket rolls and rifles they looked workman-like enough. Only their enamel drinking mugs, decorated with gaudy Communist flags and Picasso's peace dove, appeared a trifle frivolous. They were little men, their faces were young, drawn, expressionless. They had small, delicately formed hands, and wrists like twigs. They wore no insignia of rank. They carried their equipment on bicycles and bamboo poles, their rice in bandolier-like sacks slung around the shoulders of one man in each squad. And there was not an ounce of fat among them.

They were the Vietminh. As they marched into Hanoi through the *crachin*, the sad, interminable drizzle of the Tonkingese winter, with their guerrilla air of neatly patched military poverty, the booted French marched out about two hundred yards ahead of them amid the clatter of armored cars and half-tracks and overloaded lorries. But this protocolaire distance narrowed as the funeral parade crossed the city, the heavily armed losers leading the makeshift victors, and by the time the senior French officer bringing up the rear had reached the Paul Doumer Bridge, the bayonets of his diminutive adversaries were almost in his kidneys, and the look in their eyes was, for once, quite unmistakable.

The French had not trained the Vietnamese to run their own affairs, for they were not voluntarily according sovereignty—it had been wrenched from them by the wrong group. Before they left, their troops were therefore careful to pack up and take away generators, medical equipment, and laboratory instruments, to smash the furniture and unscrew all the electric light bulbs in public offices. Only later did diplomats from Paris make some restitution in a manful attempt to see that the last thread of their cultural influence was not snipped through.

After eight years in the hills and paddy fields the Vietminh found themselves moving doubtfully through this stone jungle festooned with red and gold banners and pictures of Ho Chi Minh but rustling with strange wild life—Western correspondents, Indian, Polish, and Canadian diplomats and generals of the International Control Commission, Chinese merchants and shopkeepers, Vietnamese doctors and lawyers with fluent French and sophisticated tastes, taxi girls, street hawkers, Corsican entrepreneurs and petty adventurers who were sticking their ground, even a complete Filipino cabaret orchestra. They had inherited a new and exotic world with new and exotic problems connected with tramways, timetables and price control, tap water and taxes and crime and city sanitation, the railway and the airport and all these damned foreigners.

The Vietminh opened a little press bureau, and eventually we went to them to apply for exit visas. *Visas?* They stared at us stilly, slowly tasting the word. We showed them our passports, and they fumbled through them blindly, then took them into a dusty office at the back. After five days of waiting and filling in forms run off a jelly pad for which someone had finally thought up four pages of irrelevant questions, we were given slips of paper authorizing us to leave for Haiphong. I complained about the delay to Gaston, but the difficulties of adjustment from the inhospitable bush to the sophistications of running a state were legion and started with the concept of time itself, he replied.

Gaston Pham Ngoc Thuan was a senior official of considerable prestige, but he was also a true Vietminh who preferred simplicity to ceremony. So for the purpose of this private chat we sat with our legs hunched up on the grass verge of the Petit Lac in Hanoi, eating fruit. Gaston gazed over the water, his thin, bespectacled face simultaneously earnest and dreamy. "In the resistance," I hear him telling me in his hesitant, self-effacing manner, the words coming in short, sharp bursts, "the time unit was the month. You see, it took three months for a Southern cadre like me to work his way from the *maquis* in the Mekong Delta to the Vietminh zone in the North. And after we had undergone four months of special training up here in Tonking, we spent another three getting back to the South again—clandestinely, through enemy territory, and on foot. In such circumstances, what is punctuality? What can an hour or a day more or less mean? Well, now we have got our people thinking in terms of the week as the time unit, and soon we will get it down to the day—or even the hour, as it is in Western countries. For the moment, however, you must be patient with us."

The advice was good. Off-the-cuff administration which took no account of time or convenience was the rule. A French commercial agent, whose head office in Saigon had sent him a sack of Southern piasters by air for running expenses (there were no transfer facilities), unwisely took them to the bank and was at once told that he had contravened the law by bringing them into the country. They should have been exchanged for North Vietnamese dong at the airport. He explained that he had not carried the money in personally, and suggested that he should take it back to the airport and change it. "No," the Vietminh cadre in the bank replied, "you cannot do that from *inside* the country, monsieur. What you will have to do now is fly with the money to Saigon on the plane of the International Control Commission, and then fly back here with it, duly declaring it when you come in again from the *outside*." Since Saigon was a full day's journey and a fare of thirty pounds away (for the I.C.C. plane flew via Laos and Cambodia), the Frenchman very sensibly took his cash around the corner and changed it at the black-market rate with some accommodating Indian merchant.

The Democratic Republic of Vietnam was certainly starting from scratch. But after eight years of appalling hardship and sacrifice in their astonishing fight for independence, the Vietminh did not like to be told what to do by others. Later I was able to eat Christmas lunch with the Poles and spend New Year's Eve with the Hungarians in Hanoi, and through the smog of socialist solidarity there would gradually filter the exasperation of foreign Communist technicians too often faced with an infuriating combination of ignorance and conceit in the Vietminh. And since when did debt breed love? The Vietminh owed much to Chinese instructors and experts—"But how we resented them," a Vietminh field officer at Ho Chi Minh's personal wartime hideout once told me. "We resented them for their better uniforms and higher pay, for their servants and their cigarette ration and even for their playing cards, but above all we resented them for their *advice*." He might have been echoing his Southern cousins talking about the Americans.

A scribbled half page of dog-eared notebook, once carried in the pocket of some long-forgotten bush jacket, suddenly evokes a vivid picture, a small sharp image seen down the wrong end of a telescope in time. It is the summer of 1957. Pham Van Dong, prime minister of North Vietnam, sits with me on a red-plush settee in a palace in Hanoi, pouring out a French apéritif with the grave attention he pays to all his actions, his full lips fixed in a motionless pout beneath the drawn, hollow cheeks. Dressed, as usual, in a blue tunic and slacks, he sips experimentally. A little speciously, I praise something about the administration. The expression of disbelief on his face does not change. Anyone who could drink this could say that, it seems to imply, and he answers rather wryly: "I find that particularly difficult to credit. We are struggling against so much ignorance, and our organization leaves so much to be desired. I tell you frankly, I am a very worried man. There are so many difficulties ahead, and we may face very tough opposition from the South." He looks up at me suddenly and adds: "But make no mistake about this. We are going to see that Saigon sticks to the Geneva Agreement, however long it takes, and that the elections which it provides for are held in the South. North and South need each other, for we are too poor. There can be no question of perpetuating partition." Unification, or else. It is a warning of the war to come.

Later I hear him saying: "But we have no intention of slavishly emulating China. We must examine all new steps that Chairman Mao takes, in the light of our own situation. This is Hanoi, not Peking." Pham Van Dong picked his way carefully, like a man moving through a minefield, but subordinates who followed in his footsteps at a distance knew the path was clear and showed less caution. Communist officials privately condemned "China's dangerous experimental deviations," and praised Khrushchev's predilection for open diplomacy and peaceful coexistence. There was unquestionably a pro-China seam running through the younger generation in the administration and the army of North Vietnam, but of all "friendly" foreigners in Hanoi at that time, the Chinese were the most self-effacing and perhaps the most ill-at-ease. And I remembered Pham Van Dong's words when in the following year Mao threw China into the Great Leap Forward in industry and agriculture which in fact broke the legs of both, and then created his People's Communes. Hanoi did not follow either example.

History, being the record of a marathon rat race, is a constant embarrassment to neighbors. China lorded it over Tonking for a thousand years until the tenth century, and thereafter treated the territory as a vassal. But reluctant subservience was always interspersed with bitter fighting. Vietnam's greatest historical heroes are those who raised the banner of revolt against the Chinese and gave them a good trouncing, and to this day their names adorn the squares and streets not only of Saigon but of Hanoi. The love-hate that the Vietnamese atavistically feel for the French, they atavistically feel for the Chinese.

Moreover, unlike Mao Tsetung, Ho Chi Minh himself was no smash-it-and-see sectarian about the existing order of things, and did not fire a single shot in anger in his life. Uncle Ho consistently advocated a two-stage revolution for Vietnam: a bourgeois nationalist struggle for independence, and a Communist takeover later. His prewar platform was a beguiling promise of universal suffrage and of mild land reform. ("It's like hot soup," he once said. "It should be taken slowly.") One day Mao will call him "Russian revisionist," if only under his breath.

No one distrusted Ho's agreement to open negotiations with the Americans in Paris more than the Maoists in Peking, who began by treating these peace talks like a swearword dropped in church and at first did not even tell their 700-million-strong flock of fellow Chinese that they had started at all. For Mao was the champion of the long-drawn-out anti-imperialist guerrilla struggle in underdeveloped continents, since he invented the formula, and his bid to become undisputed leader of the world revolutionary movement might depend on its successful application in Vietnam. A fundamental difference of outlook between a big, bellicose, but back-room China and a Communist Vietnam fighting in the front line for the freedom to reject "freedom" inevitably clouded their relationship further. The Chinese Cultural Revolution was unwanted in war-torn Tonking, where the enemy was no vague, ideological "revisionist" bogy, but real and round-eyed.

In 1966 a senior member of the Vietnamese Politburo attacked those who "mechanically copy the past experience of foreign countries." The Chinese retorted that "acting contrary to Mao's theory would only lead to defeat," and deplored the way in which Hanoi had escalated the war from its simple stick-and-karate beginnings by pouring regular troops into South Vietnam and provoking the Americans into bombing the North. This had made the Vietnamese increasingly dependent on sophisticated Soviet weapons, whose "false comfort" Peking condemned as "sugar-coated poison." The Vietnamese leaders were torn this way and that between Russians who used words like "negotiate" in mixed company and Chinese who staunchly supported a "people's war," which by definition meant fighting to the last Vietnamese. Nowhere else did the Sino-Soviet quarrel bring such schizophrenic anguish, for the Vietnamese were themselves divided between the two camps yet dependent upon both, and their subsequent oscillations prompted much fruitless speculation in the outside world.

Their fierce national arrogance, however, is far stronger than any ideological sympathy for this or that Communist patron. It was impossible to listen to the war stories of Vietminh veterans in Hanoi in the nineteen-fifties and not sense in them the corrupting pride that is born of terrible sacrifice. I met husbands and wives who had been imprisoned by the French and treated like mangy dogs, and who had not seen each other for nearly twenty years; radio news-readers who had performed their prim and peaceable quotidian task up to their necks in swamp water, with a microphone balanced on a bamboo raft and the enemy almost within earshot; fighting footsloggers who had defeated the French on a handful of rice a day despite the armor and the artillery and the bombers and the napalm and all the other musts of gracious modern dying. The Vietminh had no intention of selling off their national sovereignty to rich Communist friends in order to buy themselves a better life. When Russian wives moved to the head of the vegetable queue in the Hanoi market, the outraged Tonkinese monosyllables clicked back down the line: "What! We might as well have the French back. Who fought for freedom, us or all these foreigners?"

A few days after I heard this remark (translated to me by my dentist), I was on the Bay of Along in the Gulf of Tonking. This bay belongs to the realm of our dreams. It is as if half of the great wall of eccentric limestone peaks that swings up to the coast from the northwest had tumbled across the foreshore and into the green, translucent waters. The sea is studded with hundreds of huge, gray, skull-like outcrops of rock capped with shrubs and stunted trees, past whose sheer faces red-sailed junks ply like tiny bright toys. Great sponges in stone, these mountains-in-the-sea are fissured and hollowed by grottoes, some of which we visited by launch, clambering through narrow slits in the cliff walls to enter some tremendous, dripping cathedral thronged with stalagmites and hung with vast tinkling chandeliers of stalactite. And it was in one of these that someone had painted in gigantic letters: "Long live Poland!"

It was like a distorted echo from across the world of the prayer of these small yellow people, who were every bit as jealous of their independence under the shadow of Big Brother as were the men of Warsaw or Lodz. The Communist solar system has since exploded and even the East European satellites, sputniks thrown up by Stalin, begin to radiate from the Soviet sun. North Vietnam, a self-made socialist state like Yugoslavia, would never willingly become a political appendage of China or the U.S.S.R. If the second Indochina war has made Hanoi lean increasingly upon Moscow and Peking for military support, this simply means that the unfortunate Vietnamese Communists have become involved in a struggle for independence not only with the Americans but also with the Russians and the Chinese.

10 : Poverty's Child

The petite Vietnamese dentist who told me about the indignation in the vegetable queue received me in a room that was
uncurtained and completely bare except for a pedestal drill and
one of those green canvas chairs formerly reserved for film directors. It was lit on this grubby morning by a single naked bulb of
perhaps 40 watts. I handed her my loose crown, sat down in the
canvas chair, opened my mouth as if to shout "cut," and she
peered inside. "I can fix it temporarily," she said, "but you'll have
to have it seen to when you go back to Saigon. You see, I can't
get any of the things I need here in Hanoi, and I have no dental
cement. I'll just have to chance it and use the ordinary stuff."
I had a sudden ant's-eye vision of my own mouth as a huge wall
of ivory into which great holes were broken with juddering pneu-
matic drills and then filled again with shovelfuls of concrete.
Whatever she used, however, it lasted three years.

Communism is poverty's child and therefore poor itself until the day arrives, if ever, that it makes its own million. One year after the Vietminh marched into Hanoi, it was already a city of shortages. Half the shop fronts were coffined up with wooden boards, and the other half had the impersonal, empty look of the dying. It was always Sunday, it seemed. Coffee cost the equivalent of $3.60 a pound, gasoline $3.15 a gallon. Grain was scarce, for Tonking was now cut off from the main rice bowl of the Mekong Delta in the anti-Communist South. In the empty streets the traffic was orderly, for there was no traffic.

High and discriminatory taxation was smashing private business, but central cooperatives were filling little retail shops with cheap goods from China—tumblers and matches and pictures of Mao and Ho, vacuum flasks and vodka, shoddy shoes and exercise books and plastic air-travel bags—an odd miscellany of bric-a-brac upon which it might be possible to create a new and strange way of living.

Built around an oval lake fringed by tall shaddock trees, its green waters broken by two small pagoda-tipped islands, Hanoi had once been a smiling little place. But in December 1955 it seemed inconsolably mournful. At night the *crachin* slanted down into ill-lit streets whose silence was broken only by the shuffle and the solitary cry of an occasional street vender. I lived in an uncarpeted room among a number of cube-shaped Poles who found North Vietnam utterly intolerable. The Canadian armistice delegation organized a Christmas service in a tiny chapel, and a club-fisted colonel read the sermon out of *Time* magazine. A *la guerre comme à la guerre*.

Those seven words summed up the Vietminh, as I had found out when Ho Chi Minh made his first public appearance at a parade on the edge of the town. I had been given a pass to this, together with an orange and one sticky rice cake, and told to be in position by 0830 hours in the morning. My position was a numbered cross marked in chalk on a wooden platform without seats. There I stood for six slow and solid hours, eating my orange, nibbling unhappily at my rice cake, and watching the Vietnamese army, the workers, the peasants, the women, the youth, the children, and in fact most of the country, file by, holding high their red banners of praise, their great portraits of Lenin and Stalin and Mao and Ho. A guide with halitosis shouted unceasingly into my face that the trucks were Russian but the guns were American and had been captured from the French, and that the peasants were delighted with the new socialist Vietnam. It was well worthwhile, but at the end of it I felt ready to confess to anything.

Suffering becomes an addiction, however. Sitting sipping warm water in an open-sided thatched hut of bamboo up in the Tonkinese highlands while the flies ate my lunch, I asked another French-educated Vietminh cadre what he wanted. To my astonishment, he confessed to a material ambition: he was saving up for another pair of rubber sneakers. Otherwise, he owned two cotton uniforms and some miscellaneous underwear, and he was given a rice ration, a cigarette ration (about five a day), and a few dong a week. He was therefore not in need of anything much.

"I suppose you are aware," I said slowly and deliberately, as we sweated on our rough benches, feet scuffing the dirt floor, "I suppose you are aware that in Hanoi there are doctors and lawyers and other professional men who never went into the *maquis* but stayed in the city under the French and made money? And you know that they are still earning one hundred times as much as you, at least half of it paid to them by a government that won't give the price of a pair of shoes to a man who fought for Ho Chi Minh for eight years in the jungle"—or provocative words to that effect. It was quite true, and I had met several of these affluent gentlemen. "How do you accept this?" I demanded.

He did not take it amiss, but looked at me with contemptuous amusement. "Of course I accept it," he replied, as if talking to an obtuse child. "These men are technicians and we need them badly just at the moment, so we buy them with what they want, which is money. But I am a cadre and a Party member, and it is just because I spent eight years fighting the French that nobody has to buy me." His was the insidious vanity of the elite, that peculiar form of egoism which prompted British guardsmen to scorn wearing steel helmets in North Africa and American marines to fight without their flak jackets at Khe Sanh—both outstanding instances of bad, thoroughly unprofessional soldiering.

Early government-by-guesswork, woodenly emulated by a great corps of self-righteous cadres, added immeasurably to the weight of worry already laid on the shoulders of the leaders by the terrible poverty of the country. On the road southward to Nam Dinh I saw miles and miles of barefoot peasant women, the bamboo poles across their shoulders slung with shallow baskets, trotting back and forth in their conical hats beneath the persistent drizzle. They were patiently carrying the earth and the clinkers needed to put together the railway track their husbands had blown up or systematically picked to pieces during the Indochina War to annoy the French. In the cause of victory, the two sides between them had devastated the roads and railways, the few factories, and many of the villages, and it was left to the winners to put it all together again with little more than picks, shovels, and their own seamed and calloused hands. At wide river crossings the ferries had been sunk, and the ruined highways were chopped into sections by the gaps where sagging tangles of steel girder and tortured concrete were all that was left of the bridges. Like a tattered sole survivor with a crushed leg, North Vietnam was hauling itself slowly and painfully out of the wreckage of the war.

In the summer of 1955 I boarded a stifling train at Wuhan on the Yangtse River which rattled down to Nanning in South China and from there to a small terminus called Ping Hsiang on the frontier with North Vietnam. Here I was switched on to a narrow-gauge Vietnamese train which would take me to Hanoi. The single-track line, which weaved an unsteady course between the improbable peaks of Tonking, had been rebuilt shortly before by the sweat of ten thousand Vietnamese brows, and I was the first Western correspondent to travel it. The train was a push-me-pull-you toy, a miniature o-6-o switch engine back and front with a clutch of six bare wooden carriages caught between, and this contraption jolted and shimmied its way complainingly over the uneven, grassgrown track like a railway in an amusement park.

The inevitable contretemps arose when it turned out that in their slapdash generosity Vietminh cadres had given me a big box lunch and the train staff had prepared a solitary hot four-course meal for me in the otherwise empty dining car. They were flabbergasted when I declined to eat both. Vietnamese tightened their belts, yes, but everybody knew what white men were. They themselves managed on a skimpy bowl of rice and a little salt fish while I stuck virtuously to the sandwiches. The banquet in the dining car probably went to waste.

The train finally squealed its way through the outskirts of Hanoi twenty-four hours after it had drawn groaning out of Ping Hsiang—some two hundred miles away. This railway was the slender lifeline to China which was to be pulverized once more when the American jets screamed north in 1965. Like everything else reconstructed during the previous eleven years in Tonking, it was again to be cast into the kitty, to be risked in the double-or-quits gamble for South Vietnam.

The stakes lay between the tenuous fingers of a brittle match-stick of a man with a threadbare beard whose eyes were as luminous and blank as polished onyx. Yet once, when Ho Chi Minh courteously lit a cigarette for me and his face was little more than a foot from my own, I saw beneath their surface a fleeting shoal of expressions—tired watchfulness, determination, irony. "You can ask me anything you wish," he said to me, "but I certainly do not promise to answer you. I know the sort of questions you people like to think up." It was the perfect pre-emptive strike.

This disarmingly direct approach to men and headaches captivated those who met Ho, but it was the gloss on the cut-the-cant cynicism of a man who had graduated from being a kitchen hand under Escoffier at the Carlton Hotel in London to becoming a key undercover Comintern agent. He was reputed to have moved around the Far East and conspired under the noses of his enemies dressed as a shaven-headed Buddhist priest in Thailand, a blind beggar in Tonking, a tycoon in Hong Kong. He was jailed by both the British and the Chinese and led his followers through two dirty wars, and he did not go through all this to emerge as the dear old thing some made him out to be. He was tough, disingenuous. He disguised his Communist party in a sheep's clothing of national fronts just as he disguised himself to fool his foes in his earlier days. He was a patriot who saw Communism as the only salvation of his country, and he would not betray it for instant rice or instant peace.

Fading out slowly toward eternity, Ho left his indelible stamp on the state he founded. Ascetic, celibate, virtuous in his privation, he tried to discipline a whole people to glory in the name of austerity. Ho spoke Russian, Chinese, French, and English, as well as Vietnamese, was a painter, a calligrapher, a pleasing versifier, and a defiant chain-smoker, but his main vice was the cult he made of his own poverty and simplicity. His unassuming manner and impatience with formality and appearances were quite genuine, but he developed and exploited them, as a stage mimic develops and exploits his natural talent for mimicry. In short, Uncle Ho went professional.

He made a practice of turning up at places unannounced, perhaps because he "had just heard" that someone would be there whom he would like to meet. The first time I saw him do this was at a diplomatic reception in Hanoi which was magically enlivened by some unwary cadre who put on the gramophone a gross product of decadent imperialist culture, and a voice as boneless and sugared as a fried banana squeezed itself out of the disk singing: "*Gonna tay kasennimennal jernee, gonna sed mahar dadeeze . . .*"

The music was cut off when there was a slight disturbance at the door and Uncle Ho shuffled jerkily into the room in a creased, hand-me-down khaki tunic and trousers, a pair of old rubber-soled sandals on his outturned feet. As an entrance, it was a shade Chaplinesque but very much part of the mystique. He would suddenly appear in a hospital ward in the same way, rallying the patients in a jocular fashion that just stopped short of the objectionably hearty, or he would saunter into the third grade during an arithmetic class. He had a magnetic presence and in repose his still, carved face and the set of his shoulders expressed a striking poise and calm and authority.

I saw him at it again two years later, when he "dropped in" on a party given in Hanoi for Anastasias Mikoyan. It was a small buffet supper, typical of the admirable informality of the Vietminh as soon as they stopped being bureaucratic and started being simple again. Pham Van Dong introduced me to the unique mustachioed Armenian, whom not even Stalin had managed to massacre, with the words "Now you can ask him all his secrets," and walked away from us like a matador who has fixed his bull. Mikoyan's affability was up to the occasion, otherwise we could both have looked a little foolish. This mischievous trick of suddenly embarrassing people was an endearing side of a Vietminh philosophy which taught persons to be no respecters of persons.

Ho was an impulsive handshaker and joke cracker, and won hearts quickly. But he began to remind me of one of those electric heaters built to look like a pile of glowing coals—the friendly light is real enough but it has nothing to do with the true nature of the fire. The first time I saw him was at a very large dinner party. He was at the high table, and I was well below the fish sauce. But it seems he had "heard about me." In the middle of a course Ho disappeared, and a cadre whispered over my shoulder: "The president is waiting for you." Astonished, I followed him behind a curtain and was at once alone with Uncle. The glistening yet opaque eyes appraised me deliberately as we talked, but he was easy and amiable, promised to see me at greater leisure, and kept his promise—again by turning up unannounced for tea when my official host was Pham Van Dong. But for all the friendliness ("I hope you will tell us what you don't like around here"), Ho dodged any significant questions and I quickly learned that an off-the-record interview with Pham Van Dong was infinitely more rewarding than "running into" Ho Chi Minh.

It would be a mistake to think that one was softer than the other, however. When I arrived in Hanoi in the year of peace 1957, I found that a Catholic revolt had been bloodily suppressed and that cadres ordered to implement land reform had tortured false confessions out of men who did not own a square foot of soil. The atmosphere was such that when over-assiduous officials started questioning people for the purpose of compiling a census, the peasants became convinced a mass purge was coming and many committed suicide or tried to flee across the frontier to South Vietnam. The national assembly then indulged in an orgy of self-criticism, and liberalism enjoyed a short season. Publishers of a magazine critical of the army and the government were allowed to produce five issues, but by the time it had begun threatening Uncle Ho with a Hungary or a Poland if the people of North Vietnam were not accorded real liberty, the new mood of contrition had evaporated, the paper was closed down, and its editors and backers fell from sight.

Not before I had met one of them, however, for some comforts I had brought one family from relatives in Saigon opened up for me a secret labyrinth of intellectual society seething with frustration beneath the hard resonant surface of the Marxist regime. He was a tousled, tired man living among a medley of books and papers, and he was not going to enjoy his home much longer. "We intellectuals are not in any way in sympathy with the government of Ngo Dinh Diem in the South, or with the Americans," he told me. "We simply want to introduce some democratic freedom into our existing system of government here. But we are helpless. We are miserably caught between leaders who want to bulldoze their way to Communism and a mass of peasantry too cowed, apathetic, and egocentric to complain." This was the last despairing voice of protest I was to hear in Hanoi.

At dawn one week later I was driven to Haiphong to see the enthusiastic welcome to be accorded Mikoyan when he arrived there at eight-thirty. Hanoi was a gay and glittering city compared with Haiphong, for it always seemed in that depressing, gray port that the last flicker of life must die out, leaving it a pallid corpse. There were no political and military leaders here, no diplomatic missions, no signs of the bustle that surrounds the bosses. A dim phalanx of cadres in faded denims ran the empty streets, the empty shops, and the almost empty quays.

Nevertheless, on this morning there was life in Haiphong. The streets were decked with red banners of welcome, Soviet flags drooped in the heat, and the pavements were thronged with pajamaed workers and peasants mobilized for the occasion. They had been standing there since five o'clock, the mothers comforting their sleepy little children, while the cadres trotted up and down in their topees, barking at intervals and pushing people into line. Seven and a half hours after they had been turned out on to the streets, the cadres told the massed herds of humans that they could disperse. Mikoyan was not coming after all. No explanation was offered. A curious sobbing whimper echoed down the streets as, just for one moment, the crowd instinctively raised its voice in anger. But it quickly sank to a mutter that was drowned by the sound of the wretched beast's twenty thousand feet shuffling away. The potter must know the weakness of his clay and not demand from it the muscle and texture of the stuff from which he himself is made. Perhaps this is what lies between God and man, and it may be that it lay between Ho and the Vietnamese, most of whom are not starry-eyed cadres but ordinary peasants.

Communist leaders are not men to be deflected from their threats and promises, however. "Streetwalkers?" Ho had echoed when he saw Hanoi within his grasp. "We shall arrange that they walk the streets all the nights of their lives." And in the lightless capital of 1965, grim, faded Vietnamese women still moved down the avenues in aggressive pairs, never stepping aside for the oncomer. Symbols of the revolution, they had become the city road sweepers, no longer pushing sex or·drugs in the small hours, but heavy brooms. The population of North Vietnam had risen to nearly eighteen million, most of it crowded into the Red River Delta, and pretentious plans for raising rice production had failed miserably in practice. North Vietnam had remained obstinately poor and the people were told to take in yet another notch on their belts. Nationwide anti-American demonstrations were now held only on paper, for the country could not afford to waste man hours on protest.

Nevertheless, in mid-1968, the North Vietnamese were still energetically digging shelters in Hanoi, convinced that the peace talks in Paris would collapse and the Americans would start bombing

them again on a bigger scale. And behind this grim appreciation
lay the determination of the Communist leaders to be tough
and take the consequences. Their mood was marked by a kind
of serene obstinacy, it seemed, and they wanted an end to the
peculiar miseries of their struggle only if it could be bought
dirt cheap. Otherwise they would rather soldier on, for they
were more fearful of being cheated in peace than of being defeated in war. Despite much official finger wagging at faint
hearts, most cadres were neither fatalistic nor fanatical but
treated death and destruction from above as quotidian hazards
like TB and traffic accidents. "They plant flower beds, invite
foreign lecturers to come and instruct their scattered university
faculties in obscure and often rather useless subjects, and they
have even asked the French for advice on raising edible snails
when the war is won," a diplomat stationed in Hanoi told me.
"They have plans for bigger and better factories and irrigation
schemes to replace what has been destroyed. In short, they live
almost uncannily in the future."

But for millions it was becoming a little difficult to satisfy
Uncle Ho's standards of self-abnegation. Punch-drunk peasants
and workers felt their resolution slowly sinking within them by
1969, and even the armed forces were veined with the haircracks
of "negative rightist tendencies." The stony determination to
struggle on until the Americans respected the Geneva Agreements and got out of Vietnam was still there, but the years of
privation in a penurious land had relentlessly worn away at
muscle and spirit.

Where callous neglect makes men dream of drastic remedies,
Communism may have its own mystical appeal. But where they
have roofs and rice and a reasonable relationship with their
fellow men, it has been discredited as something that is no longer
social surgery, but social butchery which leaves the patient mentally lame and physically impoverished.

"Communism is for poor countries like China," a Cambodian
officer told me flatly in 1964 as we stared at the damage done to
a small thatched village on the border of South Vietnam by a
bomber or two. "It's not for Cambodia—whatever the Americans

do. We are royalists in a small kingdom most of whose subjects are happy with their prince." The Cambodian peasant is prosperous enough by his own standards and has long since fallen victim to the status symbol. Every third family has its first bicycle and its transistor radios. The people live in a lush, lukewarm land, they have all that they need of rice and fish and clothing and shelter, and they often own the fields they till. Moreover: "If Sihanouk made us work as hard as the Chinese Communists," one Cambodian murmured with a slow shake of the head, "we should simply *die*."

"Overcrowded China may need Communism," a provincial governor in Laos echoed, "but we don't need it here. Our people have a warm climate, enough to eat . . ." "The Communist movement in Thailand has to rely largely on foreign subversives," at least a dozen Thais have emphasized to me. "Our people are devoutly Buddhist and very loyal to the king. Except in the northeast, they are not poor, and we have far more food than we can eat. Now in North Vietnam, on the other hand . . ."

For the educated Southeast Asian of the late fifties democracy often appeared a delusion and Communism the reflex of despair. He was therefore tempted to turn back to his own past to find the key to his own future—a third system that was not listed among the official solutions.

11 : *"Bonjour, Altesse"*

It was certainly not beyond his resourcefulness. Necessity being the mother of makeshift, the needy Asian has a flair for improvising unorthodox, string-and-wire substitutes denied to those who can get their arms and institutions off the shelf.

I was to be reminded of this sharply when the Vietcong opened the second round in Indochina and on my first operation a South Vietnamese officer took my arm solicitously as I was about to step on a fallen palm leaf. He lifted the leaf, exposing a neatly cut trench, in which lay a spike mine, a two-foot-long upturned hairbrush of sharpened six-inch nails driven through a baseboard. The Vietcong were making bombs out of milk cans filled with rusty nails, bazookas from gas piping, grenades packed with buffalo manure (the ammonium nitrate needed only a small charge to explode it), and in 1968 they came up with the flying trashcan. This was essentially a dustbinful of TNT fired by the motor of a 122-mm. rocket but with ten times the kick, and launched from the twin rails of a seven-foot wooden ladder that could be knocked together on the spot.

Down at Sadec in the Mekong Delta I picked up a Vietcong leaflet on how to deal with "Imperialist running dogs" in the shape of Alsatians imported to track down guerrillas. This also was a model of slightly misguided ingenuity, and read: "To make the dogs lose their sense of direction when they are chasing us, confuse their sense of smell with mixed odors. Garlic, onions, perfumes like eau-de-cologne, and overripe peppercorns will all make difficulties for them. When we camouflage ourselves, we should use these items, either spreading them on our bodies or over the vent holes of our underground hideouts. When in close combat, aromatic foods like fried fish and roasted meats can be thrown to the dog to put him off. You should also discard your sweaty jacket or shirt to distract him. If the dog is up with you, give him your hand to bite and then stab him. Or use a cloth which he will start to worry and then kick him in the belly, when he will instantly die . . ." The arresting vision of a Vietcong in his undervest, a fried fish in one hand and a bottle of Chanel No. 5 in the other, kicking an Alsatian in the crotch as it worries away at his garlic-sprinkled jacket should not obscure the inventiveness of the Vietcong provincial commissar who composed these instructions.

Ingenuity was not confined to one side, however. Sitting in a command post in the swamplands of the South in 1962, I saw an odd collection of implements in a corner, and a South Vietnamese officer who had followed my eye pulled out a bundle of piping that looked as if it had come from a city scrap heap. "It's an exact copy of an American 60-millimeter mortar, without the frills," he explained. "It works just as well and costs only three thousand piasters to make." Three thousand piasters was about forty dollars, but why make copies when the originals were available? "We don't have enough," he retorted. "And also there is hell to pay if we lose an American weapon to the Vietcong, although nobody seems to care much if we lose a Viet-

namese soldier. So we keep the American mortars safe in a head-
quarter store and use these instead. A blacksmith in the district
capital turns them out for us in a converted garage."

The Asian is often refreshingly free from the bonds of Western
convention in national and international affairs. Prince Norodom
Sihanouk of Cambodia was therefore able to tell a startled Washington that he was ready to hand back American soldiers from
Vietnam caught across the border on Cambodian soil if the
United States recognized his frontiers—or, alternatively, sent him
a bulldozer or a tractor in exchange for each man. And no one
could deny that men like Dr. Goh Keng Swee think high, wide,
and handsomely. In 1965 and at the height of Indonesia's military
"Confrontation" of Malaysia we sat together in a corner of the
Adelphi Grill in Singapore, and as the island's Finance Minister
bent his puckish face over the roast pork and baked potatoes,
he suggested how he might bring President Sukarno to his knees.
It was all quite logical really (mustard, hm?), he said in his
gentle, rumbling rock-a-bye tones. Indonesia had to import about
one million tons of rice a year to feed the population. He, Dr.
Goh, would therefore corner the rice market and cut off every
possible source of supply to Djakarta (apple sauce?). The corner
would leave Indonesia impossibly dependent upon an over-
strained Communist China. The rice would be immobilized in
Bangkok, Rangoon, and other capitals and could be sold off
cheap later, mmm? I gazed at him with reverence, but shortly
afterward Singapore was dropped from the Federation of Malaysia and virtually out of the conflict.

A knowledge that outrageous fortune can only be challenged
with outrageous nerve animates Asians who come up with the
offbeat answer, or casually shrug on a new role. Sinnathamby
Rajaratnam now performed this impressive quick-change act, for
Singapore had become an independent republic overnight and
he found himself Foreign Minister.

I first knew Raja as a leader writer on the *Straits Times*, and
even after he became local Minister of Culture my mental portrait of him did not change. He was still a sandaled figure in a
Hawaii shirt, sipping a slow beer after an unfairly canny game

of badminton and kicking some subject around in a discursive way, while his eye rested half seeing on the predatory dendrobium orchids cultivated by his Hungarian wife in the sun-bitten garden of their bungalow down the road.

But on August 10, 1965, Raja was suddenly His Excellency— immaculately turned out in a sober, well-cut suit, shooting his gleaming cuffs, the touch of distinction at his temples adding to the impression of a well-poised brown man gray at the edges, in agreeable contrast to so many of his new calling who manage to look undistinguished gray men already brown at the edges. From the outset, his words matched his appearance. His first policy statements showed a fine regard for the niceties of diplomatic compromise and a good eye for the cover offered by a well-grown thicket of generalizations. "Do not ask us to take your friends as our friends," he appealed to other countries, "or your enemies as our enemies." It was the perfect expression of Singapore's desire to be little pal to all the world. Yet when Raja became the world's first instant Foreign Minister he was without an office, without a staff, and without a known policy. "He makes it up as he goes along," someone said without malice, completing the picture of His Excellency wandering around, looking for somewhere to sit and someone to give him a sharpened pencil or a cup of coffee.

Accommodation was not the only problem. Singapore had no Foreign Service, no passport office, and almost no French-speakers. Rajaratnam had to filch the prime minister's protocol expert, since nobody else was familiar with procedure. But no one flapped his hands in horror because there was no precedent for this particular nightmare. Unorthodox problems simply called for unorthodox solutions. For many Asians, niceties of procedure and principle are academic luxuries that it is not always possible to afford. And since this is true of American democracy as well as American 60-mm. mortars, Oriental leaders have also exploited their talents for confounding convention by dreaming up their own substitutes for God's Own Constitution.

Asians are nevertheless fettered by their own traditions, and these may have nothing in common with the moral and egalitarian principles of Jesus, Jefferson, and Karl Marx.

In the Malay world, the sacred Oriental principle that all men are unequal was challenged by the teachings of Mohammed, but with indifferent success. Under its thin flaking coat of Islam, Malay society retained an exquisitely intricate pecking order in which differences of birth and rank determined not only the elaborate etiquette but the form of speech, for there were quite different languages for talking "upward" or talking "downward."

The traditional Javanese would have been repelled by Christian principles of "good" and "evil," as a democratic American is repelled by the very thought of Mao Tse-tung, for the reprehensible idea of an abstract "goodness" which anyone from prince to pauper could acquire with a little practice would seem to strike wickedly at the whole hierarchical structure of society. The Javanese moral measures were *alus* and *kasar*, which carry implications of "gracious" and "ungracious," even "smooth" and "rough." And these attributes, like the uniforms and insignia, went with the rank. Kings were gracious, of course, and yokels were rude.

The Javanese village child acquires his pattern of conscience while sitting wide-eyed before the *wayang kulit*. The *wayang kulit* is the traveling puppet theater, at which coconut-oil lamps throw onto a screen the shadows of grotesque figures fashioned from polished and gilded buffalo hide as they play out stories from the great Hindu epics. These are ostensibly moral tales, but the characters are not judged by their actions so much as by their fidelity to their caste and their predestined role. Perhaps the greatest hero of all in the *wayang kulit* epics is a man who deliberately kills his own brother in battle, after flinching from the act. If he had dodged his disagreeable destiny, he would no longer be a hero at all. The young prince who shies away from butchering a beloved servant (in order to end a plague) is contemptuously dismissed for his failure to be princely. Men must above all do what is appropriate to their station.

Once, therefore, that the play actor reads murder into his

role, "Thou shalt not kill" becomes a counsel of deceit, even if he has it on the highest authority. A Javanese can easily short-circuit his own conscience, and this partly explains how the abortive Communist coup of 1965 in Indonesia was followed by a bestial bloodletting in which hundreds of thousands were slaughtered. It was all in the script, so it was all inevitable anyway.

Since there was no conception of equal rights but only of unequal roles, it was hardly surprising that British officials in Malaya a century ago found that rajahs were justifying everything they did as "Malay custom," and rewriting it to suit their own convenience as they went along. Peasants were forced to work for local chiefs for as much as three months of the year, and a prince could oblige parents to present him with their children simply by sending a messenger bearing a kris. The terrible system of debt-slavery permitted a creditor not only to seize the man who owed him even a trifling sum but to take his wife and family and even unborn offspring into bondage also—and the rajah was the one major creditor in any region. It was left to the unbelieving British to put an end to these abuses, for Islam recognized bondage, and Muslim teaching dovetailed neatly enough with earlier practices.

In Chen-La wealthy families might have a hundred slaves, who lived below the floorboards and among the stilts supporting their masters' houses. They were not called "man" and "woman" but the equivalents of "bull" and "cow," and had to kneel and bow their heads to the floor on entering the door. The tradition clings stubbornly to life. Interviewing a leading Democrat in Bangkok the first time I went to Thailand, I was startled during our conversation to glimpse, out of the corner of my eye, some poor legless creature hauling himself across the floor toward us with a tea tray held above his head in one hand. But he was not legless, and he was not hauling; he was crawling. It was the servant's normal way of approaching his master. Dr. Dooley records that since no simple Lao might hold his head higher than that of a mandarin, he sometimes found himself chasing his patients down to the very dirt floor to listen to their heartbeat.

The Laotians may say: "The lotus flower grows at the level of the lake water," but they are sticklers for servility and touchy about their dignity, and if a Lao talks to a superior, he refers to himself as "little slave." It is unsafe to call a stranger "monsieur" in Royal Cambodia and Laos, and when a British diplomat had the temerity to use this humble form of address to a rather seedy-looking individual chalking a cue in the Phnom Penh Sporting Club whom he took to be a billiard marker, he was at once corrected with a haughty: *"Altesse!"*

In a feudal society it is not unnaturally a small aristocratic clique that provides the political yeast, and the postwar anti-colonial movement in Laos was led by three royal princes, among whom were not only the future neutralist prime minister, Prince Souvanna Phouma, but his half brother and leader of the Communist-directed Pathet Lao, Prince Souphannouvong. My happiest memory of the hierarchy dates back to 1962, when the right-wing Royal Laotian Government of Prince Boun Oum in Vientiane was being challenged by a left-wing rebel "government" at Khang Khay, where the neutralists loyal to Prince Souvanna Phouma and the Pathet Lao loyal to Prince Souphannouvong maintained an uneasy alliance.

It was possible to fly over the nonexistent front line, and one glorious morning in March I climbed into a light plane at the capital clutching an overnight bag and a bottle of Scotch for Prince Souvanna Phouma, for his headquarters was out on the bare, parched Plain of Jars to the north, and I had been told he would appreciate a little spiritual comfort. The aircraft having been loaded with leaking tins of kerosene for delivery to the enemy, an unshaven Corsican pilot climbed in beside me with a half-smoked Gauloise between his lips, and we soared above the great heaving stone rollers that rear, wave after wave, over northern Laos, and into the blank blue stare of the Indochinese sky.

We landed on a dusty patch of burned plain, and I cadged a lift in a Polish jeep which was calling at Khang Khay. The seat of Prince Souvanna Phouma's "government" was an old French outpost on a hill. The floor was stone, the walls plaster and whitewash, and most of it was divided into rather small, bare rooms like cells in a particularly comfortless monastery. However, each wooden door was labeled with a magnificent legend such as *Ministère des Affaires Etrangères, Cabinet de Son Excellence le Ministre, Commandant-en-chef des forces armées, Président de l'Assemblée Nationale,* and so on, until I began to be afraid to go through any of them, in case on the other side I suddenly found myself looking on to the Place Bourbon in Paris, or the Quai d'Orsay, or the Invalides, as in some nightmare provoked by a surfeit of science fiction. Finally I found one marked *Président du Conseil: S.A.R. Le Prince Souvanna Phouma* (or words and initials to that effect). Inside was an anteroom, empty but for a decrepit chaise longue, two trestle tables, and a number of not very new cobwebs. Here I was asked to wait. His Royal Highness was out.

The two princes finally returned together, Souvanna Phouma looking, as usual, startlingly like Edward G. Robinson and smoking the inevitable cigar, while the stocky, mustachioed Souphannouvong with his oiled wedge of beard had the air of a Ruritanian forester, so that I half expected him to be wearing leggings and a frogged and fur-collar jacket. I gave Souvanna Phouma the bottle of whisky, for which he thanked me gravely. "We live simply here, under campaign conditions," he said. "However, your kindness reminds me. As it happens, we are having a little reception tonight for the delegation from North Vietnam. I hope you will stay, but I must just put some things out . . ." He wandered into his bed-sitting room next door and presently returned, his arms embracing half a case of Scotch (of a better brand than I had bought him) and a small trunk of best-quality Burmese cheroots. The contents of these he placed at intervals on the trestle tables, which orderlies then loaded with Laotian delicacies while Souvanna Phouma poured lethal measures of liquor for the three of us.

The party itself was undoubtedly the event of the Khang Khay season. The princes turned up for it impeccably dressed, and set the tone for the diplomatic corps—the Russian embassy, the Chinese Cultural Mission, the Vietnamese Communists, and the

Czech and Polish delegates. The Chinese and the Vietnamese formed their own drab little coteries in the corners, but otherwise it was one of those loud, confident affairs and I had to keep my eyes upon the stone floor, the naked bulbs, the bare bucolic walls, and the cobwebs to stop my four-dimensional nightmare from recurring. Sound parted company with sight, for while the scene was a drab fort at Khang Khay, the voices belonged to the elegant chancelleries of Europe. Glasses clinked cheerfully and fragments of French conversation straight out of *Congress Dances* rode the storm of polite chatter: "His Royal Highness has just been telling me . . ." Heels click: "Excellency, allow me to present . . ." "I assure you, my dear general . . ." A light ripple of laughter: "But certainly you are joking, Highness . . ." There was not a mister in the place except me, for even a rather gloomy-looking Slovak was apparently a *Conseiller* and had to be addressed ceremoniously as such. "We want to get this war over with, you know," Souphannouvong said to me over his Scotch and cigar. "Stop all this nonsense and get back to some good hunting." I swear, if he had been speaking English, he would have dropped the final "g." I left eventually, consoled by the thought that if I stood nowhere on the Laotian ladder, at least my name was more than twenty years old.

The Laos had had little to do with names: they had dealt primarily in titles. As men climbed, new titles smothered the old and also obliterated any rudimentary sobriquets they might have been given by misguided parents when young. These would almost certainly have been derogatory, for worried fathers deceived the evil spirits that might be greedy to possess their offspring by calling them by such unattractive labels as "Stinky," "Monkey," "Bitchie." It was only in 1943 that a law was passed compelling all Laotians to have names; they themselves were only interested in honorifics.

As in other parts of the world, classes have become confused in Southeast Asia. But the old arrogance still subtly poisons political relationships. Malay critics of Tengku Abdul Rahman, the prime minister of Malaysia, stress that he is a prince as well as a premier and has emerged from a feudal society founded on the subservience of the inferior and the patronage of the superior. In his hierarchical mind, men are either above or below each other. They cannot be equal. The Tengku therefore regarded Lee Kuan Yew of Singapore as beneath him, and when Lee claimed equality, the Tengku found it an impertinence.

Sukarno looked down his broad nose at President Macapagal ("His wife had to teach him how to use a knife and fork"), and Sihanouk despised Sukarno as a *parvenu* ("He has the manners of a peasant"). The frail unity of the Laotian neutralists was constantly endangered by Prince Souvanna Phouma's patrician disdain for General Kong Le and his somewhat frayed French. Meanwhile, on the anti-Communist side the bulky Boun Oum, Prince of Champassak, Lord of Southern Laos, is a true *seigneur*. He has been known to draw a revolver and shoot at drivers who had the effrontery to fail to pull over and let his car pass, but he doses his despotism with a kindly condescension. "We must not be nasty to them," he once remarked fruitily of his plebeian Marxist enemies. "They are only *pauvres types*, there is no real evil in them, and anyway you can get medicine even out of a poisonous mushroom."

Boum Oum is at his best in his own great domain, moving ponderously among his peasantry, yet indulging his own aristocratic whims—like making fish drunk on whisky-soaked bread, catching them when they pass out and float to the surface, and throwing them back to recover from their hangover when they come to. A good-natured elephant of a man, latest of a long line of autocrats, he dresses with deceptive simplicity. I see him lolling on the terrace of the Settha Palace in Vientiane in an open-neck shirt and white slacks, sandals on his feet, and around his magnificent circumference a leather belt whose cheap brass buckle is inscribed in large letters with the single, evocative word: *Giant*.

Perhaps that one word said all that Prince Boun Oum wanted to say about himself, doing duty for ceremonial dress and a galaxy of tinkling decorations. He was who he was, he did not have to prove anything to anybody. But most Asians turn everything into a uniform and a status symbol, and the region is already full of them: the Chinese amah proudly wears the white coat and black trousers of her sorority, the Singapore heavy-construction worker her red headdress and blue denims, the Burmese his *longgyi*, the Malay his sarong, the Vietnamese peasant her pajamas (black in the South, brown in the North) and her teeth (white in the South, black in the North).

To the uninstructed eye the Malay headdress may appear to be a glorified handkerchief, but like a damask napkin it can be folded into dozens of different shapes—some with delightful names like "eagle in the wind" and "fighting elephant"—which reveal the class of the wearer and his position in society. In Indonesia there are so many uniforms and insignia of rank that even the Indonesians themselves are bewildered and may mistake a tax collector for a colonel or a postman for a public prosecutor, but each is content that he is wearing the appropriate emblems of his station in life.

It follows that men who change may be cheats. When Tengku Abdul Rahman was invited to Tokyo by President Sukarno, ostensibly to negotiate a peaceful settlement of their dispute over the formation of Malaysia, he went hoping for the best. But with a musing, faintly aggrieved air he told us afterward: "Every day he changed his uniform. Sometimes he wore white, sometimes he wore black, sometimes blue, sometimes khaki. Here we were discussing a vital issue, and there he was changing uniforms. Now he says whoever is friendly to Malaysia is his enemy. This is how a man who changes his uniform from time to time behaves."

A change of uniform has nevertheless provided one of the colorful "third solutions" to the problem of government in Asia, where a flair for improvisation and despotic habits of thought have usually combined to insure that their highest common factor shall be the power of Number One.

The time-honored device for restoring law and order once the politicians have made a mess of things is, of course, the military coup, and this is a favorite alternative to democracy and the dictatorship of the proletariat among less imaginative Asians. The coup is habit-forming because in many countries the army not only has held the gun but has been the only disciplined organization capable of shaking up a slothful state wallowing in its own incompetence and corruption. When the soldiers took over South Korea in 1961, therefore, they very typically began by treating the place like a mutinous infantry depot, and Draconian decrees were at once issued to curb every evil from Communist subversion to overeating. But it was in Korea that the first variation on military dictatorship was played, when in 1963 General Park announced that he and other officers of the ruling military junta would don mufti and stand for election as members of a new Democratic Republican Party. The blood-and-iron hand was still there, however, if concealed within the velvet glove of civilian government. Suitable constitutional amendments were introduced to insure that no undesirable could be voted into parliament or the presidency, which would be reserved for Chunghee ("call-me-mister") Park. The Democratic Republican Party was crammed with colonels who had fought their way into lounge suits for the hustings, and in 1969 Korea was still being governed by men with curiously familiar faces and telltale ramrod backs.

General Ne Win's rule by a revolutionary council of colonels in Burma has a different flavor, however. At Rangoon Airport the immigration officer records not only the date of my arrival but also the hour. "You must be back at this desk, ready to leave the country, at exactly this time tomorrow," he warns in the clipped tones of the efficient bureaucrat—and then writes the wrong date of departure under his entry stamp in my passport, inadvertently extending my twenty-four-hour transit visa for nine days. The noncommittal mask, the nervous inflexibility, the fluster leading to the silly mistake, and the fact that the government would not allow a foreign journalist to spend more than one day in the country all belong to the new Burma—a socialist state ruled by a left-wing military junta that has its own civil service running scared.

For Ne Win has done more than change the regime by changing his clothes. He has been striving for a new form of Marxism so Burmese that it will make Titoism look as orthodox as a black bowler hat. After he seized power for the second time in 1962, he introduced his own philosophical formula for running the lives of some 25 million fellow citizens—the Burmese Way to Socialism. This doctrine condemns man's exploitation of man and all systems based on self-seeking, and advocates the nationalization of everything as the panacea for economic ills. So far, so socialist. But the *Philosophy of the Burma Socialist Program Party* attacks "dogmatic leftist imperialism with its quasi-despotic relations with the masses," allows a place for individual initiative, and is shot through with humanistic Buddhist teachings about respecting the dignity of man. It is poor fare for the Maoists. While Ne Win may have made concessions to Buddhism, however, he made none to democracy. For the first six years of his rule the list of political prisoners he held in jail read like *Who's Who in Burma*, all political organizations were abolished except for his own official party, and the government armed itself with an act that empowered it to suspend or extend any law as it pleased.

The press was "guided" rather than censored, but the trade unions were replaced with People's Workers Councils, all shops and wholesalers were absorbed into the People's Stores Corporation, fourteen foreign and eight Burmese banks became People's Banks, pharmacies became People's Drug Stores, and the rice industry—responsible for seventy percent of all foreign-exchange earnings—was also nationalized.

Unfortunately, the administration was simply not built to take the load. Rice and cooking oil were soon in short supply, a severe rationing system covering most everyday needs from soap to sarongs was introduced, and the gears of bureaucracy locked. For lack of official sanction to distribute them, umbrellas remained in warehouses until the rains stopped. Grown men applied for permission to buy a toothbrush or a pair of trousers or a bicycle tire and waited six weeks for it to be granted, while toothbrushes and trousers and tires rotted in Rangoon depots. The country drifted gently toward ruin. In a friendly game of political poker, Ne Win had proved that an officer's well-filled holster beat a politician's well-filled pockets, and had introduced his own alternative to parliamentary democracy and Communism. The only trouble with it was that it did not work.

In Saigon, President Ngo Dinh Diem was not worried by the socialistic itch among his entourage which prompted Ne Win's to-each-according-to-his-labor-while-stocks-last offer, for the Ngos —six brothers in search of absolute authority—came of a family of autocratic mandarins. Discarding democracy as "the wrong tool" for Vietnam, Diem substituted his own political philosophy of Personalism. This provided that while the personal freedoms of the individual were sacred, he should not be trusted with political freedom until he was morally educated to handle it with safety. The would-be parliamentarian, in short, must first be House-trained. His own system was based on an inner, secret political party for his trusties and an outer, "Revolutionary Movement" for the *hoi polloi*.

While hunting trophies snarled at us from the walls, Ngo Dinh Nhu, the president's brother and "political counselor," explained this plausible paternal nasty-matches-let-daddy-do-it philosophy to me on the top floor of the presidential palace, and excused the most authoritarian regime in Southeast Asia by pointing out that South Vietnam was engaged in a life-and-death struggle with Communism and claiming that "only a revolutionary party can fight a revolutionary party." The best weapon against the horrors of subjection by a ruthless, fanatical, totalitarian, brainwashed robot of a political organization was a ruthless, fanatical, totalitarian, brainwashed robot of a political organization. He made it sound very convincing, we drank tea to stifle our yawns, and in November 1963 Diem and Nhu were themselves violently depersonalized.

12 : The God-Kings

In Cambodia, Asian invention had meanwhile produced a more exotic political hybrid, whose name suggested that Prince Norodom Sihanouk had successfully crossed three philosophical concepts simultaneously, for he called the result Royal Buddhist Socialism.

Few eyebrows were raised. Little seems strange in a land whose main river flows upstream at New Year (which falls in April) and where fish can be dug out of the ground or searched for in the trees after the floodwaters subside. The "socialist" state of Cambodia had its typically untypical origins in 1955, when Sihanouk abdicated the throne in favor of his own father and proceeded to run the country under the title of "Monseigneur" (since not even Cambodia could bear both a monarch and a president). On the death of his father, the royal seat itself remained vacant. The prince was the living power. His method of establishing popular opinion was to organize a referendum whenever it looked as if someone really did not like him much after all, but until 1970 the response was always a roar for more Sihanouk.

Nearly seven centuries ago a peripatetic Chinese wrote of the customs of Chen-La: "Twice each day the king holds an audience. Whoever desires to see the king—either officials or any private person—may approach and sit down on a lion's skin. When all matters are disposed of, the king retires." But I see the prince across only a handful of dusty years, standing in the palace courtyard in Phnom Penh before a great mob of Khmers. "Buffalo tax in Battambang Province?" he is shouting at some sweating peasant. "No, I can't lower it without knowing more about this. Here"—this to some cringing court lackey—"where's the Finance Minister? He's supposed to be here—go and fetch him." Sihanouk mops his face, while the crowd surges around in the sticky heat. This is a Popular Audience, the Khmer tradition which still brings the ruler of Cambodia face to face with his subjects, to listen to their complaints about lazy and corrupt officials, nose-high seed prices, or the iniquities of the local soldiery. The prince talks it out with a line of indignant plaintiffs, and the dialogue is broadcast live to the nation in cacophonous Khmer. Later a special complaints bureau will handle most of the moaning, but the tradition remains very much alive.

Monseigneur will be overthrown early in 1970 while he is away in France, but observe him in the setting of the sixties, the autocrat of today who does not know that he is the exile of tomorrow. Ex-king, head of state, semi-divine Sihanouk is also the president of the Popular Socialist Community, a mass movement that includes the government and the civil service and almost everyone in the country with a political thought in his head, so that all differences of opinion are kept in the family and not allowed to give rise to anything so unhealthy as inter-party strife.

Cambodia nevertheless provides some of the liveliest democratic give-and-take since the days when any citizen of the Roman Republic could stand up and abuse his betters in the Forum. The

Community holds a congress twice a year at which members and provincial delegates may castigate the government, lay charges publicly against any official or even minister, and ask to see the nation's accounts. The cabinet must be present to face the music. The hero of the day is always Sihanouk, who may dress down his administrative aides there and then if untimely revelations bring a blush to the cheek. In Cambodia all is done by mirrors— the mirrors of a million dusky faces that reflect the will and the wishes of Monseigneur back upon himself, investing him at these congresses with the collective authority of the nation. Royal Buddhist Socialism adds another remarkable Cambodian paradox to the upswept rivers and the treed fish—one-man democracy.

Vox Dei Vox Populi Vox Dei. At Angkor the monarch was the Devaraja, the king who was worshipped as a god, the master of the world below who held all justice and authority in his holy hand and who would be immortalized in stone as Vishnu or Shiva or Brahma. Not surprisingly, Sihanouk enthusiastically identifies his Cambodia with the glories of Angkor, and takes every distinguished visitor to see its marvels, from Princess Alexandra to Premier Chou En-lai. "See how smooth the stone has been worn," he says lovingly, inviting the Chinese prime minister to stroke the more tempting rotundities of a heavenly dancing girl in bas-relief. "Many people have done the same before you." Chou En-lai complies, and a lucky photographer gets a unique shot of the gentleman from austere Peking in the act of forgetting his austerity and being not quite a gentleman.

A few weeks after this episode I stood with Ping amid the broken and tumbled stone of the temple-monument of Preah Khan at Angkor, a complex of long, gloomy corridors and great, still courtyards split and burst by the obscene roots of the giant banyan and silent now under a siege of jungle vegetation. As we picked our way out to the entrance, the clammy air closed over us like a soft unseen hand and the sky went black. Abruptly a thousand forest cicadas set up their sharp, shrill whistle of warning, the first heavy drops fell through an unnatural dusk that had turned the whole world to carved gray stone, and then the storm broke in a rolling sea of rain. It was impossible not to feel the spell of something dark and ancient and alien in the drowned ruin, far removed, it seemed, from the plump, smiling prince in the city suit whom I had left perched on a red plush sofa in Phnom Penh the day before.

Sipping his champagne as we talked, Sihanouk had once again reminded me of some middle-aged gossiping dandy in a Sheridan play or a Mozart opera, for his large, glossy eyes, his flamboyant gestures, and his carrying upper-register voice with its stage-French enunciation hold his audience in the same way, so that I miss the wig and the waving lace, the silken hose and buckled shoes. He had discovered that Ping and I were driving to Angkor after I had cabled my interview with him to *The Observer*, and had at once summoned his aides and given orders that the provincial dignitaries there should be told to look after us when we arrived. Later, a peremptory telephone call from Phnom Penh instructed those responsible that all our bills would be met by Monseigneur personally.

Correspondents should pay their own way, but this invitation to be the guests of the prince amounted to a royal command. When we returned, wet and tacky from our visit to Preah Khan, waiters were obsequious, and we were served a creditable dinner. It was as we were drinking an excellent wine at the prince's expense that someone switched on the news. This included an acerbic commentary inspired by Monseigneur himself on the scurrilous and tendentious inaccuracies about Cambodian policy published by *The Observer* of that day's date. These had been contained in a dispatch cabled from Phnom Penh by the newspaper's Far East correspondent, Dennis Bloodworth, and must be categorically refuted as totally false. My glass halfway to my mouth, I felt the wine slowly turning sour in my hand. It was time to pack and go.

The unshaven comments of foreign reporters regularly provoke the sore and sensitive Sihanouk to the vexed protest of a girl who gets a rasping every time she gets a kiss. He wants foreign publicity, but it makes him gasp with pain, for even the most friendly article will contain at least one observation or descriptive epithet that any right-thinking Cambodian ruler must regard as *lèse majesté* if not blasphemy. A man of boundless vitality, he spends an inordinate amount of time personally contradicting the calumnies published against Cambodia and himself.

Everything is sacrosanct. When I described an Independence Day parade in Phnom Penh, and remarked that the troops carried an assortment of French, Chinese, Russian, and Czech weapons but marched in American boots, the national news agency accused me of "ridiculing and insulting" Cambodia. There was no doubt about the exalted origin of this attack, which solemnly concluded: "There are, even so, things that our troops owe to no foreign country and to no foreign aid—their blood, their bodies, their hearts, their lives, and their unshakable will to do their duty, *even in bare feet.*" (My italics, for once.)

In November 1964 I wrote an article which was largely devoted to supporting Sihanouk's contention that he was not deliberately helping the Vietcong. But I also listed some of the absurdities of Communist aid to Cambodia, and referred to the well-organized veneration which Monseigneur enjoyed. This was evidently intolerable. On December 4 I was sent a letter embossed with the Royal Cambodian coat of arms and signed "N. Sihanouk" which began: "I have learned with profound disappointment of your article on Cambodia published in Hong Kong. I have accorded you my confidence and my friendship and had the right to hope for your comprehension or at least your objectivity." He regretted to see, however, that I had "rejoined the cohort of American journalists who dishonor their country."

I wrote back to the prince, explaining what I and my colleagues understood by "objectivity," and this drew another royal salvo six weeks later—five pages of single-spaced typing which analyzed what the prince took to be every treacherous line I had written. For example, I had described him as "flanked by Marshal Chen Yi and the Soviet ambassador" on Independence Day although the French ambassador had also been close to him: this was a dishonest distortion intended to show him up as pro-Communist. His letter concluded with a sharp twist to the conventional French ending: "Veuillez agréer, Monsieur, *l'expression de ma déception*" (the last words added in his own handwriting).

I then served three pages explaining that the point I was making was that the Anglo-Saxon powers had lost ground heavily to the Eastern bloc in Cambodia through their own clumsy policies, and moved up to the net to meet his other criticisms. In April 1965, back came still another missive, in which the prince wrote: "I see no object in replying again, for I do not wish to poison matters further—and for the rest, we shall never finish, each of us not believing himself in the wrong." Deuce. Later that year in Singapore I did a television commentary on Cambodia, reiterating much that I had said in my articles about the prince and the Vietcong. This earned me a 161-word cable from Sihanouk, thanking me "very sincerely for the objectivity you have manifested toward my country and myself . . ." and ending "with all my gratitude and my cordial memory norodom sihanouk head of state cambodia." I was, it seemed, back among the blessed again.

But for how long? If, as our forefathers believed, our personal devil stands behind our left shoulder to tempt us, while our personal angel stands behind our right shoulder to admonish us, Sihanouk's eternal problem with correspondents was that he could not give a visa to the angel without letting in the devil. And while one may have a tongue of sugar, the other is constantly tasting spilled salt.

It was enough to describe Cambodia as a little country with a population of "only" seven millions to rouse the royal wrath, and among other effusions of Monseigneur's spiky and prolific pen was a publication entitled *Open Letter to the International Press* in which he not only made the point that there are forty countries in the United Nations which are smaller than Cambodia but listed them all, giving the precise area of each down to the last square kilometer.

It might be protested that with so prickly a prince you could not win, but much of his malice was provoked by a doltish diplomacy that earlier failed to recognize in him the god-king to whom no slight should be offered. His favor sanctioned all, his fury forbade all. To court him was to court Cambodia. Yet the **first** American ambassador to Phnom Penh took his dog with him when granted an audience by Sihanouk, and a high-ranking British official once presented him with a couple of LP records in a paper bag with the bill still inside it. He does not forget these things, and it is not surprising if we find him writing venomously: "The U.S.A. and the West will always symbolize in my eyes, until I die, injustice, inequality, discrimination." He might well have added "and downright bad manners."

On the other hand, all is permitted to the prince. He will betray diplomatic confidences to the world at large when it suits his convenience, insult envoys in public speeches, insinuate on the radio that a British ambassador drinks too much.

This also has its lighter side. Diplomats are accustomed to glancing at the bottom corner of any official invitation cards they receive for the words *tenue de soir* or *tenue de ville* which tell them how they should dress for a function, but in 1960 the ingenious Sihanouk introduced a new and ominous variation on this theme—*tenue de travail* (working clothes). Since no power had offered to construct it for him, the prince had decided to build a railway from the capital to the new port of Sihanoukville with Cambodian manual labor and to augment his work force of unskilled hands by inviting the heads of some sixteen diplomatic missions in Phnom Penh to join him in laying the foundations of the track.

Every so often, therefore, an impressive convoy of shining limousines set out from the capital, carrying these polished gentlemen from their embassies to their unusual place of work. Shortly afterward sweat-stained ambassadors, wearing anything from khaki shorts and bushwhacker hats to Saville Row slacks and Charvet scarves, could be seen shoveling earth into baskets which were then passed down a human conveyor belt of senior Khmer officials. Loudspeakers filled the air with jazz, while Sihanouk himself, a round figure in shorts and white singlet, dug away briskly. At lunchtime, all retired to a marquee for a superb French meal washed down with champagne. Cynics alleged that urgent coded diplomatic messages were soon flashing to Washington, London, Moscow, and Peking, exhorting governments to present the exigent prince with his new railway as part of the foreign-aid program.

In an old notebook I find a color slide of Sihanouk, taken at the palace. Clad in a white tunic and *sampot*, with the ribbon of some intimidating Oriental order across his chest, he is smiling affably as the entire cabinet crouches before him in full cere-monial dress, heads humbly bowed, hands joined in prayerful greeting. Scribbled beside it is part of a eulogy by one of his ministers which calls him "Our August and Infinitely Engaging Leader, Worthy Descendant of the Kings of Angkor . . . Young, Dynamic, Supremely Intelligent." In 1964 he opened a museum to himself, and when he drove through Phnom Penh sirens wailed to warn the populace, and pedestrians hastened to the edge of the road to clap gently as he went by.

In 1963 Sihanouk gave up all United States assistance in mid-project, announced that foreign commerce and banking would be nationalized, and brought his country to the brink of eco-nomic catalepsy. It was a personal decision, taken by a man who looks upon the national income as his private purse. A year later he came back from a visit to Peking bubbling over with new, ambitious schemes. Everyone in the country was to be taught to read Cambodian within five months—except for the sick, the dying, the insane, and the diplomats—and the entire population was to be mobilized to plant trees. His mind was full of much else besides, from plans to socialize the entire wholesale trade to designing uniforms to be worn by all waiters, barmen, and hotel servants throughout the kingdom.

Sihanouk has had only four wives, and when in power in Phnom Penh lived in a bungalow complex on the edge of the capital, not in the royal palace. His hobbies ranged reasonably enough from model warships to playing the clarinet and direct-ing his own films. As a host he was careful and attentive, capable of personally arranging even the bowl of flowers in your room, or inquiring anxiously about your favorite dishes. But the whole court might be drafted into the cast when he made his movies, and portly ministers have been press-ganged into volley-ball teams to play against Monseigneur.

Excitable, voluble, inexhaustible, Sihanouk was a beloved prince who would dig with the peasants and share their most unsavory food and jokes and who talked and talked and talked to the masses with frankness and spontaneous charm. It is useless to judge his prima-donna whims or patent egoism by the measures of the West, for he was king in another context. "It is Cambodia they insult when they insult me," he cried of the more denigratory newspapers in the new world. He was a royal patriot, and if there had been no Sihanouk, in all probability there would have been no Cambodia today. He was only in his forties, but it was said that he observed the Hindu-Buddhist rites of his forebears, and in 1969 many still believed that we might see more stone gods erected in his country, bearing a new yet familiar face. If he charmed peasants, however, he exasperated politicians, generals, and ambitious young men frustrated by a "socialist" system run on patronage and a prince's caprice, and in 1970 he was duly deposed.

As Sihanouk reached back to the customs of Angkor, so Sukarno found in Javanese tradition his own alternative to the liberalism and license of parliaments. For the democratic system, it seemed, only encouraged further fragmentation of an Indonesia already divided by ethnic differences, by three thousand islands and the seas between, and by the three philosophical streams of Islam, Communism, and nationalism. The proliferating political parties prevented each other from ruling effectively, and cabinets flitted in and out of power every few months in the inglorious fashion of the French Fourth Republic. By 1956 the army was sick of them all, and Sukarno was able to tell them to go and "bury themselves." By 1959 he was talking of "the devil of liberalism," and announcing jubilantly in his new Political Manifesto that Indonesia had now been "completely divorced from Western democracy."

This raised relatively few hairs, for definitions of fairness change with lines of latitude. Western prejudice may demand a vote for every man: Javanese prejudice demands *musjawarah* and *mufakat*—prolonged palaver ending in a unanimous decision when the last dissenter is too hoarse or exhausted to argue further. It is a method whose origins lie buried with a million forgotten wrangles in the ancient soil of every Javanese village.

Even under the mystical hierarchs of their early Hindu kingdoms, Javanese peasants had jealously guarded their own communal custom whereby the head of a family discussed a local problem with the rest of its members until they all reached agreement, then heads of families met in council to talk themselves into a consensus in turn. This practice enabled the village chief to make up his mind without a voice being raised when he had the last word, and it prompted Indonesians to applaud when Sukarno condemned the West's "fifty percent-plus-one" vote as "the tyranny of the majority," a deplorably unfair way of making policy which ignored the wishes of up to forty-nine percent of the people. Moreover, in Java, where the land originally belonged to the entire community and the family worked together as a team under its *bapak*, or "father," the individual was nothing and the principle of *gotong royong* or mutual cooperation was the basis of society. The articulation of Sukarno's dog-French formula for government, *Socialism à la Indonesia*, came from these village principles of consultation, consensus, and cooperation.

In 1960 Sukarno dissolved the elected legislature and replaced it with an appointed *gotong royong* parliament which included not only politicians but representatives of functional groups—farmers, workers, soldiers, religious bodies, and so on. He then invented a People's Consultative Congress, a Supreme Advisory Council, a National Front, and other high-sounding instruments of "guided democracy," whose main characteristics in every case were that Sukarno was the president, there was no voting, they arrived at their conclusions by talking things out until all agreed with him, and the members swore fealty to the Political Manifesto of the great Bung above them all in his glistening white palaces. The ultimate acrological expression of *gotong royong* was NASAKOM—collaboration within all these organizations of the Nationalists, the Muslims, and the Communists.

Among the picturesque horrors of the exotic Orient the *kalis*, the evil brown canals of Djakarta, enjoy a proud place. But it is recorded that when an Australian bacteriologist tested samples of *kali* water he could not find a single germ. "They all eat each other and so cancel each other out," someone suggested to him. This was a true "Indonesian solution," with all warring factions brought together so that the prejudices of one neutralize the prejudices of the other. It enabled Sukarno to make the Communist and the anti-Communist generals "cancel each other out" for so long, and to remain above them at the apex of the state as the supreme *bapak*, the lone father-figure to end all father-figures, whose authority was absolute.

There was more to it than this, however. For the fertile coupling of earlier ancestor worship with Hindu-Buddhism bred the same supernatural license for tyrants in Java as it did in Cambodia. Hindu kings were gods incarnate and possessed mystical powers. Sukarno, some whispered, had been clairvoyant at seventeen, and when he went to Bali, he brought rain. He had healing powers, his bathwater would cure the sick, the dish from which he ate ended barrenness. There are men who still think he is Vishnu and women who have paid for sharing that belief too enthusiastically, and in various parts of the Indonesian republic people say they have seen his profile in the moon.

His basic urge to be Superman titillated by adorers and sycophants from Sumatra to Celebes, Sukarno was not slow to answer the call of Nietzsche, and we see him become Lifelong President, Supreme Helmsman, Great Leader of the Indonesian Revolution, Supreme Builder, Supreme Fisherman, Supreme Guardian of the Muhammadiyah, Supreme Educator, First Pioneer of Freedom in Africa and Asia, and Honorary Chairman of the Indonesian Rat-killing Action Campaign of 1964. On one occasion he appeared to Western correspondents fully dressed but in bare feet, explaining that a violent storm was brewing and he had been warned that he was so charged with mystical energy that he might draw down the very lightning (without his shoes he was satisfactorily grounded, he implied).

He described his repetitive speech to the millions of Indonesia as "a two-way conversation between Sukarno-the-man and Sukarno-the-people, a two-way conversation between two comrades who in reality are One." "I have been accused of megalomania, the sickness of greatness," he confessed with enormous satisfaction in 1966. "Yes, I am a great man and my power is the biggest, the biggest, the biggest." When Djakarta acquired West New Guinea from the Dutch, the main town in the territory was renamed Sukarnapura, and the Bung had the two highest mountain ranges called after himself.

He subsequently revealed that the Prophet Mohammed had inspired his decision to take Indonesia out of the United Nations. The only great leaders were Mao, Ho Chi Minh, and Sukarno, said Sukarno. Something of a name-dropper, he also remarked with approval that Hitler, Christ, and Mohammed had shared with him his own secret of success—they had all promised something to the masses. "Paint a brilliant picture of your aims," he urged his subordinates—whether these were to be the Third Reich, the Kingdom of Heaven, a paradise full of houris, or Indonesian "guided democracy." From this it may be seen that critics who accuse Sihanouk of delusions of grandeur are simply avoiding taking on someone their own size.

Sukarno promised Djakarta the biggest mosque in the world, and then built its biggest phallic symbol—a four-hundred-foot pillar in Italian marble capped with a flame contrived out of half a hundredweight of real gold and designed to "stand for a thousand years." He treated national income like mad money, flew around the world with a personal suite of thirty, moved about Indonesia in a $28,000 air-conditioned Mercedes 600 equipped with a cocktail bar and push-button gadgetry, to make hypnotic speeches about hardship and austerity. "Do you and you and you and you," he barked at one open-mouthed mob with harsh overtones of well-simulated hysteria, "do you consider yourselves Bearers of the Message of the People's Sufferings? Do you really feel to the marrow of your bones that you are Bearers of the Message of the People's Sufferings? The Message of the Sufferings of the Indonesian People is part of the social consciousness of Mankind!"

But Sukarno, of course, was not just of Mankind. There was one law for him and another for his nation of more than a hundred million debtors. When he was urged to cut his over-

stuffed de luxe government of about a hundred ministers down
to a utility cabinet which would concentrate on bringing food
and clothing to the suffering people, he contemptuously rejected
the appeal with the phrase: "Not if it's just to fill empty bellies."
No rice? The Bung said, "Let them eat corn," promised the
hungry a nuclear program, exhorted the penurious peasantry to
"love outer space." He operated in accordance with the finest
traditions of ruthless Javanese statecraft which taught the om-
nipotent monarch that true power depended upon a rigorous
self-denial of ethics or scruples, and the supreme court was told
to rule that the judiciary should be ready to break the law at
any time in order to further his Indonesian revolution.

The Bung personified Indonesia as Churchill personified wartime Britain. But Sukarno was no more like Churchill than Bali
is like the Isle of Wight. And Bali, where the bemused latter-day
Gauguins of the mid-sixties would paint bare-breasted girls carrying baskets of luscious tropical fruits that looked like overripe
bunches of swollen genitalia—Bali explained the lust of this
energetic sultan, with his moist eye for almost any well-turned
ankle.

Counting his wives is like solving one of those irritating mathematical conundrums in weekend magazines. You start off confidently enough with a total of five, of whom three are still at
least theoretically in play. Then a corruption trial reveals a sixth
for whose house in Djakarta the Bung had set aside $35,000 out
of public funds. The books are then balanced, until suddenly
there is a report of two more women to whom Sukarno is
alleged to be secretly married, and before you have had time to
feed these into the computer, the Indonesian press lists a ninth
wife, presented to Sukarno as a gift by a proud father, and well-
informed sources say that he in fact grosses eighteen marriages
(from which divorces are deductible). This does not, of course,
take into account the casuals for whom he combed continents,
both developed and underdeveloped, and much local talent in
Indonesia itself. His answer to indignant parents or reluctant
subjects was to wed the girl for the sake of form and divorce her
the next day, which in turn confuses the marriage count.

The president's will was above the law, but as with Sihanouk his love of personal power was inextricably entwined with his passionate, chauvinistic love of country. It was inevitable that, like the god-kings before him, Sukarno should dream of Empire. "God has determined that certain parts of the world should form units," he once cried. "When I look at the islands situated between Asia and Australia, I understand that they are meant to form a single entity," and he announced that in future the Indian Ocean would be called the "Indonesian Ocean." From this it was only a step to his self-appointed role as god-given champion of the underdog nations, the New Emerging Forces of the have-not continents. "We want to create not only a new Indonesia," he thundered, "but a new Asia, a new Africa, a new World!" And this was precisely what the Communists wished.

The Bung was finally compromised in the abortive Communist coup of 1965, and evicted from office. But did he jump, or was he pushed? He called himself "pro-Communist," but his answer to P.K.I. demands that he form a real coalition NASAKOM cabinet and include them in it was the royal evasion "I am NASAKOM." He was confident that he could string along the army, the Communists, and the Chinese, but he was stringing them along on a swaying slack wire. The powerful P.K.I. was able to put pressure on him, its mass organizations manipulating the mounting unrest and land hunger in the underfed republic. In 1963 the Chinese embassy in Djakarta made a direct, undercover approach to the president, warning him that right-wing parties were plotting against his life. Tengku Abdul Rahman of Malaysia disdainfully flouted him, provoking him to even more vainglorious and venomous speeches, full of sound and fury, dignifying nothing.

And beyond all this was his genuine hatred for "imperialism" and "neo-colonialism," his fear of "encirclement," of the destruction of the fragile entity of "Indonesia" which he had created out of a broken necklace of equatorial islands. Coaxed, cajoled, tricked, and tripped by his own blind pretensions, he simply lost his balance, slipped, and fell. And there was no net.

Yet there had been method in his megalomania.

13 : A Question of Identity

Dutch dogs! Get out of West Irian. It was crudely painted on a high wall in the center of Djakarta. But there was something written underneath in smaller print: *Rice—seven rupiahs. Rice—seven rupiahs. Rice—seven rupiahs.* And there was the whole sad story, I thought, as I stood teetering somewhat uneasily on the hem of a hostile mob for whom any fair foreigner might be a hated Hollander in December 1957. The Bung was in full frenzy, leading the Indonesian millions in a violent anticolonial crusade against The Hague for refusing to surrender to him the neighboring territory still so tauntingly known as Dutch West New Guinea, which lay only one hundred miles east of the last of Sukarno's coral strands. Eagerly abetted by the Communists, he tried to bully the Netherlands into relinquishing it by confiscating all Dutch estates and enterprises throughout

Indonesia, expelling all forty-eight thousand Dutch subjects still in the country, repudiating all previous agreements with Holland, severing diplomatic relations, and starting a surreptitious war for the conquest of "West Irian" with the Russian arms that Khrushchev had given him power to sign for in the Soviet super-market.

The effects were to be foreseen. The Dutch had run six hundred rubber, coffee, tobacco, and tea plantations in Indonesia, against thirty-five managed by the State Agricultural Service. Seventy-eight freighters of the Dutch KPM line had provided the main links between island and island in an archipelago which straggled across three thousand miles of sea. Holland had bought one-fifth of all Indonesian exports. *Rice—seven rupiahs?* The price trebled in the following four years and trebled again in the next three months, so that by February 1962 it was costing sixty rupiahs a liter. Exports had dropped by one-third in the preceding year, and foreign-exchange reserves were down to a ridiculous $10 million.

But Sukarno got his "West Irian" in 1963 and thereupon plowed his poverty into a new venture—the military "Confrontation" of "Imperialist" Malaysia. This extension of the Bung's guns-before-butter routine cut the republic off from the free ports of Singapore and Penang, which normally processed and sold three out of every four pounds of Indonesian rubber and two-thirds of all Indonesia's oil products. The rupiah broke into a canter and the cost of living doubled in a year. In the summer of 1963 I ordered a modest enough supper in the Hotel Indonesia in Djakarta—soup, cold platter, coffee, no drinks—and felt virtuously thrifty because it had cost me no more than an Indonesian colonel's pay for a whole month. The black-market value of the American dollar in this meaningless money was now thirty times the official rate of exchange. Two years later all foreign companies were placed under Indonesian "supervision and control," and the oil output fell sharply. *Rice—seven rupiahs?* In 1965 it was costing 200 rupiahs a liter; by 1966 it was 5,000 rupiahs a liter. But in 1966 the joke was over, Sukarno was finished, Confrontation had petered out, and new men were running their fingers through their hair in Djakarta at the sight of the outstanding bills—two and a half billion dollars in foreign exchange.

While solid citizens of the West countersunk in their own confident logic may write off the Bung as an irresponsible lunatic, however, many perceptive Asians would sympathize with his basic quandary.

As with all other continents, Southeast Asia's molten surface sluggishly rippled with the ebb and flow of conquest for centuries until frontiers finally began to settle on firm lines. Vietnam materialized only one hundred and fifty years ago. The borders of "Laos" were bulging and collapsing for century after century as Thais, Burmese, or Annamites invaded or withdrew, and at times it was two and even three kingdoms.

Then came the Western colonialists like rival land-development sharks, ruthlessly ripping out the original topography without regard for nature or the natives and neatly redrawing the maps to mark off their own concessions. The British took four provinces from Siam and added them to Malaya; the French took a fifth one for Cambodia and more miscellaneous territory to lump together with Laos. The new synthetic Laos includes territories which are not ethnically Lao and leaves out other territories which essentially are. If it were only possible, the answer for this tormented country would be a geopolitical sex-change operation whereby the northeast of Laos would be grafted onto North Vietnam and the northeast of Thailand would be added to Laos, altering the shape of the kingdom from phallic to oval.

The British mapped out the lots known as "Burma" (sixty different language groups with cultures as far apart as Scot and Slav) and "Malaya" (excluding four Muslim provinces in south Thailand), a vertical straight line with only one kink in it was drawn four hundred miles down the center of New Guinea, and the Dutch were given the western half. Later Korea and Vietnam were to be bisected by horizontal lines, and the British were to invent "Malaysia" so that they could tack on to the now sovereign Federation of Malaya the island of Singapore and a one-thousand-mile-long strip of real estate in North Borneo which they were anxious to unload. And all this neat cut-and-paste cartography was apt to leave the local inhabitant confused.

One sunny day during Indonesian Confrontation I took off from Singapore International Airport in a little Beechcraft, its doors removed to give a clear view for a camera lens, and we climbed steeply into a yellow sky over the new housing estates, the waterfront, and the ships in the harbor, when suddenly at about a thousand feet a klaxon went off in my ear with deafening urgency like the alarm in a doomed submarine. "We're just stalling, that's all," the pilot explained cheerfully. "That was to let us know. I slowed up to give you a good view, because we can't go nearer without entering enemy air space and perhaps drawing fire. There she is."

It seemed unbelievable. We had not yet passed over the crowded Singapore sea lane, and already almost below us lay the Indonesian island of Batam with the enemy guerrilla-training school on its northern headland which I had come up to photograph. The pilot swung the featherweight plane around in the international air corridor and there at once was the waterfront of Singapore again.

The Straits of Singapore and Malacca are narrow drains up which the British and Dutch drew a line in 1824, leaving one side under the flag of the Netherlands, the other under the Union Jack. And since none of the earlier indigenous kingdoms had conformed even vaguely to the new divisions these red-faced carpetbaggers now dubbed "Malaya" and the "Netherlands East Indies," traditional identities became blurred. When in 1945 the losing Japanese encouraged the emergence of an "independent" Indonesia, the sixty-four Indonesian leaders whom they called together to define its frontiers were quite unable to agree what they should include in it.

Sukarno knew that the fragile unity of his new republic, which lumped together more than a hundred different ethnic groups, rested paradoxically on centuries of common colonial subservience. Indonesia did not lack substance but identity. Seven out of every ten men lived a simple kampong existence on these fertile, sunlit islands, and the greatest danger was not famine, it seemed, but fragmentation. So, turning his back on economic problems, the Bung set out to weld his assortment cf sturdy but mutually distrustful gold-brown men into an arrogant, fiercely chauvinistic nation. Believing that a chip on the shoulder was worth two in the hand, he did not give them bread but loud, angry words and the largest armed forces of all Southeast Asia.

Imaginary external threats and proud answering challenges from Djakarta were written into his script for postwar history to divert the masses from the sorry state of affairs at home, and to make not only men of them, but Indonesians. The Bung was determined to build a nation on hatred and anger, molding his bricks with a thick shock of last straws. The Dutch presence in West Irian was a national insult. Malaysia was a "neocolonialist" creature under Western protection that had "committed an act of aggression against Indonesia" by acquiring former British dependencies on the otherwise Indonesian island of Borneo.

Malaysia was more than that: it was a living menace to the precious unity of Sukarno's archipelago republic. For its government left others to trail clouds of glory, and pursued happiness with the aid of all that the Bung had condemned—foreign bases, foreign advisers, foreign capital—and nobody was nationalized. Prosperous, pragmatic, the young federation threatened to make Indonesia look like a neighboring slum, to lure away not only the best brains in outer islands of the republic restless under the ruinous hegemony of Djakarta, but possibly some of the islands themselves. Malaysia subverted a vainglorious but threadbare Indonesia simply by existing at all.

Man may not live by bread alone, but he certainly cannot live without it, and although it has been said of many Asians that if you offer them rice or an idea, they will take the idea, the idea is very often about rice. With this nagging knowledge in the back of his mind, Sukarno became "obsessed with the frailness of Indonesia," as one of his cronies told me. And the more obsessed he became, the more he fought against the demons of division by playing dictator.

The obsession was not just the by-blow of his fevered imagination. In 1950 there had been rebellion in the South Moluccas at the southeastern edge of the republic, and in 1953 there had been an insurrection in Atjeh, at its northwestern tip. Then, five years later, the "Revolt of the Colonels" had exploded into civil war in Sumatra and Celebes, and I had found myself going into battle on a dining-room chair.

The men who split Indonesia open in 1958 were the men who had wrenched the archipelago from the Dutch in the first place: the officers of the Indonesian People's Army. Having freed the country, the soldiers not unnaturally claimed as much right to a say in its destiny as any caucus of conniving civilians. But they belonged to territorial contingents which had mainly fought the colonial enemy in their own home islands—in Java, in Sumatra, in Celebes and Borneo. Once independent, therefore, Indonesia fell naturally into a pattern of military regions, in each of which the local commanders held the ultimate source of local power— the gun.

By 1956 the incompetence and corruption of the successive governments in Djakarta, the capital of the republic on the central island of Java, had made regional military commanders in the outer islands increasingly fidgety. For overcrowded Java was not only the seat of the administration but the home of six out of ten Indonesians. It earned only a small fraction of Indonesia's foreign exchange, but it absorbed most of the national income. To the Sumatrans, therefore, Java was a cowbird in the nest. As a shock-haired politician once told me over a disgracefully early highball at Palembang in South Sumatra: "In 1956 this island earned five times as much as Java, but the government spent six times as much on the damned Javanese as it did on us. Well, as far as we are concerned, it's a case of 'no money, no love.'" Scottish nationalists would doubtless have sympathized.

Neglected by Djakarta, the outer regions developed a thriving barter trade of their own, shipping thousands of tons of rubber, copra, coffee, and spices directly to Singapore and Manila in exchange for everything from rice to road-building equipment that the central government now failed to provide. And when

Djakarta outlawed this commerce, it was transformed into a gigantic smuggling operation.

The disastrous economic consequences of throwing out all the Dutch, and Sukarno's first open steps toward a *gotong royong* administration which would logically include the Communists, further enraged the commanders on the richer islands of the republic and framed their mundane grievances about lack of money and local autonomy with a new and shining halo of anti-Communist resistance. Slowly but surely the revolts of individual colonels who now assumed absolute power in their respective regions were knitted into a pattern for national rebellion, and in February 1958 a rival "Revolutionary Government of the Republic of Indonesia" was proclaimed in Central Sumatra.

The rebel "government" was an impressive board of directors, calculated to inspire confidence in the foreign political investor. It included not only some of the ablest officers of the Indonesian army, but three former prime ministers and the republic's most brilliant economist, Dr. Djojohadikusomo Sumitro. In Celebes, seventeen hundred miles away to the east of this core of insurrection, other colonels with twelve thousand men under their command were conducting their own branch revolution in coordination with the Sumatra office. The "government" was meanwhile negotiating a wary but useful alliance with the somewhat murderous Darul Islam rebels in North Sumatra and West Java, who had been fighting for a Muslim Indonesia for several years already. Sukarno's fears about centrifugal force appeared to be justified.

At this point Singapore became the neutral bottleneck through which the traffic of all sides passed—the freighters loaded for Djakarta, the rebel blockade runners, the money, the men, and the secrets. A hundred ships rode at anchor in the harbor, their masters often tight-lipped about their destinations. There was almost a scandal when ten obsolescent British armored cars were driven straight through the city and down to the docks for forwarding f.o.b. to the revolutionaries. At night, blacked-out bombers from Clark Field in the Philippines, filled with American small arms from Okinawa and heading for Sumatra, droned in softly to refuel. The rebels needed rice, vehicles, machinery, and guns, and they had rubber and copra to sell. The town was full of couriers and agents with ready cash, false papers, and false information.

But one story was not false: Djakarta had thrown paratroops and a seaborne mobile brigade against the east coast of Sumatra, seized the oil fields, and forced the rebels back into their mountain fortress to the west. The fight was on. Robert Pepper Martin of *U.S. News and World Report*, Keyes Beech of the *Chicago Daily News*, and I decided to pool our plans for reaching the war. Pepper is a rumbling mountain of middle-aged man with hair and mustache indignantly *à la brosse*, and Keyes is a trim specimen of American Marine biology with a lightly frosted head and the collected air of a fight veteran. Together we boarded a little coaster and sailed for thirty hours across a sea of smoked glass to Palembang in South Sumatra.

Once the heart of the mighty Srividjaja empire, Palembang was the headquarters of a "neutral" colonel who stayed out of the fight himself but provided a port and a pipeline to the rebels for fuel and volunteers and other much-needed strategic commodities through the five hundred miles of swamp and jungle and mountain to the north. Our object was to get ourselves fed into this pipeline, and by devious Indonesian means we were told how to do so. We crossed the swamplands of the south concealed in the back of a plain truck and after ten painful hours found ourselves in a market town tucked into the shadow of the tremendous, overgrown, and crumbling wall of mountain that guards the twelve-hundred-mile littoral of western Sumatra. Through this range was stitched the tenuous thread of road which government troops advancing westward out of the ooze of the east were undoubtedly bent on cutting.

Within an hour we were seated in a decrepit green and yellow bus, its roof piled high with tin suitcases and fraying wicker baskets bulging with edibles dead and alive, its interior stuffed with twenty-four assorted and good-humored Sumatrans and three correspondents. The bus had gaps in the coachwork for windows, and the wooden seats were designed for the smaller

Asian femur—a foot-wide bench for the bottom and then six inches of space to the back of the next seat. A diminutive driver climbed up into the cab, the stub of a cigarette stuck obstinately to the corner of his mouth. He started the engine with an ear-splitting roar and began jolting us through the sudden potholes that combined in their tens of thousands to make up the road to the heart of the rebellion at Bukit Tinggi.

He was to keep us reeling on recklessly for forty-six hours without once pausing for sleep. Only at sundown would we stop for half an hour to swarm into some village eating house for the first meal of the day, for this was the Muslim fasting month of Ramadan. Gibbons howled and whistled from the jungle trees at dawn. At night luminous eyes reflected the headlights, and once a monstrous monitor lizard jaywalked sedately across our path. Seven times we crossed muddy, palm-fringed rivers on flat ferries that tilted and wallowed as the bus was eased down on to them, the sun burnishing the crocodile-ridden waters or our headlights probing at the farther shore through spiteful curtains of rain. Every few hours we would jerk to a halt as police and military emerged from the veranda of some dim-lit atap hut and laboriously checked all our papers but never held us up.

When the sun rose on the second morning, we found ourselves roaring through a spectacular gorge choked with unkempt jungle that thinned out to bony peaks nearly nine thousand feet up. We were already within the rebel stockade.

Sumatra is a long shark of an island nosing up into the Indian Ocean, and the revolutionary government was defying Djakarta from what might be called its underbelly—the midwest coastal area and its spectacular hinterland. The zone included the port of Padang, and also, sixty miles in and eight thousand feet farther up, the hill town of Bukit Tinggi, into which our bus snorted like a bull plunging into the arena. At such heights men see visions and dream intoxicating dreams, and this perhaps explains much. The gray-haired prime minister of the revolutionary government, the pragmatic ex-governor of the National Bank of Indonesia, told us confidently two days later: "The dislocation of normal commerce and sources of revenue, caused by our resistance, will bring Djakarta to its knees very soon. In three months' time we shall reach the turning point—and time is on our side." Within three months, in fact, the central government would have its hands on Bukit Tinggi. The rebels did not dispose of more than three thousand regular troops, and although the stockade was full of cheap rice and fat buffalo, prices were already beginning to rise and petrol was in desperately short supply.

An ancient 15-cwt. army truck was finally lent to the eight foreign correspondents in Bukit Tinggi, together with a driver and a listless young lieutenant. A great rusty drum of petrol, purchased at killing cost, was manhandled into the middle of the back, and as this left room for only three men along each side, we borrowed two flimsy dining-room chairs from the rest house which we now dominated, and tied them on to the tail-board with rope. Perched on one of these, I set off to see the war. The truck jounced past Lake Singkarak, an eleven-mile-long eye of still, mistladen water just south of the equator, and after ten hours of erratic driving swung left onto an uninviting track that disappeared into the grim mountain fastnesses to the east. Somewhere down that green gulch, central-government troops advancing from the oil fields were working toward us to cut the north-south road to Palembang and invest the rebel stronghold.

As night fell, we pulled up in the shadow of a big wooden house on high stilts, the headquarters of the rebel regiment that had been pushed steadily westward by the oncoming government troops and was now holding a river line farther down the road at a place called Lubukdjambi. "The commander of our forward companies at Lubukdjambi, Captain Azwar, has recrossed the river and driven the enemy back about ten miles," the second-in-command told us jubilantly. "We shall now go forward and retake the oil fields." Why were they lost in the first place? "Our men panicked when government planes came over bombing and strafing," he replied slowly. He reflected for a moment, then burst out sorrowfully: "We never expected Djakarta to behave like this. We never thought they would make war on us as a country makes war on an enemy state."

The Javanese were not playing fair, he implied. The whole

business was supposed to be an Indonesian charade leading to an Indonesian compromise, but Sukarno had lost his temper and pulled a real knife. In this very civil war he was not talking things out in accordance with the principle of *musjarawah*, but behaving as if all was over bar the shooting.

We slept on the floor, moved off down the road next morning, and found Captain Azwar at a command post on the hither side of the river. Characteristically, he flatly contradicted his superior at regimental headquarters. He had not attacked across the stream, and he had not pushed the government troops back ten miles. The opposite bank was still in their hands. "But you have seen what fantastic country lies behind us," he went on hopefully. "If the enemy tries to advance farther he will find this road impassable." The men from Java nevertheless crossed the river, thrust Captain Azwar off his perch two days later, and pressed on toward the Palembang road junction. The whole rebel zone was a minefield of misinformation.

The central government, having scraped together a motley collection of ships and aircraft, duly launched a model sea-and-air assault on Padang which was only briefly opposed. But meanwhile there were reports of fierce rebel resistance against government troops advancing down the six hundred miles of road that led from Bukit Tinggi to Medan, the loyalist capital of the north. This attracted Keyes, who kept repeating disgustedly: "I shan't believe there's a war on till I see a body." We therefore hired a small bus, so that we each had a whole bench to lie on, and set off one evening in this luxurious way for the battle. For fifteen hours the bus fought the ridged and rutted road through the thickly matted mountains. The night was fine, and once a flock of vampires, their great jagged wings black against the moon, flapped silently over us like a migration of demonic umbrellas. By high morning, however, the malicious wilderness had given way to calm green plains flanked by smooth rolling hills. It all looked very peaceful.

"But you cannot go all the way north by road," a rebel major warned us. "You must cross Lake Toba by boat. Carry a big Red Cross flag, whatever you do, and go by daylight. The central-government troops will fire on you as you approach Prapat. And take care in Prapat, because they are fighting there." This was another stale slice of misinformation. We climbed into our bus, and a few hours later the country coarsened equatorially again, the hills rose sharply at our approach, and suddenly before us lay the fabulous mountain lake, sixty miles long and encircled by high cliffs and escarpments. We boarded a ferry that had no Red Cross flag, and after five hours of violent tropical storm it deposited us on the northeast shore of the lake in darkness without a shot being fired.

The next morning we took off for Medan in still another hired bus. "Watch out," we were admonished by well-meaning Indonesians. "Central-government troops hold Siantar but are fighting off heavy attacks by the rebels. The hospitals are full of wounded." In Siantar we had a glass of beer in the somnolent main street with a bored army sergeant, and so bowled on up an excellent road to Medan, lunch, and a post-mortem.

We had chalked up one hundred hours of traveling by bus and truck from one end of Sumatra to the other. We had not seen a dead, wounded, or really frightened man. We had been through a dozen military and police checkpoints—government, neutral, rebel—and nobody had questioned our dubious itinerary, our right, in fact, to drive a bus right through the whole war.

I booked the one empty seat left on the Garuda Airways plane flying to Malaya. At Medan airport a Javanese immigration official asked me where I had been in Sumatra. "Just Prapat," I lied, foreseeing last-minute trouble. The loyal servant of President Sukarno looked shocked. "And you a journalist? In your shoes I would have gone to see the rebels in Bukit Tinggi," he said reprovingly. "I'm really surprised at you."

It should be added that once the government forces controlled the main towns, the rebels took their war into the hills and their guerrilla sorties and ambushes began for the first time to give their enemies a taste for aspirin. Early in 1961, therefore, Sukarno offered a free pardon to all who surrendered before October, and by August most of them had "returned to the republic." In Sumatra those killed in action officially numbered 193.

An old agency message before me reports that a provincial governor is defying Djakarta's ban on the export of unprocessed or low-grade rubber from Sumatra. This is not a flashback to Sukarno and the revolt of 1958. The message is dated ten years later. The president of Indonesia is now Suharto and the Trade Minister who imposed the ban is the brilliant Dr. Sumitro, quondam financial wizard of the Sumatran rebels. But when the safety catches are off, the real masters of the archipelago are still some fourteen regional military commanders. However, if Suharto sometimes appears to be the sort of soft tough who would drink Tabasco through a straw, his intelligence and determination should not be underestimated. Although in 1969 he agreed that general elections should be held in 1971, he severely trimmed the army structure in order to deprive the provincial warlords of distressing temptations in the future. Politicians might be a pest, but in any Asian situation he knew where the real danger to unity and peace—and president—really lay.

14 : The Sweet Smell of Corruption

Like the rigged packs of some celestial cardsharp, most Asian communities can be cut neatly into the rulers and the ruled, however much they are shuffled by well-meaning Westerners. For the Oriental answer to imperfect government has not been argument but insurrection, since he who challenged absolute power with soft words in earlier centuries was simply asking for an excruciating end. The more dictatorial powers an Asian gives himself, the more he convinces malcontents that they can overthrow him only by force; and the more he is aware of the threat they pose, the more tyrannical he becomes, and the more desperate he makes them. This is the Oriental equation, whose normal solution is an act of violence that simply replaces one clique with another.

By the time Sukarno was finally supplanted he had survived

two attempted *coups d'état* by two different chiefs-of-staff, five major uprisings, four or five miscellaneous assassination attempts, a palace bombing, and the Tjikini Affair. On Saturday, November 30, 1957, Muslim fanatics threw five bombs at the Bung as he emerged from a fund-raising fete at the Tjikini School in Djakarta. Nine toddlers and a pregnant woman died and, in all, forty-eight children fell critically wounded as the blood began to mingle sluggishly with the steadily falling rain. Sukarno was protected by two military aides, both of whom were severely injured. He was shaken but unhurt. I was the only British newspaper correspondent in the city and I had an edition going to press within a few hours. But my exclusive story rated just two column inches in *The Observer*. Distance lends no enchantment to the news, and foul play in the Far East was as common as dog bites man.

A correspondent coursing around a subcontinent of eleven Asian states cannot always be in the right place at the right time to cover every coup or killing, but he may sometimes be fortunate. One fine sunny morning in March 1962 I was working my way through coffee and croissants in my air-conditioned hotel bedroom in Saigon and glanced idly out of the locked window to see an aircraft dive silently into view and then climb out of sight again. I paid no attention, for the Vietcong had no planes and therefore all flyers were friendly. I was shaken out of this facile syllogism by a muffled, rumbling roar, and as I put down my cup and jumped to my feet a second aircraft dipped noiselessly across the air space framed by my window, there was a second juddering explosion, and from below the sill a cloud of very dirty smoke began to rise into view. The circus proceeded, the planes bobbing quietly across my vision at regular intervals as if I were counting them to cure insomnia. But it was all so dream-like that I felt sure I was already asleep.

It was no dream for the Diem family. Two young Vietnamese air-force pilots were giving a very suitable signal for a *coup d'état* by divebombing the presidential palace. Operating with commendable accuracy, they half wrecked the huge colonial structure but failed to pin down the president himself. One pilot was shot down and captured. Twenty officers were arrested, and loyalist tanks began to clatter once again through the streets of Saigon to take up positions in the park-like palace grounds.

This was the sequel to an abortive thirty-hour revolt in 1960 when seven hundred paratroops surrounded the palace and were quickly joined by infantry, marines, and artillery units in and around Saigon. But I had already ducked instinctively as the mortar bombs shrieked overhead to hit that same palace as early as 1955, when Diem's enemies had first tried to liquidate him. Later the Buddhists explored their own strange corner of the Asian map of violence by burning themselves alive in the streets of the capital to rouse men to bloody rebellion against him. They were to succeed where others had failed, and on November 2, 1963, Diem and his brother Nhu were unceremoniously butchered in the back of an armored personnel carrier in Cholon, the sister-city of Saigon.

To renounce the howitzer and the half-nelson in favor of dependence upon such dubious devices as the rule of law and the polling booth calls for a stupendous act of faith on the part of the millions. Most start by regarding a hovercraft society held up by nothing but an air cushion of civic responsibility and loyalty to the constitution as no more feasible than a flying carpet. In much of Asia the contract between men and government has been a loose, low-geared agreement-in-principle, with little obligation on either side. The government has not cared much for the people, and the people have cared little or nothing for the government. As an old Burmese saying has it, a man has five enemies: fire, water, the king, robbers, and "the one who hates him." The king is placed, it will be noted, while ordinary criminals and murderers are among the also-ran.

Moreover, dumb insolence toward authority acquired the aura of heroic national resistance once the struggle against the white colonial boss was joined, so that by the time the countries of Southeast Asia became independent sovereign states, the old habits of defiance had been consecrated. Today it is ironically the new native governments that are their target. Even when a regime conscientiously tries to sweep up the sociological mess, it is liable to be discouraged by the ingratitude of a skeptical public.

The diminutive conductress in her high-necked Burmese blouse and *longgyi* blocks the gangway as I move to get off the bus. "Back door for exit," she says accusingly. "The front door is for the entrance." This orderly canalizing is a confusing novelty in Rangoon as far as I and a million and a half Burmese are concerned, but then so is the new, shining bus, and the smooth road on which it runs, even the fact that the conductress takes the trouble to collect all the fares.

General Ne Win has been in power for nearly eighteen months and has given a convincing demonstration of the orderliness and punctuality that a little barrack-room barking can achieve. The streets are clean and a hundred thousand mangy stray dogs have been systematically destroyed, Buddhist tenets notwithstanding. The railways run on time, the passengers pay for their tickets, and trains are only occasionally blown up by frustrated insurgents. Prices of staple commodities are fixed and shopkeepers must tag their goods and not haggle. Rackets in trading licenses have been suppressed, speculation curbed.

That was in February 1960. But the stiff and scarifying military broom had already swept itself out of favor. A few days later the voters returned with an overwhelming majority Prime Minister U Nu and the party "hag-ridden by prejudice, jobbery and nepotism, muddle, delay and corruption" which Ne Win had originally replaced. The general had made the mistake of putting the intensely individualistic Burmese through a crash course in social discipline, under the erroneous impression that they would be happy if it gave them a richer, more reliable, and cleaner community. The Burmese preferred the old scramble, the dogs, the peddlers, and the garbage in the streets, so Ne Win felt constrained to seize power again in 1962 for their own good and to inaugurate rule by "revolutionary council." This has since established new standards in mutual mistrust between people and potentate.

In lands where the central government is a dubious source of comfort or protection, men naturally depend on other men of the same clan, village, class, or profession. Charity begins at home, and so does everything else. Even the Asian Christian has a somewhat clouded sense of sin, adulterated by his far greater sense of shame. He is more anxious for the good opinion of his grandfather than the good opinion of God.

Loyalties and feuds alike are determined by family rather than by moral relationships—ties of father and son, cousin and cousin, not Uncle and Thrush. It is hopeless to try to separate party rivalries in a country like Laos by using the conventional political prism, for even mass movements with resounding titles like "The Rally of the Lao People" turn out to be the instruments of some cozy clique within which everyone of note has the same name. Perhaps the most important single fact that any correspondent must bear in mind, when unraveling the contents of the bag of gentle vipers that is Vientiane, is that in the mid-fifties a man named Ou Vorovong was assassinated while sitting in the house of a man named Phoui Sananikone.

The Vorovongs are a southern family into which the former Laotian "strong man" Phoumi Nosavan is married, and Phoumi's father's elder sister was the aunt of Marshal Sarit Thanarat, the former "strong man" of Thailand. Their link with the Nosavans has enabled the Vorovongs to acquire numerous posts of power in the past, from government ministries to the chief receipt of customs. But their bitter vendetta against the Sananikones has brought them little joy, for the hated Sananikones are also great landowners, brother Phoui is a former prime minister and president of the National Assembly, brother Ngon has held every ministry but two in the succession of cabinets since 1954, and nephew Oudone is chief-of-staff of the Laotian army. More than this, Phoui's sister was the first wife of Khou Abhay, and Khou Abhay's son, Major-General Kouprasith, is commander of the Fifth Military Region, which includes the capital of Vientiane. Meanwhile, *Nhouy* Abhay was married to the sister of Prince Boun Oum, lord of the former kingdom of Champassak. Now Boun Oum . . .

At this point we drop our programs on our laps in disgust and wait for the singers themselves to unravel what is obviously one of those dire nineteenth-century operatic plots that so unaccountably inspired Mussorgsky and Verdi to compose relatively comprehensible music. That, nevertheless, is Laos.

Turn the coin over and on the back of Vendetta (you lose) we find Nepotism (we win). In 1961 at least six members of the sixteen-man Laotian cabinet were relatives of Prince Boun Oum and all but two came from his home town. The Minister of Interior was his brother-in-law, the Minister of Finance his nephew, another nephew was Minister of Public Works, and a rather backward brother was given the Ministry of Cults. Moreover, since General Phoumi Nosavan was Minister of Defense, it naturally followed that one Ngon Nosavan should be Director of Customs. Boun Oum, of course, was Prime Minister.

Seven years later most of the pieces were still on the board, although in different positions. The commanders of the five military regions remained semi-independent war lords who ran their own profitable fiefs, only intermittently scorched by the conflagration in Vietnam that was searing their eastern flank. This layout resembled the pattern in Indonesia and Vietnam, but takeover bids by military tycoons were unlikely, for the king (who commands great traditional veneration) was said to have declared officially: "All coups are banned."

The fine fretted screen of narrow allegiances and obligations through whose obscuring lattice alone Asia can be seen as Asians see it is no decoration but part of a functional structure that stiffens even the modern political party—sometimes to a point of paralysis. Every postwar group is saddled with old-guard revolutionaries whose parochial minds are rooted in the past but to whom loyalty must be given in return for long-standing loyalty. And this can produce remarkable perspectives of judgment which leave an unwary Western observer cross-eyed.

In 1964 a member of the Malaysian opposition accused the Minister of Education of embezzlement and corruption. The minister sued his opponent for libel—and lost the case with costs. The implications were obvious. But when the minister reluctantly resigned, Tengku Abdul Rahman wrote to him with a royal disregard for the courts which can only be described as princely in its generosity: "I very much regret that you consider it necessary to take this step. I would like to assure you that your colleagues and I are convinced of your innocence, having known you for this number of years. I would like to take this opportunity also of thanking you for the service that you have rendered to our party, our people, and our country . . ."

Nor was that all. Parliament was asked for a supplementary vote of £10,304. 7s. to meet the legal expenses of the unlucky minister's case, the Tengku explaining patiently to indignant critics of his open-handed gesture with the taxpayers' money that, after all, ministers' salaries were "small" compared with the earnings of business executives.

A modern Asian dictator must also reward all those who so wisely assisted him when he mounted the *coup d'état* that put him into power in the first place. In South Korea, General Park promoted no fewer than fifty-six senior officers to the rank of general for their selfless services to the state on the day he seized control of the country from its lawful civilian government. In Thailand, Marshal Sarit Thanarat paid "coup money" to the officers who helped him to take over, and thoughtfully provided his generals with unique opportunities for land speculation, smuggling, and other profitable business enterprises. These in turn allowed moneymaking options to percolate down through the ranks to their own loyal subordinates until it looked as if Thailand might die the death of a thousand cuts.

Limited loyalties encourage unlimited corruption, but in the minds of many prominent men in Southeast Asia what the un-subtle West calls graft is a natural process with an honorable history. Air Marshal Nguyen Cao Ky, vice-president of South Vietnam, once startled the Americans by saying that nine out of ten Asian politicians were corrupt, adding: "And the fact that I am one of the corrupt is obvious." He did not hang his head in shame, however, and then resign. He grinned engagingly, and got on with his work as he saw it.

Official squeeze is a custom that dates back to the days when men appointed to senior posts were expected to finance their administration by milking the millions, and were regarded as feckless failures if they asked to be given a budget to help them out. Since the millions paid few if any other taxes, this was regarded as equitable. In order to avoid the dunning that would have been beneath the dignity of the panjandrum, those seeking preference would present him with gifts. And these he pocketed.

With a little adjustment of moral focus, public funds and private purse could be made to merge, like the double image in the viewfinder of a camera, until personal expenditure became a patriotic duty. As Laotian Minister of Finance, General Phoumi Nosavan made a fortune in the early nineteen-sixties by smuggling gold into Thailand with the complicity of Marshal Sarit in Bangkok (it will doubtless be recollected that Phoumi's father's elder sister was Sarit's aunt). However, Phoumi explained that his object was not to fill his wallet but to pay the troops and the building costs of the "Monument aux Morts," a sort of stone cruet on stilts, evidently inspired by the Arc de Triomphe in Paris, which stands forlorn and forever unfinished in the middle of Vientiane.

Of the five regional warlords of Laos, one has the customs service in his pocket and is not getting any poorer, others deal astutely in rice and timber, and a fourth works hard selling opium. ("It is my duty to dispose of it," protests this oblong, garishly decorated general stoutly. "Otherwise, it would fall into the hands of the Communists.") Even the advertised strength of the Laotian army, usually given as seventy thousand must be questioned, for commanders normally draw money for far more men than they have. These nonexistent troops are called "spirit soldiers," and the angry Americans accuse venal officers of appropriating their pay and allowances, much as Chinese put food on the altars of their ancestors and then eat it themselves. The Laotians, however, indignantly reject these charges of dishonesty, and point out that this excellent practice enables them to help families of dead or crippled servicemen, since the army gives dependents nothing through official channels. Laotian officers have also been known to exaggerate the poverty of their own equipment or the strength of the enemy in order to wheedle more weapons out of the Americans and more men from the Ministry of Defense. These devious forms of private enterprise are the substitutes for equitable and efficient distribution from the center.

In 1968 the able and youthful Laotian Minister of Finance made himself unpopular by rather prissily declining to give generals money for nonexistent private soldiers, a break with tradition widely regarded with disfavor. He told me that modern methods and morals nevertheless paid, for in the old days the government could put its hands on only forty percent of all revenue, as the rest was discreetly drained off into private pocket-books. By the beginning of the year, however, he had reduced the leak to a mere trickle of twenty percent.

Intriguing details of Sukarno's generosity with cash from the national till emerged during the trial in 1966 of Jusuf Muda Dalam, ex-Minister for Central Bank Affairs in Indonesia, who had been arraigned for manipulating public funds on a colossal scale but declared firmly that he handed out money only on the specific instructions of the Bung. Drab daily existence in Djakarta was much enlivened by the court scenes, in which the action was punctuated by a parade of languorous beauties who provided eye-catching, three-dimensional décor reminiscent of a Ziegfeld Follies production, for the ex-minister was also charged with polygamy.

A twenty-seven-year-old secretary explained how she escorted five wives and three concubines to his different guest houses. "How did you have time?" the bewildered court president asked the defendant. "There is plenty of time after office hours," Dalam retorted severely. And there was plenty of money too. A raven-haired vision of twenty-six in a white shimmering dress mentioned a novel kind of gift for good girls—a $2 million import license, granted to her on "deferred payment" terms. An actress confirmed that Dalam had allowed her another vast sum on the same basis, and a third charmer described how he had given her checks worth five and a half million dollars to cash. Altogether this fast-moving man-about-town, whose name means "Joseph Young Inside," was accused of squandering more than $250 million by granting import licenses and credits to tame businessmen and pet mistresses without guarantees or time limits for repayment. He said he accepted "gifts" from grateful merchants in return, "because my salary was not enough."

Behind the trial of Dalam was the shadow-trial of Sukarno. One personable young lady confessed that Dalam had allowed her a $2 million loan after she had gone to see the president. The Bung's Japanese wife admitted that she had been given another $2 million credit, and not only a marketful of merchants but a famous woman racing driver chipped in with other stories of presidential thoughtfulness.

Sukarno also accepted "gifts," and one businessman who had been accorded a $10 million loan on orders from the palace was required to pass $600,000 of it back to the president. Small wonder that his successor, President Suharto, ungallantly told a crowd who saw his wife with him in 1968: "She was fat before I became president—don't think she has become fat since."

When Marshal Sarit of Thailand died, he was found posthumously guilty of having embezzled state funds to the value of £12 million, at least £7,500,000 of which had been diverted into his private account, most of it to be spent on "minor wives," of whom there always seemed to be a score or so around at any one time. Sarit and his family held the monopoly for importing gold and the concession for the sale of state lottery tickets and had acquired controlling interests in more than a dozen businesses, including a construction firm much favored with government contracts.

The creeping damp of Asian corruption filters downward from the top. The civil service is regarded as the ideal opening for young men ambitious not so much to slave for their country as to improve their situation and that of their family, and when a Filipino bureaucrat was caught giving special import licenses to his wife, the president himself defended him indignantly with the words: "Is there anything wrong with a civil servant providing for his future?" In 1968 another official in Manila claimed tax exemption for the "gifts" he had paid out to his own seniors and to useful congressmen, and listed them all on his assessment form.

Generations of exasperated American-aid experts in Vietnam have cursed mercenary civil servants for filching the medicine and comforts sent down to the villages to win the hearts and minds of the peasants away from the Vietcong. But the resentful petty official sees himself as the victim of a vicious system of Western discrimination whereby the peasants get free cloth or choppers or candy, and he gets nothing. By helping himself judiciously to the quantity befitting his rank, he is only ensuring a fairer distribution of foreign aid.

On the outskirts of Saigon, truck drivers with loads of innocent vegetables or concealed Vietcong pay the police to allow them through, and in Manila and Djakarta traffic police will hold up cars to exact a little casual tribute from those in a hurry. During the Sukarno era, rent-a-rifle soldiers in Indonesia would hire out their weapons to a would-be killer or kidnapper for a modest fee and ask no questions. Bullets came extra at two shillings each. In 1968 Indonesian navy helicopters were still making trips around the capital, carrying tourists ready to pay a pound a time, and army trucks ran shuttle services to the suburbs for any grateful commuter with the price of the journey in his pocket.

In countries where the system of taxation is not effective enough to collect sufficient revenue to guarantee government servants a living wage, the private citizen who has put nothing into the central exchequer finds himself paying out to the individual functionary instead. And in Sukarno's day, only one Indonesian in every four hundred paid taxes, but all needed the signatures of seven officials to be wed, and of five more to be buried.

The more complex the bureaucracy, the more numerous the toll gates and the bigger and more equitable the graft. In the Philippines this egalitarianism may be seen at its best, for a merchant may pass through fifty-four eager hands in the customs department before he is free to sell imported goods under a misleading description which will enable him to recuperate his outlay in bribes by paying less duty on them. Within this vicious circle, the customs officers make more but the exchequer makes less and therefore pays them less, so they in turn must make more by taking more tips for seeing that customs duties remain unpaid and the exchequer therefore makes less.

A simple principle underlies much of the corruption in the East: Time is money.. The official will save you precious time by putting your application at the top of the pile, or stamping your license without delay, or granting your immigration permit, or letting your car through the cordon. But you must pay, for every minute has its price. Western champions of Eastern corruption claim that it gives the administration a flexibility which enables a man to get things done without being bogged down in a bureaucratic morass. This comforting theory ignores the fact that the system favors the tycoon who can afford to pay his way through a forest of formalities in which money is cheap and documents dear, while prices are pushed up prohibitively for the small man. The lopsided licensing pattern which then develops inevitably makes for a lopsided national economy.

The managers of the big white companies do not usually soil their hands with all this sticky money, but they may employ a native fixer who knows which waving tropical palms to grease to get what they want. They themselves remain contemptuous of the corrupt Oriental, blissfully unaware, it seems, that the man who slips a Djakarta policeman a thousand-rupiah note is as venal as the policeman himself, even in a world in which the cops are the robbers.

The older Asian neither praises nor blames corruption, for its sweet smell is a part of life, like weather and hypocrites. For all his lamentable acquisitiveness, Marshal Sarit was genuinely mourned by many in Thailand, his splendid obsequies were attended by the king and the queen, and an opposition motion to deprive him of his rank posthumously was roundly defeated. He had steered his country through a difficult passage of years, and his peculations must be taken as part of his performance.

"We are not concerned with moral issues," a Manila merchant once said on the subject. "All that worries us now is that here in the Philippines graft has reached such proportions that the government has become *inefficient*." The citizen in a corrupt society has his own place on the spiral of connivance and confidence. To assure him that he will be more secure if the community is remolded into a new, exotic shape within which his equilibrium will be maintained by law and not lucre is like telling a nervous non-swimmer that if he just lies still he will float anyway.

15 : The Traffickers

As hallowed by history as corruption, the diligent practice of piracy and smuggling on a grand scale is also part of the pattern of politics in Southeast Asia. In 1969, accordingly, Lee Kuan Yew told a slightly surprised reporter in Singapore that perhaps the most useful role the United States Seventh Fleet could play after British forces had withdrawn from the area would be to check the growing piracy in the Straits of Malacca.

This occupation, regarded as reprehensible in the squeamish West by those who think in terms of the haphazard depredations of buccaneers like Blackbeard, Morgan, and Kidd, had respectable origins in Malayan waters as a form of systematic taxation. Henchmen of the local rajahs boarded ships when they sailed into the river estuaries bound for markets upstream, and exacted a toll from them. Malacca itself—one-time powerful Venice of the East—held the gorgeous West in fee by forcing ships to put in and pay in coin or cargo for the right to proceed farther, while great war fleets of Muslim rovers, proud of their profession and sanctified by their persecution of the infidel, hovered in wait for them in the South China Sea. Piracy was the flighty sister of commerce, in the tradition of the trade-or-raid policy of Vikings who importuned the English in the eighth century, landing on their coasts with a pair of scales in one hand and a two-edged sword in the other like Blind Justice herself.

Things are not what they were, and the modern Malay, Thai, or Chinese pirates make do with modest enough squadrons. But they operate in fast launches armed with machine guns or junks fitted with a row of powerful outboard motors, and hijacking smugglers or terrorizing and robbing fishing fleets are routine activities. In the uneasy waters that lie between Borneo and the Philippines, cutthroat raids on coastal towns are one of the hazards of living. In mid-1968 four boatloads of pirates armed with high-powered weapons assaulted Basilan City in the southern Philippines and fought a pitched battle with troops and police until helicopters flew in army reinforcements. This was no isolated instance, and Lee Kuan Yew's concern was quite natural. For Royal Navy minesweepers working with R.A.F. patrols have in recent years crippled flotillas of marauders infesting the notorious Sulu Sea.

Piracy and general smuggling still envenom the sometimes bilious relations between Malaysia and the Philippines as I write, but the real poison is provided by the Filipino "cigarette boats"—long, dainty fingers of open craft capable of skimming over the razor-edged coral at thirty-five to forty knots, leaving any revenue cutter or armed hijacker to feel its way gingerly around the hazard. Slipping into the small, sun-baked ports of Sabah, the Malaysian state in North Borneo, Filipino cancer merchants can cram 350 cases, each containing ten thousand "blue seal" American cigarettes, into one of these and set off safely again across the eight hundred miles of sea to Manila. Their purchases are not illegal in Sabah, and their reentry into the Philippines is made as smooth as a well-oiled palm. In this elegant fashion, 90 million cigarettes may be smuggled into the republic every month. Until recently, Malaysia made a million pounds a year out of the legal "shipping tax" on all forms of exported contraband, while Manila lost more than forty million pounds in annual revenue. The reluctant Malaysians were finally persuaded to forgo their profit and sign an anti-smuggling agreement with the Philippines in a spirit of goodwill. However, this goodwill, like all spirit, quickly evaporated when exposed to the elements and by 1969 the slim cigarette boats were back in Sabah's harbors, "smugglers" in the English of the Filipinos, "barter traders" in the English of the Malaysians. But in Southeast Asia the very word "smuggle" should be used after careful thought, for impoverished governments must resort to many unorthodox ways of raising cash. When it becomes legitimate, smuggling should be called traffic, and once it is official, it becomes trade.

In 1967 those flying over the lightly grilled Thai plains from Bangkok to Vientiane in the antique aircraft of Royal Air Lao might at any time find themselves sitting next to some unassuming individual whose sole luggage consisted of a bundle of gold bars resting on the otherwise empty seat on his far side. This gold was brought into Laos legally, subject to payment of an eight-and-a-half percent duty. It was then quietly filtered out again with the blessing of the Laotian Finance Minister, mainly to ready buyers in Saigon and Bangkok, and ultimately to India and elsewhere. It accounted for half of all that Laos earned, for it moved at a speed of up to six tons a month, and the price of a kilogram outside Laos—including in Communist Hanoi—was anything from forty to a hundred and forty pounds higher than the price originally paid.

The principal Laotian export of the past decade, however, is not officially listed. From the ideal spring-like climate of the northern uplands, the Meo tribeswomen trudge down to the markets in the plains to barter their agricultural produce for gold and cloth and salt. And their main cash crop comes from waving fields of *Papaver somniferum* which may yield sixteen pounds of crude opium per acre.

The "smoking saloons" of Southeast Asia range from utility accommodation with wooden benches for trishaw drivers and coolies to the usual plush tourist traps, but ask in any of these where the opium has come from, and the reply will be "Yunnan." Yunnan is the mountainous southwestern province of Communist China whose government in Peking, filled with sanctimonious ideological scruples, joins North Korea and North Vietnam in refusing to give any details about national production of the raw material of oblivion to the "imperialist" United Nations Opium Board. But "Yunnan," like "cognac," has become a loose generic term. It applies to the opium not only of China but of the other countries whose high frontiers converge in the same remote region of tossed hills and lush valleys—the Shan States of Burma, the northern borderlands of Thailand, the western limits of Laos—where the absurdly named "garden poppy" flourishes and multiplies.

The mule trains and caravans of porters that trek southwest from Yunnan into Burma bring out between three hundred and four hundred tons of raw opium a year, and join the general trail of poison leading southward to the Thai frontier region, where in crude "kitchens" in the mountain villages practiced hands refine much of it into powder with a morphine content of up to eighty percent. In north Thailand the commerce is organized by remnants of the Nationalist Chinese army which were forced out of Yunnan when Mao's men overran the province in 1950. While Peking and Taipei indulge their common talent for mutual mudslinging, the growers of Communist Yunnan and the former diehards of President Chiang Kai-shek cooperate—if at arm's length—in a profitable business venture in damnation.

The narcotics seep down to Bangkok and from there out into the world—in the tires of cars, in sacks of fertilizer, even embedded in the flesh of specially branded cattle. Some pass through Rangoon or are smuggled overland to Singapore. For a long time an enterprising group of French pilots ran a transport service affectionately known as Air Opium, dropping their cargo at selected points outside Saigon or parachuting it into the Gulf of Thailand to be picked up by waiting ships.

In Singapore or Hong Kong an ounce of white heroin may be worth thirty times its price in the "factories" of Bangkok, and a hundred and fifty times that price when it is peddled off Piccadilly Circus. In most countries the traffic is officially illegal, but may nevertheless have powerful protectors. In Laos military aircraft authorized by the top brass have flown the drug, and in Thailand marketing is invariably in the hands of men of distinction. Bribes buy blind eyes, and in some parts of the Far East, in consequence, the arm of the law is more golden than long.

But if minds and movements in modern Southeast Asia must be seen through filters that bring out the gaudy threads of gold and graft, piracy and *Papaver somniferum* in the geopolitical design, they must also be observed through the other influences that color them, from philosophy to superstition. For in an ignorant subcontinent, opium is not the only religion of the people.

16 : Mumbo-Jumbo Makes History

When I wrote *The Chinese Looking Glass*, certain superficial critics in England sneered at me for suggesting that superstitious belief and religious custom had survived Communism in China itself. (The Chinese Communists, being rather better acquainted with the subject, have repeatedly admitted that the supernatural has been among their most stubborn ideological foes.) But then a common Western fallacy until recent years was that the new generation born in Soviet Russia must grow up knowing nothing but Marxism, and would therefore behave like a mindless machine programmed only to repeat propaganda.

Instead, forty years of Communism produced a Russian salad of Communists, dropouts, teddy-boys, dissenting writers, protesting students, and plain ordinary patriotic youngsters, as did forty years of democracy in other countries. In fact, the technological

West might have stunned Asia into a state of amnesia more easily than the Marxist East during the same period, for it did not challenge cult with cult but offered the same collection of distracting gadgetry from the Pill to Pop Music that had emptied the churches and the consciences of the white world with an efficiency Mao Tsetung himself might have envied.

However, most people in the East are poor and ignorant and therefore cling to the habits and superstitions of their venerated ancestors. The elaborate graves in a Chinese cemetery are often decorated with photographs of the departed, so that those who cannot read the inscription in stone will nevertheless be able to identify their dead relatives. In Laos, seventeen out of twenty cannot write; in Filipino villages, only five men in every thousand buy a newspaper. It was not until 1960 that the first Dyak from the longhouses of Sarawak began to study modern medicine. He had been introduced to this strange science when a visiting English missionary had given him a dose of castor oil seven years before. But his regular family doctor had been a *bomoh*, whose stock remedy was to paint his face and chant ferocious incantations. It often worked, for his half-naked patients were no skeptics.

Dress must not be allowed to deceive in such matters, however. A smartly turned-out Lao, sipping his Scotch in the bar of the Georges Cinq in Paris, may be observed with some surprise to be wearing several frayed and rather soiled threads of cotton around his wrist in place of the platinum chronometer one might expect. The threads serve a purpose almost as important in this brisk age as telling the time: they keep his thirty-two souls inside his body and out of mischief.

When it is suspected that the souls of the thirty-two parts of the human anatomy are straying and perhaps falling in with evil companions, or when someone is sick, or marrying, or about to leave on a long journey, or has just returned home, it is customary in Laos to give him a *baci*. This is a ritualistic party to which the *phis*, the animistic spirits of mountains and flowers and water and trees and dawn and dusk, are also enticed with promises of gifts. Once the presiding sorcerer is satisfied that all are present, he calls back the souls of the guest of honor. "Be with us, return to your home of flesh, fear not, return to your body," he wheedles, and when the souls are once more imprisoned he slams the bolt home by tying the first length of cotton twine around their owner's wrist. Others present follow suit, each bestowing a wish upon him. Even Soviet ambassadors to Vientiane have been known to return to Moscow suitably abashed, with faces as pale as milk from a non-stop round of diplomatic farewell parties, and body and soul held together only by a thread.

Laos are devoutly Buddhist, Malays are Muslim. But just as the Laos will invoke primitive divinities with names like Sakke, Kamaphob, Attarikhe, and their stilted bungalows have spirit houses in the garden in which gifts of food may be placed to placate the *phis*, so the Malays believe that a kris may be the home of a *kramat* or spirit that could kill a man even if only his shadow were stabbed with it. *Kramats* are common throughout Indonesia and Malaysia, and when a few years ago the Malayan Railway Administration wanted to move an old brass cannon that was holding up the construction of a terminal near Penang, the matter had to be referred to the State Religious Affairs Department. For many believed that the cannon had healing powers, and its caretakers demanded that a medium first obtain its permission for the move.

The West also has its witches and warlocks, but they are not normally hired to keep the ball parks in shape for the World Series, or engaged to find a lost flock of sheep with incantations. The Malay *bomoh*, however, is a versatile fellow who, like Lloyds of London, will insure you against anything. In Malaysia the general practitioner will undertake to locate missing corpses, drive off ghosts, heal the sick, supply love potions, put spells on a customer's enemy, and much else besides. To him the supernatural and natural are all one, and he shows it in his contempt for both, to which headlines in the English-language press bear witness: "School Ghosts Told: Keep Off Students," one before me reads; and another: "Spirit in Tree Served Quit Notice."

Some *bomohs* are not above using their spiritual powers to gain very material ends indeed. They have been involved in crimes from confidence tricks to robbing the treasury, but their real specialty is rape. Local faith can be only too touching, it seems, and in 1969 the Malaysian Education Minister specifically advocated sex lessons in school to protect pupils because "we have all heard of those *bomohs* and religious teachers who have been brought to court for molesting girls." The record is impressive, possibly a small legacy from the ancient days of Chen-La when maidens were ceremoniously deflowered by monks before marriage, for the accent is very much on youth.

One Malaysian medium took away and violated a fifteen-year-old after telling her mother that he was going to perform a ritual which would remove eight lethal needles hidden in her body, and an eighteen-year-old wife was ravished on a beach by a *bomoh* who assured her that this treatment would "cure her husband's stomach ache." Even a blind *bomoh* has been known to take a girl out at night "to dig for gold" and then outrage her. Another told his victim that he had to see a mole under her left breast in order to forecast her future, and a third raped three fifteen-year-old schoolgirls who were under the mistaken impression that he was making sure they passed their examinations.

Not all *bomohs* are bad, however. The magical healers of Indonesia and Malaysia are often careful herbalists who will charge no fee for their services—they were, incidentally, the first to use quinine as a cure for malaria. Today *bomohs* trusted by the aborigines in the backwoods of central Malaya are being given a smattering of Western medicine and a compendium of pills to increase their powers. But while many of them are turning toward antibiotics rather than arrowroot plucked by the light of a gibbous moon, Western doctors are beginning to study their earlier methods more closely.

In 1968 an opposition M.P. tabled a written question in the Malaysian parliament asking the government if it would appoint a national *bomoh* and also seek the services of other reliable witch doctors to stop the annual floods in the peninsula. There was nothing odd about this suggestion. When the king of Malaysia (they are elected every five years) paid a state visit to Sabah, a seventy-year-old *bomoh* was flown over from Kuala

Lumpur to keep the sun shining, for it had been raining steadily for about a month in North Borneo. His timing was perfect. Everywhere His Majesty went, the weather smiled upon him, but within forty-eight hours of his departure, storms were lashing the streets of the state capital, and a gale half-scalped Sabah's oldest church.

Among educated Malaysians to whom Oxford, Cambridge, or the Middle Temple is alma mater, and whose tastes run to Jaguar cars, the stock market, and golf, far more than would care to admit call in the family witch doctor to cure suffering—or sometimes to inflict it on others. Politicians hire *bomohs* as they hire bodyguards—to protect them against the *bomohs* of their opponents. An attempt to liquidate President Suharto of Indonesia in mid-1968 was ascribed to a witch in the pay of the equivocal ex-Foreign Minister, Dr. Subandrio. Sihanouk and Sukarno both consult soothsayers, and important if mystifying political consequences may follow when prophetic words are whispered into their ears alone by some shabby old shaman. Warned that he would "die by the knife," Sukarno hesitated to commit himself for surgery when his kidneys rebelled, and drew comfort instead from acupuncture and herbal drugs prescribed by Chinese doctors from Peking. This put the Maoists in an excellent position to spread the rumor that the president was about to die, and so precipitate the abortive Communist coup of 1965.

That coup was nevertheless inevitable, and so was the bloodbath that came after it. Eight hundred years earlier, the great seer-king Djojobojo had prophesied a long period of subjection from which the Javanese would be freed after a yellow race had driven their white masters away and ruled them "for as long as the age of maize." Liberated Java would then be led for twenty years by a man with supernatural powers, but "a time of madness" would follow, in which half the Javanese would perish. Only after that would a second superman and a "prince of justice" arise to bring prosperity once more to the land. The Dutch, the Japanese, Sukarno, and the Chinese all played their roles faithfully in this predestined drama.

That Sukarno was Djojobojo's first "supernatural" man cannot be questioned, for every Javanese knows that this is why he
survived several particularly distasteful attempts on his charmed
life. In the West he was depicted as a sex-soused megalomaniac,
fumbling compulsively with girls and glory. But distance plays
tricks with values as with light, so that images may appear upside
down, and what marks a man for disgust in the Occident may
mark him for distinction in the Orient. Asian peasants, ignorant
of nations but loyal to their leaders, expect divine despots to be
demanding and the incarnation of Vishnu to be virile beyond
the potency of ordinary men.

After the 1965 coup, Sukarno was not violently wrenched from
office but stripped of his power excruciatingly slowly, as if it
were his own skin. For Suharto, advised by his own *dukun* or
medicine man, suffered keenly from sage fright. He was reluctant
to deface the god-king with whose fate his own seemed so mys-
teriously linked. Assured, however, that he and Sultan Hamengku
Buwono of Jogjakarta were respectively Djojobojo's second supernatural man and prince of justice who would jointly restore
peace to Java, he gained confidence and started to take logical
steps to see that the prophecy came true. His predestined running
mate, the sultan, was made a superminister with nine portfolios
under his control, and subsequently told the press that his plans
for the economic recovery of Indonesia would start bearing fruit
in 1970. Whether this prediction was inspired by a computer or
an astrologer is seriously open to question.

Numerology and astrology wield an arcane and incalculable
influence over public events throughout Southeast Asia, where
even house numbers may be chosen for luck rather than location,
and do not always follow each other consecutively. When Sukarno set 270 experts the task of drawing up a National Overall
Development Plan, he was not so much concerned with the content of its five thousand pages as with its form: it had to be
divided into seventeen volumes, eight parts, and 1,945 clauses,
because Indonesia had declared independence from the Dutch
on August 17, 1945. It is now possible to graduate in astrology
in Thailand after a four-year course, and it is certainly desirable

that this occupation, which regulates the very tempo of life, should be confided to properly qualified experts and not left, like politics and government, to a haphazard collection of amateurs.

A professional was consulted before the date was set for the formation of President Suharto's cabinet, and many believe that Mrs. Bandaranaike lost the general elections in Ceylon in 1965 because her astrologers goofed over the choice of polling day. The new Thai constitution was originally to have been proclaimed on June 9, 1968, but the stars said June 20, and June 20 it was. In the same year the king of Laos was advised to open the country's new radio station—a gift of the British under the Colombo Plan—on the first of August. Only at the last moment was it discovered that astrologers had been using the wrong calendar, and, to the annoyance of the heavily engaged monarch, the inauguration had to be switched to the following day.

Astrology and clairvoyance not only time events but shape them. Their exponents, when sycophantic or self-seeking, will promise their clients distinction and glory in the hope that they will then swagger forward confidently and claim the eminence predicted for them, whereupon the soothsayer will in turn enjoy even more powerful patronage. Different scheming politicians and ambitious generals, turning to different astrologers, are in this way driven upward in an ever-narrowing rivalry, for only in the context of off-peak bus services is there ever plenty of room on top.

A sibyl in Vientiane went into a trance and shrieked that Kong Le was the reincarnation of a former king. Could anything more perilous have happened to the inflated ego of the cocky little captain who had already seized the Laotian capital with his paratroops? A seer told Chaerul Saleh that he was destined to reach the highest office in Indonesia, deceitfully withholding the important rider that he would then be involved in a massacre. This revelation unquestionably fired the ambition of the arrogant Indonesian minister, who is said to have forced Sukarno to sign the declaration of independence in 1945 at pistol point, and who once ferociously felled a senior Shell Company representative to the green with a number-three iron for objecting when he failed to shout "Fore." Yet the prediction obviously clashed with those provided by the pet prophets of Dr. Subandrio, General Nasution, Suharto, and Sukarno himself.

Mysticism makes its own history. The wife of the Vietnamese warlord, General Khanh, commissions a geomancer to resite her kitchen so that it will be more fortunately oriented and in harmony with the universe. But word gets out. Other generals at once suspect that Khanh is unsure of his ground in more senses than one, and that the moment has therefore arrived to mount a coup against him. Within a few weeks, in consequence, Khanh is out and his emboldened rivals are in. Why did not Kong Le and the Communists attack the Royal Laotian capital of Luang Prabang at the beginning of 1961, as was expected? Because they would have drawn down upon themselves the vengeance of the *phis* protecting the corpse of the late King Sisavang Vong, whose uncremated body was still in the palace precincts, preserved in a large jar of formaldehyde.

Does Prince Boun Oum promise democracy as the antidote for Communism? No one cares. For a Lao villager who knows that there are sixteen hours in the day and the world is flat, the most powerful antidote for Communism is not democracy but Boun Oum's magical amulet. This loathsome fetish, which happens to be a dried human fetus, enables the prince to become invisible at will in spite of his aristocratic corpulence, and is part of the mystique which binds the Champassak peasantry to him in spite of the blandishments of the pro-Communist Pathet Lao. The ease with which magic can beat Marx in the myth-laden lands of Southeast Asia must never be underestimated.

17 : Three Thousand Million
Born Losers

"How many religious sects are there?" asked a powerful sixteenth-century Japanese overlord when the Buddhists of Kyoto begged him to suppress the new rival ideology that was being so effectively propagated by a certain Francis Xavier. "Thirty-five, Excellency," they replied. "Then it seems to me that one more is not likely to make much difference," retorted the great magnate, dismissing the plea. The feudal *daimyos* accordingly embraced Catholicism enthusiastically, finding that this act of faith won the hearts of the Portuguese, who would then furnish them with the cannons and muskets they so earnestly desired in order to kill each other off more efficiently.

The world's most dangerous weapon is not the megaton bomb or mob oratory but the label, for when it does not destroy completely, it blinds. The peoples of the Far East cannot be tidily docketed Christian or Muslim or Buddhist or "Commie." In Java alone, "Islam" covers about a hundred and fifty varieties of the faith, including one pious group that was found to have killed forty-eight people in answer to somebody's inner voice in 1968, and another which was banned in the same year for ordering its disciples to pray naked.

Every man from Goa to Nagasaki has his own worm's-eye view of God, and his own road to salvation. In Korea 434 couples are married at a mass wedding and then take off in a fleet of newly imported Swiss buses for six weeks of celibacy and evangelical work instead of a honeymoon. They belong to the Tongil Church, which was invented in 1944 and requires newlyweds to observe strict chastity for forty days after their marriage. While others whip their way through Good Friday in Manila itself, fifty miles to the north a young Filipino dressed in a purple robe and a crown of thorns has himself impaled annually on a ten-foot cross with stainless steel nails by a crowd of extras dressed as Roman soldiers.

Down in the capital, another young Filipino stretches his arms wide as he recites his rosary before a plaster-cast image of Christ on the Cross. As one member of a team of eight, he has taken the *cursillo*, a short course in instant salvation that includes a three-day retreat for what detractors have called evangelical brain-washing. From now on, he is bound to the brotherhood of his own team, and to the wider Christian fraternity of all other "Brods," as the *cursillistas* call each other. He is on call like a member of Alcoholics Anonymous to save any backsliding "fall-out," perhaps rallying him with the theme songs of the movement, including its own version of "Colonel Bogey." The *cursillo* is a society within a society. It is gradually crystallizing into a political force like the much older *Iglesia ni Kristo*, which was founded as far back as 1914 by a hatter called Felix Manalo and now has more than three million followers.

I.N.K. is a high-powered organization for godliness combining business efficiency and political punch with a Communist cell structure that has defeated the Communists themselves. It preaches popular religion in plush, air-conditioned modern chapels where the faithful may lounge comfortably in well-sprung *fauteuils*, part of the payoff from a spectacularly well-run exchequer. The Iglesia operates a system of mutual aid among its units, and this closed circuit of social insurance alone has drawn many converts. But I.N.K. also has its own firm doctrine, which demands rejection of the Holy Trinity, of Christ as God, of the Virgin Mary and the immortal soul. The brotherhood achieves emotional unity through the solace of weeping, for its oratorical preachers reduce their congregations to tears regularly once a week.

With its cells and subcutaneous political power, I.N.K. is in many ways a Christian parallel of the Buddhist Sokagakkai movement in Japan, but I first encountered modern mutations of Buddhism in Vietnam, and I could hardly have had a more exotic introduction to Asia.

I had never been east of Suez until 1954, when an Air France Constellation picked me up in Paris and dropped me down two nights later in Saigon. It was pitch dark and pouring rain. I had no local piasters and my hotel booking had fallen through. A kindly Briton put me up for the night and I found I had flown nine thousand miles to eat a supper of mock-turtle soup, bacon, and beans. The East was nevertheless at my elbow, and at dawn we drove to the Holy See of the Cao Dai sect at Tay Ninh for the Mid-Autumn Festival. The Great Temple of the Cao Dai was an opium eater's dream of Westminister Abbey, the two square towers and the ridged roof writhing with multicolored Chinese dragons and curling prodigiously at the corners, the pillars entwined by gaudy serpents, the embrasures embellished with giant lotuses. The ceiling was a mass of silver stars, and from above the altar the Eye of the Great Spirit bored down blindly upon the marble floor. But among garish sacred beasts in stone or stucco were also the effigies or symbols of Christ and Buddha, of Confucius and Lao Tzu (the mysterious master of the Taoists), and a painting of saints ranging from the late President Sun Yat-sen of China to Victor Hugo (in the full fig of an *académicien*). For Cao Daism is nothing if not syncretic, and its cardinals assured me that when he died, Winston Churchill would also be canonized and reverentially inserted into the holy calendar.

A cocktail of most great creeds, the Cao Dai doctrine was inspired by the dreams of a young Vietnamese civil servant earlier in this century, and the church was first organized in 1926. It was in that year that the elaborate ouija board, which is the means of contact between the faithful below and the rather numerous divinities above who jostle for their attention on its pointer, suddenly spelled out: "I am the Supreme Sovereign. I am the oldest of the Buddhas. I am Jesus Christ. I now take the name of Cao Dai to teach a new religion." The board was demonstrated to me later by two young mediums, but there were no revelations.

After a vegetarian lunch we stood on the balcony of the Great Temple and watched a long procession of religious floats followed by a march-past of the Cao Dai army. For this Vietnamese Vatican controlled not only the souls of 1,500,000 men and women but also the rich province of Tay Ninh, and it was defended by some twenty thousand soldiers of the Great Spirit who had been armed by the French to fight the Vietminh. Across the years, however, Cao Dai generals have shown the same genius for reinsurance with governments and guerrillas as their founder displayed with gods. They have rallied gallantly to His Holiness their Pope, or retired in revolt to the sacred Black Virgin Mountain that sticks out of their wooded plains like a vital statistic; they have intrigued against President Ngo Dinh Diem, submitted on occasion to the indelicate attentions of the C.I.A., engineered a tacit truce with the Vietcong in order to outlive and outlast them.

The Hoa Hao are different. The Vietminh rewarded them for their initial support by assassinating their beloved Master, Huynh Phu So (sensibly taking care to cut his body in two and bury the pieces far apart, in view of his supernatural powers). Huynh Phu So was a dynamic spiritual leader who preached a new, simple, ascetic Buddhism and rapidly gained renown as a great healer and prophet who foretold the Japanese invasion and the French defeat. He founded a sect which may have more than a million

devotees and whose center is Hoa Hao village, deep in the Mekong Delta. The Hoa Hao army was also equipped by the French
to fight the Vietminh and in 1954 joined the Cao Dai in defying
Ngo Dinh Diem. The Hoa Hao believe that the Communists
could not really have killed their Master forever and that he will
therefore come again. But hate is long, and in the flooded flatlands of their principal province the Vietcong have moved on
tiptoe during much of the Vietnam War.

The Cao Dai and the Hoa Hao sects, like all the strange
progeny of Hindu and Buddhist belief, trace their ancestry back
to the doctrine of Brahman, the All-Pervading spirit of the Oneness of the Cosmos. The monstrous regiment of Hindu gods and
heavenly avatars sometimes makes the devotee of this mother-
religion appear to be a polytheistic pagan, but these deities simply
provide convenient symbols for the many aspects of the One
which a plain man can then see in his mind's eye or shape into
an idol: Vishnu, the Preserver; six-armed Kali, the Destroyer-
goddess of the Thugs; Ganesa, Wisdom with the head of an
elephant. For Brahman is formless and cannot be envisaged. The
Christian is compassionately rescued from struggling with the
concept of a formless Creator by the legend that God made man
in his own image, yet even he must conjure up the picture of
an old fellow with a white beard. But to mistake this venerable
gentleman (whose features can be submitted to anthropometric
identification by any reasonably well-equipped police force) for
God is to take the picture of the apple for "A," measurable illusion for immeasurable reality, and is as futile as putting a clock
in a crypt.

The reality of the universe is that light and dark, silence and
sound, cold and heat are all part of the One, for they cannot exist
independently of each other. Good and evil are inseparable. All
that gives the illusion of individual form or contrast, therefore,
is deceit. When man measures and classifies everything, including himself, he creates an illusory world of false identities, among
which is his own ego.

Buddha was a Hindu, and Buddhism teaches that a sage asked
the Greek King Menander of Northern India, who said he had

come to see him in a chariot, to "Explain what 'chariot' is. Is the
pole the chariot? No. Is the axle the chariot? No. Is it then the
wheels, the frame, the flagstaff, the yoke, the reins, the goad?
No. Then is it the pole, axle, wheels, frame, flagstaff, yoke, reins,
and goad added together which is the chariot? No. Then is the
chariot outside the sum of these things? No. Then I can discover no chariot at all except for the sound 'chariot.' There is in
fact no chariot. So of whom are you afraid, Great King, that you
do not speak the truth?" The king replied that it was the dependence of the parts upon each other which was the chariot.
Similarly, concluded the sage with an approving nod, there is no
enduring ego. What we call "I" is not a fixed being, but simply
a collection of sensations, thoughts, emotions, and wishes. And
it is this interdependence of parts that makes all One.

His obsession with the illusory world of "ten thousand things"
is at the root of man's suffering. He can attain bliss only by
prizing his fingers away from it, whether they are clutching at
riches or reason. Until he withdraws from the mirage, shedding
the greed and hatred that it so falsely engenders and that bind
him to it, he is chained to the wheel of life. He is reincarnated
again and again, and each existence is a new settlement day for
the moral debts incurred in all previous ones. It is a terrible
world, but he has to live somewhere until he can stop pretend-
ing that he is anybody and craving for personal rewards. Right
thinking, right speaking, right acting will lead him to right understanding, contemplation, and enlightenment—his sudden, final
awareness that he is one with the universe. Since at that point
he has no further claim to a separate identity, he is excused from
further living and the flame of his mind is gently blown out.
That is Nirvana.

To the disciple of this Theravada Buddhism, whose yellow-
robed bonzes throng the pagodas of Laos and Thailand, Burma,
Cambodia, and Ceylon, we therefore live in a community of
three thousand million born losers. His creed offers no messiah,
demands stern asceticism, and promises nothing more than
blessed oblivion at the end of it all. But farther east among the
millions of China and Vietnam the comforting Mahayana Bud-

dhist doctrine, with its gentle saints, its short cuts to a heavenly "Pure Land" through simple faith and the calling of Buddha's name, its prophecy of a Buddha that is to come bringing happiness to all, long ago overshadowed the stricter sects. For Asians are not immune from man's most terrible of fears, expressed in the universal silent prayer that no church voices: "Please, God, let there be a God."

At dawn the quavering voice of the muezzin replies: "There is no God but God," reaching me through loudspeakers plugged into the tape recorder on the minaret of the stucco mosque nearby, and Malays in the kampong next door turn piously to the West to pray. Islam slashes the Buddhist yellow of Southeast Asia with a scimitar of green, its hilt resting on the border provinces of south Thailand, its great curving blade taking in Malaysia and the Indonesian archipelago, its tip lying over the southern Philippines.

But Islam is more than a faith. The Holy Koran is a transcript of the will of Allah, and since his will cannot be expressed through the fallible sense of justice of mere humans, Islam is not simply a religious congregation but a society regulated by a legal code which has been divinely inspired. There is no priesthood, and the Muslim is spared the bureaucratic frustrations of going through channels to God. But there are kathis and Shariah courts to administer Koranic law, working parallel with the secular magistrates and the civil courts of the country.

Sitting with the beauteous Che Rogayah binte Abdul Rahman in a Brunei bar and asking her what she would like to drink, I realized that this innocent meeting for an off-the-record interview about her husband (who had been detained for fomenting an insurrection in 1962) could get us both into trouble on two counts. Overzealous police of the kathi's court in this sanctimonious enclave of Islam on the North Borneo coast could catch us for technical *khalwat* (compromising proximity) and slap a further charge on me for tempting Che Rogayah to alcohol, which is *haram* (forbidden). A couple may be guilty of *khalwat* if they go to a cinema together, or link little fingers in the street, and frequently if somewhat unfairly Chinese bartenders are arrested in Brunei for serving liquor to Muslim Malays who bang on the bar and demand brandy or beer, as if all the weaknesses of the faithful were the fault of the infidel.

The Muslim may go to the mosque only once a week, as a practicing Christian goes to church, but he must pray five times every day, he must fast during the month of Ramadan, and he should make the pilgrimage to Mecca at least once in his life. In Southeast Asia Islam is inextricably intertwined with ancient Malay custom, however, and most Muslims, easygoing by nature, are only ostensibly strict in their observances for fear of the ire of their kathis rather than of the wrath of their compassionate God.

The flesh is weak. Men drink liquor in private, eat surreptitiously during the fasting month, slip into the cafes on Friday when their employers release them to go to the mosque. Imams are not immune from the more tantalizing temptations, and in 1969 one of these prayer leaders was arraigned for making love to two of his concubines while his four wives and a third concubine watched. This, it seemed, was against Muslim law, but the defendant pleaded it "kept household relations harmonious." The kathi's courts are busy with divorces. In the fervently Muslim Malaysian state of Kelantan, for example, more than seven out of ten marriages have broken up in the past. In addition the magistrates hear cases involving the abuse of women, the use of alcohol, and the eating of pork (mouse meat was also outlawed in Java during the thin year of 1963). In Brunei Muslims were jailed for adultery.

The orthodox are still strong and the bigots powerful. Some religious teachers in Malaysia insist that even to go near a dog is to be defiled, and in 1962 Muslim leaders urged the government to ban alcoholic drinks throughout the country, to forbid the showing of films on Thursday night before Friday prayers, even to arrest all who failed to attend mosque. One Mufti was obliged to admonish a teacher for calling Muslims themselves infidels if they so much as associated with unbelievers. The Islamic laws of Malaysia discourage wedlock with non-Muslims and still stipulate that the infidel bridegroom or bride must first embrace the faith. Intermarriage between Malays and pork-eating Chinese has therefore been relatively rare, and these two strong, mutually suspicious racial groups which dominate the Malayan peninsula cannot blend into one harmonious community. Islam lies between them like a sword.

Yet, like the Buddhist Sokagakkai of Japan, the Vietnamese Hoa Hao, and the Filipino *Iglesia ni Kristo*, Islam still offers a formidable challenge to creeping Communism—despite the common belief of fanatical Muslims and fanatical Maoists in the cleansing properties of that most sinister of self-contradictions: the Holy War.

18 : *Wars of Religion*

My first contact with the world of holy wars was Colonel Abdullah Taher Hussein Tyrconnel-Fay, an Irish-Canadian Muslim convert and the liaison agent of Darul Islam in Singapore. "Turk" to his friends and enemies, a curious blend of the overprecise and the fraudulent that made one think of false teeth, the "colonel" was a prized acquaintance, for it is one of the pleasures of life to deal with men whom the pious have written off as all rogue.

It is the righteous who are to be distrusted. Ambassadors are professional liars, and no one can be more preposterously dishonest than a second-rate politician, unless it is a second-rate academic. Status is no guarantee of probity. The correspondent who is always talking to well-polished premiers or clean and lightly oiled four-star generals is simply blinding his editor with giants.

Turk was the perfect example of the deceptively dubious: a long, sallow, middle-aged man whose flat, expressionless hair and eyes might have been painted on the pockmarked face with lacquer. He spoke with a Canadian burr as soft as a quagmire, but the Canadians, like everyone else, refused to give him a passport. His background was not only obscure but shifting, as the tales about him changed. People did not believe him when he said he had been in the Special Air Service and had parachuted into Greece or Albania, that he had become a Muslim in the Middle East and was in constant contact with Darul Islam rebels in North Sumatra. For he cadged drinks and borrowed money, and so he was marked down as an army deserter and a blarneying beachcomber. But his claims were true.

However improbable the colonel might have appeared, he was the boss of the Darul Islam office in Singapore. He slipped "ministers" of the insurrectionist government into the island, and on at least one occasion to my knowledge justified Sukarno's suspicions of Malayan sympathy for the insurgents in Sumatra by taking one of their leaders to meet Tengku Abdul Rahman in Kuala Lumpur in the middle of the rebellion.

A silver-studded black holster hung on a hook behind his door, his drawers were filled with shopping lists for Bren guns and British mortars, and a large framed map of Indonesia was screwed to the wall. I remember that map well. In unenlightened continents people sometimes stick pins into small images of their enemies in order to torment or kill them by proxy. This map of Indonesia was transfixed by scores of pins showing the locations of Darul Islam guerrilla forces in revolt against Djakarta. And the magic worked, if in reverse. Every time Turk thumbed another tack through some name on the map, that place in turn suffered the horrors of terrorism, murder, and arson, for he was recording the latest focus of Darul Islam interest.

Led by a white-bearded imam with headquarters in West Java, Darul Islam was virulently anti-Communist. Its followers had risen against Sukarno when he failed to make Indonesia an Islamic state after independence had been proclaimed from the Dutch, and by 1958 their loose confederacy had established the supreme authority of the Koran and the kick of the Lee Enfield rifle over great regions of North Sumatra, Java, Celebes, Borneo, and many of the smaller Indonesian islands. Their fanatical hard-core was fringed with thugs, and they burned, ambushed, massacred, and spent money abroad like water in the cause of holy war. It was they who tried to murder Sukarno with a hail of hand grenades outside the Tjikini School in 1957. I subsequently met the man who planned this peculiarly repulsive act of piety in Turk's Singapore flat. He was a Darul Islam militant working in the Djakarta headquarters of the youth movement of the legal and constitutional Muslim political party, the Masjumi.

And here lay the heart of the paradox, for the anti-Communist Muslim terrorists defeated their own object in the end. The more that tens of thousands of Darul Islam rebels extended their dominion of violence over the archipelago as disreputable partners of the Masjumi, the more Sukarno and the nationalists were persuaded that Muslim militants were a bigger threat than the Marxists to the secular state of Indonesia. In consequence, the powerful Indonesian National Party moved closer to the Communists, the Masjumi Party was outlawed, and a determined campaign was launched to stamp Darul Islam into the dust. By 1965 it was just another bloody memory.

Its instruments discredited, Islam lost the leadership of the nationalist movement which had first flickered into unsteady flame nearly a hundred and fifty years before. By 1964 it was flabbly, disorganized, split into factions, victim of its own corrupt political chiefs. By comparison, the P.K.I. looked well-knit and invincible. The moment finds its men, however. As the Communists urged Sukarno to arm the workers and peasants and the threat of a left-wing takeover bid increased, a mass movement of Muslim youth rose to challenge them. The orgy of killing that followed the Communist coup in 1965 was for many the latest stage in a *jehad* or holy struggle against Communism which the rector of Al-Azhar University in Cairo, the highest seat of Muslim learning, had urged upon the Islamic world early in 1959. Although Java, soaked in the earlier dyes of Hindu-Buddhism, was full of permissive, "lapsed" Muslims, the faith had thrown up enough militants to fight the "good" fight.

But in the other, yellow half of Southeast Asia, where Buddhist canon and not the Koran is the repository of man's beliefs, it has been otherwise.

Across the Theravada Buddhist lands, hundreds of thousands of celibate novices and monks tend the well-kept temples and live on the charity of the people, for they are allowed to own nothing themselves but three pieces of cloth, a mat, a blade, a needle, a water strainer, and a begging bowl. In Laos the housewives kneel humbly at the roadside each dawn to fill these bowls as the bonzes shuffle past in Indian file, for they may eat only one vegetarian meal a day, and that before noon. Throughout Southeast Asia it is usual for teenage boys to don the saffron toga and enter the pagoda for anything up to two years, and crown princes are not exempt from this spiritual substitute for the draft. The bonze is the village teacher. He will be consulted over the smallest decisions and he wields a moral influence that rival politicians are always anxious to win for their side.

If the lapsed Muslim is guilty of a tolerance toward his fellow humans which has tarnished Islam in Indonesia, however, the black sheep of Buddhism that have erred and strayed from the Noble Eightfold Path can be counted in flocks. In 1966 General Ne Win said the body of Buddhism was fouled by "pseudo-monks," whom he publicly accused of cheating, killing, sleeping around, and boozing. Gangsters, fugitives from justice, and common idlers thronged the pagodas in yellow robes, which gave them anonymity and sartorial sanctuary. And these were not in all cases euphemisms for men whose real crime was that they had defied Ne Win.

There was nothing new about this defiance. The bonzes of Southeast Asia inherit fine fighting traditions which in other parts of the world are normally associated with famous regiments. According to legend, it was the unarmed Buddhist monks of China who invented the ancestor of all the more terrifying pugilistic practices of the East, including karate, and one historian remarked nearly forty years ago that in Burma "no political mob was complete without its saffron-robed leader."

In South Korea celibate monks, incensed over the authority granted to married men in church affairs in 1960, burst into the supreme court in Seoul, smashing windows and sacking offices, and police squads could only quell the rioting after knocking twelve shaven pates unconscious and bundling the rest of the ringleaders off in trucks. Six of the rioters then tried to commit hara-kiri on the spot and had to be rushed to the nearest hospital. This may seem mystifying in the West, for it must be some years since cudgel-toting ecclesiastics took London's Old Bailey apart. Yet only a few months earlier Theravada monks from rival monasteries in Rangoon had gone to war upon each other with bricks, rocks, and bottles, and when the police arrived to appeal through loudspeakers for a little peace and holiness, the monks replied by combining forces to shower the common enemy with missiles for two hours. They stopped only when the riot squad unfairly started firing gas shells into both monasteries.

Nowhere, perhaps, has the potential of the pagoda as a cradle for political rabble-rousers been better exploited than in South Vietnam, where mayhem directed by militant Buddhist bonzes has so often provided a discordant urban antiphony of howling mobs and wailing sirens to the staccato ballad of battle in the countryside. Since 1963, when President Diem fell as their first victim, they have overthrown three governments and helped to edge three others toward the abyss.

As the smoke and the smell of tear gas clear for a moment from disorderly scenes of street power and strife, a man may pause to ask what has happened to the Four Noble Truths of the Lord Buddha, to the belief that all suffering is born of human passions and desires and that salvation lies in turning one's back on worldly things. But just as the casuistical Christian can find excellent reasons for condoning mass killing in wars holy or unholy, so the Mahayana Buddhist in particular has a ready-made rationalization for playing politics or pelting the police with broken glass. He must bring not only himself but all others nearer to Nirvana. If he sees misery and misgovernment thrusting his despairing fellow men into sin and corruption, he must renounce selfish renunciation, which otherwise would keep him aloof from the human tragedy, and pitch in.

Nevertheless, in some respects the cloistered Theravada monk who withdraws from the world is as unstable an element in the ideological struggle as the militant and his mob. He avoids taking sides, for fear of becoming the victim of rage and ambition. He sees capitalism and Communism as crazy if contradictory obsessions with matter. Safe in the sanctuary of his spiritual eyrie, he can coexist with either and thinks he can be master of both. Western agents who have embarked upon the terrible intellectual odyssey of trying to win Buddhism over for democracy have soon been lost in swirling sea mists of contradiction. The modern Sokagakkai sect in Japan fights Maoism with its own weapons, and in Burma there has been a defiant revival of worship and ceremony since in 1967 Communist rebels tortured bonzes and trampled on Buddhas. On the other hand, there are also Buddhists who hail Marx as the modern torchbearer of many of their own teachings, and there are complaisant priests in Communist countries ready to pay lip-service to a Lenin who, after all, is only part of the Illusion. I have clattered through the empty halls of pagodas in North Vietnam to find a solitary Superior who has been neatly inserted into the setting to greet me with bitter tea and tell me of the square deal Hanoi is giving holiness.

The desire for peace has been a passkey to the often baffling complex of relationships between the Buddhists and the Vietcong in South Vietnam. The worst mistake a correspondent can make in Saigon is to look no further than the devious intricacies of the local political weave, thinking that he has now seen everything. It is essential to turn the rug over, not only for the dirt that has been swept underneath, but for the even more unlikely system of knots and link stitches and loose ends to be found on the side you do not see.

In 1954 Wilfred Burchett, the pro-Communist Australian correspondent and writer, flew down to Saigon from Hanoi to observe how the Fascists were living, and introduced me to an agile young Frenchman with a square face, round spectacles, and a thin strip of well-mown mustache who might have been Molotov's favorite son but whose name was Charles Meyer. A few days afterward Charlie took me to a certain Mr. Tran, who in turn invited me to a tea party attended by twenty-six Vietnamese intellectuals, all members of the newly formed "Vietnamese Peace Movement." The movement was soon broken up and its leaders arrested as Communist-front agitators, but I never lost touch with Mr. Tran, and after Diem's demise in 1963 his peace-loving friends were released. These, in their turn, now introduced me to militant Buddhist leaders whom I had so far failed to meet, for they were as close to the more pugnacious priests as is glue to lacquer. Trudging through the mud of the Vien Hoa Dao pagoda in Saigon, which was field headquarters for the Buddhist offensive against the new regime of General Khanh and looked it, I would sip the inevitable tea with some bonze in his wooden hutch of an office—while typewriters chattered indignantly next door—trying to discover when the next riot would be raised and just where the Vietcong came into the matter.

I only saw the mastermind, the ambitious, sloe-eyed Venerable Tri Quang, as one of a crowd, but as time passed, the tracery of thought beneath that bony skull began gradually to show through, like veins under aging skin. Tri Quang had been accused of being pro-Communist and of conspiring deviously with the Vietcong. Accordingly, American Quang-watchers were cast down when this powerful prelate castigated their pet Vietnamese governments one after another, but uplifted when he declared staunchly that he hated "atheistic" Communism and that it "could never win." Yet these two remarks revealed his most perilous conceit—that the materialism of Marx offered no permanent challenge to the teachings of Buddha and that therefore he could sup with this devil even with a short spoon. He did not denounce the National Liberation Front, for he conceived it to be clearly divisible into a Communist minority and a "Buddhist" majority with which he was in touch.

Both parties wanted peace, for the Communists were convinced that they could then take over the country, and the bonzes boasted that they would then unite the Buddhists on both sides and leave the Communists stranded. As one Buddhist politician put it to me: "We can only lose the war, but we could win the peace." This arrogant assumption may yet cost Vietnam dear.

The Catholics of Vietnam do not, it seems, share the Buddhist belief—illusion or reality—that they can spiritually outflank Hanoi, for most of the priests in the South originally fled with their flocks from the Communist North. They are ferociously anti-Marxist, and as far back as 1965 they were already debating what to do if South Vietnam were sold to the enemy, some desperately advocating that they take to the *maquis* themselves, perhaps regrouping all able-bodied Catholics in the southernmost area of the Mekong Delta and fighting off all assailants from there.

I saw their first Exodus, but now there is no farther that they can go. In 1954 nearly a million men, women, and children bundled up their poor bits and pieces of pots and pajamas in North Vietnam and then crowded on to half-submerged rafts and leaking old tubs in the hope of reaching rescue ships waiting outside territorial waters before their own craft capsized, or were shot up by Communist soldiers along the coastline.

Life was little better for them when they reached South Vietnam. From my room in the Hotel Continental in Saigon, I could look down upon the airless oven of the main square with its peeling, fever-yellow theater, around whose withered lawn and stinking gutters were camped hundreds of Catholic families from the North, their shrill hubbub rising like the morning chatter of migrating birds. They had perched their pitiful little tents of black rags and cardboard wherever they could steal a six-foot square of soil, and there they contrived to cook, to quieten querulous children, to wash themselves and their clothes meticulously in water scooped from the drains, to fight in their misery and squalor and filth and frustration, women shrieking hysterically and tearing at each other's waist-long hair, men kicking their wives mercilessly in the rump.

Then aid began pouring in, and the government, dominated by the Catholic family of President Ngo Dinh Diem, set the refugees to work rebuilding their lives. All were sorted according to trades, sites were chosen, and neat little brown wood-and-palm-thatch villages, each with its church and school, sprang up around the country. The Catholics were on their feet again, seven hundred miles from their original homes.

At first the Buddhists watched impassively as the oligarchy in the presidential palace perpetuated the religious favoritism of the Catholic French colonialists. But later they began to complain, for promotions and plum jobs and import licenses and foreign-aid funds were flowing to this minority of fewer than two million Christians. The schools remained in Catholic hands, and the power went to Catholic heads. When the Buddhists rebelled in 1963, the disdainful Madame Ngo Dinh Nhu, sister-in-law of the president, dubbed them Communists who should be "beaten three times harder." After the first bonze had burned himself alive, she complained that the Buddhists had used "imported petrol" to "barbecue one of their monks."

The first outbreak of Buddhist violence was a protest against religious discrimination and was organized by bonzes who felt a Christian conspiracy closing in upon them, a cabal of Catholics on both sides of the world: President Diem, President Kennedy, Cardinal Spellman. With the brutal suppression of Buddhist demonstrations in Hue, Catholic became synonymous with Can Lao—the hated secret government party within the administration and army—and indiscriminate terror was countered with indiscriminate terror as Catholic villages were sacked and looted and Catholics were killed by Buddhists in their turn. By 1966 the tumult had died down. But a year later the Buddhists were again aroused when general elections threw up forty Catholic senators out of a total of sixty under another Catholic president, Nguyen van Thieu.

No religion needs Communism as a focus for hatred, for there is always another religion to fight. Little love may be lost between Catholic and Buddhist in Vietnam, but by the same token the harmony of the hammer and sickle is not for the Cross and Crescent (which they so curiously resemble). When it was rumored that a Protestant teacher had made disagreeable references to Islam in Indonesia in 1967, several thousand Muslims attacked Christian churches without further ado, damaging nineteen, and imams in many parts of the republic began making wild speeches in the mosques. The fever recurs like malaria. Two years later Muslims wrecked another Protestant church in West Java, and in 1970 a Catholic school.

In 1968 the Muslim Moros of the southern Philippines were complaining that they were neglected by the Christian government in the capital, fobbed off with meager funds and empty promises of improvements, and treated like second-class citizens. President Marcos hastily flew south to meet an ex-governor of Mindanao who threatened to create a break-away Islamic republic, gave the disgruntled Muslim dignitary his gold watch, and promised to build a mosque in Manila. It is questionable whether these handsome gestures resolved the matter, however. The Muslims jealously pointed out that there were only four congressmen and no senators or generals or police chiefs of their confession, and that they are losing their lands to Christian carpetbaggers from the north. But when plans for an uprising in seven southern towns leaked out, Filipinos blamed the Malaysians, some of whose politicians were at that very moment accusing the Buddhists in Bangkok of discriminating against the Muslim and Malay minority in the southern provinces of Thailand. Once again religious unrest was adding an extra, spicy ingredient to the stewpot of international rivalries in Southeast Asia.

Where the world of Islam and the non-world of Buddhism touch there is no meeeting of minds, as Sihanouk was distressed to find when he opened the sixth international conference of the World Association of Buddhists in 1961. Declaring that Buddhists held the "keys to international society" because they were peace-loving, showed tolerance, and knew how to master hatred, he expressed faith in U Thant as Burmese Secretary-General of the United Nations since he was a "fervent disciple of Buddha." Nevertheless, on the very evening that Sihanouk spoke, four people were killed and more than forty injured when Buddhist monks led anti-Muslim rioters on a rampage through a suburb of Rangoon.

Two months earlier Burma had become the world's first Buddhist state, and the government had celebrated this pious enactment by closing the Rangoon meat, poultry, and fish markets for three days, during which the slaughter of animals was prohibited. More than five hundred pigs, sheep, ducks, and crabs were sent to monasteries for sanctuary. Moreover, ninety-eight humans under sentence of death were also spared, for the devout Buddhist kills no living thing, however lowly.

The new law at once fired men on all sides with the worldly passions of greed and ill will so strictly abjured by the Lord Buddha. Non-Buddhists objected indignantly to the idea of a Buddhist state religion, and Buddhists were infuriated by riders in the law giving non-Buddhists freedom to teach other faiths. A confusion of righteous rioting and protest followed, with Hindus mobbing Muslims, Buddhists boycotting national ceremonies, and Christian Kachin and Karen guerrillas in the hills fitting more mayhem than ever into their working week, inspired by the earlier teachings of Baptist missionaries.

By 1966 General Ne Win had sapped the power of the native Buddhist hierarchy and its sources of income, but he had also thrown it a sop by flinging out all foreign missionaries, nationalizing their hospitals, and seizing their schools. Like the generals in Vietnam who have for years vied with one another to win either the approval or the healthy fear of the priests, Ne Win had learned the lesson to be drawn from the Judgment of Paris: it is difficult to say which is more dangerous—to arbitrate between gods, or women.

19 : Ladies Only

The jagged mountains of Central Sumatra are fissured by golden
fiords of fertile plain, and in these may sometimes be seen
the magnificent houses of the Minangkabau, standing like solitary six-horned cattle amid the growing grain. The eaves of a
small home, built of intricately carved wood and roofed with
thatch or gleaming corrugated aluminum, sweep upward steeply
at each end like the horns of a buffalo, but as the family grows,
new extensions are added, giving a second pair of glittering horns,
and later perhaps a third. Minangkabau means "Winning Buffalo," and these people proudly trace their origins to the authors
of a thoroughly questionable ruse which is said to have saved
them from the hegemony of the Javanese some centuries ago.

It seems that a certain king of Java who claimed suzerainty
over a hostile Sumatra agreed ill-advisedly that their dispute could

be decided by a buffalo fight rather than by the usual procedure which leaves these valuable beasts safe on the sidelines while the men slaughter each other over such issues. A site was marked out for the match, and in due course the Javanese fielded a herd of enormous males.

The Sumatran entry, on the other hand, raised a contemptuous laugh, for it consisted of the puniest animals the Javanese had ever seen. They looked puny, however, because they were extremely young calves. They were, in fact, sucklings to whose soft noses the sly Minangkabau had attached sharp spikes. The Javanese males, in the gentle manner of lesser species, offered these youngsters no harm, and the sucklings were therefore able to make swiftly and greedily for what they took to be the udders of their elders. After a few excruciating minutes which hardly bear thinking about, both the Javanese king and the Javanese buffalo knew only too well that they had been licked.

This humiliating legend, with its undertones of sex war, is symbolical. For the Minangkabau were matriarchal, women wielded the whip, and when an extra "horn" was built onto one of their houses, it was because a new son-in-law was moving into the home of the daughter, and the young couple would come under the care and control of the mother or grandmother. The Sam Sui women, who go out to work shoveling cement or laying bricks in Singapore, are the mistresses in their families also, and from the Nairs of South India to the Mois of Vietnam there are Asian societies in which the lady inherits the power, or at least the purse. With the demand for sex equality in a modern age and the consequent emancipation of the men, however, the matriarchs have been losing their mastery as swiftly as their sisters elsewhere have been losing their mystery.

For the rest of Asian womanhood the screw has been on the other thumb, and the lowly female must now fight her way to freedom through a fog of religious and traditional prejudice. For all Eastern confessions are marked by that disdain for women which is common among seers and sages. The Catholics do not allow them to be priests but may canonize them once they are safely dead. The Mahayana Buddhists do not usually go so far, and when Kuan Yin, Goddess of Mercy, became a Buddhist saint, this unique achievement was marred by the fact that she had started out as a male god in the first place. Women may enter the Buddhist Pure Land of Bliss above, but they have to be transformed into men for the purpose. In Burma the glory of manhood must never be tarnished by female disrespect. A wife must be meek, for Buddha himself was born a man. In old-fashioned homes, therefore, it is sacrilege for a woman to touch anything of her husband's with her feet, to use the same jar for bathing, to throw her clothes onto his bed.

In Islamic Malaya wives were formerly "the mean ones within the gate." "Women," the Koran tells the Muslim curtly, "are your tillage." A husband may beat his wives, according to the good book, for "men have authority over women because God has made the one superior to the other." Mohammed was married several times—once to a child-bride—and the Koran allows a man four wives, provided he can treat all four alike, and an unlimited number of concubines. Yet Mohammed was a champion of women, it has been said, for to commit polygamy was a charitable act in a society loaded with weak, unwanted girls. Unhappily, the liberalism of great men opens loopholes for the license of lesser ones, and for centuries Muslims have quoted the Prophet himself to justify marrying twelve-year-olds or applying Parkinson's Law to their harems. Until recently a Malay could divorce his wife simply by saying the word "Talak" three times, and men have been known to acquire a string of forty wives over a few years by starting with two and then divorcing one to pick up a third, and repeating this simple process of marital knitting until they have worked their way through three dozen or so.

Just as polygamy, condemned as a vice by the outraged West, had virtuous origins in the East, so the arranged marriage now so repugnant to the European was considered a sensible and practical custom, while the white man's freedom to choose his own mate appeared in Oriental eyes to produce comically ill-assorted couples and columns of divorce cases. For many Burmese and Laotians, the consent of the fiancés themselves is still irrelevant, and bride and groom often do not speak to each other before their wedding day.

A Chinese schoolteacher in Singapore told a divorce court in 1968 that he had slept with his wife only once, and he had been drunk at the time. His bride had been his mother's choice, not his own. But it is to be remarked that the marriage had lasted twenty years. The West has nothing to say on this subject, for the history of Europe is hideous with the howlings of beaten wives and of daughters sold off willy-nilly into wedlock. "For very need," complains the voice of one impoverished English gentleman down the ages, "I was fain to sell a little daughter I have *for much less than I should have done by possibility*." In Europe also, every price had its girl.

Southeast Asia is schizophrenic about the solid flesh. On the one hand, Muslim leaders wage an unceasing war on lust; it is not uncommon for the authorities in Malaysia and Indonesia to neutralize exotic curves with exotic curbs, and beauty contests always produce their own *crise de conscience*. In 1965 thirteen rather obviously budding Miss Malaysias competing for the honor of representing their country at the Miss Universe contest at Miami Beach were suddenly told that they could not parade in swimsuits, for this would be offensive to both the religious and the national culture of the fatherland. They therefore presented themselves before an astonished audience of eight thousand Malaysians in baby-doll nighties (which were a knockout anyway).

At the same time Rizal province in the Philippines outlawed bikinis, backless dresses, and all garments "tending to show any part of the body from the breast down to the middle of the thigh." Wearers could be sentenced to between twenty and thirty days in jail. In Kuala Lumpur, police also insisted on attending an undress rehearsal of the bare-bosomed *Ballets Africains* before sanctioning a public performance to be attended by the prime minister, although like honest witnesses testifying at the trial of their traditions the girls swore that they were "not covering up for anybody."

Yet the women of Bali have for centuries made do without

uplift, and although bare breasts are now banned, they quickly shed the irksome and unaccustomed bra when no one is looking. They will, moreover, revert to their traditional folk costume by whipping off their tops if a tourist with a camera flourishes a suitable banknote. The Mois of Vietnam also concede that one exposure deserves another, and British soldiers fighting in North Borneo during Sukarno's Confrontation of Malaysia collected color slides of dusky Dyak women that may have taken some explaining back at home in Dunstable and Doncaster.

A highly sauced mixture of poker-faced propriety and tropical heat characterizes Asian morality, tickling the palate of the Anglo-Saxon accustomed to the dull fare of his own workaday hypocrisy. The Vietnamese Secretary of State for Social Welfare, for example, announcing that special brothel quarters would be set up in the main towns of the hard-pressed republic so that soldiers could enjoy proper "rest facilities," solemnly assured his hearers that the decencies would be strictly observed: no females under eighteen would be allowed into these A-certificate precincts, and gambling would be strictly forbidden. Kissing in local films causes a furore, for it is irreligious and lustful and common, and so only to be done when no one is looking. In Thailand, where "making love in public is contrary to the national tradition," kissing on TV is not allowed. But the number of girlie bars, all-the-way massage parlors, and bookable premises for private orgies in Bangkok more than doubled between 1965 and 1966 alone.

Which came first, the phoenix or the ash? The moral laws that invite contravention, or the profligacy that calls for moral laws? "The women of this country are lascivious," remarked a visitor to Chen-La. "When a husband does not satisfy their desires, they abandon him. If the husband is called away, the wife will usually say after a fortnight: 'I am not a ghost: how can I sleep alone?'" The enthusiastic amateur is indeed not unknown in Southeast Asia, her inclinations sharpened, it is said, by eating the evil-smelling durian. One pound of this large, knobby fruit contains about six hundred calories and has a wondrously high protein value. But Asians give it credit for more than that, so that the Malays say: "When the durians are down, the sarongs are up," and the police of Djakarta on occasion find themselves ordered to restrain not only the city's ten thousand professionals but the so-called "hiding women," who demand no money but love for love of love.

The Asian Communists, supposedly dedicated to a continence far removed from the gross excesses of the licentious capitalist, are not immune to the urge. In 1964 it was revealed that the Huks frequently took an extra woman as a paramour, "provided she was within the confidence of the Party and the family." In both Indonesia and Vietnam, the Communists have not scrupled to recruit and train loose women either to corrupt and suborn officials or to seduce overgallant American soldiers and kill them when their heads are turned.

Certain literary parasites have made large sums of money by depicting the journalist as an alcoholic lay-about who invents the news in between rounds of drinking and debauchery. But even in my fancy-free days in Indochina I found myself only too often struggling earnestly to get the story in the face of irrelevant temptations pushed my way by frivolous subversives. I remember the anticipation with which I climbed into a black Citroën in Saigon one night to meet an undercover contact to the Vietcong, only to find that it was also occupied by two giggling little charmers in silk *ao-dais*. "My nieces," he explained fondly, while the girls tinkled away at this sally like windbells on a temple roof. "Look," I protested angrily, "I came out to talk, not fool around with girls." "Of course, of course," he replied, planting one on my lap. "But we need them as camouflage. Do you want us to look like a couple of conspirators? This way we are just a pair of husbands on a night out." But it was soon clear that he was simply making a necessity out of a vice.

It had all happened before. When the highway across South Vietnam was still open, I had joined two left-wing extremists on a trip from Saigon to Cambodia. I knew that the noise inside a two-horsepower Citroën clattering over the roads of Indochina would leave little margin for murmured confidences, but on arrival in Phnom Penh I hoped for an evening of interesting revelations, to be extracted painlessly during a leisurely dinner and a pleasant chat. They had other things in mind, however. After a snatched supper, they collected two girls from a house on the edge of the capital, packed them into the back of their rattletrap on either side of me, and tore off into the countryside while I fought for my composure with both hands.

Our destination was a love village, a hamlet of thatched wooden houses on stilts which could be hired by the night and were staffed by servants ready to provide drinks and light refreshment discreetly, but were otherwise uninhabited. We were served raw turtle eggs, and I was then invited to hear the musicians in a room at the back. "But I'd rather have a bit of a talk about the recrudescence of guerrilla activity," I argued despairingly. "Later, later," they said. "First, the three musicians. They're waiting." I love the liquid soft notes of Cambodian music and allowed myself to be pushed gently into a small, moonlit chamber. I emerged some considerable time later, and borrowed a comb. I had learned what the Vietnamese meant by "the three musicians," but we never did get around to talking about the recrudescence of guerrilla activity.

It was a pro-Chinese adviser to Prince Norodom Sihanouk who first introduced me to Madame Choum, on the pretext that we were going to discuss Monseigneur's last visit to Peking. "It's the best place to talk," he said. "Quiet, discreet, and the opium is of sound quality." We climbed the steep steps of the huge old stilted house and were admitted by one or two girls. "Come and say hello to Madame first," suggested my companion. We pushed our way down a dim-lit wooden passageway and he knocked on a door. "*Entrez*," answered a quavering voice, and we walked in on Whistler's Mother.

At a secretaire in one corner sat a little old Cambodian lady in black bombazine, black stockings, and buttoned shoes, wearing a cap over the neat bun of her glossy graying hair. On her nose rested a pair of round steel-rimmed spectacles, and I was not so much introduced as presented. Madame Choum ran a beady, critical eye over me and apparently decided that my credit was good. After ten minutes and one soft drink, we were gently encouraged to run along like good boys and smoke outside. The implication almost seemed to be that opium was a dirty habit and no gentleman lit up in a lady's boudoir. It was a memorable meeting. But matters seemed to be arranged deliberately at Madame Choum's to prove that opium and sex were not incompatible, and I learned little of Sihanouk's visit to Peking that evening. When I mentioned the subject, my companion thrust it aside impatiently, protesting that there was a time and place for everything. Sulking over my notes in a corner, I saw what he meant.

However, it is often in fields unconnected with their natural gifts that Asian women have advanced most swiftly toward freedom. They have burst into the men's league from all sides to become taxi drivers and trade unionists, moneylenders and real-estate manipulators, lawyers and doctors, politicians and even diplomats, so that Filipino ambassadors appealed in 1969 to their Foreign Secretary to stop "this woman explosion" in the service. The Vietcong may have their female artillery, but the South Vietnamese forces also boast tough and grimy girls in green, and in Laos women make highly trained police officers and army paratrooper nurses who jump with the men. As females fight for their rights with that supple feline ruthlessness and efficiency that is so much part of their makeup, the male retreats, so that in Singapore, for example, women are now comprehensively protected by a special charter and are given the same pay as men in the civil service—as they also are in Malaysia.

Women are perhaps regaining their ancient but stolen birthright. Funan was a matriarchal monarchy ruled by a queen until the first century before Christ, the Burmese had their feminine rulers, and the Vietnamese were led against the Chinese in A.D. 40 by a team of warrior-queens reminiscent of Boadicea and her daughters. These Trung Sisters had two spiritual successors in the postwar era. In an isolated house on the rain-soaked border of Cambodia and Vietnam I once met under conditions of uncomfortable secrecy a beautiful tigress in peasant pajamas, devoid of makeup but possessed of a pair of slim, carefully manicured hands whose short-cut nails would not snag on the safety catch of a machine pistol. Her voice was soft and warm, but as she dilated upon the unholiness of the Diem government she began biting off the ends of her words with a vicious snap and her eyes lit up with somber hatred. She was "Madame Ba Cut," the wife of the last fanatical general of the Hoa Hao sect who continued to fight a guerrilla war against the Saigon regime after all other rebels had been crushed or corrupted, and she was reputed to be a more efficient terrorist than her husband (he was caught and beheaded in 1956).

In Saigon I talked with her counterpart in the ruling Catholic hierarchy she so detested in rather different circumstances. The sad rain had been sweeping the swamps, but brilliant sunshine bathed the presidential palace in the capital. I had met Madame Ngo Dinh Nhu, wife of the president's brother, at one or two diplomatic functions and felt no pain, but this time her beauty half stunned me as I rose to my feet, like a sudden blow from a low ceiling. She had been lightly but carefully made up and then plunged into a plain scabbard of heavy, sherry-colored silk with a simple collarless neckline. She looked like an enchantress.

She did not enchant, however. She started off softly enough, pouring out tea and assuring me almost girlishly that she left politics to the men of the family, but as I raised this or that little matter of opposition to her will, it was as if the steel in her were being screwed into a tight coil. "Yes, at first the women disagreed with me," she admitted, speaking of a new ukase she had just imposed upon the community. "But I called their leaders together, and I listened to what they had to say patiently, and then"—and she fixed me with an eye that was growing cold as fast as dying ash—"and then I *explained* matters to them, and *told* them what had to be done, and after that, *they-un-der-stood!"*—and the measured monosyllables *"Elles-ont-com-pris!"* came out like four jaw-breaking slaps from an iron gauntlet.

Diem found her unendurable, but he had to accept his sister-in-law as "First Lady." She invented the Women's Army and the Women's Solidarity Movement. She gave Vietnam the Family Law, forbidding divorce and polygamy and protecting women from the weaker sex, and the Morality Law that outlawed gambling and dancing and sleeping with strangers, and she was, in consequence, much disliked.

Among her many detractors was the Doctor. The Doctor was physically a tiny man, whose feet dangled childishly if he absentmindedly sat on a high chair on a low dais, instead of the converse. Husky footballers from the C.I.A. have been known to make the mistake of slapping him on the shoulder in the hearty fashion of such fellows, only to see him skitter uncontrollably across the room with a look of durable fury on his features. The Doctor was not a small man in other respects, however, for he was the master of SEPES, another of those chilling acronyms that hide the more intimidating forms of secret police in the best tradition of the Gestapo and the OGPU. He would nevertheless wax sarcastic about the power of Madame Nhu in his own field of private public service.

"Her word is the law," he once told me with a marvelous expression of innocent indignation on his friendly little face. "She rings up any minister she likes, gives them all orders, and they have to do what she says. But worse than that—" and he wagged a diminutive index finger—"she uses her Women's Solidarity Movement as a private intelligence service. This movement is a farce, I tell you, for most of these women are simply housewives without an intelligent idea in their heads. In fact, what is happening," he piped triumphantly, "is that the government is being run on female gossip." But in spite of her own imperial waspishness and the resistance of the outraged Vietnamese male, there is no doubt that Madame Nhu personified the truth that if every dog could have his day, so could every bitch.

Throughout the subcontinent women are sidling into politics. Six were elected to Thailand's new House of Representatives in 1969, and the Malaysians made one of their three feminine M.P.'s a minister. Wives play a crucial role, and much of the mayhem in Laos may be attributable to the fact that while the neutralist Prince Souvanna Phouma is married to a French bourgeoise, his half brother the "Red Prince" Souphannouvong is married to a

Vietnamese Communist. India and Ceylon have woman prime ministers. But while the encroaching female may seem to upset traditional hierarchies, and to dislodge the pieces from their appointed places on the board, the despot and the dictator remain arrogantly male.

20 : The Broken Lands

Beyond the colorful cast of egoistical overlords and ambitious generals, of corrupt officials and pious bigots, of Communist guerrillas and nationalistic mob raisers who strut across the screen of memory is a faceless multitude—the 260 million extras of Southeast Asia. Victims of flat-chested economies, of megalomania and war and racial and religious discrimination, these are the poor and the patient whose needs should be our musts, but whose tears have become a tiresome cliché.

"Want?" asks a Vietnamese, wonderingly, stopping in the middle of a muddy village square. "What do you want me to want—a world free of Communism? A two-party system of government? A TV in every home? I want peace, that's all. I am twenty-five years old and I do not know what it is. But that's what I want." It is 1966. His country has known only occupation and reoccupation and civil war and political banditry and more civil war since he was born.

The small Asian everywhere dreams of a little security. His desires are deceptively simple—enough to eat, medicine when he is sick, schools for his sons. He does not ask for an affluent society or a welfare state. He does not know of these tourist traps for the traveler on his way to eternity. But he would like a more equitable administration. He wants fairer shares all round, and a little social justice. This does not necessarily imply that he believes he will achieve final bliss through nationalization— that economic Nirvana in which the ego of personal initiative merges into the Oneness of the state. For nationalization simply offers bigger and better opportunities for official incompetence and what is ironically known as official corruption.

He thus offends an American prejudice which has proved to be Asia's political tragedy. The natural conservatism of the American—his reverence for capital, property, and private initiative— has made him recoil violently more often than not from any suggestion of leveling legislation in Southeast Asia. A man to whom the scramble for success is sacred can only see the politician who may best reflect the modest dreams of backward millions as a dangerous radical preaching "something-for-nothing socialism," if not a crypto-Communist. But when those dreams are shattered, only the real Communists may be left to pick up the bits. This has been made all the easier for them by the anticolonialism of the Americans, which has inhibited them from putting strong pressure on Asian governments to insure that the money Washington paid out in aid did not simply slide into the fat wallets of the few. Many despairing Asians therefore see the ills of the inflamed subcontinent springing from American hostility toward the left.

It has meant that Vietnam has not been allowed to go quietly Titoist over the years. Instead, the United States has propped up a series of discredited "anti-Communist" dictators and warlords in Saigon who have consistently attacked any movement based on concepts of liberty, democracy, and equality that has incautiously raised its head. This system of "dealing with principals only," so reminiscent of Victorians buttering up local despots and calling it the administration of an empire, automatically puts age before beauty, old and corrupt ideas before younger and cleaner ideals. In Korea, Formosa, and Vietnam, Washington may most laudably save millions from Communism, but the Asians have not always liked the price.

In each case it has been much the same. I have leaned across a green baize table to reach for an ashtray, and found my hand in North Korea without a visa. The green baize table stood in the middle of a modest corrugated-steel hut on the windy hilltop at Panmunjom, and the line which marked the cease-fire boundary between Communist North and Nationalist South ran precisely down the middle of it. Here the titanic struggle between the two world blocs had reached a point of inertia. It was the South Koreans who paid for the subsequent "peace." Impoverished, separated from their natural resources, devoting nearly thirty-five percent of their budget to the maintenance of a very necessary army six hundred thousand strong, they could no longer stand up by themselves. For twelve years Washington underwrote the murderous dictatorship of President Syngman Rhee, until in 1960 the outraged young rose spontaneously against his infamous regime. The sickly parliamentary government which then emerged was killed off by *coup d'état* a year later, however, and once again the Americans found themselves shoring up a military junta.

"If you stretch out your arm," said the general—bespectacled, donnish, a product of Cambridge and the Inner Temple—"you can almost touch the other side from here." We were not on the 38th parallel in Korea. We were on the Chinese Nationalist island of Quemoy, staring at the beaches of the Communist mainland a mile and a half away. The countryside of this scorpion-shaped island in the maw of Mao's colossus looked peaceful and empty. But along the rocky coast and in the barren, boulder-strewn volcanic hills were nearly a hundred thousand moles in uniform who ate, slept, and manned their weapons in a labyrinthine warren of tunnels, bunkers, and gun positions beneath thirty, fifty, even five hundred feet of rock. Their frustration grated like a hangnail on satin—the frustration of exiles sick of dictatorship, of veterans who wanted to "return to the mainland," to go back across that tantalizing strip of water to homes all over China which most of them knew they would never see again.

"Germany? What has this situation in common with Germany?" It is not a Chinese Nationalist on Formosa but a Communist cadre in Hanoi, bitterly resenting my suggestion that the brutal bisection of Vietnam could be compared with the gentler Herr-splitting in Europe. "In Germany the people can move backward and forward across the frontiers of East and West." In Vietnam it was very different. There was no commerce between North and South, and travel between the two zones was strictly forbidden. And this was 1957, by Vietnamese standards a year of piping peace. The Geneva Agreement which ended the Indochina War in 1954 had stipulated that by 1956 the two halves of the country should hold general elections, winner would then take all, and Vietnam would be one again. But, the year before, I was already writing from Saigon: "There is much speculation as to whether the U.S.A. may not ignore the Geneva Agreement and build South Vietnam into a strong military power."

Diem duly repudiated the treaty clauses calling for elections, and in October 1956 I watched a phalanx of troops marching smartly through Saigon, boots rapping the road in time to the music, rifles at the slope, glistening black hair permanently waved. This was the women's contingent of the new Vietnamese army, and only a small part of a vast military parade to celebrate the first anniversary of the step which had turned the two armistice zones into two hostile states: the proclamation of the new independent republic of South Vietnam. Seventy-six American jets screamed over the reviewing stand. Escalation had begun.

These were the broken lands, in which the extremism of the Communist leadership supported by the Soviet bloc in the north was matched by the extremism of the anti-Communist leadership supported by Washington in the south. In each case the threat posed by the Communists in one half provided the pretext for the president to overrule his parliament and assume quasi-dictatorial powers in the other half. In each case the Oliver Twists who asked for more for the masses were condemned as Communist dupes or decoys. In each case the "strong man"—Rhee, Chiang, Diem—was defended by his apologists on the grounds that he was isolated and deceived by ambitious scoundrels in his entourage and did not know of the abuses committed in his name.

"And so we have no political leader or party or front or administration which the people trust to put the people first, and which could therefore offer a serious political challenge to the Communists," a Vietnamese diplomat said to me sadly. "Vietnamese want prosperity and a square deal and they get poverty and rule by racketeers until we are all stuck with division and war, because we cannot risk unification and peace."

21 : Our Men in Saigon

The American choice of Ngo Dinh Diem as prime minister and future savior of South Vietnam in 1954 was as honest as the word of a computer and dictated by that iron logic which does not bend but only breaks. Minister of the Interior in 1933, Diem had resigned from the imperial civil service in protest against France's refusal to grant his country a fair measure of sovereignty. He had declined to become prime minister of an "independent" Vietnam under the Japanese during the Second World War, and he had declined to take office in a postwar "provisional" government under Ho Chi Minh. He had been stamped and approved anti-colonialist, anti-Japanese, anti-Communist. Moreover, he did not even have to be dewormed of worldly ambition—John Foster Dulles had had to drag him out of his retreat in a Benedictine abbey in Bruges and beg him to take the job.

It was not the fault of Mr. Dulles that this courageous and honorable patriot had grown up a pious, humorless swot, over-fervently Catholic yet educated to the mandarinate of an empire which had been the vassal of Confucian China. The mandarinate was the civil service of scholar-officials, which had been founded on the principle that only the educated could be trusted to subordinate personal freedoms to the interests of society. The ignorant millions, on the other hand, must be restrained by laws. And it was this tradition of the divine right of eggheads, of the futility of debate with the rabble, which inspired Diem's rule.

After an absence of twenty years Diem returned to a Vietnam at the fag end of the French era and saturated with the poisons of the immediate past. The residue of the entire colonial power structure welcomed the "pro-American" exile back to Saigon with the firm determination to cut him down on the first possible occasion. This included the conspiratorial French themselves, the Emperor Bao Dai, the French-trained generals of the South Vietnamese Army, the Cao Dai and the Hoa Hao allies of the French against the Vietminh, and also the Binh Xuyen "sect," of whom, alas, more later.

Early in 1955 the emperor ordered Diem to report to him in France with his chief-of-staff and to hand over the army in his absence to the pro-French operational commander, General Nguyen Van Vy. This was to be the end of Diem. But Diem did not go, and late one evening I leaped up the stairs of the presidential palace in Saigon to find myself gaping at a curious tableau on the landing, where a group of small and rather scruffy civilians were holding one improperly dressed Vietnamese general at pistol point, while in the background other generals lounged in deep *fauteuils*, smoking and chatting in a desultory manner like spectators at Balmain. The latest creation they were being shown was the new "Revolutionary Committee," a confection of Diem's astute brother which was defying the authority of the emperor and noisily demanding that Diem reconstitute South Vietnam as a republic. This was the group of scruffy civilians. The general, his insignia already torn away by their angry revolutionary hands, was Vy. Bao Dai had lost the round.

Vy was far from being the emperor's only friend, however, for His Majesty had shown much kind condescension to General Le Van Vien (or "Bai Vien," as he was affectionately called), boss of the Binh Xuyen sect. Binh Xuyen was an autonomous fief in the Mekong marshlands, a robber barony in which the rich were plucked and the poor recruited to swell the purses and the forces of piracy and the protection racket. The Binh Xuyen had collaborated with the Japanese, the Communists, the emperor, and the French, in that order. In consequence, by the time I arrived in Vietnam in 1954 Bai Vien was enjoying his just rewards and sitting astride Saigon as the master of both its vice and its virtue.

On the one hand, he controlled the brothels, gambling farms, opium dens, and nightclubs of the capital (the "Hall of Mirrors" alone advertised a cast of a thousand personable young ladies); on the other, a grateful emperor had made his brother-in-law director of the Sûreté Nationale, so that Bai Vien might at the same time control the police and security services in addition to his own private force of five thousand well-armed thugs. Mortal man could hardly have asked for more.

But this satisfactory state of affairs was not to last, for Diem was determined to put an end to private armies and private provinces and to confine the sects to their religious function. And since all the functions of the Binh Xuyen were strictly irreligious, that would mean their extermination.

I first saw Bai Vien on the evening Diem closed down the "Grand Monde," the biggest gambling casino in Saigon, at whose twenty-odd tables pin-shanked trishaw drivers and portly French officers rubbed shoulders to lose two million piasters a night. This was Diem's first crack of the whip, and as the last customers trooped out, Bai Vien was brooding over it, a middle-aged man in an immaculate white shirt and slacks, leaning against his Cadillac and surrounded by his personal hoods. Under brush-cut hair, his face was pitted and swarthy, his eyes like stones in the lamplight. He had already deployed fighting men in and around the city, equipped with armored cars, mortars, and machine guns. "We are going to teach Mr. Diem the four truths," his aide

translated softly into French. What these were I never learned,
but the stage was now set for a showdown.

A few yards up the street from the Hotel Continental the Binh
Xuyen, barricaded and wired up within the Sûreté Nationale, their
gunners alert behind their sandbags, faced the pro-Diem troops
at the Ministry of Defense not forty yards away across Rue
Catinat. It was as if the front line ran down Bond Street. The
whole town was stippled with redoubts and makeshift fortresses,
bristling with weapons of both parties.

Diem, cooped up in his palace but "advised" by Colonel Ed
Lansdale of *Ugly American* fame, was distributing dollars adroit-
ly, and having persuaded certain of the Cao Dai and the Hoa
Hao to accept ministries in his government, he began buying up
the rest of their generals. Beneath all their plausible promises of
solidarity, however, we the watchers seemed to hear the dry
slither of treachery. The generals were watching and waiting too,
their loyalty swaying from side to side, like the cobra at La Lania.

It was Charlie Meyer who shot the cobra. Among the imperial
concessions granted to the worthy Bai Vien was a large tract of
rolling jungle near La Lania and eighty miles north of Saigon
in which he had built a shooting cabin. Here the general would
come to hunt, setting out down the overgrown tracks at night in
a jeep fitted with machine guns and searchlights, and blazing
away at any pair of eyes that shone. But on this occasion he
was not with us.

We were an improbable party of four. There was Charlie in
shorts and singlet, now a political agent employed by Bai Vien
under the curious cover of a geographer. As a geographer he was
supposed to help the second member of our group, Bai Vien's
brother-in-law, a gentle old fellow with a soft cello of a voice
whose avowed aim was to bottle the spring water that bubbled
out of these untidy hills. Next myself, six feet of sweat and
apprehension, for I had never been on a tiger hunt before; and
finally Suzie, whose presence proved conclusively that the whole
venture was a Bob Hope farce. Suzie was a gorgeous butter-
blonde with long French legs, bursting out of an undo-it-yourself
shirt that hung loose over the briefest of briefs. Formerly associ-

ated with an elegant bar off the Rue du Faubourg Saint-Honoré, she was a complaisant companion to many, for she would take most things lying down.

Thus equipped, and carrying one carbine, two shotguns, and a camera, we set off in search of prey in the late afternoon. Monkeys looped and swung along their copperplate courses in the treetops far above, the brother-in-law nearly shot his foot off by mistake, and Charlie killed a cobra that rose three feet out of the jungle grass to strike. This commotion apparently attracted a tiger, which kept discreetly out of sight but followed us all the way back to our cabin on a parallel course about ten yards off to our right, every now and then roaring throaty imprecations just when we thought we had left him behind. He reminded me of the Vietminh, watching the absurd antics of their adversaries in Saigon from the wings.

Other scenes flick through the mind briefly like siesta dreams: the bandit's brother-in-law bending solemnly by an elephant pool, tasting water from its spring and murmuring "Perrier"; Charlie and Suzie and myself in an opium den back in Saigon, Charlie whispering conspiratorially to a sect rebel who dutifully damns Diem but who is absorbed by his task, for amid the sickly-smoky odor of the pipes he is translating the Cao Dai bible into English; dining off a leg of lamb imported from Singapore in the house of the Australian military attaché as the mortar bombs scream overhead like a ragged flight of startled birds to explode with shattering futility in the grounds of the presidential palace across the road. Plaster falls into the peas. Bai Vien has begun teaching Diem the four truths, it seems.

The mortars, I believe, are sited near the Y-Bridge, which is just off the boulevard that links Saigon with Cholon. The bridge crosses a waterway called the Chinese Arroyo but also serves a long slip of an island that splits the channel into two at that point. On this island the defiant Bai Vien has set up the headquarters of the new "National Front of United Forces," which combines the armed enemies of Diem among the three sects—Cao Dai, Hoa Hao, Binh Xuyen. The front has issued a five-day ultimatum to Diem, demanding a change of government, but

Diem has ignored it. The Front has therefore attacked, and the unforgiving antagonists now slog it out with machine guns and mortars across the city.

A gimcrack cease-fire follows this inconclusive trial of strength, with the legitimate civilian population ebbing and flowing in fright as Binh Xuyen and National Army spar for the best positions. The town is choked with guns, a running fight suddenly develops in Cholon only to peter out, a Hoa Hao headquarters is blown to rubble with plastic explosive. Charlie deposits a large sealed parcel in my wardrobe without asking. "Books," he explains, avoiding my eye, "for safekeeping in case my place is searched." Suzie finds three of his hand grenades among her underwear in a chest of drawers.

During this ominous truce Diem seems to be encircled by an elusive smoke ring of enemies which we can only half perceive. Ho Chi Minh is flirting covertly with the sects through their tame representatives in the Communist North. Down at Y-Bridge headquarters two supercilious French intelligence officers whisper in a corner to a Hoa Hao general whose magnificent mustaches, it is said, are locked in a frame each night and watched by two wives, one lying on each side of him, to ensure that they come to no harm. Beside me in another corner sits Ho Huu Tuong, his soft hand tapping his knee rhythmically as he murmurs almost hypnotically into my ear. Novelist and poet, this rounded figure with the moon face, the lizard-quick eyes, and the flattened iron-gray hair is a Trotskyist in a country in which the Communists and the Trotskyists have made common cause in the recent past. For Bai Vien, under the misapprehension that politics is more respectable than piracy, has been trying to go legitimate and has acquired a little coterie of "progressist" counselors who have drawn up a socialist program for his National Front.

When it seemed certain that Bai Vien was nevertheless bent on bloodshed, his Trotskyists came to me, covertly. I was the only British newspaper correspondent resident in Saigon, they pointed out. I was therefore a neutral political observer, yet not a diplomat, who might be finicky about his friendships. I knew what the Americans thought about Bai Vien. I must tell the general the truth personally: that if he wanted to be taken seriously as a politician rather than a thug by Vietnam's rich foreign patrons, he must not start another shooting match in the capital. I agreed. My first move was to take a *cyclopousse* down to the United States embassy and talk to one of those tightly furled diplomats they turn out in Washington. This man finally conceded through a thin pink wound low down on his face that the Trotskyists were essentially right: if Bai Vien attacked, the Americans would be doubly confirmed in their support of Diem, and dollars would win the day.

At ten o'clock the next night a Citroën with three men in it picked me up in the shadows near my hotel and, after racing suicidally through the tense streets toward Cholon, eased past the armored cars and the sandbagged machine-gun nests of the Binh Xuyen guarding Y-Bridge, and dropped down to the island. Bai Vien's headquarters was in almost complete darkness. His caged tigress, to which the general was said to feed those who displeased him (when in a fractious mood), grunted once off to the right, but otherwise there was silence. I walked warily over a narrow plank bridge above the pool that led to Bai Vien's private office and could just make out three crocodiles below— smallish beasts, but reputedly with the same disconcerting eating habits as the tigress.

In a hut lit only by a flickering oil lamp, I sat down across a small desk from the enigmatic, illiterate general and talked to him for an hour through Ho Huu Tuong. He listened quietly, only moving to scratch one bare arm occasionally, his dead black eyes dancing deceptively in the wavering light. When I flagged, he prompted me with a question in Vietnamese. "You have impressed him," whispered the Trotskyist happily, as we left. "It will be all right."

For nine days Bai Vien, poised for battle, made not the slightest move. The American ambassador, General Lawton Collins, discreetly withdrew to Washington. Then Diem suddenly attacked Bai Vien. As the machine-gun bullets ripped into flimsy buildings and the mortar bombs whined down once more, the jostling Vietnamese tenements took fire, and hundreds of acres of crowded, minuscule homes were swept away in the flames and smoke. Bai Vien, his headquarters wrecked, retreated into the swamps of the Delta pursued by Diem's winning battalions. Quiet returned to Saigon-Cholon. It was May 1955.

Bai Vien escaped to live in opulent exile in an ever-friendly France, and Charlie Meyer escaped to Cambodia to become an "adviser" again, this time to Sihanouk. But Ho Huu Tuong was captured, accused of inciting the Binh Xuyen to violence, and condemned to death. Destiny had not done with him, however. After several people, myself among them, had testified that the accusation was false, his sentence was suspended. He was imprisoned on Poulo Condore, the Devil's Island of Indochina, and released when Diem fell. In May 1968 he was again whispering conspiratorially to me as a Buddhist member of the South Vietnamese National Assembly.

By 1956 Diem had bloodlessly eliminated the powerful pro-French generals who at first opposed him, and had won the National Army over to his side. He had used this army to smash the sect rebellion, and when the emperor himself tried to divest Diem of power, it was the emperor who was removed—for Diem rigged a popular referendum and, armed with the authority of its falsified results, was able to declare Vietnam a republic and become its first president. Diem resettled the Catholic refugees from North Vietnam, introduced land reform, built up impressive foreign-exchange reserves. By 1958 he had created a state out of chaos. If they short-listed his achievements and rejected the rest, the Americans could feel proud of him.

Nevertheless, when Ho Huu Tuong was released with other political prisoners from Poulo Condore on a fiery November day five years later, a festive mob armed with banners and garlands roared its welcome down at the docks. Diem was dead. Fourteen generals had overthrown the devout dictator and happy crowds were showering posies on their helmeted and booted troops in the streets of Saigon. The time had come to call at a house I had not visited for three years, the home of Dr. Pham Quang Dan.

Dr. Dan's original sin was that he had been elected as an opposition deputy in 1959. For this affront he was arrested while on his way to the national assembly to attend the opening session, and after being confined in eight different jails he, too, was shipped over to Poulo Condore. There he met the only other opposition candidate who had successfully beaten Diem's otherwise impeccably rigged ballot boxes.

Years of discretion have left on Dr. Dan a mask that is almost batrachian in its cool immobility, but as we sat in the shabby little room which makes him one with his poorer patients, the tale he told gained from his detached air and stilted English.

For months he had been shut up in a narrow, dark cell, not knowing day from night. He was interrogated endlessly, and when he protested his innocence he was tortured. They came, in their conventional way, in the smallest hours of the morning to strap him down on a hard bench and connect his fingers and toes to the terminals of a hand dynamo. Then, as the first waves of electricity throbbed heavily through his pinioned body, they poured water into his mouth and nostrils until he was bloated with liquid through which the current could jump with almost lethal impulse. When he fainted, they revived him and repeated the process.

For women prisoners under the Diem regime, strip tease came to have a second, more revolting meaning. For men there was not only the water torture, there was also the agony of the feathers. Their fingers were each pinned separately to a tabletop, with very long fine needles driven through the nails. Feathers were then attached to the needles and an electric fan directed upon them. As the quills twisted and turned agitatedly in the breeze, the needles bent and quivered in the wounds, ingeniously causing excruciating pain. Another prisoner in Saigon had told me of the cell into which Vietnamese Sûreté officers had thrown him as a left-wing suspect. The cell measured seven feet by eleven feet in area and was filled in with humanity rather as a hollow block may be filled with rubble. Eighteen men were crammed into it, and however they arranged themselves, two had to remain standing all the time. They did this in turn for three months, the shift on its feet fanning all the others to prevent them from stifling. As they were fed only two bowls of thin gruel a day, there was soon more space both outside and inside their clothes, whereupon the guards topped the cell up again.

Meanwhile, as the torturers became ever busier, many bathed and talcumed Western diplomats in their air-conditioned Saigon offices were sternly warning reporters who criticized Diem not to "rock the boat" but to "get with the team." "Aw, Diem may be a son-of-a-bitch," agreed one distinguished American with rugged loyalty, "but he's our son-of-a-bitch." Lyndon Johnson called him the "Winston Churchill of Asia." (Why not? Richard Nixon was to call the war in Vietnam "our finest hour.") Now he was gone. No doubt the new heroes would all sink back to size and perpetrate another ordinary human muddle, but just for this fleeting, golden moment it seemed as if we had reached a happy ending. Vietnam had been exorcised.

The wretched Far East correspondent who in his day has toiled up the pretentious staircase of the Independence Palace in Saigon, and then wasted two hours listening to the mechanical monologue Diem reserved for such fellows, will agree that absolute anti-Communism corrupts absolutely. Diem was mature, honest, conscientious, celibate, continent, sober, cultivated, patriotic, fastidiously dressed, and both clean and godly—like the citizens of Chen-La, he brushed his teeth and said his prayers every day. But when this good man had reiterated for the fifth time that all opponents of his regime were automatically playing into Communist hands, his victim was praying that South Vietnam would get a scoundrel for its next president, provided he had a pinch of pink in his makeup.

By 1963 Diem's secret police had picked up or pushed into the arms of his enemies nearly every prominent nationalist who had fought for the freedom of his country during the previous twenty years. He and his family suppressed all opposition, filled the jails, muzzled the press, rigged the elections, and clung to all power, so that at one point no visa for Vietnam could be issued without the president's personal permission. He chose his lieutenants for their yesmanship and promoted according to political loyalty, not seniority or merit. Vietnam had to be saved from

Communism, and therefore the Diem regime must be preserved at all costs.

In Hanoi, it was reported, leaders regarded Diem with almost affectionate approval. His regime had become a better argument for Communism than any they could hammer into the heads of the peasantry. Idling under an awning by a swimming pool in Phnom Penh, Wilfred Burchett appeared to contradict this when he said in his ironical, gravelly way that the president of the National Liberation Front had described the assassination of Diem to him as "an unexpected gift," for Diem alone had built a machine of political control and terrorism sturdy enough to enable him to run the country despite the guerrilla war. But that was exactly one year after Diem had died, and there had been time to observe what followed.

Like the jigging scribe of an electrocardiogram or a lie detector, the reporter's pen tells the story independently of the words. The measured speech of a polygamous minister opening a family-planning seminar is recorded in the fine, regular hand we associate with baptism certificates and pawnbroker's receipts, while an eyewitness account of a riot goes down in an agitated scribble that might well be a sketch of the event instead of an account of it.

My notebook labeled "South Vietnam: November 1963," the month that Diem was murdered, is faithful to this law. It is a portrait of a coup, the fighting and firepower and rivalry and disunity depicted in almost indecipherable ball-point blue, with the names of mutually distrustful colonels and generals inserted into the schizoid order of battle of an army pitted against itself: "IV corps Bui Huu Nhon," I read. "Do Cao Tri I Corps. Dinh got els 7th Div. Main force 5 and 6 para bns, one-third marines, one-third armour, 2 regts 5 div (III corps). 400-600 presidential guards surrendered midnight 20 killed 250 pws. 9 p.m. four coys attack with M-113 and 57-mm rec. rifles 80-mm MGs 105-mm Hows et 81-mm mortars. Marines half with Thao, half with Minh . . ." Then a long list of generals, followed by "Dinh

treacherous but needed, Minh feels essential oust Mai Huu
Xuan. Kim and Don with Minh, Thao pushing Khiem . . ."

It was an earnest of what was to come—Minh, Kim, Dinh,
Don, Khanh, Huong, Ky, Khiem, Thieu—the cracked carillon
of names rings the changes of regime from year to year as coup
follows coup in South Vietnam, and there is always an American
on hand to say of the latest leader "He's our boy. He may be a
son-of-a-bitch, but, by God, he's our . . ." Against a confused
background of Vietcong violence in the flooded paddy fields and
Buddhist rioting by flarelight in the city, odd, random scenes
flick into the mind like illustrations seen when riding through a
Victorian novel, and one half-expects to read an infuriatingly
cryptic caption in fine italics underneath the frontispiece: *Colonel Thao unstrapped his belt and laid his pistol on the table.
"Comme-ci, comme-ça," he replied.*

We were sitting in the muted, high-walled courtyard of his
little house in Saigon with its single, scented Malay-apple tree.
The first coup was over, Diem was dead, and the dust was set-
tling. Colonel Pham Ngoc Thao, in fresh-pressed khaki drill, had
just answered "So-so" to my question: was he satisfied with the
new government of generals announced that day? The noncommittal answer was uncharacteristic, for Thao had a trick of
hesitating, taking in a short breath as if he were thinking up an
equivocal response, and then coming out suddenly with a flat
shocking statement like a resounding slap on the cheek. And this
somehow matched the look of blank disbelief forever fixed upon
the firm, tanned, and youthful face by his wall-eye. He paused
for a moment and then, sure enough, sprung a verbal ambush
on me: "But we are organizing another coup," he added simply.

While the generals had coalesced uneasily to conspire against
Diem, Thao had worked energetically to recruit the men who
would count when the chips were down—the unit commanders
of the infantry battalions, of the marines and paratroopers.
When the storm broke, it was Thao who led a battalion of
marines into the radio station in Saigon, proclaimed the coup
to the world, and then telephoned to the beleaguered president,

shouting through the peremptory rattle of machine guns outside that the palace was encircled and he should surrender.

But now his mind was on the next phase of the plot, the second explosion which would shatter the "Military Revolutionary Council" that had replaced Diem, and fling to oblivion the old pro-French officers who had seized this chance to creep back into power. Thao was already undermining selected targets among the high brass, planting his charges of insurrection deep among their junior commanders. "Generals afraid of Thao," my scrawl of the day reads. "They begin see his power over tps, his infl among capts, majors." He was to die for that, in agony, two years later.

Coups breed press conferences. The Military Revolutionary Council assembles on the dais, its four most prominent generals behind a baize table, immaculate, beribboned, speaking out firmly from a tulip bed of microphones and a haze of cigarette smoke, the new authority, the heroes of the hour. Within months, however, one will be in exile and the others will find themselves running not a republic but a restaurant. The second coup came, but not as Thao planned, for in January 1964 Major-General Nguyen Khanh, warlord commanding the Vietnamese First Corps, seized power.

The eighteen chaotic months of rivalry and religious strife that followed have left their own unbeautiful or comic memories: in the market square of Saigon a mob of Buddhists brutally hacks at a Catholic student who staggers forward, his face streaming blood, until a small man drives a knife into his stomach, dropping him dead (Look again. It is not a small man, it is a boy of about ten); five senior generals besieged by Catholic rioters at the headquarters of the Joint General Staff telephone frantically to the archbishop to come and save them (their bodies, not their souls); the deputy premier calls Khanh a madman, a second minister is accused of treason after publishing an article calling him a dictator, and a third minister shaves his head and goes into retreat as a Buddhist; Khanh serves assembled newspaper correspondents a tasteless, indigestible mound of platitudes with the solemn air of a man clowning his way through crises: ". . . will do all to serve the country, fight the Communist lackeys and also the colonialists and neutralists, carry out the revolution, build the foundations of true democracy . . ."

There are more meetings in Thao's courtyard and two abortive coups, but Robert S. McNamara, American Secretary of Defense, shouts almost defiantly: "I want to stress . . . complete respect and support, economic and military, for General Khanh and for Vietnam . . ." There will be no American backing for any man that tries to replace Khanh, and the bearded thirty-seven-year-old is now in the same strong but fatal position once enjoyed by the autocratic President Diem.

By 1966 the United States was nevertheless supporting Air Marshal Nguyen Cao Ky with the same obdurate, abiding love for the latest general-on-the-make, but the evanescent nature of these phenomena was now recognized in Washington, it appeared, for when a colleague asked a senior American official what would happen if Ky fell, the man replied instantly: "Well, I guess we'll just have to deal with the next guy."

In 1968 I found myself attending still another press conference in the presidential palace, which had finally been rebuilt after that breakfast bombing attack six years before. Outside, the architecture of the new palace seemed to have been inspired by the old prewar cinema Wurlitzer, but inside it was all conventional red carpet and yellow drapes and great dusty chandeliers like frozen fountains of ditch water. The latest government filed onto the rostrum, natty little men with slicked-down hair, most of them dressed in what appeared to be identical dark suits and ties, for Vietnamese generals had also added this ministerial uniform to the rest of the modern military wardrobe.

President Thieu told us that his government was defending the freedom of Vietnam, and Vietnam was an outpost of the whole free world. The Vietnamese were determined to combat aggression and not give in to the Communists. If the Americans withdrew, they would be avoiding their responsibility to the free world, but the Vietnamese would fight on alone for democracy and so on.

As the familiar jargon rolled on, my eye wandered to a more casually dressed man in a cream suit at the end of the cabinet line-up, and my mind at once somersaulted back thirteen years to the old palace and this same man in his old identity, the insignia of his uniform torn off, a pistol thrust into his side by a nervous but irate little civilian. It was the pro-French anti-American pro-Bao Dai anti-Diem General Nguyen Van Vy. And he was now Minister of Defense. Beside him sat the man who had been the second Trotskyist adviser to the Binh Xuyen thirteen years before, Mr. Tran Van An, now Minister of Information. "We're not putting money on any alternatives," a man from the American embassy told me. "This is our team."

A year later members of an Anglo-American study group visited Vietnam and produced a thirty-eight-page report which found that the South Vietnamese government relied "more upon police state tactics and American support to stay in power than upon true representation and popular support. . . . Torture and brutality are widespread in the arresting and interrogation process . . . without question the Thieu-Ky government uses the words Communism, neutralism and coalition to silence dissent and weaken political and religious opposition . . ." Palace for palace, torture for torture, Vy for Vy, they were different, only they were the same. Someone had burned the phoenix again. This was where I came in.

22 : *Their Men in the Sticks*

The nineteen helicopters whir high above the watery flatlands of Vietnam's southernmost peninsula like a flight of squat ducks. Beside me in number 11 an American corporal, helmeted and visored, mans a 50-caliber machine gun pointed down through the open doorway toward the sun-stroked paddy fields below, where escorting fighters skim at hedgehopping height. But this is not a major airborne operation against the Vietcong. It is 1964 and Robert S. McNamara, United States Secretary of Defense, is paying a visit to Hoa Hao Village, accompanied by General Nguyen Khanh and a number of very large white men like General Maxwell Taylor and Mr. William Bundy.

From a balcony Mr. McNamara beams down on the Hoa Hao villagers, and the gap-toothed, teak-colored visages of the elders gaze up inscrutably at his neat, certified-accountant's face. He makes the same speech that he has made throughout this barn-storming tour of Vietnam, emphasizing that Washington is supporting General Khanh personally and exclusively. Then he descends among them and does his stuff. He clasps the hands of the adults, he clowns with the children, and in a cool, ornate pavilion he reverently puts his fingers together in a Buddhist greeting before a tiny, emaciated old lady in a green silk dress. She is the mother of Huynh Phu So, the mystic master of the Hoa Hao sect who was murdered by the Communists. Neither speaks the other's language. The old lady is very deaf. Mr. Mc-Namara ceremoniously presents her with a hearing aid. But then nobody can make it work, however much they twiddle the buttons. The lack of comprehension is complete.

It is all fantastically irrelevant. Beyond the bewildering trans-pacific bonhomie of all these big men and the impressive weight of aerodynamic hardware in which they have come lies the sad, flat scenery, as awash with Vietcong as it is with brackish water, into which one of the helicopters crashed just an hour ago. Matters will improve slowly, but at this moment it is not safe to go into more than one village in seven in the area, even in broad daylight and with an armed escort. Once darkness falls, the Vietcong dominate it almost completely. "The army can move anywhere, but it cannot stay," an American military adviser tells me bluntly. "And when it withdraws, the Vietcong come back in. We make about as much permanent impression as a ship sailing through the Red Sea."

". . . no more effective than cutting water with a sword." The similarity takes me back to 1962, when Diem was still alive and Colonel Thao was for a time military governor of Kien Hoa province. The colonel had used the expression while we were on an anti-guerrilla operation that proved a model of military futility.

Thao clung to the wheel as the little launch bounced over the Mekong Delta waterway not ten yards from the opaque fringe of mangrove and latania palms that bordered it. "Either you race by close to the shore or you keep well over on the other side," he shouted. "In midstream they get your range and strafe you." A grenade, fired from behind the screen of tangled water-edge vegetation, thudded onto the swampy bank to our left and exploded. Half a mile farther on, another burst ineffectively. "We have got the Vietcong boxed in here," he shouted. "We have flushed a hundred and fifty of their regulars and I have troops closing in all around them, not to mention"—he cocked an ear to the sudden roar of guns—"a battery of one-oh-fives to pound their hideouts."

We were on the tattered hem of Asia, where twisted threads of land reach out for the sea, and the swamps and dense coconut forests are veined with the byways of the Mekong, some of them half a mile wide. We swung left, nosed down a narrow creek, and puttered to a stop beside a command post. A company commander began to report thinly over the field telephone. Thao cursed, barked urgent instructions into the instrument. The inevitable had happened. The trapped, pajama-clad Vietcong guerrillas were shedding their battalion scarves, concealing their weapons, and hiding themselves among the local peasants by forcing all the menfolk to accompany them down their escape routes. The enemy was now indistinguishable from the villagers, whose sympathy the government was so anxious to win. It was the loyalist forces, in their American steel helmets and camouflaged uniforms, who appeared to be alien intruders. "When in doubt," Thao ordered, "don't shoot. Take everyone prisoner."

The box contracted. Forty men were killed, at least four of them ordinary peasants whose deaths would further inflame resentment against the Saigon regime. More than eighty prisoners were taken, but only eight of these were readily identifiable as Communist guerrillas. Half-naked and bound together with cords, the captured for the most part turned out to be innocent villagers. The enemy had melted away.

Covered by the automatic weapons of Rangers, we plunged into the main hamlet of the battle area. In the square stood a wood-and-plaster building, the propaganda office of the Vietcong. "We would rather die than live under the domination of American Imperialists" ran its painted slogan. We were only seven miles from the provincial capital.

An N.C.O. reported with a plastic airbag full of documents taken from the body of a Vietcong political cadre. Thao thumbed through receipt books which showed in detail the contributions to the Vietcong cause that the guerrillas had extracted from every peasant household in the area. Then he ordered a sweep to recover discarded enemy weapons. We stumbled in open order across vast squelching rice fields under a smoldering evening sky, the stinking mud sucking at our submerged boots, to find four rifles and twelve hand grenades. The place had the hallowed feel of hostile territory, but fortunately the Vietcong seemed to have gone, for they could have mown us down in minutes. A residual rattle of distant machine-gun fire faltered and died. The countryside lapsed into sardonic silence.

"You see," remarked Thao, "the enemy scatters only to return to dominate the area again once we have left it. These sweeps are no more effective than cutting water with a sword, except where we have good intelligence. And that means that until we can protect and befriend the peasants and so win their support, we will get nowhere." We listened a little anxiously in the gathering darkness for the reluctant outboard motor of the launch to splutter into life and take us away from this area which the troops had just cleaned up. Then Thao opened the throttle and we roared back along the ragged edge of mangrove that flanked the delta waters. It did not look any more friendly than it had before the operation began.

But when McNamara speaks to the Hoa Hao we are already two years and four coups further on, and all hopes of a stable central administration that will earn the respect of the Vietnamese peasant by dealing with him fairly are receding steadily into the sunset. The peasant himself—seventeen men out of every twenty in the country—is not worried or excited or elated or downcast when he is presented with a Khanh instead of a Diem. He is indifferent. Too often his district officer is a cheat and a bully, and that is all the government he knows. He owes it neither his trust nor his meager treasure. It does not protect him from the Vietcong, and it does not provide his simplest needs. It collects taxes and it takes the young men of the village away to fight. As for the riches of all these white men (Frenchmen, Americans, or whatever they are by now), they never filter down to him.

The successive upheavals in the capital threaten to shake into rubble the fragile framework of civil and military defense against Communism. The soldiers become gun-shy and think only in terms of survival, for every time there is a coup, commanders and administrators are changed, military province chiefs are shuffled around, and no man knows which will last longer—his job or the ephemeral governments for which he is so unreasonably supposed to risk his life. This in turn makes "pacification" almost impossible.

"Our 1962 pacification plan got going in July 1963," an American staff officer once told me in the deliberate, wry manner of the Vietnam veteran, "but in November 1963 President Diem was overthrown. The government changed, the provincial and district officials vital to this effort were mostly replaced, and so the campaign ground to a halt. In December 1963 we rewrote the program, but it came to grief when General Khanh seized power in another coup in January 1964. In March 1964 we drew up yet another plan, and started executing it in June, but in October Khanh was obliged to relinquish power to Mr. Tran Van Huong, and so more wholesale changes . . ." And so it went on, through project after project, until the Tet Offensive, the powerful Vietcong onslaught on Saigon and other cities at Vietnamese New Year in February 1968, wrecked the sand castle of trust that the United States was so painstakingly reconstructing once again.

All had long since agreed that the basis of this trust must be the security provided by a fortified village. As early as 1960 Diem had summarily ordered the construction of ten thousand "agrovilles"—new rural centers within which peasants would be protected and given every social amenity. I trudged around several of them, dutifully noting the watchtower and the warning drum that would bring help in case of attack, the first-aid station, the school. But the peasants were sullen. They had been recruited as forced labor to build their own agrovilles, and they would rather have been left alone in the first place.

Two years later I was trudging around the "Strathams," the new strategic hamlets of the Mekong Delta, their huddles of huts enclosed within a formidable chastity belt of trenchworks and hedges of sharpened bamboo to keep the enemy out and the villagers in. Rape was inevitable nonetheless, for the Vietcong were already inside the hamlets, "guerrilleros" who supplied the guerrillas outside with food and intelligence and the names of suitable villagers to assassinate. And they normally outnumbered the Self-defense guards.

While the government devoted large sums of American aid to flashy projects in and around the capital, the ill-armed Self-defense guard in the hamlet was paid about three dollars a week for risking his life twenty-four hours of the day, and his wife and children received nothing even when he was killed. The price of loyalty was higher than this, and in one lonely community I visited, perched on the salty fringe of the Delta and only to be approached in a steel-sided infantry landing craft, it had been possible to recruit no more than twenty-five young "volunteers" out of a population of seventeen hundred. The region was forlorn, remote, almost lost in the everglades, infested with Vietcong. A breeze blew across the stockade from the invisible sea, like a faint breath of freedom from afar.

By the time Diem and Nhu were murdered in November 1963, the whole concept of the village-fortress had been discredited in the minds of most peasants, who in many areas smashed their own bamboo perimeters or carefully picked them to bits on the principle that if you do not lock your door, the burglar will not break it down, or enter in an unnecessarily aggravated frame of mind.

With almost Oriental patience, the Americans began again, feeding their ideas through Khanh. The "New Life" hamlet was introduced for good peasants, while pro-Vietcong villages were in some cases bulldozed flat to teach men a simple lesson in good and evil, cause and effect. Instead of trying to save all the provinces simultaneously, the Saigon government developed the "oil slick" technique of using regular battalions of troops to establish complete security in a limited area, and then slowly expand it. "And it works great," an American official confided to me sarcastically, "so that out of 218 hamlets in Long An province I am now prepared to sleep in twelve at night, and maybe visit thirty during the day."

The helicopter had come to the rescue of the Vietcong, for now the South Vietnamese army could commute to and from the war, flying into battle in the morning and back home to barracks after the afternoon tea break. Air transport, which should have been used to maintain men in the field, was running a suburban shuttle service with rush hour at about sunset. It was the peasants and the Self-defense corps who had to stick it out in the villages in the dangerous hours of darkness.

South Vietnam had become a disturbing, equivocal land of optical illusion, and it was often as if the Vietcong were only on the other side of the looking glass. One village would have a headman appointed by the Saigon government. The district chief visited it regularly, it was guarded by a squad of the paramilitary "Popular Forces." It had medicines from the provincial capital, a hidden telephone for emergency contact with the South Vietnamese army, three-day-old Saigon newspapers, and American aid in the shape of a truckload of cotton cloth or a starry-eyed official with an addiction for teaching mildly surprised peasants how to build windmills.

The next village across the chessboard of rice fields would mainly be run by a lean-cheeked young man in a buttoned-up denim tunic and slacks, wearing a plastic topee with a yellow star on the front. Behind him was the National Liberation Front. The Vietcong defended the inhabitants but liquidated the unrighteous. They also distributed the rice, collected the taxes, taught everyone to brush his teeth, love Uncle Ho, and observe strict discipline. The village newspaper was *Nhan Dan*, the official organ of the Front.

A government survey of the intervening fields would show

one pattern of ownership and tenancy. But a Vietcong survey of the same fields showed another, for the Communists had redistributed the land among the more pliable peasantry. When the government ordered a call-up of young men, it was almost as if the Vietcong had done so, for many of those who shied at serving with one side dodged the draft by fleeing to the other. There were hamlets that the government controlled by day and the Vietcong by night, communities controlled by both at once. The two South Vietnams were almost superimposed upon one another.

The Vietcong were not fighting the war. They were living it. The inability to understand this led to much false analysis by the more optimistic. Whenever there was a lull in Communist activity, Saigon began to brag that pacification was paying off. But on three occasions I was able to discover the truth about these successes. In the first instance the Vietcong wanted the bridge to an isolated village to be repaired. They secretly ordered their own forces to observe a local cease-fire, and the South Vietnamese army obligingly took advantage of the break in hostilities to mend it. In the second, the Vietcong were furtively moving large quantities of supplies into prepared dumps within striking distance of Saigon. In order to beguile their opponents, therefore, they stopped all offensive action along the route. On the third occasion, everything was quiet because everything was, quite simply, under Vietcong control.

Government officials were rapacious, the police and army brutal; the Americans bombed and shelled and gunned the villages and then made up for it all by being nice to the peasant in some overcrowded refugee camp after his home had gone up in smoke, and perhaps his wife and children, too. The Vietcong gave him free land, treated him with courtesy (if also to much rather tiresome propaganda) when he showed willing, and murdered him when he did not. But the Vietcong also pointed out that if the alien Americans remained a hundred years, the war would last a hundred years. As for themselves, they were fellow Vietnamese and represented no obstacle to future peace and quiet. The Americans struggled to win the heart and mind of the peasant, the Vietcong his body and soul. It was an uneven contest, for the Vietcong were on their home ground.

The failure of the South Vietnamese government to defend the peasant against himself was matched by its failure to endear him to Saigon in spite of himself by one sure means: nationalization of all land and its redistribution to the men who tilled it. In the early days of Diem the program introduced by enthusiastic American experts to take surplus acres from the landowner and give them to the landless was converted into a gigantic racket for cheating both parties, and in 1969, fifteen years after it was first mooted, land reform was still being sabotaged in Saigon.

In February of that year the prime minister had nevertheless announced still another pacification drive, designed to win over the entire country within ten months. The looking glass was well polished at the time, for while Saigon claimed to control eighty-six percent of all the people, the Vietcong simultaneously claimed eighty percent for themselves. But at last pacification slowly began to pay off as more men with better arms were deployed to defend the villages. The anti-Communists greeted the new year in a mood of cautious self-congratulation: man had shown that he could learn from his mistakes after all, and this was a comfort to many. Except that it was now 1970, and it should have been 1960.

23 : Two Buckets of Blood

Slipping through the mirror from the Saigon of General Khanh to the Saigon of the Vietcong was a delicate operation, but in late 1964 I arrived at the last of a long chain of shy contacts and walked into a small, excessively untidy radio and electrical repair shop near the Central Market which had been chosen as my particular crossing point. I murmured a name and was simply given a time to stand on a street corner after dark. At eight-thirty that evening I was picked up in slanting rain and taken to an empty upstairs room in an Indian restaurant, to be introduced to a middle-aged mouse of a man with a balding head and a missing front tooth through which his breath whistled softly. He was dressed like a slightly ostentatious French-educated clerk in an immaculate white shirt and clip-on bow tie, gold cuff-links and wedding ring, and as we ate chicken curry and drank a glass of red wine he played his bit part as a petit-bourgeois to perfection. No one would have dreamed that he had just sidled into the city from War Zone D.

This was the first of three meetings with two senior cadres from the Liberation Front in obscure restaurants and a dusty attic above the radio shop. I saw them nearly five months before Lyndon Johnson put the first American combat units into Vietnam and nearly five years before Richard Nixon pulled them out again. At that point in time Washington's stake in the war was still limited to 20,000 military "advisers" attached to South Vietnamese fighting formations and base personnel handling the flow of American military aid. But the view from the Vietcong side of the glass is not without interest even today.

"We are ready to do everything possible to save Washington's face, so that the Americans can go home," my clerkish contact told me, sipping his wine expressionlessly as if it were the blood of Christ. "If we start real trouble in the towns, they may pour fighting troops into the South, or even attack North Vietnam. That's why we have not organized a campaign of intensive terrorism against the Americans who are already here. You realize, of course, that this is what otherwise we should be doing. We should be killing Americans as fast as we can in order to raise a storm of protest against the warmongering policies of Washington with a few thousand tearful widows and mothers at its center." If there were no negotiated American withdrawal, he said, that would have to be the next stage. "You will know when we are ready for the final push both in town and country," he added, "because part of the South Vietnamese army will change sides and fight for us, or simply stop fighting altogether."

I met my second contact at the beginning of November 1964. He was a long, stick-insect of a Vietnamese in an open-necked shirt, slacks, and sandals—cool, collected, and contemptuous. He believed that the Americans must either be persuaded to give up the war in Vietnam as hopeless or be "provoked into acts of greater and more costly terrorism which will bring such an avalanche of condemnation down upon them from their countrymen that the leaders in Washington will be able to back out with a good grace, bowing to *force majeure* at home."

Sitting and chain-smoking above the radio shop at one in the morning as the street outside fell silently to sleep, he went on: "After all, what is the danger? The Liberation Front may seem to be no more than an intermediate step toward a Communist South Vietnam which can be united with a Communist North. But the Front is nevertheless mainly made up of Southerners, and the common denominator of all its members is not Communism but nationalism. It will be many years before South Vietnam goes Communist, if it ever does. Meanwhile, it will be a democratic, neutralist state, and after eighteen months of hesitation the North has conceded the need for this neutralism, even for a coalition between the Front and a suitable Saigon government, because with that we make a concession to the Americans and can perhaps persuade them to go away sooner."

This cadre gave me a second contact address, and I took it down without comment. It was the house of Mr. Tran, the "Peace Movement" leader to whom Charlie Meyer had introduced me ten years before, and who had put me in touch in turn with the militant Buddhists. A few days later Ho Huu Tuong, the Trotskyist adviser to Bai Vien who had been released from the prison island of Poulo Condore, grasped me gently by the elbow in the tiny courtyard of his home and began a long, reasoned exposé in a hoarse mutter, much as he had done at Binh Xuyen headquarters nearly a decade earlier. He insisted that the Liberation Front leaders did not even stipulate that they must be represented in any future coalition "peace" government in Saigon: they would be content with a neutral, socialist-minded cabinet of Saigonese intellectuals at first, as long as its members were acceptable to them. Elections could come later. They did not want South Vietnam to lose American aid. There could therefore be no question of establishing a Communist regime.

It all sounded like a conspiracy to give the Americans a dishonorable discharge from service in South Vietnam, a neat pretext for begging the whole question of "Communist containment." It was obvious that the field for negotiation was sown with mines, and the question that no one in Saigon or Washington could answer for certain was to what degree the Liberation Front was indeed a "front," a booby trap whose lethal charge of Communism was concealed in an innocent can labeled "nationalism."

This suspicion reinforced the blind distrust which many responsible Americans reserved for all nationalists who opposed the son-of-a-bitch-of-the-moment in Saigon. Genuine nationalism was the only currency that was valid on both sides in the war, but they hesitated to fit the two halves of the coin together.

I remember congratulating Thao in the Mekong Delta back in 1962, as we watched the torn green curtain of lacania that screened the Island of Leaves, where Vietnamese Rangers attached to him were mopping up the remnants of a Vietcong battalion after a masterly exercise in stealthy envelopment. He rapped the resonant side of our landing craft and shook his head impatiently. "All this should not even be necessary," he replied softly. 'Nine-tenths of the men who joined the Vietminh resistance were not Reds. They were nationalists like me who collaborated with the Communists in order to end French domination of Vietnam. These men are the true Vietnamese, the force that can unify the country. Those on the other side never wanted to change French masters for Chinese or Russian ones. Those on this side have no intention of changing French masters for American ones."

He paused and then went on with a slight smile. 'Look, when I was second-in-command of a Vietminh regiment against the French, the commander of the Vietcong guerrillas we are just defeating over there at this moment"—and he waved toward the subsiding battle—"was my immediate chief. I know that man as I know myself. He is no Communist. But when I send messages to him these days urging him to rally to us, he thinks it is a trap, that the security chiefs in Saigon will wring him dry of intelligence and then push him in front of the firing squad. So he stays with the Vietcong. He has no choice. If once we had a government that men like him could respect and trust, the Vietcong problem would be solved."

He knew what he was talking about, but he was also making

enemies fast, for the foreign press was beginning to lionize him as the man who knew the answers, prompting dangerous comparisons between Thao on the ground and the powerful armchair strategists in the capital. Sensitive correspondents like Stanley Karnow, now of the *Washington Post*, and Robert Shaplen of *The New Yorker* became his personal friends, and he was unfailingly courteous to Joseph Alsop because the president had specifically told him to be ("He's supposed to have Kennedy's ear, you see"). But I had already known Thao for seven eventful years.

Thao was a Southern Catholic, born of a well-to-do family from the Mekong Delta. During the Indochina War he had joined the Vietminh, had risen to command a guerrilla regiment against the French in the Delta, had been sent North to Ho Chi Minh's headquarters, and had then returned clandestinely to become Vietminh intelligence chief for the whole Southern region. As a senior cadre but also a Catholic, he had arranged a furtive meeting with his bishop and had promised him immunity from the Vietminh guerrillas provided His Grace did not denounce them from the pulpit. Thao kept his word, but he had no means of knowing that the prelate he was protecting would become Archbishop Ngo Dinh Thuc and that his brother, Ngo Dinh Diem, would be the postwar president of South Vietnam.

I first met Thao in 1955 as "Albert" when he was paying a rare night visit to Saigon, for as a former Vietminh chief his position was still delicate and he was living almost invisibly down in the Delta, scraping along as an obscure schoolteacher. However, the archbishop was later able to pay his debt of honor, and Thao emerged from his cover to be commissioned as a major in the South Vietnamese army. He was then appointed personal adviser to Diem and his brother Nhu, and constantly toured the country in order to give them first-hand reports about the situation in the provinces. Why did he change sides? Thao was no Marxist, and his ambition was to see a popular and progressive government set up in Saigon which would capture the imagination and the loyalty of all good men in North and South. But as he watched the country on behalf of the palace oligarchy, he watched the palace oligarchy on behalf of the country, and was soon stripped of all hope that it would produce a clean administration to which nationalists on both sides could or would rally.

Thao then ran an erratic but predictable course dictated by the belief that whoever established despotic misrule in Saigon was simply driving good men after bad into the arms of the Communists. A born conspirator with a sweet tooth for undercover living, he helped organize the successful coup against Diem in November 1963, the coup against Khanh in February 1965, and a third but abortive coup three months later.

I last saw him just before the second coup and ten years after our first meeting. Knowing that Thao was against him, Khanh had first sent him into diplomatic exile, and then recalled him in order to liquidate him. Thao had therefore returned to Saigon secretly and at once had gone into hiding to plot Khanh's overthrow. The civilian prime minister, Tran Van Huong, had put out an official call ordering Thao to report to the Foreign Ministry, but had sent him a private warning to ignore it. I picked him off a pre-arranged street corner on a fine night in Cholon, after a double-take at his nocturnal dark glasses and the ridiculous beribboned nylon hat which supposedly disguised him as a Vietnamese teddy-boy. When he took the glasses off, I saw a jaunty, new-old light in his one good eye. He was his own man again—on the run, covertly contacting marine and paratroop commanders in a quest for reliable allies in his hazardous conspiracy for honest government.

As we dined frugally, he told me he had seen Air Marshal Ky, who had wanted Thao to join him against Khanh. Thao had refused ("He's just a warlord"). He had seen General Thi, the corps commander in Central Vietnam, who had made the same proposition. Thao had again refused ("Just another warlord, but that one should be destroyed"). He had seen Thich Tri Quang and other Buddhist venerables, and heard Khanh described in round canonical tones as a *vaurien* and a *salaud*. He had in mind two ex-Vietminh generals of good repute to lead the next government, "and the rest will have to be young men, perhaps unknown but at least unblemished also."

Thao then confided to me a letter for McGeorge Bundy, President Johnson's special assistant who was at that moment visiting Vietnam. We shook four hands, and left the restaurant separately. I watched his absurd hat bob away among the evening crowds, and then looked back to note the name of the restaurant —*Bahat*—for it was the same one in which I had dined with the Liberation Front delegate less than four months before. But there was nothing odd about that, for the cut-out who took me to my meetings with these two men—one in the service of Saigon, the other in the service of the Vietcong—had been the same.

How lovingly would M.I.-5 or the F.B.I. cross-index a detail like that on the cards, snapping the new and damning link into place like a handcuff. This syllogistic practice of forging circumstantial chains of guilt can lead to hideous mistakes anywhere in the world, and in Vietnam, where only the dark side of the truth has meaning, it was simply not applicable. Old comrades of Thao's seniority in the Vietminh were not only in the swamps of the South, fighting the forces of Saigon. They were in North Vietnam too, and they included his brother Gaston, with whom I had sat on the grass at the edge of the Petit Lac in Hanoi when he was director of the Western Department of Ho Chi Minh's Foreign Ministry. Gaston was a thin, staccato edition of Thao in spectacles, and had been a Vietminh political boss of South Vietnam during the Indochina War when Thao was the intelligence chief. At our last meeting Thao spoke wistfully of an imaginary Saigon regime that could rally nationalists from the Vietcong, and Gaston had spoken wistfully of an imaginary Saigon regime with which Hanoi could negotiate, when I had breakfasted with him in Cambodia just three months before.

In 1962 "Gaston" (now only known as Thuan) was the ambassador of North Vietnam in East Germany, and various scheming minds began to wonder whether "Albert" (now only known as Thao) could not contact him and try to talk him over to the side of South Vietnam. I knew nothing of this until Thao and I were standing at a window of his headquarters one dusk, looking down on the darkening waters of the Delta. Turning his disbelieving wall-eye toward me, he broke silence with a characteristic gunshot of a statement: "I have been asked to see Gaston in Berlin." "Are you going to?" He paused and then shook his head decisively. "No." Gaston was not a hard-core Communist, and if he could be persuaded to rally to Saigon and to participate in a suitable government, the effect among Southern nationalists on both sides of the nonexistent firing line would be electric. But it was useless, Gaston would not rally to Diem or any American puppet. He had already told Thao this in a message sent through an intermediary in Paris, and shortly afterward Gaston was recalled to Hanoi.

Thao never concealed his links with the Vietcong, and in the letter to Bundy he gave me in February 1965 he wrote: "I have been in districts where officers who are my friends are in charge. With them I have visited the shelters and underground Communist fortifications. The bombs and the type of military operations that we are employing at present have no chance of success."

Five months later it was as if some short-circuit in the agonized tangle of Vietnamese intrigue had blown a fuse, leaving many in darkness. In July Thao, condemned to death in absentia and with a price on his head, was lured into a trap north of Saigon, wounded, seized, and later shot dead. There is a tale that it was the new President Nguyen Van Thieu who enticed Thao into the ambush by sending him a message saying that he wanted to rid himself of Air Marshal Ky, and suggesting that they meet in secret to discuss ways and means. But the story is doubtless apocryphal, for it presupposes that Thieu did not in reality want to eliminate Ky.

Thao's letter to Bundy, therefore, rings in the memory like famous last words: "The Communists do not have entire confidence in the Liberation Front. The southern political cadres who were in the resistance from 1945 onwards have, in the majority, come back. I know them all personally. They are only Communists when occasion demands. They have all suffered from the vexations and sectarian measures of the Communists"—and he names four men who by 1969 were leading members of the Liberation Front and of its "Provisional Revolutionary Government for South Vietnam." "If we establish honest government," Thao continues, "and dare to put through profound social and administrative reforms, there is a firm hope that the ex-resistance will follow us and abandon the Communists." He urges the need for land reform, for a new tactical policy that does not involve slaughtering peasants, for a socialist government that can meet the Communist challenge.

I sealed the envelope and early next morning took it to Barry Zorthian, director of the Joint United States Public Affairs Office. "Oh, Thao," he sighed, dropping his bulk into a sturdy chair and rolling large Armenian eyes of frozen cognac toward the ceiling. "Yeah, well, all right, I'll see it gets to Bundy." And I am sure he did. Thao had timed his appeal well. This was a moment of decision. Bundy was verifying the rival reports of State Department, Pentagon, and C.I.A. on the ground, trying to help President Johnson to evaluate the chances of negotiating peace from strength or of fighting the war from weakness. South Vietnam was groggy, on its knees. If no radical changes were made in the whole rotten structure, the Vietcong would knock it out in a matter of months at most.

Having left Thao's letter with Zorthian, I walked circumspectly to the Vietcong radio shop. There are many conditions in life under which a man may suddenly doubt his sanity, and one of them occurs when his eyes simply do not see what his brain is expecting. The whole dusty, ramshackle frontage had gone. It had been replaced by a glossy façade of brass and varnished wood and lattice windows, and a neon sign on which the magic words "American Bar" flickered capriciously. The interior was decorated with a cluster of duty-free GI's and tired tarts. I stood gaping glassily at the entrance from middle of the side street, until watchful eyes within observed me, and a girl in war paint came out to lean on the lintel and lob me a soft "Hi, Joe" like an easy catch. This, evidently, was one battle General Westmoreland had won. My Vietcong contact, I later discovered, had fled to the hills around Dalat. Things had become too hot for him. I shook my head, waved vaguely at the girl, and set off to join friends at the Sporting Club.

"You notice something?" asked an American correspondent,

his eye swiveling absently toward a passing bikini on the edge of the pool. "When Uncle Sam was spending one million dollars a day on this war there were about twenty thousand Vietcong. But by the time we were spending a million and a half a day, the figure had gone up to about twenty-seven thousand Vietcong, and now that we are spending two million a day there are supposed to be thirty-three thousand of them, plus about eighty-five thousand auxiliaries. So maybe the secret of victory is financial de-escalation. By the time we get down to spending a mere hundred thousand bucks a day, the Communists will be reduced to a handful and we can buy them out anyway."

Light, forgivable laughter shimmered for a moment over the sun-flecked water, for no man could live up to the misery of Vietnam every minute. It was Tet—Vietnamese New Year— 1965, but beneath the brittle holiday mood Saigon was a tense, sick city. Nearly twenty-four thousand Americans had been fed into Vietnam, their dollars producing a morbid crop of touts and black-marketeers, gimme-five-piasters boys, and the world's daintiest whores. There was a faint, persistent racial bitterness in the air, like the taste of almonds. The Vietcong had already launched a spectacular attack against the main American air base only twelve miles away. The country was meanwhile bedeviled by military coups and kingmakers, violent Buddhist and student riots, a divided army through whose pastry-weak positions the Vietcong might suddenly push a steel fist and so end the anguish.

Most men nevertheless agreed that this was only a displeasing dream compared with the nightmare that would follow if, unthinkably, Washington tried to stave off disaster with a massive injection of American fighting troops—tall black and white aliens strange to the country, pitted against an enemy who belonged. For it could only end in a fury of frustration and indiscriminate destruction, and it must not happen.

But it did. President Johnson duly made his decision, and it cannot be said that he ignored the possibility of uniting all true Vietnamese nationalists, as Thao had urged, for its implementation pushed many of those who had sided with Saigon into the arms of the Vietcong. On February 7, the Americans began bombing North Vietnam in earnest, and in March the U.S. Marines "stormed ashore," the first of half a million American troops to be thrown into the war to win the South, while back at the ranch President Johnson waited for a "signal" from Hanoi that would open the way to negotiations. For dread of the ghost, as the Malays say, Washington was clasping the corpse.

More than one thousand days and 21,000 dead Americans later, the President was still waiting for his "signal." It was the spring of 1968. There were 500,000 Americans in Vietnam, and my colleague's thesis that Communists multiply in direct ratio to cash invested in their elimination seemed to have been borne out. The war was no longer costing $2 million a day, but $2 billion a month, and the number of enemy had therefore risen to an estimated 175,000 Vietcong, plus 55,000 North Vietnamese regular troops. Three years before, the distant grumbling of guns could sometimes be heard at night in my hotel, but now the windows and walls shook repeatedly as if with a wasting fever as the dark hours were punctuated by the heavy, flat, supercrump of Vietcong 122-mm. rockets slamming into the outer skin of the city. Curfew fell like a guillotine at 8 p.m.

The gleaming Saigon of the past had disappeared. During the day the murmur of war, like an unheeded voice of conscience, was drowned in the urgent din that rose with the diesel fumes from the stinking, rubbish-strewn streets of the sun-baked capital—the shrill chatter of the sidewalk black market in stolen army gear and PX goodies, the inferno of traffic in which monstrous convoys of army trucks and ten thousand scooters fought for supremacy. By the end of 1969 North and South Vietnam, whose respective fertile deltas had once earned them the geographical nickname "Two Baskets of Rice," could more appropriately be called two buckets of blood. The North Vietnamese and the Vietcong had sustained 580,000 mortal casualties, the South Vietnamese at least 100,000 and twice as many wounded. The Americans had lost more than 6,000 aircraft and 40,000 fighting men killed—each one of whom cost an estimated $30,000 to put and keep in the field.

As with all escalators, there had been a mechanical inevitability about the steps that led up to this platform. "The Viets were extremely difficult to defeat," I read in an official record. "They did not come out to fight, but hid in their familiar mountains and used the jungle like a weapon. In consequence, neither side could win. The security forces became increasingly fatigued, and the transport problem involved in supporting half a million men with food and arms progressively worsened. The Viets would raid suddenly, rob, and get away fast, so that just as our army obtained its supplies from the home base, the Viets obtained theirs from our army. Permanent garrisons were established, but the administration only effectively controlled the towns, the plains, and the roads."

This is not a chilling glimpse at the history books of 1980 but a fair translation of the official account of the first invasion of "Vietnam" by Imperial China. It does not describe the frustrations of the twentieth century A.D. but of the third century before Christ. Two thousand years later the Indochina War again taught that a heavily encumbered conventional Franco-Vietnamese army could not crush an elusive Vietminh guerrilla movement that merged with the countryside, any more than a swarm of ants could be exterminated with an iron pickax. Nevertheless, in 1955 the U.S. Military Assistance Advisory Group in Saigon duly began to build up another heavily encumbered, conventional army of South Vietnamese on the strictly unilateral understanding that the Communist North would not start a second guerrilla war to gain control of the South, but might march its regular divisions across the 17th parallel for a good old-fashioned stand-up fight.

The new national army consequently proved incapable of coping with the Vietminh Mark Two—the hit-and-run Vietcong guerrillas. By 1965 victory against the elusive enemy was proving as perishable as birthday cake—all glorious on the day, yet tending to crumble dryly between the fingers one week later when it was found that he had filtered back into the conquered area in undiminished strength. But the United States had modern military might and money, and the enemy did not, and these were therefore the weapons that Washington must now logically deploy. I still hear the despairing words of trapped American officials in Saigon explaining as their jets hit out at the North: "We had to escalate or get out, even if escalation could only lead to a bigger and bloodier stalemate."

It was not difficult to guess what was to come. The enemy and the peasant soon learned what a B-52 bomber could destroy on a single sortie costing no more than $60,000, what defoliants could do to their crops and napalm to their villages, and just how alike armed guerrillas and old grandfathers could look to undiscriminating troops engaged on a "partridge drive" for Vietcong across the farmlands of the Delta. In the holocaust that followed the Tet Offensive of 1968, heavy retaliatory fire wreaked havoc in towns and hamlets, and not long afterward nearly three hundred peasants were killed and wounded in one village alone when troops turned their flame throwers on it "by mistake."

Yet the war still dragged on. Why? General Vo Nguyen Giap, the "Tiger of Dien Bien Phu" and anxious father of the "People's Army of the Democratic Republic of Vietnam," had given me the answer ten years before. "The men who fought the Chinese two thousand years ago were Vietnamese fighting for Vietnam," he said simply. "And so are we." Relaxing between wars, he greeted me in 1957 in Hanoi with a quick, easy smile that the healing years had at last restored to him since his wife had died in a French colonial prison, and he radiated an intelligent, calculating confidence. His features, taken separately, were softly molded in the broad face and almost feminine, the lips full, the chin rounded, the eyebrows like black feathers. Put together however, they became the visor of the soldier, the eyes and facial muscles imposing their own discipline. Giap is unbending on duty, meticulous among the maps, a sagacious organizer, a buttoned-up man in a buttoned-up uniform who watches where he puts his small feet.

He is not infallible, however, nor are his men. His first premature mass attacks against the French in 1951 earned him a bloody nose. Yet his impatience began to creep into his campaigning against their successors in 1968, when Americans sometimes found themselves plowing into close-packed waves of North Vietnamese footsloggers with 105-mm. howitzer shells fired at point-blank range. Many of these "human sea" heroes might have been the dazed products of indoctrination courses which had armed them with a semi-automatic death wish, or they might have thrown themselves into battle only because they knew that f they dodged their destiny at the "front" they would get it in the back from their own comrades. But if Vietnamese Communists come in the usual limitless combinations of vice and virtue, patriotism and cowardice, they nevertheless have an outstanding record for violence and courage. For to the lean and hungry spirits among the mentally recumbent millions that half loved, half hated their French masters, Ho Chi Minh's call to revolution in 1946 was like a voice from the honorable past.

Obsessed by their own colonial ignominy, the Vietnamese rebels subsequently showed a masochistic capacity for self-sacrifice that left most of them rake-thin but radiant over their victory at Dien Bien Phu. Then, nightmarishly, the vanquished French were replaced by the Americans. But the Vietcong soldier was like the bird that screeches its defiance and spoils for a fight if any other trespasses on its territory, even when it is caged. Born unfree, the true patriot was driven by a desperate nationalism and could often die with facility. He did not worry that he could not take it with him. He had nothing of value to take. "I know the Liberation Front cannot gain a purely military victory," Gaston Pham admitted to me in 1964. "But you will see. The Americans will have to back down. They do not have the tenacity of the Vietnamese to win, for it is not their country."

However, it was the country of other Vietnamese who were mobilized against the Vietcong in the regular army of South Vietnam, in the auxiliary Regional Forces and the Self-defense corps. Yet by 1968 one man in every three was deserting. Even in its extreme youth the army suffered from those afflictions normally associated with aging bones, for it was stiff with incompetent officers chosen primarily for their loyalty to President Diem, and in 1969 promotions were still political, officers still clung lovingly to their authority, corruption was still rife, and incompetents still commanded many battalions. Moreover, for the Vietcong or the North Vietnamese the American was still another foreign invader on whom to strop his national will to fight; for the South Vietnamese he was often a hateful ally who contemptuously called him a "slope," a "dink," or a "gook."

Some units of the National Army fought both ably and bravely, but too many soldiers only wanted to see an end to the struggle. "How can we win," one officer asked me, hopelessly. "We Vietnamese can only lose, whatever the results. We are a nation divided, we are killing each other, and God cannot save all of us unless we stop." The whole agonizing business was futile anyway, it seemed to others. "The Communists will soon take over once the Americans go," a South Vietnamese minister commented to me bitterly. "If they cannot do it constitutionally, they will dig up their buried arms in two or three or four years' time, and rise again to seize the country by force as they did after the Geneva Agreement of 1954. It's all been for nothing." For him, the sum just would not come out. It must always leave a recurring decimal of conflict.

In the years between, I had known many heroes of the war, but also many villains of the peace—students, Buddhists, Trotskyists, socialists, nationalists, ex-Vietminh, left-wing intellectuals, neutralist monks, "non-Communists" of the Liberation Front, and men like Thao. They did not all form one vast conspiratorial ring of Marxists. Pawns or patriots, they were Vietnamese expressing Vietnamese ideas. But it was only too easy to dub them "Commie" and throw them toward the Vietcong, just as American escalation threw Ho Chi Minh back upon the arms of the Chinese and the Russians. Ironically, the salvation of South Vietnam will still depend on these twilight men and their amorphous national spirit when the last Marine has gone and the first hopes of long-term political victory may be nursed. For the nature of Communism is that it only starts to lose after it has won.

24 : The Good Guys

Scrawled upon the inside covers of buckled notebooks filled across the years are the most cryptic reminders of all: *"Maurice in gaol Saigon. Raymond no news, believed Hanoi. Michel with Vietcong, putting on weight. Jean Captain in South Vietnamese marines at Tu Duc. Jacquot, marine cadet, ordered to Saigon."* This was the blood and bones of the matter in the form of a sketchy record of five Vietnamese brothers divided by their convictions in a land split between the extremes of Communism and anti-Communism. I collected these scraps of information from time to time for an anxious sister, safe on the outside. To the Americans, Vietnam was the frontier of freedom; to these, a tortured land in which brother killed brother, and classmate classmate. The gap of incomprehension was virtually unbridgeable.

The Vietnamese and the Americans treated each other with the distrust of men with entirely different aims. The American soldier was often conscientious, imbued in the early stages with a sense of mission, machine-turned and impeccable with his weapons and his war theory. He was exasperated by the sight of the Vietnamese old-soldiering their way through the endless maze of military mayhem—"an armored battalion just stayed in a trance, our captain died trying to make them advance," as one bitter librettist put it. The Vietnamese was committed to the long struggle for the duration, and his object was to survive. He looked down on the American as a textbook soldier, a tourist who was committed for a mere 365 days plus 30 days time off and counted them off eagerly on the pocket calendar that seemed to have become standard equipment, along with his boots.

Mr. Tran Van Huong, the prime minister of South Vietnam who saved Thao from the vengeance of Khanh, was described in mid-1969 as the indispensable "darling of the Americans." But just one year before, I had gone to see him in still another of those small, simple Vietnamese homes that conspire to make the large Westerner feel like an uneconomical dinosaur. He was out of office, his face sick and tired beneath a wire brush of white hair, and he did not talk like anybody's darling.

"The experience of Eastern Europe shows that if you enter into a coalition with the Communists, your country ends up Communist," he said. "South Vietnam would go in two weeks. The idea that we would fight on alone against the Vietcong if the Americans left is just talk. But, after all, we are all Vietnamese. In Eastern Europe the Communist states have settled down to a national life that you could call nearly normal. This could have happened to us, and anyway we could not possibly have suffered so much from the Communists as we have done through this war. The Vietnamese people tend to blame the Americans for all their troubles. And perhaps they are right."

In the old imperial city of Hue on the River of Perfume in Central Vietnam, men with reason to curse the bigots of both sides might well have agreed. The Vietcong had thrown themselves into the town during the New Year offensive of 1968 and perpetrated a massacre of innocents among the local Vietnamese. But the Americans had blasted them out of it again in accordance with those humane principles of modern attack which prompt commanders to saves the lives of soldiers by first pulverizing the enemy zone with bombs and shells, reducing towns to stinking tombs of rubble and plaster commemorating the Unknown Civilian buried beneath.

All is a matter of perspective, however. For many Americans the Vietnam War was a first- and last-ditch stand against Communism in Southeast Asia. Behind Hanoi were the aggressive Chinese sectarians, rogue Marxists preaching a world revolution that would impose their totalitarian dogma on all humanity. Relentless in their conviction that the bloodiest war was "just" if it advanced the sacred cause of Maoism, they insisted that the ideological end excused the means, for theirs was the only true doctrine. Their visage was a screaming, fanatical face, full of teeth and hatred, glimpsed in a shuffle-past of Peking Red Guards.

The urbane California lawyer with whom I lunched in Singapore during the early stages of the Chinese Cultural Revolution hardly seemed to belong to the same division of mammals. But he soon proved that he did. Well-traveled, well-educated, he argued his case in a voice as smooth as sump oil while easing his way with practiced caution through a menu the size of *The New York Times*, and it went like this: The United States had the most perfect democratic system in the world. It was therefore essential that the United States remain powerful and prosperous, so that Washington could see that the American form of democracy prevailed everywhere. "So the struggle in Vietnam," he went on, "is a vital confrontation between the United States and China. It is a struggle for big stakes in which Vietnam and the Vietnamese are themselves of no importance. Even if a million Vietnamese died, it would still be irrelevant." As for the contention that defending freedom meant defending the right of the Vietnamese to choose their own form of government, "that's just a lot of semantics."

This was the kind of talk which made many Asians feel that

they were caught between two intolerant, powerful, often ruthless antagonists. The war against the enemies of democracy had become a righteous crusade, leading to the same savage abuses and brutality that had characterized all the other crusades in history. The American who believed that he and only he could build Jerusalem on earth was moving perilously close to the sixteenth-century religious sectarian who called murdering heretics "holy work." And no one would have agreed with this general principle more promptly than a Vietcong terrorist.

"Jacquot," records a later notebook, *"gone USA for course in U.S. Marine School. Jean, now major commanding battalion of SVN marines, usually Tu Duc. Raymond, with VC near Dalat, okay; Maurice, out of gaol, teaching in Saigon; Michel, in Hanoi, rumour may be sent south to fight Americans . . ."*

The Vietnamese could scarcely be blamed for beginning to suspect that preserving the American way of life was becoming the Vietnamese way of death. Obsessed with a grand global strategy, many Americans holding more immediate power than my California acquaintance appeared to be as little concerned about the fate of the Vietnamese themselves. The Pentagon used the country as a testing ground for tactics and weapons, and received news of heavy Vietnamese casualties with impressive equanimity. A proposal that the U.S. Air Force should drop a line of atomic bombs right across the 17th parallel, blasting it into a belt of scrambled radioactive jungle and effectively separating the two halves of Vietnam, was among the less lethal schemes kicked around at command level. It took a military brain at its most professional and pure to conceive the brilliantly simple alternative: to start at the southernmost tip of Vietnam and roll it up systematically, as it were, destroying everything in the process from the armed enemy to "psycho-social" targets like hospitals, schools, and churches, and leaving it all politically decontaminated and fit for democracy. It was as if the American liberator were toying with plans for converting this unconsidered trifle of a nation in the right-hand bottom corner of Asia into a second, slow-motion Hiroshima.

An outsider might admire unstintingly the American combat

soldier at his best, could recognize that devoted American field workers were risking their own lives to improve those of the Vietnamese peasant, and that in America itself millions were honestly examining their consciences. But in the minds of many Vietnamese in the middle, the American who bombed him and the American who wept over him—the hawkish and the mawkish —merged into a schizophrenic figure as unnervingly inexplicable as Jekyll-and-Hyde.

Those who would not plunge after him in his pursuit of the infidel, however, were made to feel the cutting edge of his disfavor. During a short, hot-summer visit that I made to Washington in 1967, Eugene Rostow, Undersecretary of State for Political Affairs, told me he found it extremely odd that although the Australians had come halfway around the world to help the British twice in two world wars, the British would not "go to the aid" of the Australians in Vietnam. The fact that the Australians had committed three hundred thousand men to World War II and fewer than eight thousand to Vietnam was presumably irrelevant. The struggle had assumed the ridiculous dimensions of a third world war in his mind, and he did not even realize it.

When I asked Dean Rusk, then Secretary of State, whether he thought Whitehall should act on Mr. Rostow's stricture, he replied with a quick, cold snap: "That's up to the conscience of the British government," and then added: "We know today who are our friends and who are not. And our friends are the allies who are fighting beside us in Vietnam." I also asked him whether the United States would consider halting the bombing in North Vietnam. "To please whom?" inquired Rusk, in a voice like a bastard file. "The left wing of the British Labour Party?"

I am sure that Dean Rusk was aware that a nation's first duty was to itself, and that it was this enlightened self-interest which had persuaded the United States to stay out of the First World War until 1917 (by which time Britain had taken more than a million casualties in Flanders alone), and out of the second until the end of 1941 (by which time the City of London had gone up in flames and the Nazis dominated all Europe). Washington had also prudently refrained from throwing in troops to stop the

Communists from taking over Cuba, China, Hungary, Poland, Bulgaria, Czechoslovakia, Yugoslavia, Rumania, Albania, half of Germany, half of Korea, and half of Vietnam, and in 1963 the Americans made no ill-considered moves when President Sukarno set out to destroy the democratic Federation of Malaysia with the biggest Communist Party in the free world as his ally, and the smiling approval of the Chinese in Peking.

Indonesia had a population ten times that of Malaysia and was ten times as big. Under the Anglo-Malayan Defense Agreement the new Commonwealth state was mainly protected by some fifty thousand British servicemen, but the Indonesians had more than three hundred thousand regulars under arms and the most powerful fleet and air force of any country in Southeast Asia, bought on credit from Moscow. They were well placed to make mischief for the fragile federation, whose two halves had only just been joined with little more than faith for a fixative.

One year later Indonesian personnel were still undergoing training in the United States, Washington was still giving Sukarno $40 million worth of "residual" long-term economic and military assistance. In February 1965 Sukarno inaugurated an atomic reactor at Bandung, built with the help of the U.S. Atomic Energy Commission and a U.S. government grant of $350,000. The United States government next declared that it had no objection to the sale of an American $3 million jam-proof Tropospheric Scatter Fixed Communications System to Djakarta, which would provide an up-to-date radio network linking all major military headquarters in the Indonesian republic. American armalite rifles began turning up in the hands of Sukarno's guerrillas, and Washington applied diplomatic pressure to stop the British from hitting back at their bases on Indonesian territory.

Mr. Howard Jones, United States ambassador in Djakarta, had apparently convinced the State Department that if the United States embargoed aid to Djakarta, and the British were allowed to be beastly to the infiltration forces that Sukarno was lining up on his side of the frontier to attack Malaysian Borneo, the Bung would lean even further toward the Communists. On the other hand, a friendly America could exert a soothing influence over him and might eventually "swing him round."

Few Asians were impressed. Most shared the sour conviction that Washington's conciliatory gestures evoked no reciprocal tenderness toward the United States but simply encouraged the Indonesians to think that they could with impunity intensify their terrorist campaign against Malaysia. Their fears were borne out. By August 1965 Mr. Jones, the man who "understood" Sukarno, was being accused in Djakarta of plotting aggression against the republic, and his successor was greeted with placards inscribed "Stay away from Indonesia" and a cutting lecture from Sukarno. Despite his many suitable qualifications for the job— his horror of democracy, his autocratic rule, and his corrupt government—the Bung was not to be "our son-of-a-bitch" after all.

On the other hand, Indonesian Confrontation gave a new if evanescent shine to the tarnished and blackened British image. Britain had been the victor of World War II that had led the way toward the welfare state and given India, Burma, Ceylon, and later Malaya freedom to follow if they would. But subsequently the evolving political characteristics of the Briton had begun to distort this presentable portrait. His inconstancies blurred its edges, and he became hard on the eyes. He tagged along behind the Americans, joined the Southeast Asia Treaty Organization, put troops into Korea—and then sold buses to Cuba and Viscounts to Peking. He was co-chairman of the Geneva Agreement on Indochina and advocated neutralism for Laos—but simultaneously he trained hundreds of South Vietnamese officers in anti-guerrilla warfare at his jungle school in south Malaya. Asians understand flexibility, but it must be justified by results. It fascinated them that all Britain's power, perfidy, and political wisdom could be ground into meaningless fragments of seemingly uncorrelated action.

By 1966, however, the British not only had slugged it out stubbornly with the Communist terrorists of Malaya for twelve years but had successfully blocked off the Indonesians as well. As middleweights they had proved that they carried a useful punch. "We should like the British to keep their military bases here," Rajaratnam told me at the end of Confrontation, sitting in an expensively paneled coffin of an office whose windows had been walled up against Indonesian terrorists. "The British are welcome, and for three good reasons: they are not trying to build any more empires, they are not playing power politics in this region, and they want to go home anyway."

With the lessons of Confrontation behind them, on the other hand, Singapore and Malaysian leaders said to me in almost identical words: "To the Americans, Indonesia represents more than a hundred million potential anti-Communists. That is all the arithmetic the United States wants to know. If the Indonesians attacked us again, do you really believe that they would back us and risk estranging Djakarta? You saw what happened last time. They would sacrifice us as pawns to win Indonesia's allegiance."

For Washington there was no right or wrong, it appeared, only white or red. But most Asians were not susceptible to the mental warp that automatically translated the "free political education" offered in South Vietnam into "compulsory brainwashing" when it was given in North Vietnam, or that would damn *The Nation* for a rose-red weekly twice as old as *Time* and blacklist its readers as "Commies." That kind of blinker-visioned outlook earned the United States, somewhat unfairly, a reputation for exporting more Joe McCarthy than Jefferson.

During the sixties many felt that they were being manipulated for questionable ends. There was a revulsion from the long queue of those who shambled cap-in-hand up to the American pay desk, and from the type of divisions-for-dollars deal that took forty-eight thousand South Korean troops to Vietnam in exchange for massive United States economic assistance to Seoul. In Saigon men murmured that they were no longer masters in their own house. In Thailand the Foreign Minister remarked waspishly, "We are not the fifty-first state." In Singapore Lee Kuan Yew tartly told a television audience in 1967, "I am not going to be the monkey of the American organ grinder." There was a contagious dread that control of events was rapidly slipping out of the small, weak hands of the Southeast Asians into the clutches of two Big Brothers, one the unpredictable servant of Mao, the other of the machine.

Nowhere in the entire disaster area, however, was the sense of being prodded and pinched and plucked at by foreign fingers more acute than in Laos. As the Laotians themselves say: "When the buffaloes fight, it is the grass that gets trampled."

25 : Civilizing the Natives

Nothing could have been more incongruous than that the indolent, sun-washed country of the Laotians should have become the loose hinge on which the fate of Southeast Asia was to swing, for Laos is the land of *Bau Pinh Yanh,* the "never mind" that makes *mañana* sound like *Achtung!*

Bewildered and uncomprehending, the Laos were not cut out for the task of defending the free world against the international Communist conspiracy, especially as most of them had never heard of either. Prince Souvanna Phouma once told me that he did not believe there were more than one hundred truly Marxist cadres in the whole of the left-wing Pathet Lao guerrilla movement. Prince Souphannouvong, the Pathet Lao leader, solemnly swore that his Communists were fundamentally loyal to the Laotian monarchy and the principles of neutralism.

Nonetheless, by Christmas 1960 the face of Vientiane was pockmarked with shell holes and shattered, burned-out buildings, over which festoons of twisted telephone wire hung like un-combed hair. Shops were boarded up, there was no water, and in the Hotel Constellation frayed correspondents groped their way around by candlelight. The ideological struggle had hit the Laotian capital.

This particular round had opened in April 1960 with an elec-toral victory for the "Pro-Americans" which had been so blatantly rigged that the Americans themselves had found it a little breath-taking. "We did not think our friends would go quite so far," one C.I.A. officer said in Vientiane. "But the main thing is that the right side is in." When in August, therefore, a neutralist paratrooper captain called Kong Le upset this satisfactory state of affairs by seizing Vientiane in a *coup d'état*, Washington was displeased. And when the new government under Prince Sou-vanna Phouma insisted on seeking a reconciliation with the pro-Communist Pathet Lao, the United States obliged him to forgo further aid.

Instead, American agents in Bangkok and Hong Kong began buying up all the available Laotian currency on the market in order to pay the troops of the "anti-Communist" General Phoumi Nosavan, who was bent upon throwing Souvanna Phouma out of office again. Accordingly, Souvanna Phouma, the pay of his troops and police six months in arrears, started taking aid from the Soviet Union in order to offset the American boy-cott, and the Russians obligingly airlifted to Vientiane not only food and fuel but a battery of howitzers for its defense. The right-wing army of General Phoumi then moved up from the southeast to wrest the capital from Kong Le and Souvanna Phouma, and for four days the two Lao forces hammered away at each other across the town with mortars and artillery.

Caught on the wrong foot by events, I finally reached Vien-tiane in the monstrous belly of an R.A.F. Blackburn Beverley transport aircraft feeling like some latter-day Jonah, surrounded by eight tons of medical supplies for the choked hospitals of the capital, and hoping that the airfield would be safely in the hands of one side or the other as we lumbered toward it at 130 miles an hour.

In the shell-shocked Hotel Constellation, where the soporific Laotian flies and the low canvas chairs that set one's knees about one's ears nevertheless looked much the same, I learned that my colleagues had been able to file only a short joint telegram to their agencies and newspapers once a day over the radio of the British embassy. They had, however, seized at least one opportunity to work off their frustrations, for as shells and mortar bombs fell on all sides of their unhappy headquarters in the middle of the town, a thick-skinned Australian Communist writer insulted one of their number in the bar.

While the sky spewed death outside, therefore, those gathered together for shelter within threw themselves into battle against one another. A genial American press photographer laid the Australian flat with a felicitous blow, but within minutes found himself saving the man's life by forcibly restraining him from plunging out into the inferno in the street. A woman went into hysterics and a gallant Frenchman thereupon added a deft touch of comedy amid the pandemonium inside and out by playing the role of the neutralist, reminding the disheveled Anglo-Saxons in tones of unbelievable pomposity: "Gentlemen, gentlemen, there are *ladies* present." The scene was like a miniature Laos within a Laos. For although there were "ladies present" throughout the land, the big alien antagonists were not to be deterred from treating it as their fight ring.

Phoumi captured Vientiane, and Souvanna Phouma was compelled to make common cause with the Communists to the north. "The Americans have made me utterly dependent on the Russians now," he told me, moodily chewing on a cheroot, when I met him subsequently at the rebel headquarters which he shared with the Pathet Lao on the Plain of Jars. The dismal farce was not to lose pace, however. Having suspended aid to Souvanna Phouma because he tried to unite the country by coming to terms with the Pathet Lao, the Americans now began to have second thoughts, and Washington was soon suspending aid to General Phoumi in turn—in his case because he failed to try to unite the country by coming to terms with the estranged Souvanna Phouma. But of course it is misleading to write "Washington." "The trouble with us," an elderly Lactian statesman said to me with a shrug during these stirring days, "is that we have three governments and all of them American—the State Department, the Pentagon, and the C.I.A."

Phoumi's reaction was to defy the Americans and go on a spending spree, and when I next arrived in Laos the roads of Vientiane were being widened, a set of traffic lights—the first in the country—had been purchased and put up at one arbitrarily chosen crossroads, and the "Monument aux Morts" was being completed with a large quantity of cement originally provided by the United States for the specific purpose of extending the airport runway. But in the unforeseeable future Souvanna Phouma was to return to Vientiane as prime minister, and Phoumi was to end up plotting in exile in Thailand.

The neutrality of Laos became official under the Geneva Agreement of 1962, and was endorsed by all the powers in play. Promises in writing are only on paper, however, and in 1963 I found Souvanna Phouma still stretched between extreme right and extreme left in a nerve-racking effort to bring them together and so reunite Laos as a neutral state. As I walked into his office in Vientiane, a small, boyish figure ran past me—Kong Le, now a general. "I have just told him," said Souvanna Phouma a trifle petulantly, "to go back to the Pathet Lao and start talks with them again. How can we hope for national union when all these people insist on quarreling all the time?" He looked harassed, a morose honey bear who knew in his heart that he would never find the sweet ambrosia of peace and unity. "But what is the good? The Pathet Lao are almost impossible to talk to, because they are creatures of the Vietnamese Communists, behind whom in turn are the Chinese. Meanwhile, now that I am back in Vientiane my government is again utterly dependent upon American aid, and so I am labeled an imperialist. There would be no difficulty in resolving the differences between us Laotians— if only all the foreigners would go away and leave us alone." There were Russian, Chinese, and North Vietnamese missions in the "neutral" Laotian capital, all accredited directly to the king and therefore free to denounce the prince and his government as a collection of capitalist puppets. On the way out, I passed the Chinese ambassador on his way in. Souvanna Phouma was having a trying day.

For the bemused Lao, who was faintly surprised in the first place to find that Russians were white, the struggle of the powers was scarcely comprehensible, but the war had meaning. It meant that more and more young men who should have been behind plows were now behind guns. It meant that Laos, which should have been self-supporting in grain, was importing seventy thousand tons of rice by 1968, that out of a population of fewer than three million, there were nearly six hundred thousand refugees, at least one-quarter of whom had to be fed and given shelter. The Americans paid for nearly everything, but to the Lao it seemed that the Americans were paying him just to suffer, while on the other side the Chinese and the Vietnamese Communists made him suffer without paying. By 1969 there were more than fifty thousand Vietnamese troops in the country, and Laos had virtually lost her two northern provinces.

All hope of reconciliation and reunification rested on respect of the Geneva Agreement of 1962. But even this was in turn dependent upon a settlement among nine different kinds of foreigner in an alien land—Vietnam. One thing appeared to be certain: the Laos were not to be allowed to resolve anything for themselves simply by folding their own hands in peace.

However, brother has fought brother with such distressing frequency in Asia that a fine military tradition has grown up, whereby victory and defeat may be decided by simple mathematics rather than unnecessary bloodshed. When warlords contended for the control of China in the twenties, the army which was smaller or had fewer machine guns or less money often capitulated to the larger force after firing a few shots in the air for the sake of appearances. This civilized custom was honored by the rebels in Sumatra, whose swift withdrawals enabled towns and strongpoints to change hands in a peaceful and tidy manner without classmate killing classmate. For only holy wars flout humanitarian convention today.

In Laos during the sixties the game was often geared to the

movements of the sun. If a Laotian detachment heard gunfire at dusk, it would abandon its post for the night; the Pathet Lao guerrillas would then move in, but they would leave at dawn, and the Royal Army would reoccupy the position again (after breakfast). In this way casualties were avoided but stirring communiqués could be issued and profitable indents for expended ammunition filed. When the Pathet Lao threatened the key town of Nam Bac in 1968, the defending troops promptly withdrew from it, the men dispersing in an orderly manner from the battle area and turning up a few days later to rejoin their units once all was quiet. No one was so impolite as to suggest that this was tantamount to desertion in the face of the enemy.

The Laos are not natural soldiers, and their lack of martial aptitude can be measured by the fact that even their Communist-indoctrinated guerrillas are incompetent. The principal reason for this depressing situation is that the Lao does not like to kill. The devout Buddhist knows that he should not be personally responsible for the death of any living thing—he has no right to change its destiny, and anyway a Pathet Lao (or a pi-dog) may be Grandpa reborn. Even the birds in a Laotian cockfight are not fitted with spurs, so that neither is slain.

The infantrymen that attacked Vientiane in 1960 for the sake of Phoumi and the C.I.A. fired most of their shots into the air, and mathematically minded American advisers calculated that in most circumstances Laos aimed all small arms upward at an angle of thirty degrees to make sure of missing everything. According to my slightly incoherent notes, few soldiers died in this battle, but there were at least 450 victims among the civilian spectators, and many more lost their homes, for by then a chink had been found in the armor of Buddhist scruple.

The Lao recruit was first persuaded of the essential innocence of impersonal weapons like heavy guns whose shells killed indiscriminately and out of sight, for their crews were not directly responsible for any individual death. And in time he showed that he could progress from that starting point, so that it was later recorded with some satisfaction that he was beginning to adopt a more responsible attitude generally toward the serious business of slaughtering his fellows. I saw Laotian gunners handle 105-mm. howitzers in action as far back as 1961 at a place called Phou Khoun, and by the distorted philosophy of the newspaper-man considered myself lucky to have done so.

Laos is one of the most frustrating countries in Asia to cover, for the highways are narrow, potholed tracks winding through almost impenetrable mountains of steep plaited jungle, hardly any of them are passable all year around, and much of the countryside is in Communist hands. The reporter may spend most of his time trying to get out of Vientiane, and never more vainly than when his objective is a battle somewhere in the back-of-beyond.

But in January 1961 the rebels, advancing westward from the Plain of Jars, took the strategic junction of Phou Khoun and so cut the main road that threads its way northward through the mountains for some 250 miles from Vientiane to Luang Prabang. The Royal Army then set out to dislodge them, and at that moment Fortune turned upon me her brief, meretricious smile. I happened to be on the airfield at Vientiane when a Sikorsky chopper, flown by an under-the-counter American Marine in an anonymous flying suit, dropped in for ten minutes to unload a few wounded and take on a few bags of rice for Muong Kassy, headquarters of the regiment that was carrying out the counter-attack. As no one else was in sight, formalities could be waived, so after a brief exchange of courtesies I climbed up the side of the helicopter into the seat beside the pilot, and fastened the safety straps over my thin tropical suit.

The chopper lurched off the wilting grass in a cloud of dust, fluttered north over the parched floor of the Mekong Valley, and began to weave its way purposefully among the gray, ridge-backed heights that rose abruptly from the flat plain on all sides. Deep in the hills, Muong Kassy lay astride the road some two hundred miles to the north, a cluster of wooden bungalows on stilts from which there arose into the cold blue heavens thin threads of woodsmoke and the soft, nasal lament of a solitary *khene*, the Lao syrinx that has the nostalgic quality of distant bagpipes. For the rest, the village slept. And so did the regimental head-

quarters. The regimental commander was a certain Colonel Oudone Sananikone—tall, amiable, agreeably ugly. After his siesta
he greeted me with a wry grin. I was in luck, he said, a convoy
would leave for the front in the morning. I could go with it.

At dawn next day this convoy, drawn up on the narrow, stony,
rutted farm track that turns out to be the road, gives food for
thought. It consists of two topless trucks, one loaded with fourteen sacks of rice, the other with eight open oil drums filled with
drinking water, for the colonel's troops eighteen miles farther on
through the tangled jungle and the limestone gorges are not only
hungry but thirsty. For this pitiful grocery run we are nevertheless to have an escort of two armored cars and two more open
trucks mounting Bren guns on their cabin roofs and packed with
a full platoon of riflemen in French and American steel helmets.

On the map, the road to the front is a mere kink in a brash
red line. On the ground it proves otherwise. I climb up beside
the driver of the water truck and we jolt into the first deep ruts,
over the first potholes and the first spurts of sharp shale that
make up this section of the thousand-mile long Highway Number 13 of all Indochina. The track is about twelve feet wide and
soon becomes a ledge which winds its way along the steep fall
of mountainside. The small dust-stained clutch of vehicles grates
forward, shuddering and dipping and bouncing at an average
speed of six miles an hour, and the water slops out of the oil
drums at every lurch. A small pig tied to the side of the armored
car in front of us squeals in a cross falsetto, and hens in a bamboo basket jammed behind its machine gun shift and cluck uneasily. The gunner, dressed in jungle green with a peacock feather
stuck through his beret, snatches at a tangle of convolvulus and
stuffs the stem of one delicate blue trumpet into the barrel—
just as we pass a blown-up and burned-out armored car exactly
like his. The country is ideal for guerrillas skilled in ambush, and
the enemy has Chinese mines.

We edge into a clearing and groan to a halt outside a stilted
village. Bare-breasted women are sifting grain. Raw meat hangs
from a tree, dripping blood. It is a peaceful, almost idyllic scene.
Suddenly there is a shout of warning and a man runs fast toward

the surrounding thickets. In a second our infantry escort is scattering frantically. To fight or flee? Unhappily, I think I know the answer. Then there is a laugh, another shout, and the original runner reappears, holding a squawking hen by the legs. Soldiers emerge from the underbrush, grinning a little sheepishly. The convoy comes to order, and we push on.

By midday we can go no farther. Halfway around the haunch of a hillside four howitzers are lined up across the road, firing over the gorge at the next ridge. Two officers are squatting with their backs to the mountain wall, one listening to the snarl of a small radio telephone, the other working out coordinates on a map. Sights are adjusted, the motley gun crews in sneakers and denims, butt ends of cigarettes dangling from their lips, slam home the breech blocks with almost Gallic panache and the shells scream hysterically over the valley. The target is the T-junction of Phou Khoun farther along the winding road.

Half the water in our drums has splashed away. The soldiers tumble out of the trucks and sit down at the roadside to eat balls of rice and play an obscure game of cards as the guns continue to bark from their mountain perch. Happily, the enemy has not brought up guns which can bark back, for the convoy is now an untidy cluster of vehicles and men crowding up against the howitzers. From below us rises the crackle of rifle fire, so I edge apologetically past the four howitzers and set off along the road to find the Lao infantry. But the battery commander takes one look at this chilly apparition in his polka-dot bow tie and chemical city suiting and says no. Neither the rice nor the water nor I get any farther, but, armed with the moral superiority of the thwarted, I can now sting him for a briefing.

At dusk the trucks start back toward Muong Kassy with four wounded. It is the first time the army has run a night convoy, for fear of ambushes, and hardly have we completed the first punishing kilometer, sidling forward precariously without lights along the rim of the range, when the armored car in front opens up with a machine gun, there is a cry of alarm, and once more the troops are leaping from their trucks with un-Laotian alacrity. But the convoy soon comes to order again. The machine gunner

fired by mistake, it appears. Three hours later I am back in
Muong Kassy, frozen stiff and still streaming sweat. The mission
has been accomplished. So much petrol has been wasted bringing
a little rice and water closer to the troops that regimental supplies
of fuel are now exhausted in their turn, forward units will be
without ammunition for half a week, and no more wounded can
be evacuated.

At the headquarters bungalow the convoy commander huddles
over the maps with his master, but after he has gone off into the
darkness the colonel calls me over to the porch. "Now *you* please
tell me what's going on up there," he says, glancing at the retreating back of the captain. I throw myself into what I hope is a
soldierly report, to find myself baffled by something for which
World War II experience had not prepared me: the colonel's
two war maps tell two different stories, the one often placing the
enemy where the other places own troops, and vice versa. But
I do my best. And so subsequently did he. When I last saw him
in 1968 he was not only a general, he was chief-of-staff of the
Royal Laotian Army.

On returning to Vientiane in a chopper with the four wounded
in order to cable my story, I found that I need not have gone to
Phou Khoun at all. For the Laotian Minister of Information had
already given my colleagues an admirably clear and authoritative
account of how the junction had been captured. This was the
war as we usually saw it. Had Phou Khoun really been taken the
previous afternoon, as he claimed, I could testify that the Royal
Army's victorious artillery must have been decimating the Royal
Army's victorious infantry under my very nose. But the neat maps
and facts and figures available in the capital would look fine on
the pages of the newspapers in London, New York, and Paris.

The minister produced for us a one-man war far more absorbing than the incoherent and pointless plot the opposing armies
were unraveling in the field. Shortly after his imaginary fall of
Phou Khoun, he disclosed that hordes of Chinese and North
Vietnamese had overrun a northern province, with which all
radio communication had therefore broken down. Distrustful
journalists later established that the army commander in that

region had quarreled with Vientiane and in a fit of pique had just switched off his W/T set for a few days in order to enjoy a little peace and quiet.

I preferred another minister, who found a crumpled piece of paper in his pocket while eating lunch after a press conference and remarked gently: "Oh dear! Here is a list of the army's victories I was supposed to announce. I really have no head for military matters." That seemed to sum it up. Visiting the headquarters of a Lao general with ten thousand men under command, one-third of them élite paratroopers, I was struck by a notice on the door of his office. Anywhere else it might have read "Walls have ears" or "Know your enemy." But this one said *La tranquillité avant tout:* "Tranquillity above all."

If the Lao were an arrant coward, his distaste for war might still be admirable. But he is not afraid of death: he simply does not seek it prematurely for himself or others. The Lao word for death is the same as for Nirvana, and a house bereaved is a "happy house." It is dangerous to mourn, for mourning may bind the spirit of the dead to this illusory world. A cremation is therefore an occasion for all-night parties and roistering, the house must be filled with laughter and the family settle down to drinking, dancing, and a little gentle gambling. Since final release from a long and wearisome succession of incarnations must be the ultimate object of the human operation, "Death is the most important event in thy life." And like all the best things in life, it is free.

However, a man must be sure what he is dying or killing for, the Laos would say. Any heroic impressions gained during the battle for Vientiane may have been obliterated by the spectacle of soldiers rushing into Buddhist temples in full fighting fig, only to emerge again a few minutes later dressed as harmless bonzes in saffron robes. But these did not necessarily lack courage. They simply lacked conviction. And Buddhists believe that fate should not be tempted lightly. You do not play chicken with God.

26 : *My Country Right or Left*

A perceptible shiver of dismay nevertheless fled through the sub-continent in 1968 when the Americans first showed signs of doing what they had so often been asked to do—go home. For even vociferous critics of Washington among Asian anti-Commu-nists slept easier in their beds behind the shield the Pentagon provided.

Yet local leaders were torn two ways, since Americans not only made dangerously compromising friends, but they came from a considerable distance and would therefore make safer enemies than "700 million Chinese" just over the sill of Southeast Asia. America was far, China near. Mao had unified his intimidatingly vast country. By mid-1967 the Chinese had run the nuclear gamut from A to H in the record time of two and a half years. And they were unpredictable.

No Asians were more exquisitely sensitive to the threat they posed than the Burmese, who remember what happened when their own King Sinbyushin defeated the Chinese two hundred years ago. The Chinese sued for peace, and King Sinbyushin demanded the daughter of the emperor as part of the price. In due course a retinue arrived bearing aloft in a gilt sedan chair a lady of great accomplishments. The court criers went forth and proclaimed that a Chinese princess had been received in the royal bedchamber. But the celestial lady proved to be a member of the oldest profession in the world, dressed up for the part. "And the moral of that story," a Burmese editor told me in his rat-ridden office in Rangoon, "is that with these people you cannot win."

Rangoon's attitude toward Peking had been determined by the disagreeable knowledge that Burma was an overstretched, underdeveloped state of only 25 million people which shared more than thirteen hundred miles of wild and remote mountain frontier with the Chinese colossus to the north. From the first, therefore, Burmese leaders had held out a slightly shaking hand of friendship to the People's Republic across the fence. The Chinese might give the "White Flag" Burmese Communist Party leaders asylum while their armed guerrillas continued to terrorize the Burmese countryside, and the obstreperous behavior of the local Chinese Red Guards in Rangoon in 1967 might lead to an open breach between the two countries, but in the last analysis the Burmese knew whose protestations of affection could bring them the most comfort, and at the end of 1969 General Ne Win was begging hotheads "not to give vent to anger" against the Chinese.

Malaysian and Indonesian ministers were meanwhile protesting that their governments were ready to be friends with China, if only the Chinese would just stop fomenting revolution all the time. In Manila President Marcos said that he was in favor of establishing diplomatic ties with Peking. In Bangkok, a twoheaded image of Thai policy was already engaged in cross-talk with itself. Mr. Thanat Khoman, the Thai Foreign Minister, justified a suggestion that Bangkok open the dialogue with China by saying blandly "in a world of changing allegiances, enemies

have become the best of friends, and allies the worst of enemies."
With his other voice he remained vociferously hawkish, castigat-
ing American "doves," who "aspire to withdraw into their quiet
parochial concerns." For it was still desirable that the United
States defeat Communism at a decent distance and across two
frontiers in Vietnam if possible, and the forty-eight thousand
American servicemen in Thailand had not yet ceased to be an
asset and started to become a political embarrassment. "But that
day must inevitably come, my dear fellow," a close aide of the
Foreign Minister once told me coolly in the impeccable English
they cultivate there. And it soon did.

   *Michel, no news. Raymond, okay, now with VC in the south.
Maurice, still teaching in Saigon. Jacquot, still on a course in
America* . . . I jotted it all down. "Would you say Jacquot was
pro-American?" I asked their old father as we sat by his fish pond
in Saigon, sipping lime juice and soda. "Pro-American," he
scoffed. "Pro-Western, pro-Communist, anti-Communist. How
can you presume to label us all? There are a hundred different
reasons why Vietnamese who are not Communist are with the
Vietcong, and a further hundred reasons why Vietnamese who
are not pro-Western rally to the Saigon government and the
Americans. Look at me, with all my children spread all over the
board. What do I think of all these Americans?" He laughed
softly and threw up his hands. "I cannot tell even my own
family. Do you expect me to tell you?"

   The push-button nomenclature of loyalties which demands
that an Asian be unambiguously for or against a lot of foreigners
and their alien ideologies compounds the incomprehension between West and East. The American is not automatically loved
for his big eyes or hated for his big mouth. The most important
thing about him is that he is a stranger, to be weighed cold in
the sensitive balance of Asian self-interest. "Pro-American" Thais
talk of his presence as a "necessary evil." In Vietnam, "anti-
Communist" Vice-President Nguyen Cao Ky makes it known
that he has more regard for Ho Chi Minh than for any "foreigners." But no "pro-American" better expressed the Asian's

severely pragmatic approach to rich benefactors than Diem and his brother Nhu.

Nhu defined the Americans not as friends but as "material allies." "I want their money, arms, and equipment," he said shortly before his murder, "but not them." "They have done everything to push me into the arms of Ho Chi Minh," he later complained, and like much that is veiled, this threat was not idle. One night in September 1963 he slipped down to a rendezvous in a Cholon hotel, taking only a bodyguard to stand outside one of the rooms. There he conferred until three o'clock in the morning with two go-betweens from Hanoi and several members of the Polish delegation to the International Control Commission. Within a few days Diem summoned Colonel Thao and asked him a little diffidently whether he thought Ho Chi Minh really wanted to carry on with the struggle when their two systems now had "so much in common." (Ho was soon to describe a dead Diem as "a patriot in his own way.")

Even in that moment of dubious glory when "pro-American" Phoumi had seized Vientiane with the indiscreet assistance of the C.I.A., he was already a very questionable ally in the cause of anti-Communism, for the simple reason that he was not an American, he was a Lao. Ministers to whom I spoke privately in Vientiane at that time emphasized that Phoumi's government wanted to practice a neutralist policy, and some prophesied that he would wait for the right moment and then negotiate with the Communists. There is no paradox here. "Do you think only Souvanna Phouma is a neutralist?" one asked me with a light Lao chuckle. "We are all neutralists—only we are in competition with one another."

Neutralism means keeping out of other people's fights, and it appeals to Asians, who are less anxious than the big powers might think to find out which of them is the paper tiger. If there was an awkward moment for Singapore when a trade mission from Hanoi arrived in the republic in the middle of the Vietcong's Tet Offensive in February 1968, it could easily be argued away. Only a few months before, American purchasing agents in the island had bought steel from Communist China for building bunkers in Vietnam against Vietcong attacks, and they were also believed to have ordered North Vietnamese cement through Singapore merchants for the same purpose.

Although the Singapore army is trained by Israelis, Lee Kuan Yew is a friend of President Nasser. When Israel knocked out the U.A.R. in the blitzkrieg of 1967, I therefore asked Rajaratnam how the government could take this dispassionately. He looked at me with wide-open eyes, shaking his head slightly as if I had unfairly accused him of murder. "Nasser did not consult us before moving against Israel, so we are not required to take a stand," he replied. They were the words of the immaculate neutral.

Singapore must be politically acrobatic, for it is a predominantly Chinese chip of an enclave in a predominantly Malay region. "Heaven help us if Peking offers to recognize us," Goh Keng Swee shuddered over his leg of "drunken chicken" at dinner one night. "The Malaysians and the Indonesians will think we are being converted into some sort of Maoist detonator to blow up the whole area." "A good thing President Johnson did not include Singapore in his recent tour," another minister said to me at the end of 1966. "It would have compromised us badly with Peking."

In Malaysia Doctor Ismail bin Dato Abdul Rahman stood up in parliament and proposed that his country explore the possibility of neutralizing the whole of Southeast Asia behind a screen of international guarantees from all the great powers, including Communist China. "Many people agree with me that neutralization is the answer, but they won't speak up because the Tengku is not in favor of it," Ismail told me afterward in an air-conditioned study furnished like the cabin of a somewhat bookish sea captain. He was on sick leave between two bouts of being Minister for Home Affairs, but he was not a man to mince his words. "We could start, in fact, with the neutralization of Malaya."

"Of course it would not mean anything unless the Chinese also accepted it," he agreed before I had opened my mouth. "But China need not make a positive move: it would be a beginning if Peking tacitly refrained from supporting terrorists and sowing subversion on our soil. We might make a gesture by legalizing the Malayan Communist Party. We are well placed to take the initiative in all this. We have a large Chinese population and we could make our first approach unofficially, through a suitable Malaysian Chinese businessman with standing enough to be able to meet Premier Chou En-lai." It was bold talk, but it was to have its echoes in Bangkok and Manila and in Laos, where a minister neatly fixed the timing with six words of French: "Once Mao is dead."

When anti-Communist counter-insurgency is discussed in Asia, a kind of hopelessness afflicts the infirm of spirit, for they at once point out that for years the rare achievements of half a million Americans in Vietnam were all too rare. They forget that by 1954 the country was divided into two, the Communist North was already an independent Communist state, and the South spongy with the subversion that seeped through it during eight years of anti-colonial guerrilla war against the French. No other Southeast Asian state was in this irremediably polluted condition.

It is equally fashionable for hawks to claim that neutrality is not a practical solution for Asian agonies, for the neutrality of Laos was guaranteed by all the powers concerned in 1962, yet seven years later the country was still an international battlefield. But Laos was neutralized just because it had already been carved up by warring Communist and anti-Communist forces, and this was not true of other Southeast Asian states. The foundering of Vietnam does not prove that Thailand cannot be kept afloat, and the dismemberment of Laos does not convince Asians that neutrality is necessarily an illusion. It appeals to them as a springy cushion on which the great bulk of China may be supported, the lining that could keep Communists and anti-Communists from direct, abrasive contact.

Extreme breeds extreme, and neutrality may be a safer defense against Communism than anti-Communism itself. In a world of opposites, leaders like Prince Norodom Sihanouk of Cambodia have been comforted by the belief that it is the thickness of the coin that holds head and tail apart, yet is committed to neither.

For they do not forget that when the coin is spun, one side or the other must fall flat on its face.

"I am extremely moved," Sihanouk wrote to Chou En-lai in 1968, "by the tin of Chinese lichees of an exceptional flavor which you kindly sent me. May I convey to you my warm thanks for this token of your tactful solicitude and constant friendship. I take once again this opportunity of voicing our firm solidarity with the brotherly Chinese people in the anti-American imperialist struggle . . ."

The delectable taste of the lichee is widely lauded, and more than twelve hundred years ago a doting Chinese emperor arranged for this egregious food to be brought to the breakfast table of his beloved from the far south of the Middle Kingdom by special relays of horsemen. But although Sihanouk was giving syrup for syrup, he was not to be bought into the anti-American imperialist struggle with a can of fruit.

A few months later he was urging the Americans not to abandon the region. "I need some cards in my hands to maintain a balance," he protested. "If the United States leaves Asia completely, it would be the end of my independence." He would rather have American tourists than American troops in Cambodia itself, he said ("Their dollars do not smell of policy"), but he hoped that the GI's would stay behind in Thailand and the Philippines after they had left Vietnam, so that he could "manipulate" between Communism and imperialism.

To his detractors the Sihanouk of the sixties may seem a windsock of a man, but his problems were not simple, for there are evils within evils. In the past Cambodia has been ravaged not by China but by her vigorous neighbors. It was the Thais and the Vietnamese, for the most part, who chopped up the great kingdom of the Khmers and cut it down to the Cambodia we know today. "If the French had arrived here twenty years later than they did during their period of colonial expansion in the nineteenth century," Monseigneur told me once, "there would not have been any Cambodia left for them to occupy."

Sihanouk also needs China, therefore, as a guarantee against the further greed of Bangkok and Saigon. Nothing perhaps worried him more than a secret assurance from Chou En-lai that even if he started fighting the South Vietnamese, he had nothing to fear from the Thais at his back—he was at once assailed by the horrible thought that Bangkok might have done a deal with Peking while he was still hovering between East and West. Moreover, the Vietnamese threat is two-pronged, and in the past few years he has tried to use China and the United States not only to neutralize each other but also to discourage the predatory instincts of North and South Vietnam respectively.

If this tangle of hazards leaves the reader frowning and mumbling, let it be remembered that Sihanouk had to live with it. The prince has one unwavering purpose: the survival of the Kingdom of Cambodia. This can be assured, he feels, if the frontiers and the neutrality of Cambodia are internationally guaranteed and respected. All who agree are Sihanouk's friends; all who obstruct are his foes. These are the simple ground rules of an excessively complicated game which did not end when Monseigneur was exiled.

At the coronation of King Suramarit in 1956 I stood on the high, floodlit balcony of the royal palace in Phnom Penh and gazed down with spurious condescension on the crowd of patient and humble Khmers who waited in the darkness below to see their glittering rulers and the promised fireworks. The place was full of princes, and close to the monarch himself stood the American and British ambassadors in full ceremonial dress. It was one of those moments when you feel very expensive indeed.

Eight years later the patient and humble Khmers were back again, waiting for the rulers and the fireworks in the persistent rain. But the high, floodlit balcony under its upcurling roof this time held Prince Norodom Sihanouk flanked by Marshal Chen Yi of China and Mr. Ignatov of the Soviet Presidium. The Anglo-Saxon presence was reduced to a knot of wet journalists, myself among them, in the mob below. The West had come a long way since 1956, and all of it downhill.

Out on the Vietnamese frontier it was easy to understand Sihanouk's displeasure. What was left of the little village of

Anlong Kres lay on the baking floor of the vivid green Cambodian plain, just half a mile from the border. Deserted by half of its sixty families, who had peaceably grown rice and fruit and snoozed away the oven-like afternoons until disaster struck them, the village seemed to hold only a few men armed with old French and British bolt-action rifles, a surly home guard that stared at us without love.

That was not surprising. Over a wide area the bamboo houses on stilts had collapsed completely, or stood at new, crazy angles, their legs broken and their wigs of palm thatch askew. Among them were deep bomb craters filled with scummy rainwater, and amid the rubble, twisted slivers of exploded rockets. Vietnamese air force Skyraiders had bombed, rocketed, or machine-gunned Anlong Kres twice within five days, and long-nosed American F-101's had repeatedly reconnoitered the village. Nine people had been killed, including four children. The Vietnamese claimed that they had made a map-reading error, but in fact they attacked Anlong Kres because they suspected it of harboring Vietcong guerrillas, just as they had attacked other Cambodian villages along the frontier before it.

Yet there was no doubt about the impartiality of Cambodian detestation for Vietnamese of all colors. "We distrust the lot of them," a Cambodian captain told me down on the border, with a melodramatic sneer not uncommon among Indochinese when they speak of their neighbors. "If they cross this frontier armed, we shoot them whether they are wearing the green uniforms of Saigon or the black pajamas of the Vietcong. The captain's headquarters was tactfully located well back from the Vietnamese border, and so were his troops. In the frontier area there were only militia and village home guards, who could offer little resistance to well-armed intruders. Nevertheless, to depict Sihanouk as a willing partner of the Vietcong, as many did, was to carry out arbitrary psychological surgery on the prince and leave all his instincts screaming. Ideally, he wanted everyone out of Cambodia and Cambodia out of everything. If half a million American troops could not stop the North Vietnamese from infiltrating into South Vietnam, how could his small army of thirty-five thousand men stop them from infiltrating into Cambodia across a five-hundred-mile-long border of tousled hill and swamp, he asked reasonably enough.

But Sihanouk had no affection for the Americans either. As allies of hostile anti-Communist states on Cambodia's doorstep —"these vultures which are the eternal swallowers of Khmer soil" —the Americans introduced a new dimension into historical hatreds. In modern dress, old-fashioned enemies became "pro-American" nations threatening to overrun the "neutral" Khmers jammed between them. Furthermore, in supporting the Thais and Vietnamese, the Americans were supporting "the 'Khmer Serei,'" the right-wing Cambodian insurgents who were engaged in armed conspiracy against the prince and whose insulting and belittling radio broadcasts so outraged his immodesty.

"Drink some more champagne," he cried at the end of 1963, looking around his conference table. "Steward, bring the last bottles." It came, slightly warm but of excellent vintage, and we sipped it sitting among the plush fixtures of his residence—the chandeliers, the gold-edged glass doors, the obsequious flunkies. This was a luxurious introduction to austerity, however, for Monseigneur had suddenly anounced that Cambodia would henceforth reject all American aid, cutting off in midstream economic and military assistance which was financing about twenty major national projects and generating the funds that paid for nearly forty percent of the Cambodian army. Sihanouk was cold-shouldering the West and turning for his devotions, as many do, to the East. But at the same time he warned the Soviet bloc that before his country was converted into a Communist satellite, he would either go to jail or become a simple citizen.

Monseigneur's passions and personal caprices should never have blinded foreign diplomatic observers to the essence of Sihanouk the statesman as against Sihanouk the prince. In matters affecting the sovereignty of Cambodia he was as calculating as a stockjobber balancing his prices and making sure of his turn, and he expected others to be the same. "Of course I understand that the Americans help countries like Vietnam and Thailand that are committed to the cause of anti-Communism before they will help a neutral like me," he once told me with refreshing candor and a small shrug. "But that means they fob me off with rifles dating back to the War of Secession and helicopters which are only safe when firmly on the ground. So, in the circumstances, I am naturally more inclined to trust the Chinese."

He had no illusions that Mao was interested in propping up tropical monarchies, but the better the relations between Peking and Phnom Penh, the longer the Kingdom of Cambodia would exist. "And fortunately we can be friends," he said with simple irony, "since we do not share a common frontier." Long on American goodwill, short on Chinese love, he lowered the price of the first, raised the price of the second. China was a long-term investment, America a short-term hedge.

When in 1963 the Americans refused to attend a new Geneva Conference on the neutrality of Cambodia, the prince threatened to sever relations with Washington and sign a military pact with Peking and Hanoi. And when in 1964 North Vietnam quibbled over recognizing Cambodia's frontiers, he damned the Vietnamese Communists for being "as vague as the Anglo-Saxons" and threatened to negotiate with anti-Communist Saigon. In 1965 he broke with the United States, and so brightened the faces of the Chinese, but in 1967 he promised to break with Peking also if they did not at once stop trying to export revolution to Cambodia. In mid-1969 he accused the Thais of helping the dissident "Khmer Serei" movement to set up a rebel Cambodian government, but reprieve was at hand, for the "Khmer Serei" menace was now mirrored by a "Khmer Rouge" menace of Cambodian Communist guerrillas. By the end of the year, Sihanouk had reestablished diplomatic relations with Washington and was warning Hanoi that he would break with North Vietnam and the Liberation Front if the Communists did not stop violating his borders.

The neutral leader is not a contemptible sycophant imbued with that slavish philosophy of certain dogs, "If you can't lick 'em, lick 'em." He is nobody's ally and therefore nobody's ward, and in the last analysis he must have the brazen cheek needed to flatter today where he insulted yesterday, impersonally, as part of the tasteless theatricals that pass for the defense of national interests.

"Logic demands," wrote Sihanouk in 1965, "that our independence and neutrality should be preserved always by playing off rival external influences against one another in such fashion that they cancel each other out." If one bloc attacked Cambodia, Sihanouk had to be able to turn to the other for protection. His tiffs and scenes and flirtations with both were merely the jerky arm wavings of the tightrope walker as he advances in a straight line toward his objective, and the adversaries who overthrew him in the end at once reaffirmed the neutral policy of Cambodia. They had cast him into the hands of the Communists, much as Souvanna Phouma had been forced to make common cause with the Laotian left wing at Khang Khay by General Phoumi and the C.I.A. But like Souvanna Phouma, Sihanouk could still hope to return to his capital as the indispensable waverer to whom both extremes must ultimately turn for a middleman.

Moreover, the iron logic of Monseigneur's inconstancy was sometimes a refreshing change in a region that has given the world two four-letter words for its unchallenged performances in individual and collective irrationalism—*amok* and *koro*.

27 : Cock and Bull

In the National Museum in Kuala Lumpur you may see displayed what looks like a finely made, long-handled pitchfork, the prongs judiciously set far enough apart to fit either side of a man's neck and pin him down. This is an *amok* fork, but it cannot have been used very often. For when the *amok* rushes out among his fellows, kris or parang in hand, and frenziedly cuts down all in his path in a fit of homicidal mania, the circumspect rarely seek to capture him alive.

Amok, notes the Encyclopaedia Britannica, "is the Malay equivalent of suicide." But there is also an element in it of sheer frustration, of locked brakes that provoke a mental skid. Too often the Malay can release his pent-up resentment only with a parang, and the intrepid Isabella Bird has remarked that if an insult is offered by a man of high rank and out of reach, the injured party will seize his knife and "slay all he can lay hands on."

Nations do not run amok, but the new countries of Southeast Asia—jealous of their often slender repute and conscious of condescension in others—will sometimes fling themselves into a seemingly senseless fury which bewilders the calculating West and introduces an X-factor into Far Eastern affairs that confounds all the computers. Irrational emptionalism, that ugly yet endearing quality which justifies the self-explanatory epitaph "he was only human," did not die in Indonesia with the eclipse of Sukarno.

In 1968 the Minister for Information in Djakarta announced that if two Indonesian saboteurs were executed in Singapore for killing three innocent people, the Indonesians "would have to review their friendly relations" with the island. Yet these are the facts: in 1965, two Indonesians smuggled a twenty-five-pound bomb into an office block in a busy Singapore street. The bomb exploded, killing a father of eight, a mother of six, and one other woman. The killers were dressed in civilian clothes, and although this meaningless act of murder was committed during Sukarno's Confrontation of Malaysia, no state of war existed. They were therefore tried and sentenced to be hanged, and the Privy Council upheld the judgment.

However, the Minister for Information in Djakarta was not the only man afflicted with moral strabismus. His government claimed that the two jailed bombers were marines and should be treated as prisoners of war. President Suharto made a personal appeal for clemency, and when this was rejected, a twin-engined Ilyushin bomber flew into Singapore to take the bodies back to Djakarta, accompanied by a special presidential envoy of general officer rank.

In the Indonesian capital the killers were given a hero's burial after a lying-in-state attended by thousands. Muslim imams chanted from the Koran, flags flew at half mast. General Abdul Haris Nasution, chairman of the People's Congress, swore that Singapore had insulted his country's honor. The press described the small republic as a "colony of bloodsuckers" and demanded retribution, and the commander of the Indonesian marines cried that he was ready to lead an invasion against the island. The Singapore embassy and the private homes of five of its diplomats in Djakarta were sacked. Indonesian freighters on their way to Singapore were recalled, Singapore freighters in Indonesian ports were boycotted and left unloaded. Trade between the two states slowed to a stop.

This was vengeance with a vengeance, and it was going to sting. For about sixty-five percent of Djakarta's exports normally passed through Singapore, the world's fourth busiest port and one for which backward Indonesia had no substitute. Furthermore, Indonesia was jeopardizing her chances of winning urgently needed financial support worth half a billion American dollars from a nine-nation consortium. The offer was conditional upon "signs of decided improvement" in the national economy, which a second Confrontation now threatened to wreck once again. In the end, the counsel of men in Djakarta who did not believe that the nation should be destroyed as a memorial to two terrorists supervened, and the fit passed. But that was not so everywhere.

A slightly blasphemous Philippine legend has it that when God first tried to make man, he baked the first batch for too long so that it came out black, and the second batch for too short a time, so that it came out white. Only at the third attempt did he achieve perfection—the golden-brown Filipino, crisp as they come. This pretentious version of God's last job before the first weekend may explain the rather haughty lack of logic which Manila has displayed over the Philippine claim to the North Borneo state of Sabah.

In the Public Record Office in London the Lord Chancellor has under his care a document which opens picturesquely: "We, Sri Paduka Maulana Al Sultan Mohamet Jama Al alam, Sultan of Sulu and the dependencies thereof, on behalf of ourselves, our heirs and successors, grant and cede of our own free and sovereign will to Baron de Overbeck of Hong Kong and Alfred Dent of London, their heirs, associates, successors and assigns forever and in perpetuity all the rights and powers belonging to us over all the territories and lands being tributary to us on the mainland of the island of Borneo . . ." Under the terms of this agreement, the "successors and assigns" must pay the sultan's heirs five thousand dollars a year, and the grant must never be transferred to any nation other than Britain without the sanction of the British government. It is dated January 22, 1878, and is an object lesson in the importance of keeping correspondence.

The territory in question became a British protectorate in 1888 and in 1946 was ceded to the Crown. The Spanish and American masters of the Philippines successively recognized Britain's right to this northeastern shoulder of the island of Borneo, and international law does not concede that a change of regime invalidates an agreed frontier. Then in 1962 the British, who were liquidating their empire in the East, proposed to appoint the new independent Federation of Malaya as their "successor and assign" and to incorporate it into a wider Federation of Malaysia.

It stood to reason (unfortunately) that the Philippine Republic would accept the change with equanimity, even pleasure. The white colonial power was ebbing from Manila's doorstep. In its place would come a young Asian state of fraternal Malay stock. Yet, although Manila had laid no previous claim with the British, the Filipinos now began to insist that the sultan of Sulu had only leased the territory to Overbeck and Dent. Since Sulu was part of the modern Philippine Republic, it should be ceded without further ado to Manila, or the case be taken to the International Court. The British ignored this peremptory demand, however. The dependency was signed over to Malaysia and was renamed Sabah. The Philippines then joined Indonesia in boycotting the formation of Malaysia and diplomatic ties with Kuala Lumpur were suspended.

The Philippine Republic was chipping away at its own favorite image of the Philippine Republic as a truly anti-colonial Asian state, keen to develop friendly regional cooperation with its neighbors. For it was ogling with unsuitably imperialistic acquisitiveness a territory whose people had been granted self-determination and whose wish to join Malaysia had been established both by United Nations investigators and in free general elections. These considerations, other Asians felt, should override any historical claims based on dubious nineteenth-century deals in real estate. But although Indonesia's Confrontation of Malaysia died a natural and therefore lingering death in 1966, the Filipinos were still in oral action three years later, for any one Manila lawyer can talk the hind leg off another.

There was to be more than talk, however. In 1968 details of a secret training camp for Filipino terrorists, who were being groomed on Corregidor for military operations against Malaysian Sabah, were suddenly exposed when harsh conditions on the island provoked a mutiny and a minor massacre, and a lone escapee told all. Faced with an international scandal, officials in Manila produced a quick flurry of contradictory explanations— that the men were training for an offensive against the Huks in Central Luzon, that they were to combat Indonesian infiltrators in the southern Philippines—and the astonished Malaysians were then told sharply that anyway it was all a "purely internal affair." Filipinos were caught illegally ashore in Sabah, some of them with arms, Filipino jets buzzed ships in Malaysian waters, and an influential Muslim congressman in Manila demanded a holy war against the new Federation. The National Security Council was given a comparative evaluation of Philippine and Malaysian armed services, and a somewhat optimistic intelligence officer was quoted as saying that Sabah could be taken in two weeks.

Filipino fantasy was far from exhausted, however. In September of that year President Marcos signed a bill which referred to Sabah as territory "over which the Republic of the Philippines has acquired dominion and sovereignty." Western reasoning might suggest that if, by way of a casual subordinate clause, Britain were to record the annexation of Calais in a bill solemnly passed into law, France might have grounds for complaint. But when Malaysia sought further clarification, Manila's official reply read: "This unwarranted interference of the Malaysian Government on a matter which is essentially within the domestic jurisdiction of the Philippines Government constitutes a flagrant violation of the United Nations Charter." Three days later the Philippines demanded an immediate explanation from Britain because five R.A.F. Hunter jets had flown over the state capital of Sabah and so had notionally violated "Philippine" air space. But when Malaysia suspended diplomatic relations again in protest over the bill, Mr. Narciso Ramos, the Philippine Foreign Secretary, wailed in New York: "What hurts is that we considered Malaysia a friend and neighbor and did not expect her to act contrary to the rules of fair play."

Soundly based on human characteristics of monetary greed and political ambition, the entire script was nonetheless a masterly piece of unreason. Relations between the "anti-Communist" powers—Malaysia, the Philippines, the United States, and Britain —were curdled by the squabble, and the strain thrown upon ASEAN, the new five-nation partnership in regional cooperation which included both Malaysia and the Philippines (as well as Indonesia, Singapore, and Thailand), was threatening to break its back. Overzealous Filipino interception of Malaysian patrol boats meanwhile sabotaged their joint anti-smuggling agreement, which had been particularly welcome to Manila since the illegal cigarette traffic profited the Malaysians but grievously pained the Philippine treasury. The Filipinos had protested that Sabah was only eighteen miles from the nearest of their own islands and that they must be responsible for seeing that it did not "go Communist"; yet they explained the guerrillas training on Corregidor in terms of their own inability to control illegal armed insurrection, subversion, or aggression by Marxist Huks or Muslim hotheads at home. Unquestionably the most irrational aspect of all to the humdrum Western mind, however, was the exotic proposition that people of a state which was safely outside the frontiers of the Philippine Republic might actually want to join it.

But then collective delusion can take peculiar forms.

In the fine autumn of 1967 strange, hallucinatory scenes are enacted in Singapore, noteworthy even in the days of the psychedelic happening and the general release of blue films. In a coffeeshop lavatory a small crowd, drawn by cries of anguish, gapes helplessly while a middle-aged soap boiler clamps a pair of chopsticks over his exposed male organ to stop it from retreating into his body. The chopsticks snap. Some quick thinker substitutes a pair of market-stall steelyards, but these prove too unwieldy. Panic! One bystander seizes the reticent gender and starts pulling; another rushes off to dial 999; a third runs for a Chinese doctor.

This is no isolated event. Similar little dramas are being played in hundreds of homes, and sometimes in public. A young fellow is hastily carried down a village main street in h s bed while his father jogs alongside, clutching the prostrate youth's masculine member. Another trots down a lane, his retiring nature in the firm grasp of a friendly pacemaker. Men arrive at the outpatients' entrance of hospitals with their sex stretched downward by dangling weights, or held in an improvised wooden vice, or captive on the end of a piece of string or a loop of wire. For Singapore is in the grip of an epidemic of fear—the fear induced by *koro*, a condition whose principal symptom is a sudden, disconcerting shrinkage of the penis (which the Chinese somewhat pretentiously call the "Sun-tool").

Western medicine regards this as a purely psychological affliction, a hysterical condition producing a real or imagined contraction of the male organ. But since worry can cause shrinking and shrinking in turn causes worry, Singapore has been caught on a spiral of alarm. The Medical Association therefore sets out to allay public fright by making a few interesting disclosures, if in somewhat monumental English. "The physiological causes," a press conference is told "are cold weather, getting into bed, and anxiety. Those afflicted are beset with the great fear that should the retraction be permitted to proceed, the male organ would eventually be drawn into the abdomen, with a fatal outcome [*sic*]. The Medical Association wish to reassure the public that the condition of *koro* leading to death is definitely unknown. Medical science indicates this retraction is not possible, as the male organ is fundamentally an external appendage," the doctors conclude comfortingly.

The rumor flies around that the *koro* comes from the meat of pigs vaccinated against swine fever, and although assured that the phenomenon is illusory and could not poss bly be produced by pork, many still cling to their old-fashioned fallacies, and slaughter in the abattoirs falls from thirteen hundred pigs a day to one hundred. Even at a banquet thrown for doctors in a smart downtown restaurant, pork is—symbolically—conspicuous by its absence. We give a buffet supper and Ping decides to label the boiled ham "Ladies only." For ten days of pandemonium, Singapore is the Land of the Shrinking Sun.

Mysterious epidemics are not unknown in the West, it may be protested. In 1968 men all over the United States complained that when they ate won-ton soup in a Chinese restaurant, they began to feel giddy and numb, their necks ached, their heads throbbed, and their hearts palpitated. "Chinese restaurant syndrome" was traced to a chemical flavoring, however. The narrowminded Westerner insisted that there must be a reason—and so he duly found it. But *amok* and *koro* are freakish embroideries upon a psychological pattern which has been sewn with a freer hand than the stencils of Western rationalism usually allow.

Since Asians do not regard life as a theorem of Euclid, there is no Q.E.D. and in consequence their reasoning and their objectives are sometimes mysterious. In 1961 U Nu, then prime minister of Burma, revealed that Buddhist candidate monks preparing themselves for holy orders not only cheated and cribbed their way to the cloth but ostentatiously pulled out daggers and coshes in the examination hall to intimidate their invigilators. All men are prone to syllogism, but the Asian often deals in rope-trick logic. He likes his argument open-ended. One day when I returned from lunch to the Hotel Indonesia in Djakarta I found myself double-locked out of my room. The reception clerk refused to give me a key, and referred me to a Javanese assistant manager. "But you are no longer staying at this hotel," this dignitary told me. "You checked out a week ago. So, of course, you cannot go into the room."

"And who do you think has been living in it ever since?" I demanded. "Who has been sleeping in the bed, sending out laundry, ordering breakfast, putting through telephone calls, picking up and depositing the key, asking for mail, signing chits? Whose possessions are in there right now?" He shrugged. "You paid your bill a week ago," he reiterated. "You are not on our books." "That was last week's bill," I protested, but the rope of reason had come to an end in mid-air, and it was half an hour before I was back in my room. "*Will* you get off this phone!" yelled an infuriated woman who had mistakenly called our number in Singapore three times in succession under the impression that it was that of a friend.

All is flexible in a flowing cosmos, many Asians contend. Truth, if left-handed, must be made to conform to changing circumstances, and history can if necessary be rewritten. The Minister of Information in Vientiane, importuned by correspondents who complained that they were receiving conflicting reports of what was happening in the Laotian war, remarked with asperity: "If you *will* talk to different officials, naturally you get different answers." Another minister, asked if it was really true that seven North Vietnamese battalions were attacking Phou Khoun as officially announced, replied readily enough, "Well, it's only *partly* propaganda."

The Vietcong have twisted the malleable truth of Asia into their own form of folk art. Doubtless anxious to please their superiors, they have submitted statistics of such slaughter to higher echelons that their general staff claimed that 162,000 Americans had been killed in the first half of 1966—nearly ten times the real number. Two years later I learned in Saigon that Vietcong units were being further encouraged to file false returns by instructions from above which laid down minimal killing quotas: "In February the division will eliminate one thousand of the enemy, shoot down fifty American helicopters . . ." History was being written in advance this time, for back came the same figures from below at the end of the month, proving that all quotas had been fulfilled.

It is Asian to tell a man what he wants to hear, or to refrain from telling him what he does not want to hear. Dr. Dooley wrote of a Lao assistant: "He was not a liar, he was just congenitally unable to say no." The courteous Malay who does not want to answer your inconvenient request with a brusque and final negative replies "*Belum*," and it is understood that this vague and elastic euphemism spans all future time, from "not just yet" to "never."

The white man who accuses the Asian of double-talk is simply failing to understand what he is being told in plain, straightforward innuendo. Southeast Asia is a polite subcontinent in which you say a man has short legs by calling him tall in the saddle. "How many members do you have?" I asked the leader of a moderate political party in Brunei once, as we sat barefoot in his bungalow. "About twenty thousand," he replied. "All staunch supporters?" I pressed on, in my brutal Caucasion fashion. "Let me put it this way," he answered with a plump smile. "About eight hundred of them would probably have the sense not to join the extremists if there were another insurrection." "And how many pay party dues?" "We do not levy dues," he said loftily. "We rely on well-wishers for our funds." It was a painless way of saying that the party was being bribed from behind but if it came to the crunch about ninety-five percent of its members would desert it.

In the East words are often uttered only because, without them, it would be more difficult to read between them, whereas in the West one is actually expected to take them at their face value. What is a subtle guide at one end of the world, therefore, may become an unsubtle disguise at the other. Unlike the Asians, the Americans do not spell out their fantasies in words of four letters, but pad out their truths with the polysyllabic falsies in which their national language is so rich. At their distorted five-o'clock shadow of the Vietnam War known in Saigon as the daily press briefing, a helicopter attack becomes a "vertical envelopment," failure to catch the enemy is a "pursuit operation terminated with negative results," and raining five-hundred-pound bombs and napalm on Vietnamese peasants by mistake is an "accidental delivery of ordinance which impacted on an inhabited area." A communiqué dated March 16, 1968, reads: "In an action today American divisional forces have killed 128 enemy near Quangngai City." That's the massacre at My Lai, that was. The unpleasant realities of war are often carved down to a set of deceivingly manly clichés until the name of the game becomes the name of the game.

"Joint project." The words fall through from six years back, uttered in the lazy-river voice of Barry Zorthian, who chairs the daily briefing in his Saigon office. It is November 1964, and Zorthian reveals that the Vietcong have smashed or damaged at least twenty-seven American aircraft in a mortar attack on Bien Hoa air base. He hopes to get away with a deceptively candid statement of losses, but he is not to be left in peace, for now Joe Fried cross-examines for the New York *Daily News*. (Joe Fried, veteran of a thousand briefings, has the long, sad face of a dead-pan comedian into which some careless smoker has burned two angry eyes, but he writes his own patter. Zorthian is a hostile witness, and Fried is ready to tear him apart.)

PROSECUTION: Weren't there any bays or revetments to protect these aircraft?

WITNESS: There were some revetments, but not where the planes were.

PROSECUTION: You're saying there were not enough revetments for every plane?

WITNESS: That is correct.

PROSECUTION: Was there a shortage of sandbags then?

WITNESS: No, they had enough sandbags up there, and they were being filled as fast as labor and other commitments permitted.

PROSECUTION: But the B-57 jets have been at Bien Hoa three months, how do you account for the fact that no revetments were built for them?

WITNESS: There was no time with the labor available.

PROSECUTION: What's the labor problem?

WITNESS: Well, this is a joint project . . .

PROSECUTION (*Pounces*): A *joint project?* What's "joint project"? You mean an American holds a sandbag while a Vietnamese pours in the sand, or a Vietnamese holds the . . .

(Leading question: objection sustained. Fried retires and a recess is declared.)

Even with Fried present, the Public Affairs staff can refuse to answer questions on the grounds that they may incriminate someone, and too often the court scene turns into a commercial.

There has always been a strong Javanese element in all this: reports should be "appropriate." On his departure after more than four years in Saigon, Barry Zorthian said straightforwardly that American officials had made mistakes in dealing with the press. They should have admitted, for example, that the air strikes against North Vietnam had sometimes hit civilian houses. This changed little, however. The department still worked with the precision and aplomb of a cuckoo clock, and the Javanese could look to their laurels. Their former Foreign Minister, Dr. Subandrio, might have personified the heroic Indonesian struggle with truth. But others could be sub-android too.

28 : The Tortoise and the Terrapin

Asians are not like or unlike Europeans. They are both. They are possessed of the human conscience, the sex urge, five senses or so, and forty-six chromosomes per cell nucleus. They are hard-wearing, edible, combustible, and they float when inflated. But their programmers—history, environment, belief, tradition, prejudice—have not been the same. Since, therefore, magnanimous man is quickly convinced that his neighbor is mad when he is shown evidence that the fellow's morals and customs are different from his own, Oriental and Occidental are vulnerable to each the other, and as the first superficial similarities give way to hidden surprises, narrow eyes may grow round, and round eyes narrow.

The Javanese with his Leyden degree, talking fluent English and Dutch, Russian ballet and vintage cars, may slowly reveal himself as a man of rigid principles who does not, however, believe in any universal moral excellence, and whose regard for Lady Macbeth is increased by the fact that she stabbed Duncan in his sleep (for Macbeth he has only contempt). Nothing is more futile than to try to impose the West's standards upon the East, for the Asian has his own knife-sharp sense of what is fitting. A young Indonesian has himself buried alive "to save his country." A young Malaysian Chinese, sentenced to prison for armed robbery, earnestly begs the judge to have him whipped as well. In North Borneo a Sea-Dyak laborer indignantly accuses an army unit of paying him for a day's work he did not do. (In a less disordered world he would still be in his jungle longhouse, planning to decapitate some unsuspecting stranger at night from behind and hang up the head as an honorable trophy.)

Since culture wags the tongue, and not the other way around, languages of East and West often refuse to fit. In Burma "jewelry" is not an optional adornment but "apparel for the arms," a lack of which would be shameful. The Westerner recoils quite unfairly, therefore, from the vision of the overdecorated Eastern seductress up to her elbows in bangles. Each end of the world is quick to suspect the other of the worst and the dirtiest. The Christian lingers aghast before the sacred pornography in stone which Hinduism seems to inspire, and listens with pursed lips to accounts of sexual orgies in Buddhist temples. But sex with a "spiritual wife" was once part of the strenuous ritual of certain forms of yoga, one of many religious exercises designed to bring the devotee to Nirvana.

The Asian, on the other hand, is often puzzled by what appear to be subtle distinctions in the Mysterious West that make Botticelli's "Birth of Venus" Art, but girlie-magazine cheesecake Filth. On one occasion the postmaster-general of Manila raised a storm in the press when he warned off a local newspaper for reproducing the Venus, and banned as "obscene" an issue of *Time* magazine that carried a color print of Goya's "Naked Maja." Those who defended these works he described as "public enemies of civilized society who simply want to cater to the animal instincts of the lascivious."

Nothing separates men from men faster than money, however. "It is no good," said Ping, sinking back in her window seat with a sigh after vainly attempting to wade through the free champagne cocktails, the caviar and Strasbourg paté and smoked-oyster snacks, the five-course menu and the wines and liqueurs served at the front end of a jet liner across five hundred miles of South China Sea. "It is nice to try once. But we Asians are *reary* born economy class." A minority of Orientals may be wealthy, but in the East any Westerner is the poor man's rich man. He lives in the dream world of that contradiction, the instant age, surrounded with enough plug-in gimmickry and gadgetry to blow a minor power station. His house could accommodate fifteen Malays, twenty Vietnamese, and his car is as big as many an Asian home. His cornucopia economy can shower him with all his heart may desire, from machine-stitched Bayeux tapestry to a prefabricated swimming pool.

The militant Vietnamese Buddhist leader Thich Tri Quang had his own quaint image for this abundance: "The Americans are giants who will become bloated and die if they eat but do not defecate. This defecation is their aid. If they cannot find ways of granting aid they will have no place to sell the goods they produce. If they cannot sell the goods the plants will have to shut down. If plants shut down, hundreds of thousands will be out of work. America will then be in danger. That is why we can insult the Americans as much as we please, and they must still do our bidding and grant us aid."

Yet sadly, "Green Imperialism"—the influx of the American dollar with the American soldier—has tended to make the rich of the subcontinent richer, the poor poorer. By the end of 1965 rents in Saigon had risen by as much as four hundred percent. Landlords refused to let premises to haggling Vietnamese, and taxis refused to stop for them, for they could charge Americans five times the correct fare. United States agencies overpaid the labor they hired, inflation took wings, and Vietnamese on fixed salaries found themselves angrily tightening their seat belts. By 1968 the cost of living in Saigon had nearly doubled in three years, and Thailand was also beginning to feel the windy discomforts of financial flatulence. The Americans had descended on the subcontinent like the northeast monsoon, but their fantastic torrents of goods and gold seemed to wash away more than they irrigated in terms of human life and happiness, and the unimaginable wealth and wastage alike confirmed the more uncharitable Asian in his bitter, often supercilious belief that the Westerner was not Superman, but Supermonkey.

The overbearing Occidental who struts through the subcontinent as if it were a condemned slum is balanced by his humble and unctuous brother who is forever prostrating himself before all things Oriental and apologizing for the unpardonable existence of the billion or so barbarians to the West. If he does it for kicks, he can expect them. For the Far East is full of pretentious arrogance and pretty conceits.

In a Japanese garden, we read, we may find in summer "a tinkling contraption to listen to because only the Japanese can believe that a special sound can be cooling." This is typical of the simpering school of Asian writers that lends to the Japanese a vocabulary of sensibilities which the crude Westerner cannot be expected to understand. The pinball parlor in the Times Square area is dismissed, of course, as typical of the trash-can period in Western culture, but it seems that the pachinko parlor in Tokyo, crammed like its American counterpart with idle, vacuous youth, is only one remove from a Zen school of archery, and should be treated with due reverence. The vertical pinball machine, notes one writer loftily, "perhaps appeals only to the Japanese mind" because "the game is a test of manual dexterity, a trait the Japanese attach great value to," and it offers an entertainment suitable for "the Japanese virtue of quiet concentration."

There are many occasions on which I feel constrained to remark loudly that some of my best friends are British. "You cannot possibly understand us," Asians have told me woundingly. "But with us it is different. We know you Europeans only too well." This is frequently a ludicrously unjustified boast. The older Asian tends to see the white as a rather simple piece of apparatus for grasping, destroying, and building, like one of his own mechanical grabs, the strictly materialistic product of a two-dimensional television culture thrown up by broad civilizing influences ranging from cowboys to Coca-Cola. Christianity, with its improbable tales of mystery and imagination, seems to fall ignominiously into the category of the pop Asian religions so disdained by the Confucian intellectual or the Buddhist ascetic. The mystics and the philosophers, the awesome and virginal conceptions of Greece and Rome and Nazareth that made men free, the swelling paean of European art and life, are often ignored.

The East cheerfully murders the muses of the West without even knowing it. It is, for example, always instructive to listen to the background music for television programs in Southeast Asia, and compare it with the subject. Among my specimens are: Liszt's "Liebestraum" for an announcement warning the public to lock their cars and houses against thieves; "Humoresque" for a newsreel of a motocycle race; Mussorgsky's "A Night on Bald Mountain" for a fashion parade of fur coats; Gilbert and Sullivan for a Catholic funeral procession.

But it is only too easy for a Westerner to offend. A Cambodian or a Burmese, a Chinese or a Lao will be loyal to the polite hypocrisies of an outwardly imperturbable society, and the first thing you learn when treating with Malays is to smile, damn you, smile. The Anglo-Saxon only puts himself in balk if he becomes irritated by Asian obliqueness, by the habit of the Indonesian of hiding behind much tittering and the dark glasses which are his modern substitute for the traditional impassive face—"the hangman's hood of the common man," as Ping puts it. It follows that a rush of blood to the head and a display of true feelings and temper must be looked upon by the educated Asian as evidence of a contemptible lack of self-control. Passions that slop over into the watching world are for animals, small children, ignorant peasants, and white men. His is a society that deals uneasily with invasions of Anglo-Saxon sailors raised on roaring traditions of rum and Pensacola, or of great bony Australasians, their powerful vocal chords twanging like banjo strings as the beer flows faster.

Even the most sober and circumspect can fall into error, and ignorance of the lore is no excuse. In many parts of Southeast Asia it is offensive to pat a child's head, for the head is the repository of Buddhahood. Backslapping and pointing with the index finger are resented, shoes must be taken off on entering Japanese and Malay houses, and it is widely regarded as impolite for a man to sit with one leg over the other so that the sole of his foot faces his host, or to sip the coffee or tea or lime juice that is set in front of him before he has been invited to do so. Among the Faithful, the quicksands are even more treacherous. The Koran must always be treated with a special reverence, and it is sacrilege not only to smoke or drink while it is being read, but to put another book or anything else on top of it at any time. And it must not be touched with the left hand, which is, of course, unclean.

There is more to this matter of cleanliness. Strangers attributed the many cases of leprosy to be seen among the people in Angkor during the thirteenth century to "their excessive passion and their habit of taking too many baths." Marco Polo, returning to the West at about this time, writes with astonishment of the Indians: "Another of their customs is that all of them, male and female, wash their whole body in cold water twice a day. One who did not wash twice a day would be thought an ascetic." A strict obligation to wash before praying is imposed on every Muslim, and upon this the finicky Mohammed commented: "Were it not for fear of troubling disciples, verily I would order them to clean their teeth also before every prayer" (which would have meant five times a day).

The Buddhists are believers in the bath and at New Year throw themselves into an orgy of drenching, for all must be purged of impurity at this time. As the week washes by, the siphons, pumps, buckets, and syringes come out, the children enter into the spirit of the Thingyan (as it is called in Rangoon), a war of water develops and everyone gets a daily dousing. On two occasions when Chou En-lai conferred with Premier U Nu of Burma, the Chinese prime minister needed all his well-developed self-control to keep his temper, for since the conferences coincided with the water festival in both Burma and neighboring Yunnan, he emerged from both experiences soaking wet.

Asia is an insanitary continent, reeking of ineradicable dirt and poverty, but famous for its laundering and inhabited by different peoples who wash thoroughly before getting into a hot bath, or who bathe in running streams, dance under a shower (if in public, fully clothed), or throw bucketfuls of water over themselves from great vats or jars. To them, the white man is disgusting, for he sits in a tub of water and rinses himself in his own filth. As to left-handed cleansing operations, the Chinese used paper before the West, but preferred goose feathers in the heyday of the hedonists, and many Orientals claim that water, sand, or even stones are more hygienic.

If the Westerner is unclean, he is also ugly, and his customs sometimes take much explaining away. American soldiers are no more brutal or licentious than others, but when they are unleashed on Taipei or Bangkok or Tokyo for five days of leave from the Vietcong, they are quite naturally less concerned with national manners than country matters, and since the evil that men do lives after them, by 1963 they had fathered more than two thousand "red-haired" Thais alone.

It is useless to protest that while the Americans were increasing the mixed population of Thailand, the Thai "Queen Cobra" Regiment was doing the same in Vietnam at the average rate of one baby for every thirteen men, or that in a given year seven unlucky Americans out of ten in some units had caught the "Vietnam Rose" (which, by any other name, may be identified as a particularly stubborn form of clap). Asian prejudices have been hardened by scenes of public necking and drunkenness and brawling, and by the insults offered to their wives by white men for whom every pretty girl was a prostitute. Even the best-behaved American serviceman, walking sedately down a Bangkok street arm in arm with some permissive little piece, is a shameless *farang* who fans hidden fires of cultural indignation. For, strictly speaking, it is inadmissible for boy to touch girl in public in Thailand, even if the girl has fainted.

Little credit goes to thousands of Westerners who set out to please. Yet if the British can be courteous and accommodating to local custom, to the point of letting the natives hack each other to bits, a really conscientious American behaves as if he had majored in manners. The Peace Corps, above all, presents in principle a new Western visage—bland, smiling, helpful, and understanding sometimes beyond all understanding as far as the bewildered Asian is concerned. In 1964 a Peace Corps volunteer invigilating a high-school class in Thailand politely began eating his way through nearly three dozen plates of food which the students, one by one, presented to him with a note in Siamese. He was finally saved by a Thai teacher who explained that they were not gifts from the girls, but their examination entries in the finals of a food-preparation course.

His behavior contrasted agreeably with that of the late Marshal Sarit, who sipped his carefully chosen wine as guest of honor at a severely protocolaire dinner given by the British ambassador in Bangkok, screwed up his face in disgust, flung his glass down on the table, and called for a bottle of brandy. Too often the touchy, thin-skinned Asian behaves as if everyone else had the hide of a rhinoceros.

Moreover, the Westerner cannot be blamed for the suspicion that in some countries Oriental etiquette is overrated as a mechanical substitute for common consideration. I remember no better example of this habit of stifling courtesy with too many courtesies than an occasion in Hong Kong when Ping and I waited patiently in an elevator with four American ladies of indiscreet age, while two Japanese men bowed at each other a dozen times before one would be good enough to get in and allow us to go up. The itch to leave them bowing for another three or four minutes simply by pressing the button was almost irresistible.

However, the vices of the inventive white, yesterday damned for poisoning the wells of wise living in the Orient, are adopted by Asian governments today provided they show a profit. The anti-colonial urge to fulminate against the foreigner as if he were the sole originator of all pot, sex, booze, and gambling is giving way gently to a tacit admission that he is not the only man who is vile, after all. But there is still much room for misunderstanding in all matters of morality.

Like most of his Asian neighbors, the Lao lacks the Christian's sense of guilt. In his philosophy, Man did not first come on stage against the setting of the Garden of Eden to perform Act One Sin One, for to him good and evil are inseparable. In consequence, as long as a man's actions are not motivated by a possessive urge, he may accept all opposites—the pleasure that is defined by pain, as well as the pain that is defined by pleasure, since they are all one and the same. This is the middle way between the guru and the gourmand. The Lord Buddha himself condemned excessive asceticism. The enlightenment which eluded him for six long years of self-denial and meditation embraced him finally after he had disgusted five fellow sages by eating a square meal and taking a bath. That inspired the outlook which gives to millions of Asians their sense of perspective today.

But, as at least one devout Lao commentator has plaintively remarked, Buddhism can easily become the doctrine of lethargy and self-indulgence. If to reason is to destroy the true vision of the cosmos, don't think. If to strive is to bind yourself to this deplorable world of illusion, then don't strive. Moreover, as all Buddhists wish to "gain merit" by performing charitable acts, and so edge nearer to Nirvana, it may be kinder to take than to give.

The Buddhist bonze who holds out his begging bowl to the Thai housewife and lets her fill it with food is doing her a favor, for she is gaining merit. The pagodas bless the community by allowing themselves to be showered with candles and flowers and fruit and children. How many times Westerners have embarrassed or bewildered Asians by thrusting things upon them and expecting gratitude in return, it is hideous to contemplate. Asian leaders who have taken the dollar aid and damned Washington afterward have also assumed that in the unsentimental commerce of international relations the donor in any case gives because he needs the recipient. The recipient, therefore, renders service twice over.

The Orient produces its own fine strain of hypocrisy, however, and while the Muslims and Buddhists of Southeast Asia may remain strictly loyal to their faiths, they will argue that to cut corners is to take the straightest path. "Fish?" an old peasant in Thailand once echoed, grinning toothlessly. "No, I don't fish. I am old and will die soon. Why should I risk losing merit by killing living creatures? I leave fishing to my son. He's still young." An angler caught in the act protested, "But I only take the fish out of the water. If they die, that is not my doing." In Malaya, Chinese Buddhists will happily eat the bird that has been decapitated out of sight by some other unfortunate. In Burma the rule that monks may not touch money was side-stepped long ago when people began giving the bonzes cylinders of silver coins contained in long nets. The Theravada Buddhist usually wears his hair shirt open at the neck, as it were.

The rigid morality designed for use in a Western universe of fixed ethics is often replaced in Asia by a flexible casuistry more suitable for an Eastern cosmos in a constant state of change, just as the tortoise has legs for two-dimensional land, the terrapin flippers for three-dimensional water. They are cousins under the carapace, but the Westerner on his solid philosophical ground believes he can manage his universe, while the Oriental knows he must give way to tides and currents. He is more resigned to the liquid factors beyond his control, and therefore often more happy-go-lucky. To him, the white man with his feverish determination to measure and master everything always seems to be letting his nerves get on his nerves.

Gliding and eluding the disagreeable in what the West often regards as deceitful fashion, a Malay would rather say "*Belum*" than refuse or contradict, while with Indonesians one always seems to be surrounded by much nonchalant shrugging and self-deprecatory laughter. Yet behind this is the discipline of bland-ness which they believe leads to spiritual enlightenment. It is not weakness but a way of life, as the hippies discovered in Laos.

"The Third Eye" on the outskirts of Vientiane was a barn of a hippiedrome whose circling psychedelic lights flashed through rotating Chinese umbrellas of torn paper suspended from the ceiling, while the current throbbed through the guitars and the cats gave out their weary ectoplasm of song. But by 1968 it was living on borrowed time. The Laos had not taken to the Western hippies, who had flocked into their lotus land unbidden and unwashed. They saw nothing transcendental in filthy Europeans dressed in matted hair and jingling beads, and when these appeared with blackened faces and danced at the Laotian fertility rites, the prime minister took it as an offense to his people and their religion. The chagrined hippies had quite mistakenly assumed that they would find the Buddhist Laos as feckless and sloppy and permissive as themselves. The Laos regarded them coldly as a case of too many kooks.

The legend of laziness in Southeast Asia must be examined, like all legends, for its inner meaning. "How slothful they are," sighs the newcomer to the East, watching gardeners listlessly cropping the grass or a cook sitting in a cane chair, fanning herself in slow motion. The simple cure for this sense of superiority is for the energetic Westerner to try hanging a picture on a wall on a fine Sunday in Singapore or Saigon. Long before he has rammed his rawl plug home, he is soaked to the skin, his sweat has made a puddle on the floor, and he needs a long drink and a shower and a change.

It is quite unjust to imagine that Oriental idleness is the same as the dishonest scrimshanking of the Western worker who slacks on the job while the foreman has his back turned. The white man is a thief who steals paid time, but the indolent Asian would rather have the time than the money. Slowness and the siesta are his secrets of survival in the steamy tropics, and his philosophy leaves him with simple demands and a preference for leisure over lucre.

Buddhism has taught the Lao that he must cast off ambition, that nothing fails like success, and this suits him down to the ground. When provided by solicitous Americans with new strains of seeds that would double his rice crop, he remarked with pleasure that now he need sow only half his usual acreage. "What would I do if I worked harder and earned more money?" repeated a Cambodian farmer, when told he, too, could double his yield. "I don't know. I already have a bicycle and a radio. Get another wife, perhaps?" It was obvious he did not think that it was worth the effort. Furthermore, the Hindu sages have preached that life is divided into four phases, and in the last a man should grow old gracefully, indulge in the quiet contemplation that leads to release from material existence. By forty-five a man may already be in the third state and loosening his worldly collar. He is not lazy, but he simply declines to lead the life of Reilly or Richard Nixon any more.

If there is work to be done, the Asian will do it. The Lao peasant must sharpen his plow, mend his harrow, repair his cart. He must plait his own ropes, thatch his own roof, weave walls of palm, and split bamboo for his house. He must make fish traps, kitchen utensils, spinning wheels, and looms for the cotton he grows and dyes. He must look after his buffalo, raise poultry and herbs, plant and reap, and help his neighbor, for this is a do-it-yourself economy demanding diligence from all. But to ask the Lao for "urgent" will raise a laugh, for that is another matter. The sensible man sees that straining to solve one problem only creates another, and may entangle him inextricably in the web of this world. It is not surprising if many Laos look askance at modernization and miracle rice, for instinct tells them correctly what will next come to pass: the bumper crops will demand more fertilizer and insecticides, then more roads and carts and trucks, then more mills and silos, more credits, more consumers at home and buyers abroad, more human involvement, and so, of course, more metempsychosis.

Man should not meddle. The West applies this principle to science fiction, postulating that the fool who takes a time machine back to the Upper Jurassic and massacres all the megalosaurs may come back to the present to find Mao Tsetung in the Vatican and Chi-Chi winning the Derby. The East applies it to life: it may be dangerous to save a drowning child, for then you will certainly be responsible for changing not only its own destiny but also the karma of all others, as its every move during the rest of its existence makes the ripples shudder outward to the ends of the earth and forward to eternity. It is better, therefore, to avoid fiddling with the fate of strangers. Who ran to catch little

Adolf Schicklgruber when he fell? Whoever did has much to answer for, many Asians would say.

Most Muslims believe that all is decreed in advance, and the Buddhist sees the world of illusion rolling blindly forward beyond his control. Man's illness is terminal from birth, and the patient must accept with mild resignation all the funny and unfunny things that happen to him on his way to the cemetery. "Now it is wet, now it is fine," say the Malays. Fate, like England, does not have climate, but weather.

29 : The Numbers Game

Napoleon was only just born a Frenchman, Mohammed only just founded Islam, and it is accidents like this that persuade so many Asians that it is better to accept destiny than to try to change it, to consult an astrologer rather than a computer. True, Asia has had its own enthusiasts for programming Fate and manipulating history mathematically, and it was the fudged calculations inspired by a preparatory war game in Tokyo which persuaded the Japanese to attack Midway in 1942. "The battle cost the Japanese two-thirds of their big carriers; it also cost them the war," as Andrew Wilson noted with curt finality in *The Bomb and the Computer*.

But for the West, cold logic and mechanical calculation seem to dictate increasingly today that sheer weight of men and money and machines can simply crush the elusive imponderables of life.

Nowhere has this been more clearly applied than in Western military response to Eastern military mischief during the recent past, and an observer in the Straits of Malacca on one searing day in 1965 might have concluded that in defending Malaysia against Indonesian Confrontation, the British were emulating the eagle-beats-ants philosophy of their American cousins in Vietnam.

It is high noon. The whole universe seems to screech in agony when the Sea Vixens, each wrapped in its own wicked glimmer of condensation, rip viciously over the flight deck as H.M.S. *Eagle* sails like a matronly monarch through the heat haze, her foaming train falling carefully into place, her retinue of three more aircraft carriers in line astern. Up on top the world is flat. But prize open this ingenious metal container for fifty aircraft and three thousand men, drop down a few decks, and pass through a steel door. The big Ops Room is in sepulchral darkness except for the glowing moon-faced dials of thirty different radar sets and other automatic registers, their revolving traces watched by mute shadows of men. Near one gloomy corner stands SINS (Ships Internal Navigation System), a fancy-looking slot machine that automatically plots the ship's course and position.

In the control room directly below this nightmare pinball parlor are more rows of radar and, within a gyroscopically balanced solid-steel cell, the masterminds themselves, the computers of ADA—Action Data Automation. ADA sifts all the information pouring in through these round electronic pupils, distinguishing friend from foe, identifying the type of approaching enemy and his speed and position. It then automatically selects from the whole floating armory the correct combination of weapons to kill the threat at a comfortable distance, perhaps two hundred miles away. The giant has not only its brains but all its sixty-odd blinking, cataracted eyes in its stomach. We are guided not by the stars above but by our SINS below. Nobody looks at the sea.

I photograph the great beast as we rattle back to the palm-fringed Malaysian coastline in a Whirlwind helicopter. It has the doomed look of the stegosaurus, the armor-plated monster with brains in its bottom as well as its head, whose world the small, scurrying, subversive little mammals inherited several ages ago. For the threat to Malaysia comes from guerrillas in the jungle of North Borneo—a motley mix of Indonesian regulars disguised as "volunteers," Chinese Communist terrorists, and Malaysian rebels in jungle green or shirts and slacks. It comes from agents smuggled into Singapore with bombs and booby traps, and from sneak troops sea-landed or parachuted into West Malaysia to set up revolutionary bases, panic the population with acts of savagery, or foment internal rebellion with false rumors and undercover political agitation.

I first saw *Eagle* from the bridge of H.M.S. *Maryton* as she sailed majestically toward us down the Straits of Malacca, decked out in all her man-killing finery, and swept by with a condescending wink from a signal lamp. But it was the wooden-walled 470-ton minesweeper and not the sophisticated 50,000-ton flattop that was the queen of the seas in this furtive battle. More than seventy British naval units were deployed to screen the long, vulnerable Malaysian coast from intruders, and *Maryton*, like all other minesweepers in the slender chain of patrols, was equipped for a strange guerrilla war on water with armed junks and prahus that tried to cross the narrow gulch separating the Indonesian archipelago from the shores of Singapore and the Malayan peninsula. The crew soon discovered that their most useful ironware consisted of four Vickers machine guns that were about to be thrown to the scrap heap when Sukarno first threatened to "crush Malaysia." *Eagle* could keep her science-fiction strike potential.

January 1965. It is deep night. Behind the blackout curtain of the tiny chartroom a bespectacled midshipman, motionless and unblinking in the dim light, watches the radar screen as a small white blob crawls across its surface like some obscene, sun-shy bug. This is a contact. The ever-swiveling scanner atop the bridge has picked up something out in the starlit Straits that is trying to move *across* the overcrowded channel, instead of up or down it, and is therefore suspect. Diesels whine, and a perilous game of blindman's-buff begins for the fragile minesweeper as she cuts through the treacherous waters of this slit of an international sea lane at maximum speed and with no lights showing, amid a flurry of small islands and a stream of freighters and giant tankers oblivious of the war at their skirts.

The trace on the radar screen suddenly shows another white blob scuttling between *Maryton* and the first suspicious pinhead. Uneasy, I step back on to the bridge, and my eyes at once cling to the towering shadow of a freighter ahead, the wide, fixed grin of its bridge windows seemingly halfway up the sky as it bears down on us at speed. Bells ring urgently. The blacked-out minesweeper heels over on a sharp turn, swerves around the freighter on the blind side with feet to spare, and comes up neatly upon the unsuspecting quarry. The captain calls "Boarding stations!" A hollow explosion shakes the deck and there is an airburst to port as an old two-inch mortar filched from the army fires a starshell that casts a reddish glow over the onyx waters—and, like an apparition, a long, rakish Indonesian prahu, powered by big outboard motors. Abruptly, the twin Vickers on the bridge smash the momentary silence with two sharp bursts across the intruder's prow, searchlights snap on, and men move to the rail to cover the boarding party, Stirling submachine guns at the hip. No chances are taken. It is not long since a similar raider met the challenge of H.M.S. *Ajax* with a bouquet of hand grenades. But there is no unpleasantness this time. A police boat materializes out of the Stygian swell around us. The Indonesian infiltrators are handed over to the Malaysian security authorities. The minesweeper pulls away tactfully, back to her beat.

The night is not through with us, however. Another bug crawls across the radar screen, the mortar slams a flare into the sky, and binoculars snap on the suspect. It is a log of wood. And this very Indonesian log of wood is the essence of Confrontation. In its own inert way it abets Sukarno's policy of making warless war, of putting the defense to a maximum of trouble, danger, and expense with a bare minimum of prompts and feints. But if the shadow-fighting is far removed from the hypothetical hell of a computerized conflict, it is characterized by its own precise military niceties, as I first saw at some anonymous point in Borneo in September 1963.

On the map it was reassuringly marked "Landing Zone." On

the ground it was a twenty-yard ledge above a dark river, a tiny clearing of brushwood and tree stumps backed by a high wall of tangled hill. The Wessex helicopter skimmed over the rolling sea of treetops at ninety knots and dropped hesitantly onto this uninviting shelf like some fastidious insect, the tips of its whirling blades almost slashing the foliage. It was a place without a name, a mere map reference along more than six hundred miles of border between Sarawak and Indonesian Borneo where precipitous, jungle-covered mountains alternated with deep, river-seamed ravines in insanely repetitive waves. But a few days before, a group of armed terrorists from Indonesia had asked the chief of the nearby Iban longhouse for rice, whereupon the chief had paddled downriver for five hours to warn the Gurkhas of the enemy's presence. Patrols now went out, ambushes were laid, and the guerrillas were duly flushed. In the immensity of this wilderness where troops can move only on rivers and overgrown jungle tracks, the Gurkhas had struck with almost uncanny accuracy.

It was the helicopter, the ubiquitous chopper, that made such operations possible. From the nearest battalion headquarters in the village of Song, the iron fans clattered out over the frontier area like hands moving over a chessboard, picking up a patrol here, putting down an ambush party there, sometimes hovering low over the screen of trees while troops slid down the fifty-foot rope from which they could drop to the ground for the next phase of the hunt. In three minutes a helicopter could fly a patrol to a position that it would have taken men up to three days' march to reach through the thick underbrush.

British officers nevertheless said that they were resigned to "losing slowly," and one day in June 1964 I saw what they meant. Dominating the uneasy ocean of Sarawak jungle, the last and highest crest loomed above the transparent bubble of the diminutive Hiller helicopter, and the pilot beside me suddenly pulled it into a tight turn. For up there, shimmering in the damp tropical haze, was the border of Indonesian Borneo. No more than five miles beyond the watershed lay the safe jungle camps from which the terrorists launched their raids into Malaysian Sarawak and

Sabah. British, Gurkha, and Malaysian troops were responsible for defending nearly one thousand miles of frontier to stop the enemy ahead of them from linking up with the enemy behind them—the Chinese Communist guerrillas along the coastal strip —but they were not allowed to cross that border and destroy the enemy in his tantalizingly close bases. Frustrated commanders therefore prophesied that they would have to go on parrying his attacks with their elbows until a political solution ended Confrontation—perhaps in ten years' time The prospect was grim.

Only in theory, however. Sukarno had sworn that he would "crush Malaysia" before the cock crew on January 1, 1965, and as the day when his bluff would be called came closer, Djakarta escalated the war with cold-blooded inefficiency. Indonesian regulars in jungle green or paratroop mottle and armed with mortars and machine guns hit the beaches of the southwest coast of the Malayan peninsula itself in a series of seaborne assaults. They were soon eliminated. In September 1964, accordingly, blacked-out Hercules transports (for which Americans had recently delivered much-needed spare parts) flew a crack force of Indonesian paratroopers with renegade Malaysian guides into south Malaya, dropping them some ninety-five miles north of Singapore. At Labis, focus of the operation, I found small Malay and Chinese children clinging like flies on a meat cover to the wire fence around the police station. On a patch of grass inside was a neat row of Indonesians in camouflaged uniforms. They were flat on their backs, their wrists and ankles trussed to carrying poles, their Javanese faces discolored in death. Concise killers from a Gurkha battalion had shot them down with surgical precision a few miles north of the town. They had been among the last to be liquidated.

The cock crew in January 1, 1965. The Indonesians had failed miserably. The whole untidy business of Confrontation, had cost the Commonwealth forces 114 men killed in action before it whimpered to its own ignominious end. In a war whose potential hardly bore thinking about, most of the dangers proved hypothetical. The crewman on a chopper skimming over green waves of Sarawak jungle hooked a safety strap on to me, and I sat beside him on the edge of the floor to photograph the longhouses beneath, legs dangling in the cool slipstream outside. More than one thousand American helicopters were to be shot down in South Vietnam, but here there was scarcely a chance in a million that anyone would fire at us. And when H.M.S. *Maryton* loomed unfairly over the low Indonesian prahu, I was reminded suddenly of the last years of the anti-Communist emergency in Malaya, and the operations room of the South Wales Borderers in Johore.

"We've half a battalion working this area," the second-in-command had told me, pointing to a vast expanse of rubber and scrub on the map, "but the terrorists are devilish elusive." "How strong is the enemy then?" I asked. "Oh, just him and her. They're a married couple, you see." And he pointed to two snapshots of a Chinese man and woman pinned to a board above their names, their full descriptions, and their biographies. "That's all that's left. We've knocked out the rest. Pink gin?" Ten years later the Americans were still struggling against a quarter of a million unfriendly Vietnamese. Why did the British always seem to come off lightly?

Some British make facile and invidious comparisons between their own success against the Communist terrorists during the Malayan emergency and Washington's predicament in Vietnam which first interest, then irritate, and finally just bore the Americans. For as the real experts know, the two problems may have been similar, but the attendant circumstances were certainly not. Malaya was inhabited by two principal communities, Malay and Chinese, and as nearly all the Communist terrorists were Chinese, the British could automatically count on the loyalty of most of the Malays; but the Vietnamese Communists and the Vietnamese people were of one race, and anyone else was a foreigner. The Communists in Malaya with experience of guerrilla warfare numbered a few thousand, and they had no friendly base across the frontier; but the Communists of Vietnam had provided the hardened spearhead of a vast nationalist movement which had fought the French colonial power for eight years, the

Vietcong had North Vietnam behind them, and North Vietnam had China behind her.

The British started on firm ground and all square with their enemy; the Americans inherited a battlefield already soft with years of subversion. The British could undermine the resistance by offering Malaya independence; the Vietnamese had already won independence for themselves from the reluctant French, and owed it in large measure to the Communists. Even so, the Malayan emergency lasted for twelve long and gruelling years.

To compare Indonesian Confrontation with the war in Vietnam would be equally ludicrous. Had the roles been reversed, the Americans would probably have succeeded in suppressing the Malayan terrorists and the incongruous ambitions of Sukarno, and the British would probably have failed to suppress the Communists in Vietnam. All three situations nevertheless held similar seeds of disaster, and the scenario and the final fade-out in each case might have been very different. For the British, afflicted with the national change of life from imperial past to parochial future, are perhaps less confident of their own righteousness than the Americans, and recognize more readily that the peoples of the East are pragmatists concerned with their own immediate interests who do not love Indonesians or Americans or democracy or the Queen as such. And this unromantic approach may make for a sounder relationship than one based on ideological breast-beating. It certainly did in North Borneo.

As helicopters whirred over the undulating mat of trees deep in the interior, long black holes would appear here and there, like cigar burns in an ill-used green rug. In these slots were the great, raised longhouses of the Ibans, or Sea-Dyaks, accommodating twenty-five or thirty families under a headman in a G-string and with much elaborate blue tattooing. The Ibans drew comfort from the British presence and pinned up Union Jacks next to their sometimes gruesome trophies, having snicked the heads off any dead Indonesians they could lay their hands on when the troops turned their backs.

In remote jungle along the Indonesian border I once found two different tribes living amicably enough in adjacent, almost identical settlements of tin-roofed houses built of rough-cut logs and raised on stilts. The inhabitants were also similar in many ways. They loved good guns and good liquor. They were in excellent physical shape despite the oversimple, overheated conditions of the Borneo back-of-beyond. Both groups were in many cases heavily tattooed and both stuck feathers in their headdresses for formal occasions. But while the Ibans had their wives with them, the First Battalion the Royal Ulster Rifles did not.

The grinning Ibans were queueing up at a busy little dispensary of bamboo where the R.U.R. company medical orderly handled thirty native cases a day, dispensing anything from aspirin to eye drops. He had made a name for himself by saving the life of an Iban with a bad spear wound, chopping out the blade and then remaining with him far out in the rain forest until they were both picked up by helicopter. There were similar stories to be heard everywhere. An R.A.F. medical orderly delivered an Iban baby during the flight of a light single-engined Pioneer, and a hovercraft saved a woman's life after a difficult birth in a midnight dash up the "M. 1"—the great Rejang River that is the only highway in an anarchy of peaks and jungle completely devoid of road or rail. Inevitably, the helicopters provided the main shuttle service of this welfare system, and in 1965 No. 845 squadron R.N. took the unusual step of asking the army to train two men as midwives. By that time the squadron had already carried more than five hundred civilian emergency cases out of the jungle to the nearest town and hospital, including about three hundred direly pregnant females, many of whom had given birth within minutes of landing, and the odds were growing uncomfortably short.

The maid-of-all-work choppers evacuated longhouses on the border, lifting pigs and chickens and jars and gongs, carried water tanks into villages in the interior, brought out cholera victims. One pilot was adopted by a longhouse, renamed Booboo, and allowed to go on leave only after much lamentation among the locals (there was a scurrilous rumor that he used his machine not only for moving men, rations, ammunition, and the wounded, but for taking "Ma," the headman's wife, to market in the nearest town every week). At one isolated village a Scots corporal became the virtual chief of one hundred gentle, primitive Punans and taught them not to wash in the same water into which they relieved themselves.

All this casual neighborliness was as nothing when set beside the highly organized American charity drives in Vietnam. But it was subtly different. In Borneo the hearts-and-minds campaign was not something for the specialists. Doing good was not a profession, but the hobby of half the servicemen in the forward areas, and some pilots passed almost as much time playing ambulance and postman and errand boy for the people as they did dropping off and picking up patrols. Their superiors thought it well spent. Furthermore, the population was never tempted to feel that it was playing host to a Jekyll-and-Hyde general staff that dealt out candy with one hand and catastrophe with the other. The Director of Operations, General Sir Walter Walker, made certain that extreme precautions were taken to avoid shelling or bombing the ordinary people. "It was indelibly inscribed on our mind that one civilian killed by us would do more harm than ten killed by the enemy," he has since written. Nevertheless, "every time we defeated the enemy we took every precaution to ensure that he could not exact retribution on the nearest village."

The British had the advantage of poverty. If you do not have a hundred heavy bombers to spare to hit "suspect" hamlets, or a computer to work out how to be human by numbers, or a billion dollars to do the job of brains, it may be easier to preserve a sense of proportion and of flesh-and-blood values. Riches in resources, on the other hand, can encourage a wild spending spree on gadgets and facts and figures that only obscure reality and create their own world of illusion. Too often the conviction that truth is a *deus ex machina,* born of the punch card and the programmed computer, misleads to false and over-optimistic conclusions that deceive planners in war as in peace. In short, the desire to tidy up unkempt reality and express it in neat mathematical terms produces so much *pi-in-the-sky.*

In the villages of Vietnam the charts of statistics multiply, recording local loyalty in terms of the number of tons of fertilizer distributed by the Americans, and political prejudice expressed as medical aid received by the peasants, until even "1,505 haircuts offered free of charge since 1963" are weighed in the balance. But the enemy remains obstinately lethal, and this prompts another spoonful of polysyllabic slush: "Much more must be known of the behavioral and attitudinal responses of the villagers to externally imposed changes." How? One American answer was AGILE, a computerized war game to measure the factors governing the "loyalty rating" of Vietnamese villages. Hearts-and-minds were fed into the machine, so to speak, and converted into tape.

In 1967 the 12,722 hamlets scattered over the war-ravaged face of South Vietnam were reduced by H.E.S. (Hamlet Evaluation System) to a security index of figures and percentages. In January 1968 this index was released, and it showed that by December 1967, 5,340 hamlets (42 percent) were "relatively secure" from the Vietcong, 3,500 (27.5 percent) were "contested," and 3,882 (30.5 percent) were dominated by the Vietcong. Therefore, 11.5 million people out of a total population of 17.2 million were living in secure towns or under "reasonably good security conditions" in the country. This was an increase of 4.8 percent over the previous eleven months, thanks to the work of pacification and the expenditure of $350 million. "Let me say briefly I don't see how we can fail to do somewhat better in 1968 than we've done in 1967," added Robert Komer, adviser on the South Vietnamese pacification program in Saigon on January 24, 1968. The Communists launched their Tet Offensive just a few days later, and soon any new-found sense of security the peasant had enjoyed was shattered. For all the figuring, the confidence trick had failed again.

But even without the Tet Offensive, the adding-machine evaluation system was suspect, for while it could measure the number of sheets of corrugated iron roofing supplied to pleasantly surprised villagers, and translate this into love, it took no account of all the secret personal factors that influenced the infinitely more complex human computers in their own heads. The impact of material aid on political allegiance cannot be sold by weight as a winner of wars, for the minds of rich donor and poor beneficiary so often do not meet anyway. In some parts of Vietnam, American-inspired farming techniques proved so profitable that landowners started evicting their tenants in order to cultivate the land themselves, and the main by-product of "technical assistance" turned out to be a growing army of discontented and landless laborers. Elsewhere, United States aid officials have distributed gifts of rice and salt and cloth to needy refugees on one day, and South Vietnamese officials have moved in and carted them all away on the next. In Thailand, local administrators not only have "requisitioned" American largesse but have told peasants that American volunteers who give them free injections are in reality selling them, and have then furtively demanded cash in payment for the shots once the white nurses were out of sight.

As the supersonic jets from giant computerized carriers rained bombs on Tonking, yet small, skinny Vietnamese Communists fought on doggedly in the South, the war in Vietnam began to symbolize a wider contest between Western invention and Eastern intention. And in the hearts and minds of Asia, every day that the might of modern America failed to annihilate her diminutive enemy was a licking for the West. No intelligent Asian underestimates the enormous value and potential of the electronic brain, but many have become increasingly suspicious of the electronic blunder. They distrust a slide-rule civilization that will ask its gadgets anything from the name of the greatest heavyweight champion in history to the political and military alliances to be expected among forty-two countries with "space capability" in a notional nuclear crisis in 1985. And they are waiting to see if the computers have got the second one wrong too.

30 : Small Brother Is Watching You

By 1968 the affluent world of the white appeared to many Asians to have acquired the character of one of their own traditional despots—it was remote and rich and powerful, calculating but incalculable, often callously indifferent to poverty and suffering yet given to unpredictable, sometimes misguided gestures of generosity.

Parsimonious aid and timid investment from the haves accounted for only about twenty percent of the foreign exchange of which the have-not countries disposed to buy the machines and the know-how that should one day enable them to "take off." Meanwhile, the export drives upon which they depended to earn the other eighty percent were often cold-bloodedly blocked by protective tariffs in the West. Backward Southeast Asia merited a little charity, it seemed, but not a fair chance. A censorious

Occident pointed to the evils and idiocies of the undeserving continent, to the repellent spectacle of impoverished millions being sacrificed to the political and pecuniary ambitions of corrupt or incompetent bosses, to the ugly tangle of chauvinism and violence within which this corner of the market seemed inextricably caught. Yet who were the white men to talk?

On television Singaporeans watched documentaries about destitute Londoners living in grimy tenements with leaking roofs and broken windows, surrounded by broods of nine or ten unwashed children and sleeping four to a bed. Newspapers told literate Asians that one person in five in the United States was a poverty-stricken squatter sunk without trace in some filthy slum, and that ten million Americans went hungry on the day Apollo 11 hit the moon.

The West might write off Sukarno as a chauvinistic megalomaniac who had missed several good opportunities to die, but the East observed how Charles de Gaulle strove to put the *gloire* back into Gaul, demanding a hundred million Frenchmen by the year 2000 (while Asians were being urged to keep their copulation counterproductive if they wanted to eat), and behaving in Quebec and Montreal as if Canada were some sort of transatlantic Malaysia whose creation had cheated him personally of his rights. Had Sukarno denounced jeans and Beatle cuts as un-Indonesian? In 1968 the French solemnly removed the Mona Lisa from its place of honor in the Louvre because in future the whole of the Grand Gallery was to be reserved exclusively for French painters, and the works of mere foreigners were relegated to lesser rooms.

Vietnamese read of America's other dirty war at home between black and white, and Malaysians opened their newspapers to find stories from Britain with headlines like "Landlord Hired Dogs to Evict Negro Tenants" ("I am having no niggers in this house," he said). Indians in Singapore heard with disgust that when Sikh bus drivers and conductors were finally allowed to wear turbans as their religion stipulates, two hundred ill-mannered English morons of the London Transport Board turned up for work sporting sarcastic headgear that ranged from dirty towels to deer-stalker hats with feathers on the side.

As rival Catholic and Protestant mobs attacked each other with petrol bombs, bricks, and bottles in Belfast, the brown and yellow men took note that intolerance of color, race, and creed in the patronizing West yielded in nothing to exacting standards set by the East. And the same held true of violence itself. In 1967 there were some forty million guns in private hands in the United States, eight thousand murders, seventy thousand armed robberies, and a shooting every half hour. The following year bitter argument within the Democratic Party over the war in Vietnam led to the Battle of Chicago, in which the police struck out blindly at demonstrators and innocent onlookers alike, clubbing and gassing with egalitarian impartiality and yelling "Kill 'em, kill 'em."

Other aspects of Occidental political philosophy also repelled. In Britain industrial relations based on demands for unfair shares for all encouraged workers in a Northamptonshire factory to down tools because one of them had been asked to have his hair cut for his own safety, and the Ford Motor Company disclosed that it had enjoyed only twenty-three days free of strike threats during 1968 (which was a leap year). Under the British parliamentary system, the nation was the prisoner of the ruling party, and the ruling party was the prisoner of any group of parliamentary rebels that could threaten its majority, for its first concern was to stay in power. The caucus came before the country —and certainly, therefore, before any other country, as Lee Kuan Yew was to discover.

It was noon on a fine sweaty Saturday in January 1968. Upon the lawn in front of the prime minister's official residence in Singapore two men in white shirts and shorts sat at a table, gazing speculatively at me as I walked toward them. Lee Kuan Yew greeted me with a small, freezing grin, while Goh Keng Swee ordered more beer. The prime minister was obviously in an ominous temper and elated by his own fury. He had told his people that they would be safe from aggression "with our British friends remaining until 1977," and now word was out that they were aiming to close all their military bases on the island and abscond by the end of 1971.

Goh Keng Swee, who habitually submits all British promises anyway to the cold, impersonal appraisal of a pawnbroker conning a seed pearl through his jeweler's glass, rumbled gently from time to time but seemed to take it all as a matter of course. Lee, on the other hand, was brimming over with pugnacious arithmetic, totting up the stiff bill that he was going to make Britain pay for this treachery if the story proved true. He would take the republic's £2 hundred million worth of reserves straight out of the sterling area, and the British would also lose the £70 million a year that they earned from their industrial and commercial enterprises on the island. No new British business would be allowed into the country. The Singapore government would not pay one cent for the bases, no one would buy the land, and Whitehall could bloody well abandon it, what? Moreover, he was not sure that he would be able to promise to protect British subjects from the fury of the people once they learned . . .

"Hey," protested Goh, suddenly less somnolent, "don't talk like that. They'll think we are a bunch of gangsters." Lee stopped and smiled thinly, looking about as abashed as Vito Genovese. "I am not saying anything against Britain," he went on. "I am talking about a small group of Labour leaders who are ready to jettison everyone's interests, England's as well as ours, because the left wing of their party wants them to pull out all their forces East of Suez, and they need the support of that left wing if they are to be reelected. But don't quote me," he added, his eyes like fine slivers of obsidian and his syntax shaking with anger. "We don't know if it's true yet, isn't it?" Next day he did. After much rough and ready discussion, however, tempers slowly subsided, and if Singapore's sterling reserves started sidling off into other currencies, it was not because Lee had a tough spleen but because Goh had a hard head.

That was not the first time that the Far East had had occasion to sweep broken British promises into the rest of the litter of shattered illusions about the excellences of Western civilization, as everyone in Singapore knew from the cabinet to our cook.

Just two months earlier, her eyes watchful but sorry, Ah Fu had unlocked a drawer, pulled out a battered purse, and emptied its contents on her dresser. Twenty slightly flattering pictures of Her Gracious Majesty Queen Elizabeth II fell out—a thousand old Malayan dollars. Ah Fu was not the only one to have been caught by British devalution. Prime Minister Harold Wilson had said on thirty-three different occasions that the pound would not be unpegged, but this had inexplicably failed to arouse suspicion in the minds of many. Now the value of the old colonial dollar, which had been freely convertible at par into the new national currencies of Singapore and Malaysia up to that moment, was cut to eighty-five cents because it had been pinned to the pound.

The ghastly irony of it was that many uncomplicated Asians had put their faith in old bills stamped with the illustrious imprimatur of the great British raj, spurning all later issues. Fifty-dollar notes bearing the crowned heads of the United Kingdom had actually commanded a higher price than their face value and had been sold for profit. Now they were emerging all over the area like dishonored promissory notes, and Britons had much to blush for on that day. Those slightly crumpled royal faces symbolized a wider devaluation of the white which nevertheless gave pleasure to many. For some Asians are incurably color-conscious and compulsive racists themselves.

The compulsive racist is that poisonous animal, the man who will read racial discrimination into any fact or fiction, innocent or ugly, on the flimsiest pretext. In Singapore people have protested against Westerners because they "glorify the white man," and in Sukarno's Indonesia, Tarzan was banned as propaganda deliberately designed to prove that one illiterate Caucasian was a match for ten thousand black Africans. An Indian publication closely associated with Krishna Menon has found that the most significant thing about the destruction of Hiroshima was that the Americans did not try out their atom bomb on their blond German enemies. They dropped it on the yellow Japanese. It escapes the attention of self-righteous Asians that racists—whether white, black, brown, or yellow—are the same trash under the skin.

The prism of color prejudice east of Suez refracts tints more subtle than the black-and-white contrasts of the West, however. For where the white man is resented for his race, he may be envied for his whiteness, and where the black man earns sympathy as the victim of white oppression, he may be despised for his blackness. The Negro in Asia can find a landlady's door slammed in his face as surely as if he were in Notting Hill or Little Rock, and in 1968 a Committee of the Concerned for Equal Housing was set up to fight discrimination—not in either of the Birminghams but in Bangkok. The Asians sympathize with the black man's struggle for civil rights in the United States, as long as it stays there.

In the East caste and color became confused with the passage of centuries, but the great Hindu epic, the *Mahabharata*, told the men of India long before the birth of Christ: "Brahmins are fair—and sudras are black." Brahmins are the teachers and priests of the highest caste, sudras are peasants and servants. An Asian country is a land of many hues, in which the basic principle of prestige is the lighter the better. Dark Indians, dark Cambodians, dark Indonesians suffer silently the disdain of their paler compatriots. In Singapore and Malaysia, Eurasians come in all shades from ivory to ebony and yet will make cruel distinctions among themselves, off-white denying his mixed-blood brotherhood with dark-oak. Many struggle purposefully up the color chart toward an alabaster Nirvana, deliberately seeking wives fairer than themselves so that their children—the next incarnation—will be a shade closer to the ultimate bliss. Moreover, in a multicolored subcontinent, difference of pigmentation sharpens the sense of racial superiority, and as the tide of Western colonialism ebbed in Asia, it left exposed the *Herrenvolk* instincts of those who had been quickest to complain of oppression by their former European masters. And none felt this more promptly than the minority hill tribes.

I first saw them in June 1955, when Ngo Dinh Diem accepted the Oath of Fealty in Central Vietnam from the human remnants of ancient cultures that had been driven up the disheveled mountains as successive waves of conquering Thais and Vietnamese rolled into the fertile valleys and plains below. M'nong, Nung, Rhade, Djarai, Tho, Curu; the Vietnamese lumped them together contemptuously under the generic term Moi—"savage." They had dressed for the occasion in a riot of native silver and copper, beads, belts and bangles, embroidered turbans and blouses and woven blankets of flaming orange and red and black. As undulating girls, each shining poll supporting a single tall black feather, beat a soft, liquid flow of caressing notes out of five gongs, the main ceremony began in a grassy clearing on the edge of the Annamese jungle, framed by skeletal buttress trees and feathery tamarinds.

Diem—immaculate, shy, somewhat pink of face—sat on a wooden elephant head in a small open-sided pavilion and moved his arms and legs like a reluctant marionette in accordance with the whispered instructions of a ritual expert. Five menials threaded their way through the watching crowd and placed before him the bloody severed heads of a male and female buffalo freshly sacrificed, together with selected parts of their bodies. The eyes of the female were closed in quiet resignation. Those of the male leered emptily into the middle distance. At Diem's feet was a large banana leaf on which had been placed an ax head and a cup of blood. The arch-sorcerer took up Diem's well-shod right foot and placed it on this leaf (the gesture of a victorious and supreme chief). He then dipped a thick wick into the cup of blood and touched Diem's shoes with it. Chanting in Rhade, he next passed a thin gold bangle over Diem's wrist and swore allegiance to him. He was followed by a long line of tribal chiefs, more oaths, more blood and bracelets.

After the tribal chiefs came the elephants, prized possessions whose act of loyalty would symbolize the sincerity of their Moi owners. Two hundred and sixteen of the great gray beasts, piggy little eyes peering, trunks sweeping the grass, passed the pavilion in majestic Indian file. As each drew level with the new master of Vietnam, its mahout, perched barelegged on the vast wrinkled cranium, pounded it with a heavy goad to make it kneel before the man in the white sharkskin suit. Thirty minutes nearer death and just as this repetitive procedure began to pall, one vast fellow, evidently suffering from either stage fright or decided views, started to turn toward Diem obediently but suddenly swung about and knelt in the opposite direction, presenting the startled Vietnamese leader with an enormous expanse of uplifted pachydermatous rump which he then declined to remove. The gesture was unmistakable: "Thine impudence," remarks the Caliph in Flecker's *Hassan*, "hath a monstrous beauty, like the hind-quarters of an elephant." The old beast seemed to express the feelings of all the minorities of Southeast Asia.

The Mois hated and distrusted the Vietnamese, and the Vietnamese too often treated them arrogantly as expendable sub-humans whose sufferings and privations were irrelevant. In the middle-sixties the hill peoples mounted two armed revolts, demanding that the upland tiger-country in which they lived should be granted regional autonomy. In 1969 *montagnard* villagers were still complaining bitterly that when schools, food, and title to land were handed out, they were conveniently forgotten by Saigon. On their side, the Vietcong plundered villages and shot tribesmen in Central Vietnam in an attempt to frighten them into fighting for them, and kidnapped them at gunpoint to make them act as their porters.

Shans, Kachins, Karens, Mois, Thais, Meos, Nagas, Sakkais, Papuans, Dyaks, Dusuns, Muruts, Igorots, ranging from primitive aborigine to early settlers of a distinctive civilization, the minorities straddle the neat national boundaries that others have drawn straight through the troughs and crests of their mountainous territories, and ignore the borders that ignore them. And in most cases they have until recently been cheated, bullied, and sometimes enslaved by new Asian masters for whom "Freedom" is a war cry when used against the West but a dirty word when directed against their own brown or yellow power.

During the war against the Communist terrorists in Malaya it was the New Zealanders who were filtered into deep jungle to win over the Sakkais, the aborigines whom the Communists recruited as farmers, guides, and spies, for it had been found that the Kiwis had the knack of winning their confidence and friendship. The Australians were trusted next, then the British, then the Gurkhas. Inevitably, the last on the list were the Malays, the new Asian overlords of the land. But the Malays have been models of magnanimity compared with the Burmese.

Most Burmese live in the lower reaches of the Irrawaddy valley and its delta; the great uplands in the north and the coastal area to the south are the domains of big minorities. But when in 1947 the country stood on the threshold of independence from British colonial rule, nearly all of these peoples agreed to join a sovereign Union of Burma governed from Rangoon, provided they enjoyed certain autonomous rights. Separate Shan, Kachin, and Karen states were duly created, each with a minister in the central government and representation in the two Houses. The senior Shan ruler, Sao Shwe Taik, became first president of Burma.

Almost in a matter of months, however, the Burmese were showing that they were determined to dominate the entire country—by force if necessary—and militants among the minorities took to the hills in open armed rebellion. The Burmese then tossed out the constitutional right of the Shans and Karens to secede, and their trigger-happy troops moved into the mountains, sacking villages and brutally shooting or manhandling the hill people in their homes.

When he was not up in his Shan capital of Taunggyi, Sao Shwe Taik lived in a rambling old house in Rangoon, and here I first met this good and gentle old man, who was dividing his time between translating Buddhist texts and feeling his way like some political osteopath toward a quick and painless constitutional twist that could end Burma's racial agony. But in February 1962 General Ne Win seized power. Soldiers surrounded the ex-president's house after dark, shot his son dead when he opened the front door to see who was outside, and then arrested the father. Sao Shwe Taik died years later in lonely custody and his widow lives in exile.

In 1966 a British television team was able to spend five months with the Shan rebels without being challenged by the Burmese military authorities, who could maintain only a tenuous hold on towns and roads in the north. Three years later the fight that need never have started was still flickering over the fissured and splintered land whose title—the Union of Burma—was now nothing more than a sour joke.

In Thailand, where three hundred thousand restive Meos live astride the northern border, the government reacted to the depredations of fewer than two hundred armed tribesmen in 1968 by ordering air strikes on "suspect" villages and by treating all who did not subsequently come out of the hills to be resettled in the plains as Communists. The Communists were indeed wheedling their way into the hearts of some Meos, enticing them for guerrilla training across the border in Laos with promises not only of all manner of good things from guns to girls but—most significantly—of autonomy and of revenge against the Thais. But it was only after the Thais had bombed, burned, and evicted the Meos that the Communist recruiting program began to show really satisfactory results.

Meanwhile, like the dark side of the moon, the western half of the vast tropical island of New Guinea consistently shunned exposure to the light after it became the Indonesian province of West Irian in 1963. There were muffled reports of sudden armed uprisings by discontented Papuan natives in this territory which Sukarno had "liberated" from the Dutch, but in that huge enigmatic wilderness the truth was not easy to determine. However, I remember how Lieutenant-General Djatikusomo—Javanese soldier, diplomat, prince, and presumably gentleman—had spoken of Indonesia's compassionate task of freeing the oppressed Papuans from their colonial fetters as civilizing the dirty natives "if necessary at the point of the bayonet."

The New York agreement, concluded between Holland and Indonesia in 1962 through the good offices of the United Nations, permitted Djakarta to take over the territory provisionally but stipulated that in 1969 the Papuans must be allowed their own "act of free choice" between independence and permanent incorporation in the Republic of Indonesia. But in 1969 Djakarta refused to organize a referendum, and instead only consulted members of the appointed councils in West Irian's eight regencies. In the best traditions of *musjawarah*, this carefully chosen selectorate voted unanimously for West Irian to remain in the republic, one servile delegate claiming a little boldly: "Since the time of Adam and Eve we have been part of Indonesia." Djakarta had had no intention of ceding the territory from the outset, whatever the natives thought about it. President Suharto had declared that he would regard any decision by the people to leave the republic as "treason against Indonesia."

The betrayal of trusting tribesmen has become a cliché of modern Asian history. The British handed their loyal friends over to the incoming brown or yellow sahib, and the French and the Dutch did the same. It was expedient to sacrifice them in order to keep on friendly terms with the new emerging master races in the capitals of Southeast Asia. The corollary of this, however, was that the minority peoples spread untidily across the high frontier lands of the subcontinent became prime prey for the Communists, until each of the new states began to fray and discolor at the edges.

31 : The Wandering Chinese

Undeterred by the sometimes sad results of arbitrarily chopping up and combining the pieces and populations of Asia in new surrealistic patterns—a head severed down the middle here, an ear attached to a navel there—the British invented "Malaysia."

The existing Federation of Malaya was a drooping finger of peninsula on the mainland of Southeast Asia peopled principally by indigenous Malays and by immigrant Chinese and Indians. Dangling from it by a 1,200-yard causeway, however, was the island ministate of Singapore, in which the Chinese dominated and Malays were in the minority. And along the northern strip of the otherwise Indonesian island of Borneo, several hundred miles away across the South China Sea, Britain had other dependencies which she was also anxious to shed—two great undulating carpets of jungle and coastal mush, now known as

Sarawak and Sabah, whose native inhabitants were upriver tribes like the Dyaks and the Dusuns. As their empire came under the hammer, the main problem before the British was how to unload this ill-assorted geographical bric-a-brac. The only answer was to lump it together as a single job lot and knock it down to the one obvious buyer. And in this they succeeded.

Sitting next to him at a public lunch on May 27, 1961, I asked Tengku Abdul Rahman of Malaya whether his recent trip to the North Borneo territories had persuaded him to move into them politically. He cut cautiously into his gaudy sweet with a small spoon and replied: "I was very touched. Everywhere I went, people who felt that the British were going soon seemed to be looking towards Malaya for leadership. But I shall have to think more about it first."

Apparently it did not require too much thought, however, for as coffee was served, he rose to address the Foreign Correspondents' Association of Southeast Asia and spoke for the first time of a possible political "association" which would include Malaya, Singapore, and the North Borneo states. Two years later, after much acrimonious last-minute bargaining, this new expanded Federation of Malaysia came into being under a predominantly Malay central government in Kuala Lumpur. But in Sarawak only one man in five was a Malay, in Sabah one man in twenty-five, and although the upcountry Dyaks and Ibans and Dusuns and Muruts had voted for union with Malaya (since they could not go it alone), they viewed their change of chiefs with some foreboding. They had unpleasant racial memories of the days when they had been administered by the callous minions of the sultan of Brunei, and they imagined that all Malays were much the same. The takeover was quiet enough, but the surface smoothness was as deceptive as a Dyak longhouse on its high stilts, which looks clean because all the rubbish and ordure fall between the polished slats of the bamboo floor to the midden beneath.

A venomous stream of whispers fled zigzag through the apprehensive valleys of North Borneo. The Muslim Malays were going to force the people to give up eating pork and to submit to circumcision. They were going to make Malay the compulsory national language for all by 1967, and only those who spoke it would be accepted into the police and administration. They were going to take over all key posts, exclude the natives, strip the country, and put nothing into it. These spurious rumors lent a long shadow to any small incident that seemed to confirm them, and the Malays did on occasion give cause for a certain uneasiness. In 1963 an angry general privately complained to me of the insolence of Malay troops, who contemptuously slapped and kicked the Dyaks and insulted their women, and later there were to be scattered skirmishes between soldiers and civilians. By 1967 the Dyak paramount chief who had become Malaysian Minister for Sarawak Affairs was openly accusing Malay ministers of favoring Malays and completely neglecting the Dyaks. "I don't care if anybody kills me, but I have to say the truth," he declared defiantly.

When the third new state of Singapore proved intractable, the Tengku cut it loose from Malaysia. But he did not deign to consult the elected state governments of Sarawak and Sabah beforehand, although they had joined the Federation on the understanding that Singapore would also be part of it. Non-Malay political leaders in North Borneo were outraged, for given the autocratic attitude that the princely prime minister had instinctively adapted toward the constitution over the matter, they themselves might be stripped of their autonomous rights at twenty-four hours' notice if it ever suited Kuala Lumpur.

It was fair to say, however, that if discontented natives were suspicious of the Tengku's government, the Tengku was equally unhappy. Already in 1964 he had spoken to me sorrowfully about the ungrateful Borneo states as we took tea in his old residence in Kuala Lumpur. "The British did not train an efficient local civil service there before they handed over to us," he grumbled gently over the biscuits. "These people are not always easy to deal with, and some of their politicians will not keep their big mouths shut. The trouble is, you see, they are rather a primitive lot."

Once again a good man had been fooled by figures. It had been accepted that Malaya and Singapore, split apart by the British colonial power during the nineteenth century in the unnatural course of events, should be reunited. But this meant that in their combined territories there would be more "immigrant" Chinese than indigenous Malays, which was unthinkable. However, by adding all the "proto-Malay" natives in Sarawak and Sabah to the ingredients (said the British slyly), the balance would be redressed, leaving the Malays with a comfortable lead of 407,000 head of population (four percent) over other races. In reality, only a minority of the natives of North Borneo were Muslim and most of them should have been counted among the non-Malays, but at the time the price seemed right to the Tengku: the important thing was that the Overseas Chinese, the "Jews of Asia," would be safely outnumbered.

The Chinese called it Nanyang, the South Seas, this exotic subcontinent of aromatic spices and healing herbs along the tropical sea route to the Buddhist shrines of India, and their pilgrims trickled through its narrow waters and ancient cities at least fifteen hundred years ago. They were followed by enterprising traders who oversold things Chinese so successfully that in the thirteenth century the Dragon Throne decreed that the commerce must be cut back, and some celestial exports (notably grain and girls) were forbidden altogether.

But as the acquisitive European conquistadors sailed into these tepid seas and overran the coasts, Chinese mercantile communities sprang up in counterpoint in the Spanish Philippines, the Dutch Indies, Portuguese Malacca, and when the British settled Singapore and Penang it was the immigrant Chinese who flooded in to become the main inhabitants. Later many brought their own womenfolk from China and preserved the clannish customs of their homeland, until the entire demographic map of Southeast Asia was mottled with alien, unabsorbed Chinese life.

In 1830 the tin mines of Malaya began drawing peasant labor from the impoverished villages of South China, and the soulless "pig trade" in indentured workers, shipped out like so much merchandise, brought thousands of penniless contract coolies into Nanyang to join the Chinese carpenters and goldsmiths, the market gardeners and merchants who had already settled abroad —"yellow, lean, smoothshaven, keen, industrious, self-reliant, opium-smoking, gambling, hugging clan ties, forming no others, and managing their own matters even to the post and money order offices," as Isabella Bird puts it.

Forbidden by imperial edict to leave their own country, the Chinese had not traveled for love of the trip. Hard-working, thrifty, astute, they were driven by a desire for the security of wealth that frequently manifested itself in unscrupulous avarice and sharp practice. They became the village shopkeepers and moneylenders, the pawnbrokers and the bankers, and eventually the bosses of trucking services on which local farmers and fishermen depended for the distribution of their crops or catch. Sullenly envied by their less business-like hosts, they privately despised the indolent native and distrusted the white overlord.

Their domination of the retail trade in Indonesia dates from the eighteenth century, when the Dutch East India Company used them as managers and middlemen, and the Malay mercantile class was edged out of business altogether. The Chinese ran and rigged the markets, bought up cheap the local rubber, tobacco, coffee, kapok, and rice, and sold them dear. They gave the impecunious Indonesian producer credit but slapped on interest at the rate of up to twenty-five percent a month. By the time the archipelago had become an independent republic, some two and a half million Chinese controlled two-thirds of all trade, nearly all inter-island commerce, and up to ninety percent of all small and medium industry.

To resentment of this rich alien infusion that had filtered into the finest capillaries of the subcontinent was now added angry suspicion. The peoples of Southeast Asia began to fear that the strong sense of brotherhood among the 14 million Chinese scattered like fertile seed over their soil might most admirably suit the purposes of Mao Tsetung.

Communist China sedulously cosseted her errant sons, for their remittances through Hong Kong alone to relatives still living in the home country contributed £50 million a year to foreign-exchange reserves. Local branches of the Bank of China in Southeast Asia extended generous credit to merchants buying goods from the mainland, and Peking accorded to selected Overseas Chinese traders in Singapore and elsewhere the exclusive right to handle this or that Chinese product on highly advantageous terms. A trellis of Chinese merchants and shopkeepers dependent upon the favor of Peking was built up—to carry the vine of subversion, many bitterly declared.

Chinese operations knew no frontiers. The Chinese in Cambodia smuggled Communist Chinese goods to Chinese merchants in southern Laos, and the Chinese in north Malaysia smuggled Communist goods to Chinese dealers in southwest Thailand. Money talked Maoism. Until 1965, every time a Chinese living in Indonesia remitted money to needy parents on the Communist mainland, the counterpart which he paid in Djakarta went into a special fund held by the Chinese embassy. The fund accumulated about £6 million a year (at the official rate of exchange) for financing "revolutionary movements" in Indonesia itself, and it was swollen by voluntary contributions exacted from rich businessmen. Peking actively encouraged violence, and in 1967 militant young Overseas Chinese could look back on weeks of riotous living inspired by Mao's Cultural Revolution in China, where Juvenal's bread-and-circus formula for keeping the masses happy had been translated into a modern combination of rice-and-rampage. Emulating the Red Guards on the mainland, they had fought off police and beaten up bystanders in the streets of Hong Kong, Djakarta, Malaysia, and Singapore, amid showers of brickbats and burning debris, bottles and rotten eggs, hose-piping and dustbin lids.

Ardor is always a matter of age, however. The disorderly behavior of an impetuous minority of students may have suggested that the "Great Cultural Revolution" was a danger wherever two or three Chinese were gathered together. But it would be wrong to mistake the froth for the beer. The unassimilated Chinese may champion their national culture, but to identify Chinese culture with Communism is absurd, for nowhere is it more fiercely defended than in Chiang Kai-shek's Nationalist stronghold of Formosa. Most Overseas Chinese in Southeast Asia are not revolutionary animals. They are pragmatic fauna who want peace and quiet.

In 1967 the Indonesians revealed that out of a million and a half "People's Chinese" in Indonesia who theoretically owed allegiance to Peking, only twenty thousand had registered for repatriation to China. Thousands were applying for Indonesian citizenship and were ready to buy it if they could—the Supreme Court had already been obliged to sack four judges for "irregularities" in dealing with naturalization demands. In Bangkok their new readiness to be assimilated is demonstrated by the fact that few Chinese under twenty-five years old speak Chinese or have Chinese names any more. At least fifteen Thais in every hundred have Chinese blood in their veins, on the other hand, and they include the king and most of the cabinet. In Cambodia, the Chinese showed how steady an eye they kept on the main chance rather than Mao Tsetung by crowding the Chinese embassy at receptions when Peking was popular with Prince Norodom Sihanouk but tactfully forgetting its existence when he talked darkly of Communist conspiracies against him. Most Overseas Chinese want a relationship with China which will be profitable, apolitical, and free of friction. So do the British, the Americans, the Canadians, the Australians, and most of the rest of the world besides.

But as the new nations of postwar Southeast Asia took their first, uncertain steps in sovereign rule, it was inevitable that they should turn censorious eyes upon the Chinese among them, with their hideous economic strength and their dubious political loyalties. The flamboyant shop signs with their dancing ideograms disappeared from the streets of Saigon-Cholon in 1957, to be replaced by neat notices in Roman-lettered Vietnamese, and the old air of faintly guilty gaiety was gone. President Ngo Dinh Diem had decreed that all Chinese born in Vietnam must become Vietnamese citizens and adopt Vietnamese names. Those who did not were barred from engaging in eleven of the most profitable and important trades, including the milling and distribution of rice. Chinese schools were allocated Vietnamese supervisors, who made sure that classes were taught in the Vietnamese language for sixteen hours a week. Chinese wives applying for their new identity cards were firmly advised to present themselves at registration bureaus wearing Vietnamese costume. It was the first attempt to convert one race into another at short notice by putting another language into its mouth, a sheaf of new identity documents into its pocket, and a strange if admittedly fetching new costume onto the backs of its women.

In Thailand and Burma and the Philippines the Chinese were the victims of similar measures, but Indonesia enjoyed the blackest record. When Djakarta ordered the Chinese to abandon their village stores in 1959 in an abortive attempt to break their hold on the economy, troops were called out to herd them into the crowded towns, and thousands of their homes and shops were burned down or wrecked by vengeful Javanese (many of whom seized this golden opportunity to set fire to all the IOU's in the hands of these alien moneylenders). Vicious anti-Chinese rioting flickered over the republic in 1963 and 1965, and in the grim autumn of 1967 Dyaks went berserk in Indonesian Borneo, butchering or burning entire Chinese families in their beds and forcing more than fifty thousand to flee to the coastal towns, abandoning everything they owned. (Exports from the island dropped by forty percent. Cash flows out with the blood when the Chinese are attacked.)

By 1968 it was illegal to speak Chinese in Indonesia, to use Chinese characters on shop signs, to celebrate Chinese festivals publicly, or to have a Chinese name. Parliament then passed a law prohibiting Chinese without Indonesian nationality from putting capital into any form of trade. The law was designed to encourage assimilation and to end Chinese domination of the Indonesian economy once and for all. But it will only come into effect after 1977. For if the business acumen of shrewd and grasping Chinese has been their downfall, it has also been their salvation: like most of the flabby countries in the South Seas, Indonesia cannot do without them yet, any more than man can do without muscle.

In Malaya, the different races learned to live side by side amicably enough on any ordinary day, but embers of distrust and enmity smoldered and flared from time to time, and after World War II the overbearing behavior of "victorious" Chinese who regarded the Malays as stooges of the hated Japanese prompted some savage fighting.

This was the unwinding brown-and-yellow scroll of past insult and injury in the region against which a predominantly Malay Malaya and a predominantly Chinese Singapore were merged in 1963, amid much public shaking of hands and private shaking of heads.

32 : The Mythical Malaysians

The merger was strictly a marriage of convenience that ended in a divorce on grounds of incompatibility of temperament. In Singapore the Malays were outnumbered six-to-one by tiresomely vigorous Chinese who overshadowed them in government and administration. For the most part they were the philosophical poor—fishermen, gardeners, postmen, and messengers living in combustible kampongs—as they were on the mainland. In Malaya, however, the king was a Malay sultan, the prime minister a Malay prince, all political portfolios in the government were held by Malays, and the constitution recognized their "special position" as the "sons of the soil." Within the Malayan Alliance, the coalition that administered the Federation, harmony between Malays and Chinese depended upon their prince-and-merchant relationship. The privileged Malays dispensed favor; the rich

Chinese, funds. The Malays held the power; the Chinese merely the purse strings.

But while the Alliance was a troika of three separate racial political groups—Malay, Chinese, and Indian—the ruling People's Action Party in Singapore was an integrated organization of all races. The Alliance was conservative, the PAP socialist; the Alliance was bent upon defending Malay privilege, the PAP demanded a "Malaysian Malaysia" in which all races would have a seat in the sun; in Malaya the Alliance governed and the PAP was in opposition; in Singapore the PAP governed, and the Alliance was in opposition. Within six months of the merger the hostile PAP had advanced into Malaya to put up candidates against the Alliance in the general elections of April 1964. The Alliance, fearful that Lee Kuan Yew planned to become the first Chinese prime minister of the entire Federation, damned him for "a hungry dog" whose "itching hands" were bent on "pulling down Malaysia" and whose party was "ready to collaborate with the devil." The brief, frigid honeymoon was already over.

The PAP called the Alliance leaders racists for protecting Malay rights at the expense of all others; the Alliance called the PAP leaders racists for calling them racists. Everybody was in the right, as usual, and so everybody was in the wrong. "I have warned Tengku that there can be no Malaysian nation until all men are treated equally as Malaysians, and that otherwise there will be racial trouble," Lee Kuan Yew told me in June 1964. "But the old boy simply pooh-poohs the idea, tells me I don't understand Malaya properly and it will never happen."

Within the two incompatible states were two incompatible prime ministers. Tengku Abdul Rahman was born an Oriental Edwardian, a Muslim prince from a royal family that was a thousand years old even on paper, who spent his years at Cambridge avoiding study in the expensive company of girls and horses and flashy cars. By now over sixty, he was the master of Malaysia, a quasi-feudal father-figure of partly Siamese origin with the face of an elderly seal point who believed in the inalienable right of man to pursue happiness (for which his personal recipe included poker and golf and football and the turf and adopting children of different races). He moved through the world of politics with the casual aplomb of an aristocratic amateur, taking life at an easy, patrician pace like a man willfully avoiding a coronary.

Relying on rank, the Tengku remained aloof from the scramble for success, had no pretensions to arid intellectual brilliance ("I don't understand all this cultural stuff," he once remarked of the new National Art Gallery in Kuala Lumpur, "but if it makes people happy, let 'em have it"). He had the bluff common-sense manner of a plain prince, urbane but not suave, and there was something magnificent about the careless impartiality with which, a few years ago, he described Lee Kuan Yew as "that bloody Communist Lee" and the Muslim secretary of his own party, who was Lee's bitterest enemy, as "that bloody fellow Albar"— all in one sentence. He could turn the tables on an adversary as gently as another might turn his cheek. "Malays lazy? But all the nicest people are lazy," he once remarked. It was his philosophy. When an English journalist aroused wrath by writing that the Malays had no culture, "no literature, no history except piracy," the Tengku waited until the angry hubbub subsided and then asked: "What's all the fuss about? The British are proud of all their pirates, and we should be proud of ours."

Like all the best with blue blood, the prince-premier had the common touch, the air of a benevolent uncle who filled his pockets with sweets for the kiddies and was ready to throw any Communist suspect into jail at the drop of an "h." But he avoided acrimonious discussion, for it was beneath his dignity to raise his voice, and he was always ready to let the past bury the past. He also allowed it to bury all his enemies, and he was to chop out of political power in Malaysia not only Lee and "that bloody fellow Albar," but half a dozen other leaders who were so disloyal as to challenge his paternalistic rule, displaying on these occasions all the characteristic Malay indolence of a whip-lash. He would then set off for Penang or Singapore amid much tremulous speculation as to what these further moves meant. But he was only going to watch his horses run.

The Tengku was known as a firm enemy of racialism, and

although in 1964 he remarked: "Wherever there are Chinese, there are Communists," the assessment was correct. He got on famously with them all, provided they kept their place. Lee was another matter, however.

The prime minister of Singapore was the son of a moderately successful merchant and just forty years old when their two territories were joined. A brilliant, pugnacious lawyer and politician with an absorbent memory and a mind like a cheese wire, he was feared for his incisive, often ironical argument in the legislative assembly, but for mass meetings and alfresco hecklers he reserved an open shirt, a closed fist, and a fiery I'll-fix-you delivery. He was a socialist, yet no easy mixer, a man of sudden, arrogant tempers who suffered fools badly. Within Lee the intellectual was always at war with the tough, the democrat with the political bronco-buster. Born to politics, he had the ability to rationalize questionable decisions that successful members of this disagreeable profession must acquire. His detractors called him ruthless and dictatorial, his admirers the very epitome of a Chinese hero (who must almost by definition be a bit of a thug).

A news reader on Radio Singapore once made a slip that jeopardized Lee's political calculations, so the prime minister summoned him and bawled the man out in front of his colleagues. The undaunted news editor yelled back at Lee, whereupon Lee started to tear off his jacket, it is said, shouting, "Why, you little pipsqueak, I'll break you in half," or some unexpurgated version of these words. Others present intervened and the fight was called off. Lee admired pluck, however, and the man not only kept his job but became head of the news division. Lee's cold intelligence and hot furies threatened to combine to destroy him, but with the disciplined tenacity with which he did everything, he applied himself conscientiously to the task of learning to be tactful and tolerant with the slow and the stupid. It was a long, painful business.

The Tengku liked an informal understanding as between men of honor. Lee preferred agreements in black and white. The Tengku was intuitive, Lee cerebral and pragmatic. "They play poker up there in Kuala Lumpur," Lee used to say. "Down here we prefer bridge" (he did not realize that in that one sentence he had revealed that he might never have made a successful premier of a federation held together by flair and not logic). The Tengku thought Lee blunt and indiscreet, prone to dissect nasty little problems that he felt should have been left in the woodwork, a leftist, a twister, and no gentleman. Lee found the Tengku permissive, feudal, politically superannuated, and there was no sympathy between them. Lee reacted to the "treatment" of girls, gambling, and big balloon glasses he found awaiting him in certain houses in Kuala Lumpur like a purse-lipped twentieth-century Savonarola threatened with seduction. "I'm not throwing in my hand just so's I can go to bed with a Thai actress," he growled to someone after one visit, back in Singapore and doubtless intact.

Yet to Lee the Tengku was the only man in sight who could keep the peace between Singapore and Malaya. "If Tengku went and someone like Albar became prime minister, there would be nothing left for us," he said to me in August 1964. "We would have to take to the jungle, and Malaysia would become another Vietnam."

This Syed Ja'afar Albar showed what he thought of the concept that a man must be a "Malaysian" whatever his race by declaring "Whatever I am, I am a Malay," and the boast was all the more curious since he was not only "that bloody fellow Albar," but an Arab, and indeed descended from the family of the Prophet himself. It should not be thought, however, that Albar was a Muslim fanatic to whom the presence of the pork-eating infidel was an intolerable affront. He has since been profitably associated, in fact, with a millionaire who in theory is everything he has been said to detest—a Chinese chauvinist and a left-wing champion of Chinese culture.

In 1963 Albar was a slightly corpulent gentleman with all the hallmarks of aristocratic distinction—a graying mustache, a fine sloping forehead, a long cigarette holder, a plausible, quick-witted charm—and as secretary-general of the Tengku's party, he made his philosophy clear to me in a reasonable, let's-face-it voice on two occasions. The Tengku was weak. The native peoples of

North Borneo were ignorant and unreliable and no friends of
the Malays as he had been fooled into thinking. The trouble with
the Chinese leaders in the Alliance was that they were incapable
of keeping their people "under proper control." As for "that
Communist bugger, Lee Kuan Yew," he ought to be put in jail
out of harm's way. Something would have to be done about all
this.

Ten days after our second meeting Albar organized and addressed a Malay and Muslim convention in Singapore headed by
a "Malay National Action Committee" whose object was to make
more demands for special privileges for Malays on the island, and
to prepare for a mass rally to protest against their "victimization"
by the PAP state government. The Malays must unite, Albar
stressed. "Then not even a thousand Lee Kuan Yews can break
us." Those Malays who had accepted Lee's invitation to thrash
out their problems with him peacefully were condemned as
"traitors."

Lee had already been accused of brutal discrimination in favor
of the island's 1,200,000 Chinese, of evicting Malays from their
homes to make way for new blocks of cheap flats, of neglecting
to build schools for them, and of failing to respect their "special
rights." The Singapore government in vain retorted that under
current housing-development plans, eight Chinese were being
evicted for every one Malay, and that only the Malays enjoyed
free education in the state up to and including university studies.
Many Malays wanted more, for they felt unable to stand up to
the dynamic Chinese man-to-man unless they were given false
heels—an assured quota of jobs, free schoolbooks, subsidized
rents, reserved lands. I picked up a leaflet headed "Singapore
Malay National Action Committee" and addressed to "Malay
brothers and sisters" which urged: "Let us unite to resist the
Chinese, who want to kill us Malays. Before Malay blood flows
in Singapore, it is better to flood the state with Chinese blood."

One week later I stood at the end of a long, silent Singapore
street covered with a glittering carpet of shattered bottles. Knots
of sullen youths watched from the shadow of the arcaded side-
walks. A car burned quietly. The knives and the machetes had

been out. Nearby, hooligans had gouged a man's eyes from his head and then disemboweled him. Night in the critical district of Geylang was punctuated by screams and the alarm beat of mosque drums as white, Sikh, Chinese, and Malay officers of a mixed Singapore battalion led their men through the kampongs of wrecked or half-burned shacks to stop Malays from killing Chinese, and Chinese from killing Malays. The worst race riots in Singapore since the war had broken out, on Mohammed's birthday. I cabled the story of Albar's convention and the leaflet to London, and *The Observer* ran it under the headline "Malaysia Premier's Party Extremists Inflame Killings."

Albar composed an open "Letter to Dennis Bloodworth" and sent copies to *The Observer*, to a number of interested parties, and even to me. It was, of course, typed and unsigned. Relevant sections read:

> I was amazed and utterly shocked when I read the heading of your article. I did not believe that I still live in the world that has been contaminated with falsehood and full of lies that have been spread by people like you.
>
> In the Party that is led by the Tengku there are no extremists . . . Moreover I do not believe that there is a single sane person who would say that there are extremists among the Malays who want to kill the Chinese.

The riots over, I was summoned to Kuala Lumpur by Tun Abdul Razak, the deputy premier who would succeed the Tengku when the old paterfamilias finally retired from the scene. Razak was no colorful personality, but his pale, owlish gaze and tenderized handshake concealed an able administrator and a formidable fixer. He complained about my article and hinted that Malaysia might have to start "treating correspondents as they do in Ghana" if they published inaccurate and unfair reports. There had been no racial incitement in Singapore. "The trouble began when someone threw a bottle at the procession on Mohammed's birthday, that's all," he said, the light glinting blindly on his round glasses and the words implying that the culprit was not a Malay.

He was sorry to see me writing in this way. I said I was sorry he was sorry, but we parted without regret.

In an earlier interview Razak had told me that Albar was "the greatest friend of the Chinese." His appointment as secretary-general of the ruling party in Malaysia was "a good thing" because it meant that "a firm front will be preserved against Lee." If Lee Kuan Yew did not cooperate fully with Kuala Lumpur in future, he would be "put in his place." Later, he quietly gave the Communists in Singapore an assurance that they could come out and vote against the PAP in an important by-election without fear of arrest. One of the political bosses of the Chinese party within the Alliance then went behind the wire to see Lim Chin Siong, the young Chinese detainee whom the left-wing students and workers on the island regarded as their private Mao Tsetung. A former senior police officer who had found politics infinitely more rewarding, this prison visitor with admirable professionalism extracted from Lim a written promise that he would fight Lee Kuan Yew for control of Singapore if Kuala Lumpur sprung him.

But nothing was being left to chance. As the police prepared to shelve the old dossier on Lim, they received orders to open a new one on Lee, and the "ultras" in the Alliance began to press for his arrest. Contingency plans for dispatching more Malay troops to the state to overthrow his regime had already been drawn up in the federal capital. At the beginning of August 1965 the Tengku told Lee that pressure groups within the Alliance were insisting that he use "totalitarian methods to force the rebellious state of Singapore into submission." "Things had gone so much out of hand," the Malaysian premier said afterward, "that my colleagues and I were left with no alternative but to legislate Singapore out of the Federation." If it had remained part of Malaysia, violence would inevitably have ensued, he explained.

The paternalistic Tengku did not deem it necessary to consult parliament about snapping the Federation in two at the causeway, however, and he deliberately avoided discussing his intentions with the British, who had confided Singapore, Sarawak, and Sabah to the care of Kuala Lumpur in the first place and were defending them at that very moment from the ire of the Indonesians. Harold Wilson sent a message through the British High Commission in the Malaysian capital, strongly urging the Tengku to delay the ejection of Singapore from Malaysia, at least for twenty-four hours. Lord Head, the High Commissioner whose blunt talking sometimes dismayed the Malays ("Real plush nineteenth-century feudalism here," he remarked to me once as we watched his pet gibbons at play. "They've even got a race course that makes Newmarket look like a chicken run") was deflected so that he ran Razak to earth at a reception only on the evening of the last, crucial day, and the Tengku then refused to wait. On August 9, 1965, Singapore became an independent republic.

Albar, furious that the Tengku had made the terrible mistake of giving freedom to his enemies, began a round of private, silver-tongued little talks with prominent men in the Alliance in Kuala Lumpur whose general burden was that it was time the "Father of Malaysia" retired. The benevolent eyes of the old prince went suddenly still when he heard this, it seems, and Albar was duly sacked.

The mud-slinging between Malaysia and Singapore that followed was accompanied by an economic slugging match with much wild hitting on both sides. This reached a point at which a Malaysian state minister solemnly suggested that the sale of sand to Singapore should be stopped in order to sabotage the island's housing program, and the Singapore government began talking of taxing lorries from Malaysia to pay for wear and tear on the roads of the republic. The common currency shared by the two territories was split into separate issues, to the enormous inconvenience of everyone.

No morphine muffled the agonies of amputation. The Singapore police force was full of Malaysians, and more than five hundred had to be dismissed and sent home if the republic was not to open for business with a built-in fifth column. "That's nothing," Goh Keng Swee told me. "Not only are half the men in our two regular army battalions Malaysians, but the battalions are under command of a Malaysian brigade with headquarters still on this island. And you heard about the fleet? Well, we have this one ship, but of course it has been under command of the Malaysians. We don't even know where it is at present. So we've lost the whole damned Singapore navy before we start."

Matters were not to rest there, however. The "Jews of Asia" were to push the analogy to its illogical conclusion, and in the minds of many, Singapore was to become "Little Israel," a diminutive, bellicose, indigestible socialist state bracketed by the bigger, predominantly Muslim sister-nations of Malaysia and Indonesia. The basic suspicions which made these neighbors see eyeball to eyeball rather than eye to eye remained. A secret appreciation ordered by the Malaysian government in 1968 described Singapore as a potential base for Chinese Communist activity and the subversion of Malaysia. In the same year officials in Djakarta, angered by the execution in Singapore of two Indonesian terrorists captured during Confrontation, attributed the act to "the influence of Peking."

Moreover, Lee had not only to lead a nation, he had to create one out of an ex-colonial immigrant community with about as much corporate sense as a mob of women commuters at a downtown remnant sale. The hostile-seas-around-us, every-man-a-soldier philosophy suited his purpose admirably. Israeli military instructors were brought in to train a tough citizen army but were referred to in polite circles as "Mexicans" in order to abate alarm and anger in Muslim capitals from Djakarta to Cairo. The Israeli victory in the Six-Day War of 1967 was greeted with ill-concealed satisfaction and relief. "We'd have looked a proper bunch of Charlies if the Jews had lost," as one Singapore minister put it in his refined way.

All eighteen-year-olds and all those who joined government service were drafted, and the cream of the call-up, the ten percent off the top, was allocated to the regular army for two years of intensive battle training and ten years on special reserve. When in August 1969 the island celebrated the 150th anniversary of the foundation of the settlement, its pocket army had grown to seven regular battalions and the tanks of its first armored regiment grumbled their way past the reviewing stand. Jet pilots were back at school in Britain, a mosquito navy of fast patrol craft was in the making, the first munitions plant had opened, and Singaporeans were learning to operate sophisticated radar and Bloodhound missiles. Two hard-worked Scotswomen had converted half a hundred petite Asians into a kilted pipe band, and Dr. Goh had only just been dissuaded from raising a squadron of ceremonial cavalry when the Indians tempted him with an offer of eighty horses.

Fortunately, however, hard self-interest had meanwhile worn hatred a little smoother, as both parties began to realize the extent of their economic and military interdependence. There followed a delicate exercise in gamesmanship whose object was to prove that neither needed the other. The Singaporeans stood off with raised eyebrows and played hard to get, while the Malaysians pretended that an impoverished and chastened Singapore was begging for readmittance into the Federation, and the Tengku visited the island republic as if it were a vassal state. But gradually they shook down into a wary, tacit truce, as the worst of good neighbors will.

Racial relations continued to be frail, sometimes febrile, however. Having failed to mix a Malaysian Malaysia, Lee was now concocting a Singaporean Singapore, and although some Malays responded capably to the challenge, for too many the trouble with this society seemed to be that all men were most unfairly being given an equal chance. In Malaysia it was otherwise, for the "Bumiputra" or "son of the soil" enjoyed preference and privilege—and for the purposes of the exercise, "Bumiputra" was simply a euphemism for Muslim Malay.

Four out of every five posts in public service had to be given to Malays (unless none qualified for them). In Kuala Lumpur taxi licenses were issued only to Malays. For a new industrial company to obtain the tax exemption that went with "pioneer status," thirty percent of its employees had to be Malays, and the Public Works Department automatically favored Malay contractors. The state of Pahang adopted a report recommending that fifty percent of all scholarships be given to Malays, irrespective of performance, and mining licenses should be granted only to firms with Malay capital and staff. Private companies throughout the country were obliged to keep up to twenty percent of their shares for Malays. In 1967 Malay became the national language of Malaysia.

The indignant Westerner is prone to see in all this a conspiracy to cheat the non-Malays of their birthright. This is to fall into the error of egalitarianism. Each man has his place in the hierarchy, and his particular role to play, Malays argue. And if this can be true of the individual, it can be true of the race. The Chinese nevertheless felt themselves treated as second-class citizens. The older businessmen might accept their inferior merchant status, buy themselves a Bumiputra with a trading license (Malays make marvelous sleeping partners), and pile up a million dollars behind this legal if listless front. But many young Chinese-educated Chinese were lured by the siren voices of left-wing subversives, eager to smash a society which seemed to present them with nothing but open doors to dead ends.

Some enlightened Bumiputras felt humiliated by their self-inflicted wound, the admission implicit in their privileges that they could only qualify to compete with the rest in a handicap. But frustrated non-Malays were nonetheless matched by frustrated Malays, the anachronistic products of Muslim schools and colleges more devoted to Koran-reading than calculus, misfits incapable of challenging the Chinese and Indians or of qualifying for jobs in a modern, secular administration. "The Malays complain, but this year six Malays have been appointed to government jobs for every one non-Malay," a Chinese objected to me in 1967, when I made this point. "The Chinese complain, yet today they hold at least half of the senior posts in the civil service," retorted a Malay. And they were both right. If the frustrated Chinese became the recruits of left-wing extremism inspired by the Thoughts of Mao, the frustrated Malays became the recruits of right-wing extremism theoretically inspired by the Thoughts of Mohammed.

In May 1969 Malaysia felt the sudden jolt of a political gear-change when the Alliance, which had ruled the Federation since its leaders negotiated independence from the British twelve years before, was returned in the general elections with a severely reduced majority. Even the Tengku only scraped by in his own home state with a lead of 3,500 votes, against 11,600 in 1964, and three ministers lost their seats. More than fifty percent of the voters supported the opposition, and the real winners were the mixed parties in which Chinese candidates predominated.

These jubilant opponents held a provocative victory parade in Kuala Lumpur, the Chinese sometimes obscenely insulting the Malays but offering them no violence. On the next day busloads of Malays armed with well-sharpened parangs rode into the capital for a counterdemonstration. This rapidly turned into a ghastly orgy of killing and burning in which young schoolchildren were brutally cut down while waiting for their after-school buses, and families were incinerated in their own shop-houses. The Chinese secret societies rallied, carrying the war to the Malays, whereupon troops were called out to restore order. Some of these blatantly ignored illegally armed Malays but fired with alacrity into Chinese houses if anyone so much as showed his face at a window.

The tragedy was complete. Five years before, I had asked the chief-of-staff in Kuala Lumpur whether the Ministry of Defense would "multi-racialize" his almost exclusively Malay infantry by recruiting Chinese and Indians. "That is impossible," he replied briefly. "The security risk would be too great." Now, however unfairly, up to one half of the people in the Malayan peninsula might well regard their own national armed forces, in which Malays outnumbered non-Malays by two to one, much as the Irish had regarded the British Black-and-Tans in 1920. According to miniaturized official figures, 196 people were known to have died hideously in the riots. Of these, 143 were Chinese and only 25 were Malays.

But the election results had panicked Malays, who saw their political mastery thrown into hazard. Democracy had turned nasty and had to be curbed. Parliament was therefore suspended and an overwhelmingly Malay "National Operations Council" took over control of public order and security as the curfew crept across the map like a black blight. Malay leaders of the Alliance lashed out nervously at their rivals. The violence had been the work of "disloyal" Chinese. The opposition parties were racist groups financed with secret funds from Singapore and from Communist agents who used them as a cover for terrorist tactics. The electorate had been "threatened and intimidated" into voting for tainted traitors, who had provoked the rioting "to overthrow the government by force of arms and spread terror and panic throughout the country." This fascinating farrago of inaccuracies was disproved by the known fact that the Communists had tried to bully the public into boycotting the elections altogether, and therefore those who voted for the opposition parties had not abetted the Maoists by doing so: they had defied them.

For the Malays, however, truth had to be "appropriate." In a hierarchical world, furthermore, truth went with rank. After the riots, Malaysian ministers angrily dismissed as ignorant, malicious, and irresponsible lies, the reports of foreign correspondents who wrote that Malay troops had victimized innocent and defenseless Chinese civilians, and conscientious police reports that seemed to confirm these hideous stories were rigorously edited. The fact that the correspondents and the police officers had been eye-witnesses, while the ministers had scarcely ventured outside their doors, was irrelevant. Accuracy must be in direct ratio to the importance of the speaker. Having cast the island out of Malaysia four years before, therefore, the moderate Tengku was able to claim with a straight face in 1969 that it was he and not the British who "gave Singapore its independence." There is an unhappy parallel here. The Tengku's hand had been forced by Malay extremists on that occasion, and now reasonable men had once again felt compelled to echo the ravings of the racists in order not to lose the confidence of the mob—just as the sane feel compelled to humor the mad, but never the other way around.

Did the Malays ever intend to abolish their split-level society and bring into being that legendary creature, a true "Malaysian" irrespective of ancestry? "Not for a hundred years," one Malay politician once assured me. As a fabulous animal, he can already be said to exist. Why make more trouble by creating him? But the trouble is there, and the future looks forbidding. The phrases filter back from the innocent past to the guilty present. I hear

Lee's voice saying *"I have warned the Tengku there will be racial trouble. But the old boy simply pooh-poohs the idea, tells me I don't understand Malaya properly and it will never happen."* And Albar: *"In the Party that is led by the Tengku there are no extremists . . . Moreover I do not believe that there is a single sane person who would say that there are extremists among the Malays who want to kill the Chinese."*

Pontius Pilate might have laughed, but he was, after all, just another uncomprehending Caucasian. The entire Malaysian Dream itself has depended on the readiness of local politicians and local press to tell it the way it isn't.

33 : The Seventies: Adults Only

Facts rarely flatter the national *figura* and usually fit only where
they touch. They have therefore quite understandably been
trimmed to suit the self-styled image of many new independent
countries in Southeast Asia. Britain and the Commonwealth
fielded eighty percent of the regular troops that fought the
twelve-year jungle war to cleanse Malaya of Communist guerrillas and drive the last remnants of them across the Thai border,
but the Tengku has since declared that a handful of Malay
battalions dealt the terrorists the final, decisive blow after "the
might of the British army had not succeeded." His party newspaper added that the Anglo-Saxons had run helter-skelter from
Malaya, but the "sons of the soil" had then heroically defended
the plantations and tin mines of "foreigners like the Australians
and British."

This twistory was to repeat itself. The Malaysian army was still a pocket force when Sukarno launched Confrontation in 1963, for Kuala Lumpur had a military agreement with London which threw the burden of defending the Federation on to Britain, and when he was asked whether there would be a general call-up of Malaysians to serve their country, the Tengku said no, he did not think the time had yet come to "deprive the chaps of their pleasures." The Commonwealth soldier was spared the embarrassment of any effusive gratitude or false bonhomie from those he shielded, however. Relations were unhypocritical, and toward the end of 1965 Malaysian national trade-union leaders proposed a general boycott of British military, so that troops returning to mainland Malaya for rest from the Borneo jungle would be refused service in bars, restaurants, and shops and prevented from using public transport.

Once Sukarno's star was safely on the wane and Confrontation faded into peace, the wretched British caused grave offense by declining to grant the Federation additional military aid worth £75 million. Mr. Tan Siew Sin, Malaysia's pragmatic Finance Minister, compared them with the tottering, imperialistic playboy that they had just been defending him against, and added rather unamiably that Britain was nothing more than a "toothless old lion." His first peacetime gestures were to switch the parity of his currency from sterling to gold and then abolish Commonwealth preference on a large number of imports. The British had only been guarding their own investments in Malaysia, he said. The arithmetic of this argument was the subject of much fudging on all sides, but it was undeniably weakened when the Labour government decided to close all military bases east of Suez by 1971. The failure of the British to continue protecting their interests was seen as only more treachery, however. The Federation had "gloriously fought for its independence," but it was still Britain's duty to defend it and to uphold the Alliance government.

In 1965 the parsimonious attitude of the United States also deeply hurt those thoughtful Malaysians who felt that Britain was poor and played out and that in the national interest their country should now turn to a richer patron. For when Kuala Lumpur appealed next to Washington for additional defense aid, the Americans answered with an offer of a seven-year loan on standard terms at five-percent interest. The press enlarged sarcastically on Malaysia's "five-percent friends," and an outraged government-party leader accused the United States of making a profit out of the fight against Communism.

The mistake of the West has been to imagine for some reason inexplicable to most Asian leaders that there should not be one law for the poor and another for the rich. The principle applies in the exacting world of the income-tax assessment, where the poor get preference and the rich are cut down to size. And it can apply outside, they say. It was therefore quite seemly in the eyes of South Koreans that although the dollar was worth 1,450 *hwan* on the open market in Seoul in 1960, the long-suffering Americans, who still had five thousand troops committed to the defense of their country, should make all local military purchases at the official rate of 650 *hwan* to the dollar. The Thais may tell the Yankee dogs in most insulting terms to go home, but will attack with almost serpentine sibilance any Western slight upon their own godliness, girls, cleanliness, or clear soup as slanderous and scandalous distortions of the truth. The Filipinos demand an end to the special privileges enjoyed by the Americans in their republic, yet stress that the special preferences accorded to Philippine produce in the American market must be maintained.

If alms or investment are not forthcoming, Asian Finance Ministers are quick to cry shrinking fisc, and to threaten the niggling Occident with the specter of Communism. In 1966 Razak told the Western powers that if Malaysia was not given more than $600 million in loans and aid, it might go red, and in rare harmony Singapore chimed in with a similar warning. Although hands have been raised in horror at the massive deployment of American troops in Vietnam, the massive deployment of the American dollar has not always come amiss, and the delicate moral decision taken by disapproving Asian governments is best expressed in the sad old music-hall song about the girl gone bad in the wicked city:

For her parents in the country
She buys cases of champagne.
They may curse the hand that sends them
But they drink it just the same.

Why not? The Western colonialists had outraged and exploited the tender and defenseless states of the East. The world owed them a living.

Professional anti-colonialists are cheap and abundant in Asia, for any fool can flog a dead horse, and it was typical of the breed that when Singapore celebrated its 150th anniversary in 1969, voices should be raised against homage to the founder of the settlement, for he was a white man. Malay sociologist and Chinese editorialist alike protested that Sir Stamford Raffles had not settled the island "for the benefit of the indigenous people" and that it owed its success and prosperity not to the colonialists but to the "sweat, blood, and tears" of its Asian settlers. As these human anachronisms well knew, Singapore had become precisely what Raffles had intended it to be—one of the greatest ports in the world. Had the white man stayed away, it might have dozed through the future, as it had dozed through the past.

However, Rajaratnam retorted with a short and pithy paragraph of miniaturized philosophy which left the dust to bury the dust and contained the precious seed of all Asia's salvation: "When our People's Action Party first came into power," he said, "it was so anti-colonial that the statue of Raffles was earmarked for removal. But now we have polished him up. He has an honorable place, and we are celebrating the 150th anniversary of the founding of Singapore by him. To pretend that he did not found Singapore would be the first sign of a dishonest society."

It was no accident that it should have been Rajaratnam who so promptly laid the ghosts of the past, for he is a new Asian with a new look. His words can be as hard as his voice is soft, and they reprove the old invertebrates whose political life has consisted almost exclusively of whining and dining. Those who rummage amid the myths of history to justify the glorification of their race or land or religion he calls "political archaeologists."

"Neo-colonialism" is a fiction, an intellectual subterfuge of incompetent, outmoded nationalists. What these superannuated patriots do not realize is that "the younger generation never experienced Western colonial oppression, but they are acutely conscious of the oppression, corruption, and ineptitude prevailing among their own indigenous rulers." Empty nationalistic braggadocio has given youth only "disintegration, decadence, and misery."

Rajaratnam's formula for the future is to stop blaming the evils of the white past for the ills of the polychromatic present. There must be a new philosophy of "development nationalism" that builds instead of destroys, inspiring people to assume responsibility for their own shortcomings. "Anti-Communist postures and alarmist cries about a Communist takeover will not in future bring Western money and Western troops rushing to our side," he warned. These would be made available only to help a Southeast Asia that was already strong, stable, and prosperous and did not look to others to fight its battles for it.

In Kuala Lumpur, Tan Siew Sin gazed at me through gold-rimmed spectacles and produced his rueful, almost imperceptible auditor's smile. "Cooperation with Singapore is now a must," he said. "It seems a pity that Lee Kuan Yew and the Tengku are hardly on speaking terms." In February 1969, however, Lee promised to send a detachment of Singapore infantry to Malaysia if the need ever arose, and the Tengku described this offer as "a gesture of friendship on his part, which I appreciate very much." While the British danced with impatience on the sidelines, the two sister-states edged tentatively and suspiciously toward the military *gotong royong* without which any regional defense system would simply fall apart at the Straits of Johore.

What had happened? At the beginning of 1968 the Labour government announced that it would withdraw all troops from Singapore and Malaysia by the end of 1971. If these Commonwealth partners were attacked thereafter, Britain would fly in fire-brigade forces from Europe. VC-10 troop transports, "Nuclear bat" V-bombers, and supersonic fighters practiced dry runs to show just how quickly they could be back in their old Asian bases in an emergency. But although the British might go through the martial motions, they would never fight again in the Far East, it was objected. "They may come back for exercises, but they won't come back for a war," said one minister. A demonstration drill of their technical ability to deploy men from Europe, therefore, promised no more protection than a pistol in the hand of a pacifist parson.

Tan Siew Sin had words of comfort: "The British won't die for Southeast Asia, but the Americans will." One year later, however, it became evident that the Americans felt that they had died quite enough for Southeast Asia already. The Southeast Asians must learn to do more of their own dying in future. The Americans would help them. The first Marines were pulled out of Vietnam, the first U.S. engineers and airmen out of Thailand. After years of frantic bailing and pumping and damming and blasting, Washington was at last preparing to give the subcontinent a chance to find its own level.

The more perceptive local leaders began to realize that salvation could lie only in social revolution and regional solidarity among themselves. Their peoples had squabbled and cheated and sulked behind a nursery wall of Western defense, but the wall was coming down and they were going to be exposed to the world outside. It suddenly seemed as if, in holding them together, their white protectors had in fact been holding them apart. In a new and chilly age of nuclear superpowers, Europe had been compelled to bury its innumerable hatchets and start creating "Europe." However wild the idea, Southeast Asia must now start to create "Southeast Asia."

Like the first ice of winter, cooperation crystallizes almost imperceptibly, in small unmatching fragments that have only broken the surface tension here and there. New sets of initials in an acronymic age sprawl over the maps of the Far East: ASPAC, covering nine Pacific countries bent on "greater cooperation and solidarity"; ASEAN, covering five bent on "accelerating economic growth, social progress, and cultural development through joint endeavor and partnership"; ADB, the Asian Development Bank "to promote investment, finance regional, subregional and national development projects . . ." These are the civilian Asian sons of the older soldiers—ANZUS, ANZAM, SEATO—whose business has hitherto been with "armed attack" and whose color is more Anglo-Saxon than Oriental. Talk slowly coagulates into joint action on scholarships, fishery promotion, airlines, coordination of tourism, standardized spelling, but it will be years before the surface is solid enough to take any weight.

As Thanat Khoman of Thailand has warned, however, peace cannot be guaranteed solely by the countries of the region. It must be underwritten by the big powers. As the first U.S. Marines to leave Vietnam in 1969 happily packed their kitbags for home, the small soft states of Southeast Asia were finding that a new dimension had been added to the problem of survival. Like men juggling two spirit levels simultaneously in an effort to build soundly on a slope, they now had to calculate their position of maximum stability not only between the Western and Communist camps but also between the Soviet Union and China.

The Russians—determined to insure that if the Americans followed the British out of the subcontinent, Peking should not fill the vacuum—were feeling their way artfully into the area. They had already appointed as ambassador to Malaysia a genial, well-dressed shoulder-patter who could play golf with princes and talk nicely to the peasantry, and within months were to dispatch another ambassador to Singapore. By now the Soviet Union was the biggest single buyer of Malaysian rubber, and its ships were calling at Singapore at the rate of forty a month. As Russian commercial missions and shipping offices moved into position in the two territories, Thailand and the Philippines began practicing in the mirror those conciliatory speeches and taut little smiles which might later establish for them a new relationship with the white Communist world. Later Soviet diplomats insinuated themselves into the hearts of certain leaders in Kuala Lumpur as the "best friends" of the Federation by telling them not only that they hated the Chinese but that the Soviet Union would always back a Malay Malaysia against a Chinese Singapore.

Moscow must nevertheless fight an uphill battle. The Russian invasion of Czechoslovakia reminded the wiser men in the East that a bear whose muzzle was dripping with honey was still a bear. Others have balked at the idea of repeating Indonesia's unfortunate mistake of buying naval and air power and industries and irrigation wholesale from the Soviet Union, and thereafter being dependent upon Moscow's political goodwill for everything from mechanical replacements to the rescheduling of debts. The Russians are caught at the intersection of two lines of prejudice —one because they are white and the other because they are red. Moreover, when Leonid Brezhnev, the Soviet Party Secretary, spoke of "the task of creating a system of collective security in Asia," Asia reacted cautiously, anxious not to be dragged into any confrontation with China. The Russians had feared that the states of the region wanted to stay neutral. And they were right. It was not surprising that all powers, both great and small, were feeling their way toward the future like men in a moving maze of glass, for amiable enemies might soon prove preferable to dubious friends as the situation revolved. Which way was Southeast Asia to look?

Australia teetered uncertainly on the edge of this rowdy playground like a new boy of the wrong color who wants to be loved by all adversaries simultaneously. Although Canberra promised to keep troops and jet fighters in Singapore and Malaysia after the British pulled out, the Tengku disgustedly wrote these arrangements off as "useless," for twice in six years enemies had threatened the North Borneo states of Malaysia, and twice in six years the Australians had refused to commit combat troops to their defense—in 1963 for fear of angering the Indonesians, in 1969 for fear of angering the Filipinos. Nothing had been more consistent than this Antipodean hedging. The Australians were ready to station battalions in Singapore provided they never became involved in a fight, it appeared. "If our neighbors attacked us, the first thing they would do would be to pull out," one minister put it to me.

At the other end of this tangle of nations lay Mother India, but it was unlikely that the states of Southeast Asia would turn with much confidence toward New Delhi for either military support or economic cooperation. The patronizing airs and loquacious arrogance of many Indian politicians and diplomats hardly appeared to be justified by events in their own country, where every sordid problem of the East from starvation to sticky palms seemed to be magnified a hundred times, and China's ability to invade India with impunity in 1962 increased the impression that the Indians might be good for gods but not for guns.

The impending British military withdrawal from Malaysia and Singapore and President Nixon's dismaying doctrine of disengagement were meanwhile cutting small lines of worry on faces in Japan, the world's biggest importer of oil. For ninety percent of this oil came through the narrow gullet of the Malacca Straits and across the South China Sea. In 1969 and for the first time since World War II, accordingly, a destroyer squadron of the Maritime Self-Defense Force (exquisitely polite Japanese for the ocean-going navy which the postwar constitution expressly forbids) sailed out of Tokyo to make a 24,000-mile "goodwill" tour of the entire region. This had American blessing, for Tokyo's economic power and military potential seemed to offer a pair of long Asian tongs with which Washington might one day be able to manipulate the critical mass of the Orient from a distance. The Japanese already had more than 250,000 men under arms, an air force of nearly six hundred combat aircraft, a navy of ten submarines and about fifty destroyers and frigates. Moreover, bigger and better weapons were on the way to enable them to play policeman in Asian waters—to help keep the peace stable and the traffic moving.

However, in spite of the obvious reluctance of the Japanese government to assume any form of international responsibility that did not show a clear margin of profit, and the power of the peacemongers in a land that had both sown and reaped so much death and destruction only a quarter of a century before, Southeast Asians watched Tokyo through narrowed eyes. The new concern about the Straits of Malacca brought to Singapore a curious succession of inquisitive Japanese journalists and "journalists," their cameras as eager as their questions, who visited the naval base and assiduously interviewed officials. Many were middle-aged men with somewhat middle-aged ideas. One of them deplored the mood of the Japanese young, who were so careless of their country's "national interests." The peoples of Singapore and Malaysia might not like to see Japanese troops on their soil again, but surely a few Japanese warships on the skyline would be acceptable? After all, had it not been for the atomic bomb . . .

Throughout the region, memory dies hard. A tall, stiff, bone-white pylon of stone in the center of Singapore, paid for out of a £6 million "blood debt" grudgingly conceded by Tokyo, reminds citizens of the fifty thousand victims of the "Greater East Asia Co-prosperity Sphere" whom the Japanese massacred on the island. More significantly, perhaps, no one in the region has forgotten the *kaishas*, the big Japanese combines that moved into Southeast Asia during World War II to set up protected monopolies, and whose shamurais ruthlessly fleeced the subcontinent until it was red and raw.

By 1969 there were faintly unhappy faces among finance ministers as the Japanese economic invasion began to look to many like the beginnings of a second takeover bid. The airborne army of investors that now descended on Asian capitals from Tokyo was polite, sometimes apologetic. "But we must watch them like hawks to make sure that they are not turning us all into industrial satellites," one senior official told me. It was already established that the Japanese wanted to harness the subcontinent to their own economy as a cheap work horse, investing money in labor-intensive industries in countries where wages were lower while reserving highly sophisticated production for Japan itself. In Manila the Filipinos voiced a thinly veiled suspicion that Tokyo only wanted to mine the area for raw materials and ready buyers of cheap Japanese goods, and when at an international conference in Singapore the Japanese Foreign Minister suggested that a permanent committee be set up for the development of Southeast Asia, the idea was at once thrown out as a possible ruse to get the wolf in among the sheep. Instead, the Philippines proposed that the underdeveloped countries should work to create a Southeast Asian Common Market from which Japan would be rigorously excluded.

Dr. Adam Malik, the Indonesian Foreign Minister, prophesied

that in the seventies Japan might be "more of a vexing problem than China" and an object of "envy, suspicion, and fear among its Asian neighbors." The Japanese, he added, "have themselves to blame for this." "When they first came back to Southeast Asia," another minister told me, "they bowed low. Now they merely nod. God help us the day they don't even nod." In 1969 the Japanese promised to double their aid to Asia within five years, and Asia will take the cash and give Tokyo the credit for this belated generosity. But responsible political leaders share a healthy determination not to allow Japan to reconquer with bank drafts what she could not hold with bayonets. And this may be the making of the subcontinent.

34 : The Adhocracy

In accordance with the inexorable law that the better you learn
to build, the better you learn to break, the older Japanese have
outstripped the rest of Asia in establishing a modern state and
therefore the younger Japanese have mounted the most spectacular of rebellions against it. But the war of the generations hit the
Far East long before student guerrillas seized sixty universities
in Japan in 1969.

The spectrum of the postwar generation was as multicolored
in Asia as it was in Europe, and ranged from Trotskyist to teddy-
boy in Saigon as in Southampton. But there was a broad band
of young men and women for whom the colonial era and its
"democratic" aftermath seemed all part of the same pattern of
degradation. Ashamed of their parents for their preoccupation
with money and its glossy, wax-like fruits, they wanted to purge

themselves spiritually by proving their capacity for honesty, industry, thrift, and self-sacrifice, and they were inevitably attracted by the demands and disciplines of Communism (although most of them could not have told the Theory of Value from Capitalist Encirclement). These were only prototypes, however, and by 1968 their successors were swinging left or right according to circumstance.

Like spontaneous fire from rotting hay, student power in Asia kindled from corruption—the corruption of a dream. In the eyes of cheated youth, the bright postwar promise of a brave new world for men born free was translated at best into government by middle-aged nationalists still steeped in the discreditable conventions of the past. At worst it yielded a mess of crooked or sick-in-the-head dictators and military juntas with barrack-square answers to the problems left by abortive experiments in democracy. The reaction of many students to the constraint imposed upon them by those so sardonically referred to as their elders and betters was therefore characteristically savage. "Make Love" is the motto of disillusioned youth repelled by the deceits of overstuffed Western societies, for a hippie is a child of an affluence that the young Asian does not know. The Asian is square, politically minded, still imbued with old-fashioned ideas about fair shares and social justice and morality.

In their self-appointed role of national conscience, umpire, and scandal-breaker, the students of Asia have proved salutary, sometimes infuriating watchdogs, and their methods have often been picturesque. In 1968 they distributed a manifesto in Manila condemning the "lavish display of wealth" put on by the vice-president of the Philippines for his fortieth wedding anniversary and listing some impressive statistics: one thousand guests, a fifteen-piece orchestra imported from America, a twenty-five-foot-high fountain of champagne, ten buffets, eight bars. In Indonesia they have published details of the luxurious villas and limousines owned by high-ranking officials, on the principle that by definition upright men, like upright pianos, take up little space.

In the fight against speculation and profiteering they have jammed telephones, seized rice stores, appropriated the keys of fuel depots, and in 1970 they plastered official cars with notices asking "Where does the foreign aid go?" Attacking decadence and immorality, they have raided brothels, closing fourteen at the port of Belawan in East Sumatra in spite of the furious objections of local authorities that foreign ships would no longer call there and the entire province would suffer a severe loss of revenue. By 1969 they had obliged a reluctant attorney-general in Djakarta to set up an anti-corruption task force, and they were demanding a louder voice in a legislature in which their appointed representatives already sat as a "functional group."

The young are sometimes exploited as political pawns, or misled by megalomaniacs, but in a subcontinent in which too often the elected legislature has been faked, bought, suspended, or ignored, the irreverent barracking of schoolboys in the gallery is frequently the only effective protest that can limit flagrant abuse of authority. Americans who resigned themselves too early to financing the unedifying capers of potentates disguised as popular government, like monkeys in mink, were isolating themselves on the wrong side of the generation gap. Student power put the cutting edge on the axes that felled three of the strongest dictators in the Far East—Syngman Rhee in South Korea, Sukarno in Indonesia, and (with other forces) Ngo Dinh Diem in South Vietnam.

The young are not entirely alone, for new values are emerging among their fathers. Hallowed traditions of official extortion and graft are under attack, and although the die-hard opposition to the newfangled morality is naturally stiff, there are at least some signs that Southeast Asia may be jerking awake instead of nodding off soporifically into another permissive decade of pocket-lining. In Vietnam special anti-corruption committees have been created, and in Thailand graft was the main campaign issue in the 1969 elections. In Malaysia civil servants are now forbidden to receive gifts, may be arrested for accepting complimentary tickets to a cinema, have been warned to think twice before taking even a cigarette from a member of the public. In Singapore, Rajaratnam attacks the "kleptocracy"—the society of the corrupt, for the corrupt, by the corrupt—and Lee Kuan Yew tells a Commonwealth conference pointedly that Afro-Asian administrations should take a look at themselves "when instead of dams and power stations, roads and railways, we have Rolls-Royces and executive mansions, not to mention golden bedsteads." Do these censorious islanders have the right formula for the future?

In their little laboratory-state they have been carrying out a bold experiment, which could prove to be the pilot scheme for immunizing Asia from the grosser attractions of Marxist materialism and Mao Tse-tung. Lee Kuan Yew and his People's Action Party have taken the unusual step of regarding government as hard work, and public money as something to be spent on the public. Capital and confidence pour in, but Lee lives in the same old rambling family house in which I met him a dozen years ago, and Rajaratnam lives in the same three-and-a-half-room bungalow which he bought when he was a journalist.

Another modest fellow who has not moved house is my neighbor Dr. Lee Siew Choh, chairman of the left-wing Barisan Sosialis, or Socialist Front. "You British are here to suppress our people and to sabotage democracy," he tells me at our first meeting, "and the PAP government of Singapore is merely the stooge of the Anglo-American colonialists." We are sitting together on his small lawn, drinking Tiger Beer from his battered old refrigerator, and Dr. Lee is being his usual affable self. Friendly but frank, a Western-trained doctor with an all-wool bedside voice, he produces the strip-language of Communism as effortlessly as a conjurer pulling yards of ribbon from between his teeth. But Dr. Lee is not a happy politician. It is not easy to play the militant in Singapore.

He complains that the twenty-nine left-wing unions that support the Barisan Sosialis are split. Some of them are ready to fight it out in the streets, but the others believe that the prime minister will keep his promises of a bright future. How many unionists can he trust at a pinch? "Your guess is as good as mine," he answers gloomily, putting his head in his glass. "Perhaps little more than half of them. It looks as if what we'll have to do is simply be patient and let time prove that the government is not really sincere." But the government does not suddenly stop building Singapore and abscond with the funds, and this is Dr. Lee's problem.

His frustration is understandable. The relationship between Premier Lee Kuan Yew and these left-wing extremists, who also started public life within the PAP, was for years like one of those energetic *pas de deux* during which it is hard to tell whether the partners are supposed to be fighting or fornicating. But whichever way you look at it, Lee Kuan Yew emerged on top. The break-away came when the pro-Communists walked out of the PAP and formed the Barisan Sosialis, after which most of their leaders were thrown into jail without trial as security risks. His detractors are quick to point out, therefore, that Lee did not beat the Communists in a straight contest for the minds of the masses.

However, six out of every ten men in Singapore were Chinese-educated Chinese, chauvinists proud of Mao's achievements in their homeland, many of them as red and ripe for trouble as Eve's apple. Balancing his special security powers against his special security problem, Lee Kuan Yew can still claim to have proved that Asian Communism can be killed with Asian kindness. For his government has done more than lock up the left wing. It has swept away slums and given the people towering blocks of low-rental flats, new networks of roads, a new port, a new industrial complex, nearly one hundred new schools, a new social security system, a new face, and a new future. In the summer of 1969 Lim Chin Siong, the darling of the Singapore Maoists whom the Malaysians had tried to use against Lee Kuan Yew in 1965, became the latest of a long line of left-wing detainees to capitulate and recant. (He was then released and dispatched to England to study law, for ex-colonial Singapore is taking poetic revenge upon its former masters. In the days of empire, Britain's black sheep were bundled off to distant tropical dependencies to live useful lives, but now the tropical dependencies get rid of their red sheep by bundling them off to Britain.)

It says much for Lee Kuan Yew that bold and outspoken men have accused him of being, at different times, a Fascist, a Communist, even a democrat, and at those different times all of them have ostensibly been right. For Lee, ideology is not contained in sacred books: it is written by a moving finger in the shifting sands of the political arena. English democracy, like the English language, grew up naturally in a changing cosmos—untidy, flexible, and durable because it was spared the otiose attentions of pedants and academics. In a changing cosmos, Lee Kuan Yew's democracy also twists and evolves with the passage of years, assuming unorthodox new shapes as he and his political partners adapt and tropicalize this alien northern concept on an *ad hoc* basis.

In 1965 Lee and his team began trying to knock their small island and its two million miscellaneous inhabitants into a serviceable and coherent nation. The raw material was 225 square miles of low-lying equatorial estate and an ex-colonial mince of money-minded Asian immigrants to whom "home" was not Singapore but the land of their respective forefathers—distant India, unfriendly Malaysia, Mao's China.

In the early stages, the drive for a new, unaccustomed civic and national pride produced some elegant planning for the prime minister promised the people "a garden city beautiful with flowers and trees, tidy and litterless," and he set about providing it. But one must suffer to be beautiful. He also promised them compulsory standardized trash cans whose rental would be added to their electricity bills, and fines ranging from £17 to £120 for shopkeepers who flung their refuse into the streets. The courts started ordering citizens to pay a painful price for dropping even an empty peanut packet out of a car, and tenants of the new government flats were warned that they would be evicted if they proved incorrigible litterbugs.

"Keep Singapore Clean" was followed by "Keep Singapore Fit." Morning physical jerks for all were introduced, and one thousand teachers were especially trained to supervise compulsory toothbrushing after meals for the pocket state's 400,000 primary-school children. The watchwords of the government were "discipline," "survival," the "rugged society." On TV Singapura pretty little speakerines with sanitized voices warned the public weekly against dirt, dodging the draft, bad driving, too many babies. Determined that the young state should be lovely and therefore loved, the administration created an all-year-round cleansing organization under an act that also abolished weekend overtime pay for employees in essential services of this type. The public was not going to be made to carry the can for the night-soil worker.

In "socialist" Singapore the trade unions might no longer negotiate about the dismissal or retrenchment of staff. Workers must do a forty-four hour week and retire at fifty-five, and they were allowed an annual holiday of only seven days until they had been ten years at the job. Four public holidays were struck from the calendar, and the tight labor laws left a man little purchase with which to lever himself more pay for less work in the fatally luxurious traditions of the British trade-union movement. Workers who rebelled were accused of "high treason," and Lee warned troublemakers that they would be sacked, kicked out of their houses, possibly deprived of citizenship and deported back to those "homes" abroad from which their forebears had originally come. Strikes whimpered out. The employer was made master in his own house, so that Singapore could attract much-needed foreign capital, and as fast as it won private investment, the government paradoxically advanced a policy of "creeping socialism" by going into business on its own account and also becoming a partner in more and more joint industrial ventures.

In "democratic" Singapore, the PAP held all the seats in the parliament, the Communist Party was outlawed, a Security Ordinance allowed the government to detain political "undesirables" indefinitely without trial, and students entering the university were screened for reliability. Daintier democrats might understandably wince, but men like Lee pointed out that they were manhandling the muck of Asian social realities, not teaching political theory in an aseptic classroom.

It was true that Singapore had become a one-party state solely because the legal left-wing opposition had boycotted the general elections, but PAP leaders were still faintly uneasy, like men improperly dressed for democracy. Back-benchers, exhorted to political self-flagellation, began to strike out heavily at their own government. Contingency plans were drafted for splitting the party into two so that it might fight itself more effectively if the need arose. A presidential council of nominated members was fabricated to protect the citizen against the parliament he had elected. Sacred beliefs were nevertheless held up to scrutiny and flouted. Abortion and voluntary sterilization were introduced, and juries were abolished. A man on trial for his life must now appear before two judges of the High Court, and his fate depends upon their unanimous verdict.

This new law was attacked with characteristic ferocity by David Marshall, ex-chief minister of Singapore and a brilliant criminal defense counsel who might well have been invented by Erle Stanley Gardner had he not already existed. He argued that a venal government could more easily put pressure upon the judges it appointed than upon a random jury of independent citizens who, given their practical common sense and knowledge of the world outside, were in any case better qualified to weigh the truthfulness of testimony affecting the conduct of the ordinary mankiller-in-the-street. But Lee objected that the English of Asian jurors was frequently unequal to the rigors of legal jargon, and that they were often confused or intimidated and overreluctant to convict. He had his way, of course—and then invited David Marshall to become a member of the presidential council.

No one mentions words like "nationalization" in polite society in Singapore today, and even "equality" is on the way out, for Lee and his ministers are determined to place the destiny of the island in the hands of a politically pure elite with a pride and stake in the republic. The government has opened its first "Singapore Eton," a character-forming super-school that accepts "loyal and dedicated" students chosen for their sense of social discipline, their initiative and physical fitness, as well as for their academic ability. Three more of these colleges are to be built to turn out the bilingual, all-round leaders modern Singapore needs.

Some will enter the civil service and the army, but many will become key cadres of the organized, nationwide youth movement. Their function will be to keep the young fit and free from the sins that stretch from prurience to pink-think in a new, brash society nearly sixty percent of whose citizens are under twenty-one. Socialist Singapore is creating its own indoctrinated aristocracy, but there is more than that to the subtle machinery that gears the government and the party to the masses.

The PAP has conventional party branches in all districts of the island, but these are far outnumbered by the 187 community centers of the "People's Association," which ostensibly has little to do with politics and is partly financed by the people themselves. However, the overwhelming majority of the one thousand full-time organizers of these centers are PAP members in regular if discreet contact with the local party branch. The main business of the centers is to draw and hold the public within a light and attractive web of welfare services. They organize sports and gymnastics for the young, run some six hundred courses in everything from sewing to soldering, and had opened four hundred kindergartens and crèches in outlying rural areas by 1969. They provide cheap fertilizer for the farmer, arrange for free inoculations for his livestock. But every community center is also fitted with the square cyclopean eye of a television set, the voice and view of the state-run broadcasting division, which comes under the political direction of the Ministry of Culture.

This exotic, liberty-gibbet synthesis of capitalism and socialism, authoritarianism and freedom, is the product of Lee's urge to create a tightly organized, dynamic, and disciplined community in a diminutive cockleshell of a country that must somehow ride the uncertain seas of the seventies. Almost inevitably, he is at his unhappiest with the students. He has chastised them humiliatingly for "lacking guts" when they have stayed out of the political arena, yet arrested or banished them if they have then entered the lists but ill-advisedly shown their left hands in attacking his administration. Of the curious social quagmire to the West, he has said bluntly: "We cannot and will not allow this permissive, escapist, drug-taking, self-indulgent, promiscuous society to infect our young."

The universities must be assets to the republic, he insists angrily. Graduates must link their interests to those of Singapore. "You mean the interests of *your* Singapore," reply rebellious students, for every turn of the screw drives the iron deeper into the soul, and they turn huffily to Law or Philosophy, dreaming of post-graduate years in England and Australia, where they will not be cheek by jowl with this domineering, exasperated juggernaut of a man.

Lee's Singapore is a success story, nonetheless. If the republic's leaders are imaginative manipulators of the democratic system, they are also energetic and uncorrupt, and they deliver the goods. By 1969 the small Singaporean seemed to be enjoying a prosperity and a security he had never before known, on an island that was being transformed so fast that it was as if the cake of mud had miraculously come alive. Detractors complain not only that the PAP regime is undemocratic but that it is opportunistic and "has no ideological basis whatever." This probably means that it will stand an excellent chance of survival in a world painfully stiff with political pedantry and prejudice. If Lee can show that he has achieved a miracle and not just a mirage, his "rugged society" may be the working model for other modernizing Asian states in a world made safe for Adhocracy.

35 : Dangerous Liaison

Across developing Southeast Asia tall shoots of concrete and glass thrust skyward like some alien crop, while new ribbons of road unfurl, smooth six-lane streamers laced with gas stations and soft-drink cafés, shacks, shops, and saloons. The neon signs flicker and multiply and the sparse, spiky hedges of television aerials thicken with the passing years. In Bangkok a great temple with golden spires takes on the dignified but defensive air of a dowager in a discothèque as the old city of canals is relentlessly rebuilt into a series of deep grooves for deafening traffic jams. Hong Kong appears to sink beneath the weight of its new stone colossi, and in low-lying Singapore rain brings flash floods as the spreading cement encases more and more of the absorbent soil beneath.

Ah Fu, the old amah who cooked with a pair of chopsticks and a couple of blackened pots, disdaining to use even an egg whisk, has been replaced by young Ah Yook, whose small hands play with professional competence upon electric cooker, washing machine, refrigerator and deep freeze, waffle iron and toaster and coffee percolator and floor polisher, as if they were all related percussion instruments and she the star drummer doing her daily solo.

The accelerating tempo of a West agonizingly caught up in the breathtaking age of the blast-off is beginning to subject Asia also to the first incipient moral and material strains. The young Chinese flock out of the schools looking vainly for work worthy of their literacy; the Malays move from the kampongs to the big towns and the bright lights, and fall into feckless delinquency. But a new middle class pushes its way forward, greedy for gadgetry and gracious living, and in highly organized cities the worker is not far behind. Asia is taking its first steps down the dead end to the junk yard of accumulated wealth, possessions, and prestige so well symbolized by the mountain ranges of rusting, abandoned cars that characterize the landscaping of the affluent age in America.

It follows that, as in the West, faith is in retreat. Fewer Muslims make the pilgrimage to Mecca from south Thailand (you can buy a second-hand car for the same money), and many young Malays cut mosque. "How can we compete if we have to stop everything and pray five times a day?" one expostulated to me. Buddhists are also sidling slowly away from their earlier piety, neglecting the rites and slaughtering ancient images of the Lord Buddha, chopping off sacred heads and hands for sale to collectors and curio dealers.

For the more the Asian learns to want scooters and stereo, sex and similar status symbols, the greater becomes his devotion to the dollar. And this inspires reverence for new gods of wealth like Tourism, whose manifestations as Creator, Preserver, and Destroyer are today enslaving Southeast Asia. The demand for a handy mock-world for the package-tour pilgrim is slowly but inexorably transforming the Far East into the Exotic Orient, since the fascinating if sometimes grisly reality is not good enough for him and he must be presented, rather, with a deodorized

Technicolor dream, all kimonos and Kleenex and Quaint Old Customs.

Change Alley, the long, narrow slip of a street market running down to the Singapore waterfront and choked with a mass of struggling humanity haggling over a few cents, was for long a raw, pungent slice of Asia. But in 1965 men put up illuminated arches at each end of it "to give it an Oriental atmosphere," as one well-meaning Chinese solemnly explained. Stallholders were asked to arrange their goods tidily, to be polite, to turn Change Alley into "Change-Alley-World-Famous-Shopping-Center," part of the modern mirage that could be purchased with a round-trip air ticket and a sheaf of traveler's checks. The island's ramshackle trishaws, pedaled by gaunt, mahogany-faced Chinese with calves like veined iron, ceased to be painful anachronisms due for the scrap heap and were reclassified as Genuine Tourist Attractions.

Singapore called itself "Instant Asia" and began assembling all the marvels of the East in convenient clumps for the harassed holidaymaker. Not to be outdone, Malaysia started constructing a two-hundred-acre Far East of its own with Chinese and Japanese gardens and traditional houses and kampongs and temples, with a sample rubber estate, rice farm, and tin mine, and an orchard full of all the fruit trees of Malaysia, plus genuine jungle (no plastic), equatorial lake, waterfalls, and many other extras, the whole to be served by monorail and cable car.

There are air-conditioned hotels in Hong Kong so crammed with *chinoiserie* that by the time you have had a drink at a long bar designed like a red and gold dragon-boat, unloaded your cigarette ash into a fake Chou-dynasty bronze sacrificial vessel as big as a beer barrel, eaten in a grill hung with Chinese paintings and silk lanterns, and strolled through a disinfected foyer decorated to resemble the tomb of a Han emperor, the Chinese town beyond the glass doors looks like the less inspiring end of Tottenham Court Road.

Not all prefer the palm-studded lobbies to the palm-studded beaches of the Orient, however, and the energetic are being systematically relieved of their surplus on Bali, at Angkor, even at the Great Temple of the Cao Dai in South Vietnam, where,

Vietcong permitting, the priests are ready to switch on the lights, open up all doors, and advise the three-eyed invader not only on the best angles for his pictures but on what exposures to use.

All over Asia, the pagoda is becoming a tourist trap for festivals and faith can be big business. Hundreds of camera shutters blink impersonally as the Hindu penitents of Singapore dance down the streets at Thaipusam, chest and back pincushioned by the fifty sharp needles of the metal arches of atonement they carry on their shoulders, and the event is listed in the local tourist guide. The canny globe-trotter who times his moves correctly may then snap the Christian penitents in Manila on Good Friday as they in turn whip themselves through the city or are flogged by obliging friends until the blood flows.

Some Asians object, but others show much ingenuity in satisfying the morbid urges of the mob. Indonesia, justly famed for its many volcanic disasters, now has a seven-thousand-foot drive-in crater for the curious. As early as 1960 Panmunjom in the demilitarized zone between North and South Korea, scene of permanent tension and sporadic violence, was taking nearly twenty thousand visitors a year. When Sukarno dropped his crack paratroopers into south Malaya during Confrontation, Australian trippers with box lunches were almost breathing down the back of my neck as I tried to reach the battlefield. And then there is Quemoy.

A Chinese colonel leans over the dazzling concrete wall of the sty to poke a large and exceptionally ugly pig with his sunshade. "A countryman of yours," he murmurs to me slyly. "He's come from England for cross-breeding with our local hogs." The pig and I look at each other with the barely concealed antipathy of fellow Britons meeting abroad. He is used to strangers, however. Quemoy may be the Gibraltar of the East, an embattled, shell-raked Nationalist fortress in the mouth of the Communist mainland. But Quemoy is also an island of Riviera-like beaches, golf courses and tennis courts, seven cinemas, five faintly girlie tea-houses and five jive bands. There is a punctual bus service, and two private taxi companies run comfortable American cars.

Courteous officers conduct the visitor around the sights—the underground tunnels leading to the big coastal guns, the nearest point to the mainland, the ceremony of releasing gas-filled balloons carrying propaganda to the Communists across the way. Quemoy is famous for its excellent pork and its kaoliang wine, a small glass of which will burn brightly for five minutes if lighted instead of drunk, and bottles may be bought duty-free on departure in the underground waiting room at the heavily bunkered airport. A black Dakota from Formosa, almost skimming the choppy sea to flummox the enemy radar, drops onto the airstrip, its windows blocked by steel shutters. It is the daily bus that will take you back to Taipei. And you are still not sure which is uppermost in your mind—the picture of the grim offshore bastion, or "Come to Sunny Quemoy."

One day I find that selected pretty girls are being paid to walk about in Singapore in *cheongsams* and sarongs and saris because, although there are thousands of other pretty girls walking about in *cheongsams*, sarongs, and saris, they are doing it naturally and not as color-slide models for tourists. In a Hong Kong hotel I ask for the menu, and a Chinese waitress offers me "Ye Olde English Breakfast Piping Hot from the Skillet: Crispy Toast and Choice Marmalade, Two Fresh Country Eggs with Slice of Hickory-Smoked Ham, a Good Old Cup of Tea or Coffee, and Newly-Squeezed Orange Juice." The whole world is nothing but illusion, say the Buddhists. If that is not already a fact, it may well turn out to be an accurate prophecy.

It might be thought that the last citadel of Oriental culture must be the stomach. The Burmese use the phrase "I grew up eating rice" to mean "I wasn't born yesterday," for rice is the basis of all the delicate, subtle, or brutally hot cuisines that overlap across a continent in which a cook is still prepared to spend an afternoon crushing chilis in a stone mortar or subjecting a duck to the full treatment for females—to be massaged and bathed, perfumed and dressed, and stuffed and finally served. The Chinese can prepare anything delectably from bird's nest to fish lips; the Laos like chicken stuffed with peanuts and cooked in coconut milk, ant's eggs, and placenta from the mother cow; the

Thais work wonders with red-hot peppers and lemon grass; the Burmese make cocktail crisps out of deep-fried buffalo skin. The poorer Vietnamese survives on rice and *nuoc mam,* a vivid sauce made by packing salted fish in a jar and leaving them to rot, and the Korean loves *kimchi,* three-month-buried pickled vegetables which can give him a breath that takes everyone else's away.

A six-month-long publicity campaign in Singapore in 1968 to persuade families to change from rice to cheaper wheat converted less than one in fifty, and even these turncoats ate bread only for breakfast or tea. But this stubborn defense of rice is essentially a rear-guard action. Switch on the television and Dr. Kildare with Malay subtitles is interrupted by clattering Cantonese voices urging hitherto happy islanders to buy American fruit juice and British baby foods, bottled essence of chicken and extracts of beef, deep-frozen fish fingers and tinned Scotch broth. Children brimming with black-currant juice are shown diving into sparkling pools, tired husbands sip their reconstituted mushroom soup and assume slow, lecherous smiles.

The Asian audience is unsuitably impressed, and eating habits begin to alter. The supermarkets of Singapore, originally opened for white men raised on bottles and cans, paper cartons and similar unrewarding fodder, are full of eager yellow and brown faces and hands. As the edibility gap closes, peoples who thought that one of the most sinister aspects of the Westerner was the way he went on drinking milk long after he should have been weaned now have cream and butter in their own refrigerators at home.

Japan, farthest of all to the East, leads the way toward the West in all things. Japanese are forgetting tea and taking to coffee, and there are about a hundred thousand coffee houses today in their narrow islands. They are also forgetting rice and taking to noodles and meat and milk and even cheese. By early 1969 more than five hundred rice dealers had put up their shutters in Tokyo alone. The Japanese are beginning to import great quantities of mutton and lamb and beef, because the steaks from their own magnificent ale-fed herds can no longer meet domestic demand. But in order to eat gross Western food it is necessary to use gross Western methods, and among the white-collar workers of Tokyo chopsticks are going out, and the knife and fork are coming in. *O tempura, o mores!*

Not only the food of the screw-top civilization, but its science and sport, its dress, and its culture are increasingly tempting Eastern appetites. The West is building its biggest empire after the colonial era has slipped into history. In 1968 a Malaysian minister suggested that television had helped to reduce the birth rate, for it had given the masses something else to think about after dark. More often than not, what it gave them to think about in between commercials would be Perry Mason and the Wild West, the problems of Peyton Place and the F.B.I., the vicissitudes of the Avengers and Coronation Street.

In Southeast Asia the arts are drawn from rich and varied cultures, for Islam and India and China are all foster fathers of the subcontinent. Like early Celts and Saxons, the ancient Buddhists carved geometrical designs rather than the living form, and built their holy shrines of stone but their homes of wood. From these beginnings came the magnificence of Angkor and Borobodur, intricately wrought giants that dwarf the temples of the West. And out of the past flowed the liquid music of the gong and gamelan—"the sound very strange, but pleasant and delightful," noted Sir Francis Drake—the statuesque dances of Bali and Thailand and Cambodia, the love-courts of Laos and Malaya at which girl and boy nimbly toss impromptu verse to and fro.

But in Laos there is no literature of note, in Thailand intellectual life is at low ebb, and a Malay remarks sadly but truly that almost everything written about Asia has been the work of people who were not Asians. This constitutes a puny barrier against the onslaught of an industrialized, mass-producing Occident that can pour out culture as easily as it pours out cars. The graceful, touchless dancing accompanied by antique songs that was common to most countries of the region has today been adulterated with soul music, miniskirts, and the mini-thoughts of modern lyrics. The cinema heavily influences the traditional Indonesian shadow play, breaking down its classical philosophy into the trite idiom of Western romance and violence. And the choice of films is narrow. Spreading out the entertainment page of a Singapore newspaper, I find the following fare: "The Devil's Brigade," "The Brain Stealers," "Killers Five," "Coffin for a Gunfighter," and "The Tramplers." The only serious challenge comes from the Chinese sword-fighting film—the sole authentic Eastern Western.

Western rape or Eastern urge? It is always difficult to place the responsibility for seduction. But as the more striking manifestations of modern Western culture from muck books to Beatle cuts first streamed into the area, governments hit back. Singapore banned the jukebox, Korea the pinball machine. In Indonesia rock-'n'-roll records and tapes were burned, youngsters were arrested for wearing winkle-pickers and bandleaders for playing Beatle music, while troops armed with scissors chopped off overlong hair and slashed overstretched jeans.

Indonesia was perhaps the only country in the world in which the tight skirt was elaborately defined—in terms which reflected rather curiously on the customs and pastimes of Indonesian women. The elders of Makassar ruled that it was a skirt in which the lady could not run when chased by a dog, could not pick up a fallen handkerchief, could not step into a jeep without help, and could not have a beer bottle placed between her knees. Miniskirts were frowned on in both Bangkok and Djakarta. Formosa, Indonesia, and Laos all cracked down on the flower people, native or imported, and Thailand banned hippies from the country until they shaved off their beards and cut their hair. The way-out was on the way out from the start.

However, the West was also giving of its best, and the undiscriminating Asian housewife who today opens a can of stew instead of cooking her own curry is paralleled by the discriminating Asian intellectual who opens a can of Scriabin rather than make his own music. And he is matched in turn by the man who would rather deal in a modern international language than his own inadequate mother-tongue. In consequence, one of the greatest imperialists of the post-colonial era has been the English language.

Nearly one hundred years ago King Mongkut of Siam hired a certain Mrs. Leonowens (thereafter to be known as Anna) in a letter which ran: "We wish the School Mastress to be with us in this place or nearest vicinity hereof to save us from trouble of conveying such the lady to and fro almost every day also it is not pleasant to us if the School Mastress much morely endeavour to convert the scholars to Christianity than teaching language and literature etc. etc. like American Missionaries here because our proposed expense is for knowledge of the important language and literature which will be useful for affairs of country not for the religion which is yet disbelieved by Siamese scholars in general sense."

The king's reservations expressed with the eccentric elegance of a smooth linguistic skid the feelings of generations of Orientals to come who wanted English to be a simple harmless tool, not the sharp end of an insidious alien culture. But it advanced steadily in spite of all opposition from local postwar chauvinists imbued with new-found national pride, and by 1969 seven countries had set up a regional language center in Singapore to improve the teaching of English as a second (or first foreign) tongue in nearly all the states of the subcontinent.

It could be argued that the center met a long-felt want. In 1960 Air Vietnam advertised itself as "The Most Experimental Airline in the East" (the French for "experienced" being, rather unfairly, "*experimenté*"), and when the former president of South Korea visited Saigon a felicitous banner read "Welcome Syngman Rhee, Fighter of Freedom." Even more subtly, a Singapore telegraph clerk made me pay extra for a quick query to *The Observer* which began "Canst cable soonest weekend requirements . . ."—despite all my expostulations. " 'Canst' is two words," he declared firmly, "and so is 'soonest.' "

It remains to be seen who laughs last. The invader who strikes boldly across strange territory inevitably risks being cut off and mauled piecemeal, and English, like Latin before it, has been no exception. The impeccable thin red line of language was first broken by *pidgin*, the speech of nineteenth-century Chinese who somehow found it easier to understand "Makee fire here chop-

chop number one" than "Make a good fire here quickly." The
Chinese have abandoned this extreme case of spastic syntax as
hopeless, but it survives nonetheless, and is the talk of New
Guinea.

A copy before me of the newspaper *Nu Gini Tok Tok* announces "Nu Ailan Transpot Sasaiti Ltd istap long Kavieng i-bin
baiim wanpela sip i-kosim ol olsem $140,000, kamap pinis long
Pot Mosbi long las wik." My guess is: "New Island Transport
Society Ltd at Kavieng been buy-him one-fellow ship cost-him
all all-same $140,000, come-up finish along Port Moresby along
last week." *Nu Gini Tok Tok*, which sold "Fo Tausan kopi" and
"i-kos 5 sen tasol" (that's-all), also carried an item about tinned
"pusikat bilong Australia" (which happily turns out to be Neo-
Melanesian for rabbit). It is to be noted that the Asians played
their variations on the English tongue back on the white man,
who found himself gabbling in turn about "Catchee one piecey
manee" or writing "Sekretari-Jeneral U Thant bilong Yunaited
Nesin."

The Japanese are masters at swallowing English and regurgitat-
ing it as a poor thing but their own. Consider the unlikely man
in a suit and overcoat drinking a cocktail while watching a sex
film on television in his hotel at Christmas. He becomes an even
more unlikely man in a Saburo (Saville Row = suit) and Oba
drinking a Kakateru and watching an Ero on Terebi in his
Hoteru at Kerisumasu. And what of the Japlish for cross-eyed:
"Lonpali" (one eye on London, the other on Paris)? Some Asians
are beginning to ask why they should speak English this way or
that. What is English, anyway? There is Australian English and
American English and English English. Why not Malaysian English, and even more pronounced mutants like Vietlish, Thailish,
Angloporean?

However, most not only want to learn conventional English,
but they bring a fresh, tropical taste to a tongue jaded with stale
jargon. In a Burmese newspaper an indignant letter writer described an accident in 1959 like this: "Then, bang, one car coming to city hit the poor woman with mudguard and the woman
fall spinning in the middle of the road. We stop, but the other

dirty dog he's only small red light fading into distance. The woman make no sound and no more." With a mistake in every line, it compares well with an example of contemporary English literature that was received on the same day from a local European publicity writer: "Hi folks. This is B.H. and with a big new piece of news. Under the aegis of the old scribe now comes that fabulous territory, the Federation of Malaya . . ." Ten years later an American told me seedily that there were "all kindsa things we haven't got which I don't know why." This somehow seemed to sanction Ping's sprightlier references to dieting: "You are not allowed to lose more than too much," and to bad laundering: "Why the people wash the shirt so dirty?" And to libraries: "Rows and rows of books up to the floor."

Who, in fact, is doing what and to whom? One hundred years ago the Duke of Beaufort played a novel game that derived its name from his seat in Gloucestershire: Badminton. Today the world champions are drawn with almost monotonous regularity from Indonesia. On the other hand, great was the consternation in Tokyo in 1961 when the international judo championship was won not by a Japanese but by a Dutchman. Singapore painters show the influence of European techniques and European clichés; the Cambodians are preserving their traditional monastery music by transposing pieces into Western notation, and they are updating their traditional dances with Western postures. But Australian companies engage Japanese and Chinese singers for the operas of Puccini and Poulenc, and a Japanese is commissioned to produce the designs for a production of *King Lear*. White audiences acclaim Chinese pianists and Chinese conductors devoted entirely to serious Western compositions, while in England records of Indian classical music sell like hot discs. The East opens a can of stew but the West crowds into thousands of Chinese restaurants to eat the chop suey which is its Oriental equivalent, and if the Asian earnestly dismembers English, the Anglo-Saxon has taken to butchering Chinese.

Yet the young are not just cultural transvestites, borrowing each other's clothes and parading in their Oriental or Occidental drag. There is the beginning of a new and deeper understanding that, like all else, the *yin* and *yang* of East and West are part of the universal Oneness. The impoverished little materialist from the spiritual East turns eagerly to the West for the good things of life. The heavily beaded and bearded and besandaled Buddhist from the suffocatingly affluent society of the West turns to the East for the good things of death. But the young West also learns slowly that the Orient can be practical as well as pious, and the young East learns that the Occident has not only riches but values.

The youthful Asian wants freedom, perhaps an Asian democracy like his Asian English. He is being drawn into the rat race away from his traditional philosophy that problems are hydra-headed and since to dispose of one is simply to create two others, it may be better to do nothing. This is a triumph for the West. But the Asian is not the only one learning and adapting. When I flew into Southeast Asia sixteen years ago, the Americans were just taking their first confident steps into the quagmire of Vietnam, and the British in Singapore were debating just how they could rid themselves without revolution of a turbulent left-wing menace elected to the legislative assembly called Lee Kuan Yew. Ngo Dinh Diem faced Ho Chi Minh across the 17th parallel in Indochina, Sukarno strutted in Djakarta, Syngman Rhee dictated in Seoul, Dulles dictated in Washington, and power came out of the barrels of guns pointed in all directions simultaneously.

A generation, fortunately, is an elusive, transitory affair, and the elder statesmen of the era are on the edge of eternity, if they have not already disappeared into the silence. In East and West the demagogues of yesteryear are deadweight today, the times call for bureaucrats more than barricades, and "hero" is in danger of joining all the other four-letter words. Despite setbacks, freedom has been scoring points, if below the line. In South Korea President Park tried to rewrite the constitution in 1969 so that he could stand for a third term, but he was shouted down by enraged politicians and students and obliged to abide by the decision of a popular referendum. General Ne Win of Burma released his principal political opponents from detention and started searching almost guiltily for a new constitution in which to clothe his naked power. The Thais went to the polls and a partly elected parliament opened again in Bangkok for the first time in ten years. In Indonesia President Suharto finally agreed that general elections should be held in 1971. And we have witnessed the twilight of the god-kings.

Whether the East will go Communist, or fall among despots, or work its own elaborate variation on the simple one-finger-one-note theme of democracy, will depend on many things—above all, perhaps, on the yawning sociological gap between the high-rise, Hiltonizing cities and the hungry villages. Even modern Japan's gimcrack, Potemkin-like structure is like a sad skit on the century, for it suffers simultaneously from a ridiculous glut of gadgetry and a lamentable shortage of elementary plumbing (only nine homes in a hundred have a flush toilet, against ninety-eight in Britain and thirty-seven even in France). In Southeast Asia Bangkok may begin to look like Broadway, yet many a Muslim in southwest Thailand still lives in primitive squalor and earns no more than sixty pounds a year.

But the destiny of the whole world may depend upon the greater understanding that must grow between its two halves. In this context, the flirting and prying and filching and cannibalizing that make up the latest, slightly obscene chapter in the long, brutal story of interplay between East and West must be welcomed. It may be the prelude to a respectable and responsible relationship. For the most dangerous liaisons of the past often lead to the safest marriages of the future.

Synopsis of the Plot

B U R M A

Definitions
Kachins, Karens, Shans: minority peoples of non-Burman stock, mainly living in the mountainous north

The Events
January 1948 Burma becomes an independent, sovereign state following postwar negotiations with British. U Nu is the first prime minister. The constitution provides for autonomous Shan, Kachin, and (subject to referendum) Karen states with their own local government and own civil service.
1948–1951 There are Communist—and Muslim—uprisings, followed by an insurrection of the Karen minority.

October 1958   General Ne Win, army chief-of-staff, compels U
Nu to relinquish power and establishes rule by military
junta.

1959–1961   Active Shan rebels increase from eight hundred to
three thousand. Karens and Kachins are also still in revolt.

February 1960   General elections: General Ne Win steps down,
U Nu becomes premier again.

October 1960   The Sino-Burmese frontier agreement and Treaty
of Friendship are signed.

January 1961   Premier Chou En-lai of China visits Burma, and
offers a £30,000,000 credit.

1961   Buddhism is made the state religion.

March 1962   Ne Win seizes power by *coup d'état* and sets up
a military government under a "Revolutionary Council"
with himself as chairman. U Nu and other political leaders
are arrested.

1963   The Burma Socialist Program Party is formed to implement Ne Win's "Burmese Way to Socialism," which includes progressive nationalization of all capitalist enterprises
and eradication of foreign investment and economic power.

All rebel groups are invited to negotiate a peace, but the
Shans demand a federal state with the right of secession,
the Kachins want to leave the Union of Burma, and talks
break down in November.

Mid-1967   Provocative acts of local Chinese Red Guards in
Rangoon lead to anti-Chinese rioting. Peking attacks Ne
Win's "Fascist regime."

1968   Forty percent of Burma is troubled by armed insurgency.
Ne Win releases U Nu and other political leaders and asks
thirty-three of them to advise him on a new constitution.

1969   Ne Win rejects the suggestions of these political leaders
for a return to a multi-party system. U Nu goes abroad and
declares that the Ne Win regime will be overthrown, by
force if necessary.

November 1969   Ne Win reveals five hundred men have been
killed in major clashes between the Burmese army and rebels
in the north near the China border.

INDOCHINA

French Indochina consisted of the three regions of Vietnam known as Tonking, Annam, and Cochinchina, and the kingdoms of Cambodia and Laos:

CAMBODIA

Definitions

Cambodia: successor of the earlier Khmer kingdoms of Chen-la (sixth to ninth century) and Angkor or Kambuja (ninth to fifteenth century)

Khmer: the Cambodian people, their language, etc.

The Events

1941 Prince Norodom Sihanouk becomes king of Cambodia.

November 1953 Cambodia becomes independent of the French.

March 1955 Sihanouk abdicates in favor of his father, Norodom Suramarit, and becomes prime minister. He creates the Sangkum Reastr Niyum (Popular Socialist Community).

May 1955 Cambodia enters into a military-aid agreement with the United States.

September 1955 The Sangkum wins all seats in the national assembly in general elections. Sihanouk announces a policy of neutralism.

March 1956 Norodom Suramarit is crowned king.

July 1957 Cambodia recognizes Communist China.

April 1960 King Suramarit dies. There is no successor. Sihanouk is head of state.

November 1963 Sihanouk announces rejection of all further American economic and military aid.

1965 Sihanouk breaks off diplomatic relations with the United States.

September 1966 General elections are held, with candidates from the Sangkum only.

April 1967 Khmers Rouges (Cambodian Communist guerrillas) launch armed attacks in Battambang province. As Maoist subversive activity intensifies, Sihanouk turns on Peking and threatens to recall the Cambodian ambassador. Premier Chou En-lai smooths matters over with a reassuring response.

1968–1969 The Khmer Rouge threat to Cambodia increases, and Sihanouk also estimates that up to forty thousand Vietcong have violated his frontiers.

Sihanouk reestablishes diplomatic relations with the U.S. He is nevertheless the only non-Communist leader to attend the funeral of President Ho Chi Minh in Hanoi in September 1969.

March 1970 Sihanouk is deposed during his absence in France by right-wing neutralists, who announce that Cambodia is to be a republic.

L A O S

Definitions

Lao: the dominant race in Laos, their language, etc. Plural: Laos
Laos: the country. Adjective: Laotian
Pathet Lao: "The Lao State"—the Communist-directed guerrilla movement under Prince Souphannouvong

The Events

July 1949–1950 The French accord partial sovereignty to Laos. Of the leaders of the Laotian independence movement, Prince Souvanna Phouma accepts a ministry in Vientiane; Prince Souphannouvong forms the Pathet Lao with the help of the Vietminh and takes up arms against the Royal government and the French.

1953 Laos becomes independent.

July 1954–1957 The Geneva Agreement ends the Indochina War. Souvanna Phouma becomes prime minister and forms a government of national union with Pathet Lao participation in Vientiane.

1958 The Pathet Lao score heavily in supplementary elections. Alarmed, the Laotian right-wing force Souvanna Phouma to resign. A new government is formed without Pathet Lao ministers.

1959 Vientiane announces Communist North Vietnamese troops are moving into Laos. The new right-wing prime minister is given "special powers" to deal with the Communist threat. The Laotian government asks United States to provide military technicians to train the army. Souphannouvong and other Pathet Lao leaders are arrested.

January–June 1960 Rigged general elections. The right wing scores a heavy victory and all Pathet Lao candidates are defeated. A new government is formed with General Phoumi Nosavan as Minister of Defense. Prince Souphannouvong and other arrested Pathet Lao leaders escape and rejoin their guerrillas upcountry.

August 1960 The neutralist paratrooper Captain Kong Le seizes Vientiane by *coup d'état*; Souvanna Phouma becomes prime minister, announces that he will negotiate with the Pathet Lao again and asks for Soviet aid.

December 1960 Right-wing troops of General Phoumi throw Kong Le out of Vientiane. Boun Oum becomes new prime minister, with General Phoumi as Defense Minister and the real "strong man."

March 1961 Souvanna Phouma, still recognized as prime minister by Communist powers and supported by Soviet airlifts, sets up headquarters with the neutralists of Kong Le and the Pathet Lao under Prince Souphannouvong at Khang Khay on the Plain of Jars.

1961–1962 A second Geneva Conference is held and guarantees the neutrality of Laos. Boun Oum, Souvanna Phouma, and Souphannouvong agree to form another provisional government of national union. Souphannouvong and Phoumi Nosavan are vice-premiers under Souvanna Phouma, holding finance and economy portfolios respectively.

1962–1964 There is no true reconciliation. Fighting resumes. Souphannouvong leaves Vientiane and returns to his headquarters on the Plain of Jars, and later withdraws the remaining Pathet Lao ministers from Vientiane.

January 1965 Abortive right-wing coup in Vientiane. General Phoumi flees to Thailand.

January 1967   General elections are held without the Pathet Lao, and a new Souvanna Phouma cabinet takes office in Vientiane without Pathet Lao participation.

1968–1969   Intensified military action between the Royal Lao Army and the combination of Pathet Lao and North Vietnamese troops in Laos, who are now estimated to number forty to fifty thousand. Heavy American bombing helps government forces to recapture much of the Plain of Jars. The Communists nevertheless dominate most of the territory.

V I E T N A M

Definitions

Annam: the central region of Vietnam, the former center of the empire

Tonking: the northern region of Vietnam, now Communist

Vietcong and Vietminh: apart from their precise meanings ("Vietnamese Communist" and "League for the Independence of Vietnam," respectively), these terms have been used loosely for the Communist-led Vietnamese insurgents. The "Vietminh" fought the French; the "Vietcong" the Americans

The Events

1946–1954   The Indochina War. The Vietminh defeat the French at Dien Bien Phu in May 1954.

June 1954   Ngo Dinh Diem becomes prime minister of Vietnam with the reluctant consent of the Emperor Bao Dai.

July 1954   The Geneva Agreement divides Vietnam into North and South zones at the 17th parallel, pending joint general elections in 1956 and reunification.

November 1954   The Vietminh take over Hanoi from the French. The North becomes the "Democratic Republic of Vietnam" under President Ho Chi Minh.

March–May 1955   A sect rebellion under the leadership of the Binh Xuyen is mounted against the Diem regime in Saigon. Diem crushes it. The emperor makes an abortive attempt to appoint General Nguyen Van Vy commander-in-chief and to remove Diem.

October 1955 Diem organizes a referendum and South Vietnam becomes an independent republic with himself as president; the emperor is deposed. The Americans start reorganizing the South Vietnamese army.

1956 South Vietnam refuses to hold joint general elections with North Vietnam to unify the two halves of the country.

1959–1960 The first major acts of terrorism are committed by the Vietcong. "Agrovilles" are created to protect the peasants from the guerrillas (they will be followed by "Strategic Hamlets" and "New Life Hamlets" as the struggle intensifies).

November 1960 An abortive military coup is organized against Diem.

January 1961 Hanoi Radio announces the formation of the "National Liberation Front" in South Vietnam.

February 1962 The U.S. Military Aid Command is set up in South Vietnam. Rebel Vietnamese air-force pilots bomb Diem's palace in Saigon as the first move in a second abortive coup against him.

May–August 1963 Buddhist demonstrations in Hue are brutally suppressed by the Diem regime. More demonstrations follow. The first Buddhist monk publicly burns himself to death in Saigon. The government carries out numerous arrests of Buddhist monks and students. Tension mounts.

November 1963 Army generals organize a successful *coup d'état*. Diem and his brother, Ngo Dinh Nhu, are assassinated. General Duong Van Minh ("Big Minh") heads the country as the leader of a new "Military Revolutionary Council."

January 1964 Major-General Nguyen Khanh seizes power.

August 1964 North Vietnamese torpedo boats attack American destroyers. The Americans bomb North Vietnamese naval bases.

Khanh attempts to make himself president of South Vietnam but is discouraged by Buddhist and student riots.

October–November 1964   Mr. Tran Van Huong forms a new government. Khanh remains commander-in-chief.

The Vietcong attack Bien Hoa air base, twelve miles from Saigon.

December 1964   Khanh acquires the real power again at the head of an "Armed Forces Command."

February 1965   The repercussions of a coup against Khanh mounted by Colonel Pham Ngoc Thao force him to resign as commander-in-chief and to leave the country. The Americans begin regular bombing of North Vietnam.

June 1965   The military take over again from the civilians. Air Marshal Nguyen Cao Ky becomes prime minister. Major-General Nguyen Van Thieu becomes chief of state at the head of a "Council for the Leadership of the Nation."

July 1965   There are now seventy-five thousand American troops in South Vietnam. Colonel Thao is caught and shot on government orders.

September 1967   Thieu and Ky are returned as president and vice-president in general elections.

February 1968   The Vietcong launch a major Tet Offensive at Vietnamese New Year against fifty-four towns of South Vietnam.

May 1968   The Americans open negotiations with the North Vietnamese in Paris.

Tran Van Huong becomes prime minister of South Vietnam for the second time.

November 1968   The Americans stop bombing North Vietnam.

February 1969   There are 543,054 American troops in South Vietnam.

June 1969   The Americans start to withdraw their troops.

August–September 1969   Huong is replaced as prime minister of South Vietnam by General Tran Thien Khiem.

President Ho Chi Minh of North Vietnam dies.

INDONESIA

Definitions

Indonesia: former Netherlands East Indies. The main islands are Java, Sumatra, Borneo, Celebes

Papuans: the people of "West Irian"

West Irian: former Dutch West New Guinea, now part of the Republic of Indonesia

The Events

August 1945 The Japanese surrender. Dr. Sukarno proclaims the independent Republic of Indonesia before the return of the Dutch colonial power.

September 1948 An uprising of the Indonesian Communist Party (P.K.I.) is quelled.

December 1949 After two "police actions" against the nationalists, the Dutch finally concede sovereignty to Indonesia, but leave open the question of the future ownership of Dutch West New Guinea.

1950 Indonesia adopts a Western-style parliamentary constitution.

1951–1953 An uprising of the fanatical "Darul Islam" movement gains momentum in protest against President Sukarno's failure to make Indonesia an Islamic state.

September 1955 General elections. Nationalist, Muslim, and Communist parties dominate the parliament

February 1957 Sukarno proposes to introduce "Guided Democracy" to give the executive strong central power and as an alternative to Western democratic practice.

December 1957 In his campaign to wrest Dutch West New Guinea ("West Irian") from The Hague, Sukarno breaks off diplomatic relations with Holland, expels all Dutch subjects, and begins appropriating all Dutch interests.

February 1958 Regional military commanders rebel in Sumatra, where a "Revolutionary Government of the Republic of Indonesia" is declared.

1959–1960 Sukarno announces his "Political Manifesto," which is the basic document of "Guided Democracy," and becomes head of government as well as head of state.

Sukarno dissolves the elected parliament and replaces it with a *gotong royong* (mutual cooperation) assembly of his own choosing and subordinated to his authority. The new policy of NASAKOM (cooperation between Nationalists, religious parties, and Communists) is confirmed.

February 1960 Khrushchev visits Indonesia.

1961 The Sumatra rebellion peters out.

Indonesian troops begin infiltrating "West Irian" to harass the Dutch.

1962 The New York agreement gives Indonesia provisional control of West Irian under the aegis of the United Nations but stipulates that the population must be granted their own "Act of Free Choice" in 1969.

The Darul Islam revolt is finally suppressed.

September 1963 Sukarno launches serious military "Confrontation" against the new expanded Federation of Malaysia.

January 1965 Sukarno takes Indonesia out of the UN in protest against the admission of Malaysia.

September–October 1965 An abortive Communist coup in Indonesia is followed by a widespread massacre of Communists by the military and the Muslims.

1966 Muslim youth movements organize massive demonstrations against Sukarno, the Communists, and the Chinese. General Suharto assumes effective power.

June–September 1966 Confrontation is ended by signed agreement. Indonesia rejoins the UN.

February–March 1967 Suharto officially becomes acting president.

August 1969 After consulting only one thousand appointed representatives, the Indonesians announce that West Irian has opted for permanent incorporation in the republic.

October 1969 The army is reorganized into six territorial defense commands. Authority is concentrated at the top and at the center, and the powers of regional commanders are severely curtailed.

MALAYSIA
Definitions
Dyaks: natives of Borneo, divisible into Land-Dyaks, and Sea-Dyaks or Ibans (who are in reality upriver people)
Malay: the dominant race in the Malayan peninsula and Indonesia; their language, etc.
Malaya: the Malayan peninsula, whose eleven states formed the independent Federation of Malaya from 1957 to 1963. Adjective: Malayan
Malaysia: the wider Federation created in 1963, taking in not only Malaya but Singapore and the North Borneo states of Sarawak and Sabah. Adjective: Malaysian

The Events
September 1945   The British return to Malaya following the Japanese surrender.
June 1948   Communist terrorists murder three British planters, and a state of emergency is declared. The campaign against guerrillas of the Malayan Communist Party (M.C.P.) continues until 1960.
1955   The Alliance Party of Tengku Abdul Rahman wins all but one of the fifty-two elected seats in parliament under a new constitution.
August 1957   The "Federation of Malaya" becomes an independent, sovereign state. The Tengku is prime minister.
1960   The emergency is declared over. The remnants of the M.C.P. terrorists are now hiding on the Thai side of the Thai-Malayan frontier.
1961–1962   The British intend to liquidate their colonial dependencies in North Borneo (Sarawak and, as it is to be called, Sabah), and discuss with Tengku Abdul Rahman the possibility of his incorporating them with Singapore into a larger "Federation of Malaysia."
Mid-1962   President Macapagal of the Philippines lays claim to Sabah.
1962–August 1963   UN delegations satisfy themselves on the

ground that the peoples of the North Borneo dependencies think their best course is to join the proposed "Federation of Malaysia." Pro-Malaysia parties are returned in local elections in both territories.

Mid–September 1963 The Federation of Malaysia comes into being. The Philippines and Indonesia withhold recognition, and Indonesia launches economic and military "Confrontation" against Malaysia as a "neocolonialist" invention.

April 1964 General elections: the Alliance wins 89 out of 104 seats.

August 1965 Deteriorating relations lead to the expulsion of Singapore from Malaysia.

June 1966 Confrontation is ended by a signed agreement between Indonesia and Malaysia. But Communist terrorists are again active on the Thai-Malaysian border.

August 1967 Malay becomes the sole official language.

1968 Malaysia learns that Filipinos have been undergoing training on Corregidor Island for terrorist operations in Sabah.

Manila enacts a law to include Sabah constitutionally in the Philippines. Malaysia suspends diplomatic relations.

May 1969 The Alliance suffers a severe setback in general elections. Fierce race riots between Malays and non-Malays follow, a state of emergency is declared, parliament is suspended, and a National Operations Council takes over control under Deputy Premier Tun Abdul Razak.

THE PHILIPPINES

Definitions

Moros: Muslims of the southern Philippines

Tagalog: the dominant ethnic group of the Philippines; their language, etc.

The Events

1942 The "Hukbalahap" (People's Anti-Japanese Army) is formed, and its strength is subsequently built up to thirty thousand.

July 1946 The Independent Republic of the Philippines is inaugurated. Manuel Roxas is first president. The Bell Act provides for preferential trade between the Philippines and the United States, and Americans are granted equal rights with Filipinos within the republic.

1947 An agreement is concluded whereby the United States may maintain bases in the Philippines for ninety-nine years.

1950 Ramon Magsaysay is appointed Secretary of Defense in view of the increasing Communist Huk menace, and rapidly destroys its central organization.

1953 Magsaysay is elected president (Nacionalista Party). He attacks the Huks effectively, reducing their fighting strength to about 650, and introduces reforms to abate discontent.

March 1957 Magsaysay is killed in an air crash. He is succeeded by vice-president Carlos Garcia.

November 1961 Presidential elections.

January 1962 Diosdado Macapagal (Liberal Party) becomes president, with Emmanuel Pelaez as vice-president.

1962–1963 Macapagal officially advances the Philippine claim to British North Borneo (Sabah). Manila refuses to recognize the new Federation of Malaysia, which includes Sabah, and diplomatic ties are suspended.

November–December 1965 Presidential elections. Ferdinand Marcos becomes president (Nacionalista Party).

1966 Relations with the Federation of Malaysia are restored. President Marcos visits Washington. The lease of the U.S. military bases in the Philippines is cut from ninety-nine to twenty-five years as from 1966.

1968 The Philippine Congress passes an act constitutionally including Sabah within the frontiers of the republic. Malaysia suspends relations with Manila.

November 1969 Presidential elections. Marcos is reelected after a campaign marred by much violence.

December 1969 Malaysia still does not agree to submit the Philippine claims to Sabah to the World Court, but tension eases and the two countries agree to resume diplomatic relations.

SINGAPORE

The Events

May 1959 The People's Action Party (PAP) of Lee Kuan Yew wins forty-three out of fifty-one seats in the first fully elected Singapore Legislative Assembly under a new constitution granting the island internal self-government.

February 1963 Lim Chin Siong, secretary-general of the pro-Communist Barisan Sosialis, is detained with some other party leaders.

September 1963 The PAP wins thirty-seven seats in general elections, the Barisan Sosialis thirteen.

Singapore merges with Malaya and becomes part of the new Federation of Malaysia.

July 1964 Race riots between Chinese and Malays break out on Mohammed's birthday.

August 1965 After an increasingly abrasive relationship, Malaysia expels Singapore from the Federation. Singapore becomes an independent republic.

October 1966 Under the chairmanship of Dr. Lee Siew Choh, the Barisan Sosialis boycotts parliament and "takes the struggle to the streets."

April–May 1967 The Barisan Sosialis calls for a general strike and for a mammoth demonstration on Labor Day. Both are failures.

November 1967 The old British Straits dollar is devalued, following devaluation of the pound.

January 1968 The British disclose that they intend to withdraw their forces and close their military bases in Singapore and Malaysia by the end of 1971.

April 1968 Snap elections are held in Singapore. The Barisan Sosialis boycotts them, and the PAP wins all fifty-eight seats in the legislative assembly.

July 1968 A stringent Industrial Relations Bill is introduced, stipulating a forty-four-hour week for all.

1969 Bills are introduced to legalize abortion and to abolish juries.

July 1969 Lim Chin Siong, detained secretary-general of the Barisan Sosialis, recants, is freed, and goes to the U.K.

August 1969 Singapore celebrates 150th anniversary of the founding of the settlement by Sir Stamford Raffles.

T H A I L A N D (formerly Siam)

The Events

January 1942 Marshal Pibul Songgram, the Thai premier, declares war on the Allies.

1944–1946 As the Japanese begin losing the war, Pibul resigns, and is later jailed for one year as a war criminal.

November 1947–April 1948 Pibul seizes power again in a military coup, and becomes prime minister.

1950 United States military assistance begins.

1951 Pibul suspends the constitution and the fully elected parliament in view of the "Communist threat."

1954 The headquarters of the Southeast Asia Treaty Organization is established in Bangkok.

September 1957 Marshal Sarit Thanarat, commander-in-chief of the army, overthrows Pibul. Elections are held.

October 1958 Sarit assumes direct power in his own name, dissolves the new national assembly and cabinet imposes martial law, abrogates the constitution, and bans political parties.

December 1963 Sarit dies. Field Marshal Thanom Kittikachorn becomes prime minister.

1964 The Communists announce the existence of a "Thai Patriotic Front" fighting for "liberation" in northeast Thailand.

1965 The decision is taken to establish a joint Thai-Malaysian headquarters in south Thailand in view of the increasing terrorist activity of the Malayan Communist Party guerrillas on the border.

1966–1967 The United States builds up its forces in Thailand and its bases for bombing Vietnam.

Thailand sends the Queen Cobra regiment to fight in Vietnam. Foreign Minister Thanat Khoman urges relentless bombing of North Vietnam.

Communist-trained Meo guerrillas become active in northern Thailand.

June 1968   A new constitution is promulgated. Political parties are legalized.

September 1968   Municipal elections are held. Only twenty percent of voters go to polls.

February 1969   General elections. Marshal Kittikachorn forms a new government.

Thanat Khoman, the Foreign Minister, expresses readiness to hold talks with Peking.

September 1969   Thai-U.S. discussions on the future withdrawal of forty-eight thousand American servicemen in Thailand begin.

Bibliography

SOUTHEAST ASIA GENERAL

A *History of Modern South-east Asia*, by John Bastin & Harry J. Benda
Federal Publications
Kuala Lumpur
Communism in South-East Asia, by J. H. Brimmell
Oxford University Press
People and Progress in East Asia, by Eli Ginzberg
Columbia University
New York
A *History of South-east Asia*, by D. G. E. Hall
St. Martin's Press
New York
Asian Drama, Vols I–III, by Gunnar Myrdal
Pantheon, Random House
New York

East Asia in Old Maps, by Hiroshi Nakamura
    East West Center Press
    Honolulu
The Revolution in South-east Asia, by Victor Purcell
    Thames & Hudson
    London

INDOCHINA GENERAL

The Struggle for Indochina, by Ellen J. Hammer
    Stanford University Press
    Stanford, Calif.
The Emancipation of French Indochina, by Donald Lancaster
    Oxford University Press
See also CAMBODIA, LAOS, and VIETNAM.

PHILOSOPHY AND RELIGION

The Sayings of Muhammed, by Allama Sir Abdullah Al-Mamun Al-Suhrawardy
    John Murray
    London
Buddhist Scriptures, translated by Edward Conze
    Penguin Books
    London
Islam, by Alfred Guillaume
    Penguin Books
    London
Buddhism, by Christmas Humphreys
    Penguin Books
    London
The Wisdom of China and India, by Lin Yutang
    Random House
    New York
Buddhism: An Introduction, by Luang Suriyabongs, M.D.
    The Buddhist Council of Ceylon
    Colombo
Hinduism, by K. M. Sen
    Penguin Books
    London

Malayan Buddhism, by Teng Eng Soon
  Eastern Universities Press
  Singapore
The Way of Zen, by Alan W. Watts
  Random House
  New York

BURMA

The Union of Burma, by Hugh Tinker
  Oxford University Press
Outline of Burmese History, by G. E. Harvey
  Orient Longmans
  Calcutta
Burmese Family, by Mi Mi Khaing
  Orient Longmans
  Calcutta

CAMBODIA

Angkor: An Introduction, by George Coedes
  Oxford University Press
A History of Cambodia, by Manomohan Ghosh,
  J. K. Gupta
  Saigon
Angkor: Art and Civilisation, by Bernard Groslier and Jacques Arthaud
  Thames & Hudson
  London
Cambodia: The Search for Security, by Michael Leifer
  Frederick A. Praeger
  New York
Cambodge, compiled by Charles Meyer
  published by the Ministry of Information of Cambodia
  Phnom Penh
Cambodia (Country Survey Series), by David J. Steinberg and col-
  laborators
  Human Relations Area Files
  New Haven, Conn.

INDONESIA

Sukarno: An Autobiography, as told to Cindy Adams
    Gunung Agung
    Djakarta
The Mythology and the Tolerance of the Javanese, by Benedict R.
  O'G Anderson
    Monograph Series
    Cornell University, Ithaca, N. Y.
Indonesian Communism, by Arnold C. Brackman
    Frederick A. Praeger
    New York
Indonesia, by G. A. Chatfield
    Eastern Universities Press
    Singapore
Indonesia, by Bruce Grant
    Melbourne University Press
    Melbourne
Indonesian Upheaval, by John Hughes
    David McKay
    New York
Indonesia, by J. D. Legge
    Prentice-Hall
    Englewood Cliffs, N.J
Indonesia: A Profile, by Jeanne Mintz
    D. Van Nostrand Company
    Princeton, N.J.
Rebels in Paradise, by James Mossman
    Hillary House
    New York
The Smiling General, by O. G. Roeder
    Gunung Agung
    Djakarta
The Fall of Sukarno, by Tarzie Vittachi
    Frederick A. Praeger
    New York
The Republic of Indonesia, by Dorothy Woodman
    The Cresset Press
    London

LAOS

Aspects du Pays Lao, by Nhouy Abhay
    Editions Comité Litteraire Lao
    Vientiane
Kingdom of Laos, by René de Berval
    France-Asie
    Saigon
Conflict in Laos, by Arthur J. Dommen
    Frederick A Praeger
    New York
The Edge of Tomorrow, by Thomas A. Dooley, M.D.
    Farrar, Straus & Giroux
    New York

MALAYA

Malay Customs and Traditions, by Alwi bin Sheikh Alhady
    Eastern Universities Press
    Singapore
Essays on Indonesian and Malayan History, by John Bastin
    Eastern Universities Press
    Singapore
The Golden Chersonese, by Isabella L. Bird
    Oxford University Press
Malaya's Eurasians—an Opinion, by C. H. Crabb
    Eastern Universities Press
    Singapore
Sarawak, Brunei and North Borneo, by Nigel Heyward
    Eastern Universities Press
    Singapore
Land Below the Wind, by Agnes Keith
    Little, Brown
    Boston
A History of Malaya, by J. Kennedy, M.A.
    Macmillan and Co.
    Kuala Lumpur
Menace in Malaya, by Harry Miller
    George G. Harrap & Co.
    London

Prince and Premier, by Harry Miller
    George G. Harrap & Co.
    London
Costumes of Malaya, by Katharine Sim
    Eastern Universities Press
    Singapore
Piracy and Politics in the Malay World, by Nicholas Tarling
    Donald Moore Gallery
    Singapore
Malaysia and Singapore, by K. G. Tregonning
    Donald Moore Press
    Singapore

THE PHILIPPINES

The Philippines, by G. A. Chatfield
    Eastern Universities Press
    Singapore
The Philippines, by Albert Ravenholt
    D. Van Nostrand Company
    Princeton, N.J.

SINGAPORE

The Singapore Story, by Kenneth Attiwill
    Frederick Muller
    London
Sinister Twilight, by Noel Barber
    Collins
    London
Lee Kuan Yew, by Alex Josey
    Donald Moore Press
    Singapore
The First 150 Years of Singapore, by Donald and Joanna Moore
    Donald Moore Press
    Singapore
Singapore: A Popular History, by H. F. Pearson
    Eastern Universities Press
    Singapore
Raffles of the Eastern Isles, by C. E. Wurtzburg
    Hodder & Stoughton
    London

THAILAND

Thailand, by Noel F. Busch
   D. Van Nostrand Company
   Princeton, N.J.
The Rice Bowl of Asia, by David M. Davies
   A.S. Barnes
   New York
Thailand, by M. Palmer
   Eastern Universities Press
   Singapore
My Country Thailand, by Phra Sarasas
   Mazusen
   Tokyo
   Reprinted privately in Bangkok
Politics in Thailand, by David A. Wilson
   Cornell University Press
   Ithaca, N. Y.

VIETNAM

Histoire du Viet-Nam, by Philippe Devillers
   Editions du Seuil
   Paris
Ho Chi Minh on Revolution, by Bernard B. Fall
   Frederick A. Praeger
   New York
The Two Viet-Nams, by Bernard B. Fall
   Frederick A. Praeger
   New York
The Making of a Quagmire, by David Halberstam
   Random House
   New York
Ho Chi Minh, by Jean Lacouture
   Random House
   New York
Vietnam between Two Truces, by Jean Lacouture
   Secker & Warburg
   London
Vietnam: The Lotus in the Sea of Fire, by Thich Nhat Hanh
   SCM Press
   London

Visages et Images du Sud Viet-Nam, by A. M. Savani
    Saigon
Trip to Hanoi, by Susan Sontag
    Farrar, Straus & Giroux
    New York
The Last Confucian, by Denis Warner
    Penguin Books
    London

GENERAL

A *History of the Chinese in California*
    Chinese Historical Society of America
    San Francisco
The Travels of Marco Polo, translated by Ronald Latham
    Penguin Books
    London
The Bomb and the Computer, by Andrew Wilson
    The Cresset Press
    London
The Asia Magazine, Hong Kong
The Far Eastern Economic Review, Hong Kong

Index

Abhay, Khou, 150
Adzhubei, Aleksei, 72
Aguinaldo, Emilio, 37
Ajax, H.M.S., 307
Albar, Syed Ja'afar, 338, 340-4, 350
Alsop, Joseph, 236
Amboina, 15
An, Tran Van, 222
Angkor, 9, 10, 12, 19, 29, 30, 121-2, 126-7, 375, 378
Annam, 10-2, 15
Australia, 251, 323, 333, 351, 358, 371

Bali, xiii, 13, 21, 70-1, 129, 131, 195, 374, 378
Bandaranaike, Mrs. S., 170
Bandung, 66, 68, 252
Bangkok, 13, 25, 49, 107, 153, 161-3, 190, 196, 257, 268, 272, 274, 297-8, 321, 333, 372, 384
Batam, 136
Beech, Keyes, 140-1, 143
Bennett, Gordon, 22
Binh Xuyen, 209-5, 234
Bird, Isabella, 16, 18, 279, 331
Borneo, xiv, 18, 45-7, 59, 135, 138, 160, 168, 178, 183, 196, 252, 281-2, 306-8, 311-3, 327-30, 334, 341, 352, 358
Borobodur, 69, 70, 78
Brezhnev, Leonid, 358
Brunei, xiv, 179, 288
Buddhists, xv, 12-3, 70, 104, 117, 127, 129, 148-9, 166, 174, 176-8, 180, 183-191, 193-4, 221, 234, 261, 299-301, 373
Bukit Tinggi, 141-4
Bundy, McGeorge, 238-40
Bundy, William, 223

Burchett, Wilfred, 186, 218
Burma, xiv-v, 11-2, 17, 20-1, 23-4, 50, 54-5, 61, 79, 116-7, 135, 149, 162, 177, 185-6, 191, 194, 199, 253, 268, 286, 297, 300, 324-5, 334, 383, 385-6

Cambodia, xiv-v, 8, 10, 33, 60-1, 73-4, 89, 107, 111, 119-7, 129, 135, 177, 197, 199, 215, 238, 272-8, 321, 332-3, 378, 387-8
Cao Dai, 174-6, 209, 211-2, 375
Celebes, xvi, 73, 129, 138-9, 183
Ceylon, 12, 54, 61, 71, 170, 177, 202, 253
Champa, 8, 11-2
Champassak, 114, 150, 171
Changi, 23, 30-1
Chen-la, 8-10, 12, 110, 120, 167, 196
Chen Yi, 123, 274
Chiang Kai-shek, 55, 162, 207, 332
Chicago Daily News, 140
China, xiii, xv, xvii, 4, 8, 10-2, 25, 55, 58-9, 61-3, 90-3, 95, 97-8, 103-4, 107, 112-3, 132, 161, 164, 168, 177, 184, 199, 206, 209, 243-4, 246, 249, 252, 259-60, 265, 267-8, 270-4, 277, 296, 310-1, 330-7, 339-43, 345, 347-50, 357-9, 361, 366-7, 378
Chinese Looking Glass, The, xvii, 164
Cholon, 148, 212-5, 237, 270
Chou En-lai, 29, 121, 272-4, 296
Clark Air Base, 37, 82-3, 139
Collins, Lawton, 214
Communists, 50-1, 53-5, 58-63, 67, 72, 74-5, 77, 83, 85-6, 91-3, 95, 99, 101, 103-4, 117-8, 127-8, 132, 139, 164, 171, 176, 180, 183, 186-8, 197, 205-7, 210, 218, 221-2, 227, 230,

Communists (*cont.*)
  234-5, 239-41, 245-6, 248-9, 252-3,
  256, 258-60, 262, 268-70, 272, 277-
  8, 306, 309-11, 314-5, 323, 325-6,
  332, 338-9, 343, 345, 351, 353, 363,
  366, 376
Czechoslovakia, 72-3, 113, 252, 357

Dai, Bao, 209-10, 222
Dai Viet, 11
Dalam, Jusuf Muda, 154-5
Dan, Pham Quang, 215-6
Darul Islam, 139, 181-3
David, Benedicto, 41-2
de Gaulle, Charles, 15, 317
de Overbeck, Baron, 281-2
de Souza, Eddie, 23
Dent, Alfred, 281-2
Diem, Ngo Dinh, 47, 49, 52, 101,
  118, 147-8, 175-6, 185, 187-9, 200,
  207-22, 224, 226-8, 231, 236-7, 239,
  245, 270, 321-3, 364, 383, 390-1
Dien Bien Phu, 85, 244-5
Djakarta, xiv, 6, 62-3, 65, 67, 73-4, 78,
  107, 128, 130-3, 137-41, 143, 145,
  147, 154, 156, 182-3, 197, 252-4,
  280-1, 309, 325-6, 332, 334, 345,
  364, 383
Djatikusomo, 325
Djuanda, 72
Dong, Pham Van, 90-1, 100
Dooley, Thomas, 79, 110, 287
Dulles, John Foster, 208-9, 383
Dusuns, 46, 323, 328
Dutch West New Guinea, see West
  Irian
Dyaks, 45-6, 165, 196, 311-2, 323,
  328-9, 334

Eagle, H.M.S., 305-6
Eisenhower, Dwight, 67
England, 3, 15-8, 21, 23-4, 28, 34, 54,
  70, 135-6 164, 170, 251-4, 282-4,
  298, 305, 309-11, 318-20, 323, 326-
  30, 333, 343, 347, 349, 351-2, 355-
  6, 358-9, 371, 383

Fidel, Benito, 40
Formosa, 205-6, 333, 376

France, 15-6, 28, 33-4, 85-7, 91-2, 96-
  7, 120, 135, 175-6, 208-10, 215,
  235-6, 244-5, 272-3, 310, 326
Fried, Joe, 289
Funan, 7, 8, 12-3, 199

Geneva Agreements, 85, 89, 103, 206,
  246, 253, 259-60, 277
Giap, Vo Nguyen, 244
Goh Keng Swee, 107, 271, 318-9, 344-
  6
Gujerat, 13

Hague, The, 16, 33, 133
Haiphong, 85-6, 88, 101
Hanoi, 60-1, 85-103, 161, 186, 188,
  206, 238-9, 242, 244, 249, 270, 277
Hatta, Muhammed, 24
Hindus, 13, 70, 109, 127-9, 176, 183,
  191, 321
Ho Chi Minh, see Minh
Hoa Hao, 175-6, 180, 187, 200, 209,
  211-3, 223-4, 226
Hong Kong, 4, 20, 30, 78, 81, 98, 123,
  163, 257, 281, 331-2, 372, 376
Hue, 189, 248
Hukbalahaps, 25, 55, 81-4, 197, 284
Huong, Tran Van, 227, 237, 248, 392

Ibans, see Dyaks
Iglesia ni Kristo, 173-4, 180
India, xiii-iv, xvii, 11-3, 17, 31, 61, 78,
  161, 193, 202, 253, 321, 330, 347,
  358-9, 367, 378
Indian Ocean, 4, 10, 15, 132, 141
Indochina, 4, 11, 15, 20, 27, 30, 61,
  105, 197, 215, 253, 263, 383
Indochina War, 85, 97, 206, 236, 238,
  243
Indonesia, xiv-v, 4, 10, 16, 20, 24, 30,
  33, 35, 48, 50-1, 61-7, 69, 70, 72-5,
  79, 107, 110, 115, 127, 129-34, 136-
  9, 143, 145, 151, 154, 156, 166-70,
  178, 182-4, 190, 197, 252-4, 268,
  271, 280-2, 284, 305, 307-9, 311,
  320-1, 325-6, 330-4, 344-5, 358,
  364, 375, 384, 393-4
Islam, see Muslims
Israel, 271, 345

Japan, xvii, 4, 20-1, 23-5, 54, 136, 168, 174-5, 180, 186, 208, 210, 304, 350, 360-2, 377
Java, xvi, 10, 12-3, 16, 22, 33, 55, 64-5, 69, 73-4, 109-10, 127-9, 138-9, 142-3, 168-9, 173, 179, 182-3, 190, 192-3, 290, 333
Jesselton, 46
Jogjakarta, 68-9, 169
Johnson, Lyndon, 36-7, 217, 233, 238, 240-2, 271
Johore, 310, 355
Jones, Howard, 252, 353

Kachin, 191, 323-4
Kalb, Bernard, 72
Karen, 191, 323-4
Karnow, Stanley, 236
Kelantan, 179
Kennedy, John F., 189, 236
Khang Khay, 111-3, 278
Khanh, Nguyen, 171, 187, 220-1, 223-4, 226-8, 232, 237, 248, 391-2
Khe Sanh, 97
Khmer, xv, 8-10, 30, 60, 74, 120, 273-4, 276-7
Khoman, Thanat, 268-9, 357
Khrushchev, Nikita, 65-72, 74, 90, 134
Knox, Rawle, 4
Komer, Robert, 314
Kong Le, 114, 170-1, 257, 259
Korea, xvii, 11, 116, 173, 205, 252-3
Krishna Menon, 320
Kuala Lumpur, 47, 51, 56, 168, 182, 195, 279, 282, 328-9, 338-40, 343-4, 346, 348, 352-3, 355, 357
Kuching, 45
Kunming, 55
Ky, Nguyen Cao, 152, 221-2, 237, 239, 269, 392

La Lania, 211
Labis, 309
Langkawi, 6
Lansdale, Ed, 211
Laos, xiv-v, 5, 6, 8, 11, 33, 47, 50, 60-1, 79, 89, 104, 111, 113, 135, 150-1, 153, 161-3, 165-6, 170, 177, 184,

199, 201, 253, 255-62, 266, 272, 299-301, 325, 332, 378, 388-90
Laurel, Jose, 41
Lee Kuan Yew, 31, 34, 47, 114, 159-60, 254, 271, 318-9, 337-41, 343, 345-6, 355, 364-71, 383, 398
Lee Siew Choh, 365-6, 398
Lim Chin Siong, 343, 366, 399
London, 3-5, 62, 78, 98, 126, 281, 352
Luang Prabang, 171, 262
Lubukdjambi, 142
Lukman, M. H., 62-3
Luzon, 81, 84

Macao, 3, 4
Macapagal, Diosdado, 27, 42-3, 80, 114, 397
MacArthur, Douglas, 24-5
McNamara, Robert S., 221, 223, 226
Madiun, 55
Madjapahit, 10, 12-3
Magsaysay, Ramon, 397
Makassar, 73
Malacca, 4, 15-7, 28, 159, 330
Malacca, Straits of, xiv, 17, 136, 305-6, 359
Malaya, xiv, xvi, 4, 8, 10, 13, 18, 21-4, 54-7, 110, 135-6, 144, 166-7, 182, 194, 253, 271, 282, 300, 309-11, 323-4, 327-30, 334-8, 340-2, 346, 351-2, 375, 395-6
Malaysia, xiv-v, 27, 31, 34-5, 46-8, 51, 59, 78, 80, 107, 113, 115, 132, 134-5, 137, 160-1, 166-7, 178-9, 190, 195-6, 199, 201, 252-4, 268, 271, 280, 282-4, 305-9, 320-1, 327-9, 332, 337-8, 340, 342-7, 349-50, 352-53, 355, 357-60, 364, 366-7, 374, 395-6
Malik, Adam, 360
Manila, 24, 35-41, 44, 80, 82, 138, 155-6, 160-1, 190, 268, 272, 281-4, 360
Mao Tsetung, 31, 58-61, 84, 90-2, 95-6, 109, 130, 162, 165, 206, 255, 261, 272, 277, 331-3, 347, 365-7
Marcos, Ferdinand E., 36, 84, 190, 268, 283

Marshall, David, 369
Martin, Robert Pepper, 140-1
Maryton, H.M.S., 306-7, 310
Masjumi, 183
Medan, 143-4
Mekong, xiv, 5, 8, 77, 88, 95, 106, 176, 188, 210, 225, 228, 235-6, 244, 262
Meos, 59, 60, 161, 323, 325
Meyer, Charles, 187, 211-3, 215, 234
Mikoyan, Anastasias, 100-2
Minangkabau, 192-3
Mindanao, 44, 190
Minh, Duong Van, 391
Minh, Ho Chi, 55, 88-9, 91, 95-6, 98-103, 130, 208, 213, 236, 238, 245-6, 269-70, 383
Miri, 46
Mois, 193, 195, 322-3
Moros, 13, 16, 190
Moscow, 57-8, 66-7, 72, 74, 93, 125, 166, 357-8
Muong Kassy, 262, 264-5
Muruts, 46-7, 323, 328
Muslims, xv, 13-6, 63, 110, 127-8, 147, 166, 173, 178-80, 182-4, 190-1, 194-5, 284, 300, 330, 345, 373, 378

Nam Bac, 261
Nam Dinh, 97
Nam Viet, 11
Nanning, 97
Nasser, Gamal, 271
Nasution, Abdul Haris, 63, 171, 280
National Liberation Front, 229, 233-5, 238-9, 245, 277
Nepal, 61
Netherlands, The, 13, 16-7, 28, 33, 130, 133-9, 168-9, 182, 325-6
New Guinea, 135, 325
New York *Daily News*, 289
New York Times, The, 72
New Yorker, The, 236
Nhu, Ngo Dinh, 118, 148, 228, 236, 270, 391
Nhu, Ngo Dinh, Madame, 189, 200-1
Nixon, Richard, 217, 233, 359
Njoto, 63

North Korea, 162, 205, 375
North Vietnam, xiv-v, 11, 60-1, 80, 90-3, 95, 97, 101-2, 104, 112, 135, 162, 186, 188, 206, 215, 233-4, 238, 242-4, 246, 251, 254, 259, 265, 271-2, 274-5, 277, 287, 290, 311
Nosavan, Ngon, 151
Nosavan, Phoumi, 6, 150-1, 153, 257-9, 261, 270, 278, 389
Nu, U, 149, 286, 296, 385-6

Observer, xvii, 5, 42, 122, 147, 342
Okinawa, 139
Ong Eng Guan, 32
Oum, Boun, 111, 114, 150-1, 171, 389

Padang, 141, 143
Pakistan, 50
Palembang, 6, 10, 138, 140, 142-3
Panmunjom, 205, 375
Panomyong, Pridi, 25, 54
Papuans, 323, 325
Paris, 15, 60, 87, 91, 102, 174, 239
Park, Chunghee, 116, 152, 383
Partai Kommunis Indonesia, 62-4, 131, 183
Pathet Lao, 60, 111, 171, 256-9, 261
Peh, Mary Ann, 58
Peking, 12, 17, 57-9, 61, 63-4, 67, 90-3, 121, 125-6, 162, 168, 198-9, 252-3, 268, 271, 274, 277, 332-2, 345, 357
Pelaez, Emmanuel, 41-2
Penang, 17, 134, 166, 330, 338
Peng, Chin, 54
Perak, 18, 53
Philip, Prince, 45-7
Philippines, xiii-v, 10, 13, 16, 21, 24-5, 27, 31, 34-9, 41-4, 55, 78-80, 82, 84, 139, 156-7, 160-1, 178, 190, 195, 281-4, 330, 334, 353, 357, 360, 375, 396-7
Phnom Penh, 6, 32-3, 73, 111, 120, 122-6, 197, 218, 274, 277
Phou Khoun, 262, 264-5, 287
Phouma, Souvanna, 6, 33, 111-2, 114, 201, 256-60, 270, 278, 388-90
Phoumi, see Nosavan
Pibul, see Songgram

Ping Hsiang, 97-8
Plain of Jars, 111, 258, 262
Poland, 72, 113, 252, 270
Portugal, 4, 15-7
Prapat, 144
Pridi, see Panomyong
Puthucheary, James, 34

Quang, Thich Tri, 187, 237, 293
Quemoy, 205, 375-6

Raffles, Thomas Stamford, 6, 17, 70, 354
Rahman, Ismail Abdul, 27, 80, 113-5, 132, 151-2, 178, 182, 271, 328-30, 337-40, 342-4, 346, 348-52, 355, 358, 395
Rajaratnam, Sinnathamby, 107-8, 254, 271, 354-5, 364-5
Ramos, Narciso, 284
Rangoon, 19, 55, 107, 116, 149, 162, 185, 190-1, 268, 324
Razak, Tun Abdul, 342-4, 353, 396
Red River, 86, 102
Rejang River, 312
Rhee, Syngman, 205, 207, 364, 383
Rostow, Eugene, 251
Roxas, Manuel, 24, 397
Rusk, Dean, 251
Russia, 58, 66-8, 72-4, 92-3, 112, 134, 164, 246, 257-60, 357-8

Sabah, xiv, 59, 160-1, 167-8, 281-4, 309, 328-30, 343
Sadec, 106
Saigon, 4, 6, 8, 26, 29-30, 32, 49, 85, 89-91, 94, 101, 118, 147-8, 156, 161-2, 174, 186-8, 197, 200, 206, 209-13, 215-7, 219-20, 225, 227, 229-32, 234-39, 241-44, 254, 269, 274, 287-90, 293, 314, 323, 333
Sailendra, 12, 70
Samy, Solomon, 58
Sananikone, Ngon, 150
Sananikone, Oudone, 150, 263
Sananikone, Phoui, 150
Sarawak, xiv, 45, 59, 165, 308-9, 328-30, 343
Semarang, 69

Seoul, 185, 254, 353, 383
Shan, xiv, 11, 162, 323-4
Shaplen, Robert, 236
Siam, see Thailand
Siantar, 144
Sibu, 46
Sihanouk, Norodom, xv, 33, 60, 104, 107, 114, 119-7, 131, 168, 190, 198-9, 215, 272-8, 333, 387-8
Sin, Tan Siew, 352, 355-6
Singapore, xiv-v, 3, 4, 6, 17-8, 20-3, 28, 30-2, 34, 48, 51, 59, 107-8, 114, 124, 134-6, 138-9, 162-3, 181-3, 193, 195, 212, 249, 253-4, 270-1, 280-1, 284-7, 306, 318-21, 327-30, 332, 335-46, 349, 353-5, 357-60, 364-72, 374-7, 383, 398-9
Singkarak Lake, 142
Sjahrir, Sutan, 33
So, Huynh Phu, 175, 224
Songgram, Pibul, 24-5
Souphannouvong, Prince, 111-3, 201, 256, 388-9
South China Sea, xiv, 160, 293, 327, 359
South Korea, 48, 51, 116, 152, 185, 205, 254, 353, 364, 375, 383
South Vietnam, xiv-v, 30, 48-9, 60-1, 90, 92, 95, 98, 101, 118, 152, 185-6, 188, 197, 199, 206, 208-9, 217, 219, 222, 229-31, 233-4, 236, 238-40, 242-3, 245-6, 248, 253-4, 272, 274-5, 310, 314-5, 364, 374
Spain, 13, 15, 17, 19, 35-6, 282
Srividjaja, 10, 12, 30, 140
Stalin, Josef, 93, 96, 100
Straits Times, 107
Subandrio, 168, 171, 290
Suharto, 51, 63, 145, 155, 168-71, 280, 326, 384, 394
Sukarno, 24, 27, 55, 62-3, 65-70, 72, 74, 107, 114-5, 127-37, 139, 143-7, 154-6, 168-71, 182-3, 196, 252-3, 280, 306-7, 309, 311, 317, 320, 325, 352, 364, 375, 383, 393-4
Sullivan, William, 60
Sulu, 281-2
Sulu Sea, 160

Sumatra, xvi, 10, 12-3, 21, 129, 138-41, 145, 182-3, 192, 260, 364
Sumitro, Djojohadikusomo, 139, 145
Surabaya, 70, 72
Suramarit, Norodom, 274, 387

Taik, Soo Shwe, 324
Tapei, 162, 297, 376
Taruc, Luis, 83
Taunggyi, 324
Taylor, Maxwell, 223
Tet Offensive, 227, 244, 248, 270, 314
Thailand, xiv-vi, 10-1, 21, 23-4, 47-51, 54, 59-61, 77, 79, 104, 135, 150, 152-3, 155, 157, 162-3, 169-70, 177-8, 190, 201, 254, 259, 268-9, 272-4, 276-7, 284, 297-8, 315, 321, 325, 333, 335, 353, 356-7, 364, 373, 384, 399-400
Thailand, Gulf of, 162
Thanarat, Sarit, 49, 150, 152-3, 155, 157, 298, 399
Thant, U, 190
Thao, Pham Ngoc, 219-20, 224, 226, 235-41, 246, 248, 270, 392
Thieu, Nguyen Van, 189, 221-2, 239, 392
Thuan, Gaston Pham Ngoc, 88, 238-9, 245
Thuc, Ngo Dinh, 236
Tjikini, 147, 183
Tjipanas, 65
Toba, Lake, 143
Tokyo, 115, 297, 304, 359-61, 377-8
Tonking, 8, 12, 20, 55, 77, 88, 91-2, 95, 97-8, 315
Tonking, Gulf of, 93
Tran, "Mister," 185, 234
Tran, see An
Tuong, Ho Huy, 213-5, 234
Tyrconnel-Fay, Abdullah Taher Hussein, 181-3

United Nations, 62, 124, 130, 162, 190, 282-3, 325
United States, 24, 33-4, 36-8, 44, 49, 52, 82, 91-3, 101-3, 125-6, 154, 204-6, 208-9, 213-5, 221-2, 227-8, 230-1, 233, 241-54, 257-60, 267, 269-70, 272-7, 282, 284, 286, 293-4, 298, 305, 310-1, 313-5, 333, 352-3, 356-7, 359, 383
U. S. News and World Report, 140

Vien, Le Van, 210-5, 234
Vientiane, 5, 8, 33, 60, 111, 114, 150, 153, 161, 166, 170, 256-9, 261-2, 265-6, 270, 287, 300
Vietcong, 48, 60, 105-6, 123-4, 147, 156, 175, 186-7, 197, 199, 219, 223-33, 235, 238-46, 248, 269-71, 275, 287, 289, 297, 311, 314, 323, 375
Vietminh, 55, 61, 85, 87-9, 92-3, 95, 98, 100, 175-6, 209, 212, 235-6, 238, 243
Vietnam, xiii, 4, 8, 11, 47-9, 55, 60, 77, 79, 85-6, 89, 91-2, 96, 102-3, 107, 135, 151, 156, 174, 176, 188, 191, 193, 196-7, 199, 200, 204-10, 214-5, 217, 221-4, 230, 233, 235, 238, 241-5, 247-52, 254, 259-60, 269, 271-6, 293, 297, 305, 310-1, 313-5, 321-3, 333-4, 353, 356-7, 364, 383, 390-2 (see also North Vietnam, South Vietnam)
Vorovong, Ou, 150
Vy, Nguyen Van, 209-10, 222

Walker, Walter, 313
Washington, 60, 62, 107, 125, 205-6, 214, 221, 224, 233-5, 241-2, 251-4, 257-8, 267, 277, 310, 353, 356, 359, 383
Washington Post, 36
West Irian (West New Guinea), 130, 133-4, 137, 325-6
Westmoreland, William, 240
Wilson, Harold, 320, 344
Win, Ne, 116-8, 149, 184, 191, 268, 324, 383, 386
World War II, 30, 77, 80, 208, 251, 253, 335, 359-60
Wuhan, 97

Yangtse River, 97
Yunnan, 161, 297

Zorthian, Barry, 240, 289-90

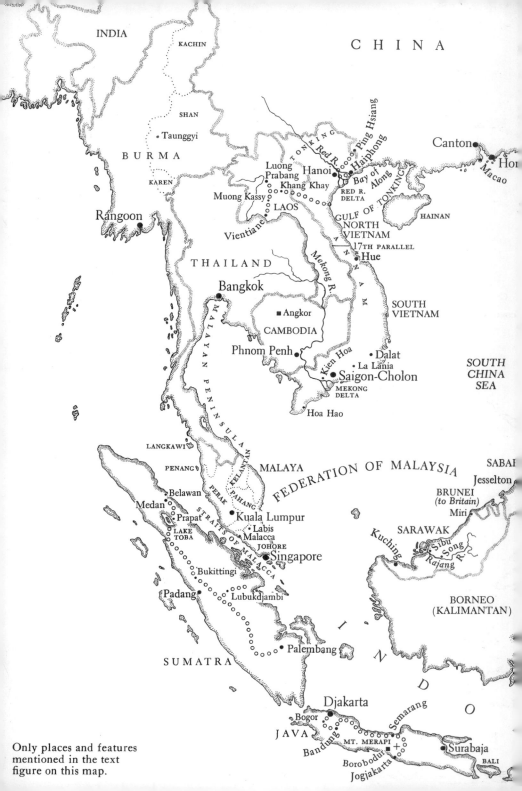

INDIA

CHINA

KACHIN

SHAN

• Taunggyi

BURMA

KAREN

Rangoon

Luong
Prabang
Khang Khay

Muong Kassy

LAOS

Vientiane

THAILAND

Bangkok

■ Angkor

CAMBODIA

Phnom Penh

Kien Hoa

MEKONG
DELTA

Hoa Hao

TONKING

Red R.

Ping Hsiang

Haiphong

Hanoi

Bay of
Along

RED R.
DELTA

GULF OF
TONKING

NORTH
VIETNAM

Canton

Hoi

Macao

HAINAN

17TH PARALLEL

Hue

Mekong R.

ANNAM

SOUTH
VIETNAM

Dalat
• La Lania

Saigon-Cholon

SOUTH
CHINA
SEA

LANGKAWI

PENANG

MALAYAN PENINSULA

KELANTAN

PERAK

PAHANG

MALAYA

FEDERATION OF MALAYSIA

SABAI

Jesselton

BRUNEI
(to Britain)

Miri

Belawan

Medan

Prapat
LAKE
TOBA

Kuala Lumpur

STRAITS OF MALACCA

Labis
Malacca

JOHORE

Singapore

Kuching

SARAWAK

Sibu

Song

Rajang R.

BORNEO
(KALIMANTAN)

Bukittingi

Padang

Lubukdjambi

Palembang

SUMATRA

I N D O

O

Djakarta

Bogor

JAVA

Semarang

Bandung

MT. MERAPI

Surabaja

Borobodur

BALI

Jogiakarta

Only places and features
mentioned in the text
figure on this map.